Karl Leonhard Reinhold
Human Capacity for Representation

Essay on a New Theory of the Human Capacity for Representation

Karl Leonhard Reinhold

Translated by Tim Mehigan and Barry Empson

With an Introduction and Notes by
Tim Mehigan and Barry Empson

De Gruyter

ISBN 978-3-11-048177-8
e-ISBN 978-3-11-022741-3

Library of Congress Cataloging-in-Publication Data

Reinhold, Karl Leonhard, 1758–1823.
  [Versuch einer neuen Theorie des menschlichen Vorstellungsvermögens.
English]
  Essay on a new theory of the human capacity for representation / K.L. Reinhold;
translated, with an introduction and notes, by Tim Mehigan and Barry Empson.
     p. cm.
Includes bibliographical references (p.   ) and index.
ISBN 978-3-11-022740-6 (hardcover : alk. paper)
1. Representation (Philosophy) I. Title.
B3081.V472E5 2011
128'.3—dc22   2010051845

Bibliographic information published by the Deutsche Nationalbibliothek
The Deutsche Nationalbibliothek lists this publication in the Deutsche
Nationalbibliografie; detailed bibliographic data are available in the
Internet at http://dnb.d-nb.de.

© 2011 Walter de Gruyter GmbH & Co. KG, Berlin/New York

Printing: Hubert & Co. GmbH & Co. KG, Göttingen

♾ Printed on acid-free paper
Printed in Germany
www.degruyter.com

Acknowledgments

A number of colleagues have helped bring about this volume. We are indebted to the advice and assistance of Ernst-Otto Onnasch, Karianne Marx, Paul Franks, Karl Ameriks, Alberto Vanzo, Peter Anstey, Amanda Cole, Mark Seymour, Brittany Travers, Dan Breazeale and three anonymous reviewers. The University of Otago provided financial support with two research grants. We gratefully acknowledge these. We also wish to thank The Australian Research Council, which has supported Tim Mehigan's work on the German Enlightenment. Thanks, finally, to Gertrud Grünkorn at De Gruyter for her interest in our project, and to Ulrike Swientek for her able assistance with the copyediting.

Tim Mehigan and Barry Empson

Contents

Acknowledgments v

Introduction ix
Tim Mehigan and Barry Empson

Essay on a New Theory of the Human Capacity for Representation 1
Karl Leonhard Reinhold

On What has been Happening with the Kantian Philosophy (1789) 3

Book One: Treatise on The Need for a New Investigation
of The Human Capacity for Representation 29

Book Two: Theory of the Capacity for
Representation in General 89

Book Three: General Theory of Cognition 151
Theory of Sensibility 167
Theory of the Understanding 203
Theory of Reason 243
Basis of the Theory of the Capacity for Desire 275

Appendices
  Glossary 289
  German Thinkers Mentioned by Reinhold 293

References 299
Name Index 305
Subject Index 307

Introduction

I.

Karl Leonhard Reinhold, a towering figure in German philosophy of the late eighteenth century, is a little known name today. His contribution, when it is noted at all, is usually recorded in studies charting the complex history of ideas in the period coextensive with, and immediately following, the appearance of Immanuel Kant's three great Critiques, the *Kritik der reinen Vernunft* (*Critique of Pure Reason*) (1781/1787), the *Kritik der praktischen Vernunft* (*Critique of Practical Reason*) (1788) and the *Kritik der Urteilskraft* (*Critique of Judgment*) (1790). In this context Reinhold is usually accorded a – albeit not insignificant – place in the passage of thought linking Kant's Critical philosophy to the birth of German idealism, especially in the form given it by Fichte, thence to the early German Romanticism of Schelling, Novalis, Friedrich Schlegel and, still later, to Hegel. That Reinhold came to fame as an expositor of the Kantian system and for a time was even more famous than the great philosopher from Königsberg himself, is from today's vantage point a remarkable fact.

Reinhold was born on October 26, 1757[1] in Vienna. After attending the Gymnasium in Vienna, he entered the Jesuit seminary of St Anna in 1772 as a novice. Soon after Reinhold's arrival in the seminary, however, Clement XIV's papal bull "Dominus ac Redemptor Noster" was issued, which aimed at suppressing the Jesuit order throughout Europe. While the Jesuits were permitted to continue their work in education in Prussia as individuals, their seminary in Vienna was closed. As a result of the closure, Reinhold returned for a short time to his father's house before joining the Barnabite seminary in 1774. The Barnabite order attended the sick, preached, taught the young

---

1 Manfred Frank: *"Unendliche Annäherung." Die Anfänge der philosophischen Frühromantik* (Frankfurt: Suhrkamp, 1997) and Martin Bondeli: *Das Anfangsproblem bei Karl Leonhard Reinhold* (Frankfurt: Klostermann, 1995) give 1757, but Horst Schröpfer: "Karl Leonhard Reinhold – sein Wirken für das allgemeine Verständnis der 'Hauptresultate' und 'der Organisation des Kantischen Systems'", in Norbert Hinske et al. (ed.): *"Das Kantische Evangelium": Der Frühkantianismus an der Universtität Jena von 1785–1800 und seine Vorgeschichte* (Stuttgart-Bad Cannstadt: Frommann–Holzboog, 1993), 101, gives 1758. Fuchs notes that documents about Reinhold's birth were discovered in 1983: Gerhard W. Fuchs: *Karl Leonhard Reinhold – Illuminat und Philosoph* (Frankfurt am Main: Peter Lang, 1994), 13, and fn 5, 145, and that the error arose from Reinhold himself – whether deliberately or not remains uncertain.

and worked in Austria on the conversion of Protestants. Reinhold was engaged to teach philosophy there in 1778 and was ordained as a priest on August 27, 1780. One of his students reported later that Reinhold retained the characteristic gait of a monk even when he was teaching philosophy in Jena.[2]

In his early years in Vienna Reinhold came in contact with several thinkers associated with the Austrian Enlightenment, with advocates of the Emperor Joseph's reforms and with the "Vienna Friends", a focal point of intellectual life in Vienna. These contacts acquainted him with freemasonry. In the house of Johann Michael Kosmas Denis (1729–1800), a former Jesuit, Reinhold was introduced to Ignaz von Born, a highly regarded poet in Vienna[3] and head of the Masonic lodge "Zur wahren Eintracht" ("True Accord"). Reinhold joined von Born's[4] lodge on 30 April 1783.[5] He began working anonymously for the *Realzeitung*[6] at this time, writing book reviews and articles. These writings indicate a growing distance from Roman Catholic dogma. As he later reported in the foreward to the *Essay on a New Theory of the Human Capacity for Representation,* he found himself unable to accept the religious teaching he had received "blindly". Reinhold seems to have endorsed the Emperor Joseph's reforms, revealing himself to be a strong supporter of the progressive goals of Enlightenment and of religious toleration[7].

---

2   Forberg: *Lebenslauf eines Verschollenen,* quoted in Frank 1997, 201.
3   Fuchs 1994, 147.
4   Ignaz von Born is thought to have provided a model for Sarastro in Mozart's *Magic Flute.* Mozart himself became a Master Mason in the same Lodge in January 1785. See H. C. Robbins Landon (ed.): *The Mozart Compendium: A Guide to Mozart's Life and Music* (London: Thames and Hudson, 1990), 132.
5   Freemasonry played an important part in the "radical Enlightenment". See Margaret Jacob: *The Radical Enlightenment* (London: Allen and Unwin, 1981). The papal bulls denouncing it were not published in Austria. Theoretically it was impossible for a practising Catholic to be a freemason. Haydn and Mozart were admitted as members of Viennese lodges in 1784, however, and the Emperor Francis I was himself a member. Interesting reflections on freemasonry in Vienna in the 1780s can be found in Daniel Heartz: *Mozart's Operas.* Ed. Thomas Baumann (Berkeley: University of California Press, 1990), 257ff. Goethe was a freemason as well. Reinhold spoke at a masonic meeting for midsummer (Johannisfest) in 1805 and pleased Goethe. Voigt reported in a letter to Böttiger of 25th June: "Reinhold gave a well conceived lecture to amalgamate the sanctity of the festival with the destiny of the Lodge. His old father-in-law [Wieland] and the hero G[oethe] were well pleased." Robert Steiger (ed.): *Goethes Leben von Tag zu Tag* (Zurich, Munich: Artemis, 1988), vol. 5, 321.
6   This newspaper, which first appeared in 1770, reported on a range of matters including literary events, new inventions and commercial happenings. It also provided commentary and analysis on topics such as livestock, botany, finance, literature, music and the arts.
7   For further discussion of Reinhold's connection to the Enlightenment, see Karianne Marx: *The Usefulness of the Kantian Philosophy: How Karl Leonhard Reinhold's commitment to Enlightenment influenced his reception of Kant* (diss. Amsterdam 2009).

In this new liberal atmosphere Reinhold soon felt the restrictions of his position as monk and parish priest. He left Vienna precipitously on November 19, 1783, in the carriage of a Professor Petzold who was returning to Leipzig. In Leipzig he began to study with Platner, who of all the Wolffian philosophers was later to be among those most open to the work of Kant[8]. Following the advice of friends from Vienna to seek help from Christoph Martin Wieland, the eminent man of letters known among other things for his editorship of the influential literary journal *Der Teutsche Merkur*, Reinhold arrived in Weimar from Leipzig in May 1784. He was received there warmly by Wieland. In Weimar he encountered the philosopher, poet, and historian Johann Gottfried Herder, who was to play a key part in his conversion to Protestantism[9]. This conversion took place formally in the month of his arrival. Within a short time Reinhold began collaborating on Wieland's journal, and in 1785 married Wieland's daughter, Sophie.

There was nothing assured about Reinhold's early success as a philosopher. He seems to have had no substantial knowledge of Kant's philosophy before 1785[10]. The first reference to Kant came in the form of a defence of Herder in a review of Herder's *Ideen zur Philosophie der Geschichte der Menschheit* in 1784[11]. In this review Reinhold contrasted Herder favourably with Kant, whom he considered to be nothing more than an old-fashioned metaphysician. When he later realized he had seriously misjudged Kant, Reinhold apologised to Kant directly. The record was corrected, and Reinhold's reputation as an expositor established, in eight letters on the Kantian philosophy published in *Der Teutsche Merkur* in 1786 and 1787 – letters which were subsequently extended and republished under the title *Briefe über die Kantische Philosophie* (*Letters on the Kantian Philosophy*) in 1790[12]. Not only did the *Letters* provide a readily accessible

---

8 Ernst Platner (1744–1818) taught anthropology, physiology and philosophy in Leipzig. His *Handbuch der Physiologie* impressed J.M.R. Lenz, who recommended it in a letter to Jakob Sarasin, 12.12. 1777. Platner's later work *Philosophische Aphorismen* (1793) was to serve as a basis for Fichte's comments in his lectures on philosophy in Jena.

9 Cf. Karl August Böttiger: *Literarische Zustände und Zeitgenossen: Begegnungen und Gespräche im klassischen Weimar*. Ed. Klaus Gerlach and René Sternke (Berlin: Aufbau, 1998), 293.

10 In the foreward to the *New Theory* Reinhold indicates that he began a formal study of Kant in 1785.

11 Published in the journal *Der Teutsche Merkur*, vol. 2 (1784), lxxxi–lxxxix.

12 A second set of letters on topics ranging from law and politics to the will was published as volume two of the *Letters on the Kantian Philosophy* in 1792. For a brief overview of the additions and revisions Reinhold made to the original version of the *Letters*, see Alexander von Schönborn: *Karl Leonhard Reinhold: Eine annotierte Bibliographie* (Stuttgart-Bad Cannstatt: frommann-holzboog, 1991), 70–1, and Karl Leonhard Reinhold: *Letters on the Kantian Philosophy*. Ed. Karl Ameriks, trans. James Hebbeler (Cambridge: Cambridge University Press, 2005), xlviii–l. The major additions to the 1786-7 letters in the first volume of the *Letters* published in 1790 are excerpted and translated in the immediately preceding above, 124–226.

commentary of Kant's *Critique of Pure Reason*, which, burdened with the
reputation of being difficult to approach, had been languishing by the mid
1780s after some harsh criticism. The *Letters* also adjudged Kant to have
found a way out of the Spinozism dispute – a debate that had started in
1785 when Jacobi alleged that Lessing, the esteemed writer of the German
Enlightenment, had been a "Spinozist", a label that amounted to the claim
that he had been an atheist. Jacobi had wanted to show that Enlightenment
and the unassisted use of reason inevitably lead to atheism and determinism.
Reinhold championed Kant in the *Letters*, no doubt partly also in defence
of his own strong belief in Enlightenment ideals, on the grounds that Kant's
philosophy had effectively resolved the Spinozism dispute. He argued that
Kant had shown the impossibility of proving or disproving the existence of
God by reason, and at the same time argued that belief in God is no mere
superstition, and does not depend simply on "blind faith". As Reinhold
argued, Kant had demonstrated that there is no necessary conflict between
reason and faith. In offering an interpretation of Kant's philosophy of
which Kant himself later approved[13], Reinhold showed that a way out of
an impasse that threatened both rational thought and religious faith could
be found. As Reinhold argued, philosophy in the form given to it by Kant
could be restricted to, and emerge from, the material concerns of this world
without ultimately abandoning its otherworldly commitments[14]. Moreover,
the *Letters*, written on the basis of Kant's first *Critique*, could also appear
prescient, as the moral grounds of religion that Reinhold diagnosed as being
central to Kant's philosophy were indeed to become the focus of Kant's
second *Critique*, the *Critique of Pure Reason*, which appeared in 1788.
Reinhold's *Letters* on Kant's philosophy, therefore, had seemed to anticipate
a direction that Kant was in fact to take in his development of the Critical
philosophy. Such was the success of the *Letters*, Reinhold was able to obtain

---

13   Kant's letter to Reinhold of 28th and 31st December 1787 makes this clear. Kant also praised
     Reinhold in his *Über den Gebrauch teleologischer Prinzipien in der Philosophie* (1788),
     ending the essay with a congratulatory acknowledgement of Reinhold's position at Jena:
     "I have just learned that the author of the aforementioned letters, Councillor Reinhold,
     has been for a short time Professor of Philosophy in Jena; an addition which can only be
     advantageous to this celebrated university." ["Ich erfahre eben jetzt, daß der Verfasser
     obbenannter Briefe, Herr Rat Reinhold, seit kurzem Professor der Philosophie in Jena sei;
     ein Zuwachs, der dieser berühmten Universität nicht anders als sehr vorteilhaft sein kann"],
     cf. Frank 1997, 231.
14   Reinhold makes this claim explicit in the second letter. In reference to "the Kantian
     answer" Reinhold says the following: "Its arguments, which lead to faith, are forever
     secured against all objections of skilled reason, the sources of these objections are cut
     off, and all dogmatic proofs for and against God's existence – by which faith was made
     either superfluous or impossible – are annihilated": Karl Leonhard Reinhold: *Letters on
     the Kantian Philosophy*, 23.

a chair of philosophy at the University of Jena in 1787 without having published anything else of consequence.

Reinhold's *Letters on the Kantian Philosophy* set out an understanding of Kant's philosophy based on the first edition – the so-called "A" version – of the *Critique of Pure Reason*, which had been published in 1781. The revised and extended second edition or "B" version of the *Critique* appeared six years later in 1787 and clearly could not have been consulted by Reinhold when he was writing the *Merkur* letters. (The difference between the two versions of the first *Critique* appears to be of some importance for the reception of Kant's thinking and will be discussed later below.) While some evidence for Reinhold's focus on a faculty of representation can already be found in the last two *Merkur* letters published in 1787[15], the development of Reinhold's thinking culminating in the *New Theory of the Human Capacity for Representation* mainly took place after Reinhold had taken up his appointment at the University of Jena in 1787. The *New Theory* appeared with Widtmann and Mauke in Prague and Jena in 1789. A second edition was later to appear in 1795[16].

As a teacher in Jena Reinhold was popular and esteemed. By 1793 when the university was recorded to have a total enrolment of 892 students, some 600 students attended lectures[17] he gave on Kant's *Critique of Pure Reason*, on logic and metaphysics, on aesthetics, and the history of philosophy. Caroline von Beulwitz has observed that the study of Kantian philosophy under Reinhold had attracted many bright people to Jena[18]. The philosopher Forberg – thinking of Sophie Mereau who was later to write a poem on Reinhold's departure from Jena[19] – said that Kant and Reinhold could even be studied successfully by women (!)[20]. While in Jena Reinhold had contact with Friedrich Schiller – the founder, along with Johann Wolfgang Goethe, of the literary movement known as Weimar classicism. Reinhold guided Schiller's reading of Kant's philosophy.

---

15 In the eighth and final letter Reinhold discusses the role of pure sensibility in supplying the form of intuition, and intuition, which, in turn, supplies the content for the the form of the understanding. He is here clearly quite close to articulating a formal theory of representation, but stops short of doing so. See Karl Leonhard Reinhold: *Letters on the Kantian Philosophy*, 115.

16 Karl Leonhard Reinhold: *Versuch einer neuen Theorie des menschlichen Vorstellungs-vermögens* (Prag: C. Widtmann, 1795). As Ernst-Otto Onnasch reports in personal correspondence, the second edition is identical with the first, except for a minor change to the title page and changes to the table of errata. It may fairly be considered a reprint rather than a new edition.

17 Schröpfer in Hinske et al. 1993, 110.

18 Quoted in Eberhard Lange: "Schiller und Kant", in Hinske et al. 1993, 125.

19 Theodore Ziolkowski: *Das Wunderjahr in Jena: Geist und Gesellschaft 1794–95* (Stuttgart: Klett-Cotta, 1998), 74.

20 Ziolkowski 1998, 71.

In 1793 Reinhold was called to the professorial chair in philosophy in Kiel (then belonging to Denmark) to replace Tetens, who had moved to Copenhagen. The chair he vacated in Jena was in turn filled by Fichte. Among the remarks made by Goethe about Reinhold is a note in his *Annals* for the year 1794: "After Reinhold's departure, which was justly seen as a great loss for the academy, Fichte was called to his position, with boldness, indeed with rashness."[21] Reinhold left for Kiel with his family in 1794. His students in Jena were sorry to see him go and gave him several ovations. In his later career his capacity to attract students to his lectures and to his thinking remained undiminished. He continued to search for a philosophy, as he called it, "without epithet", turning to the work of Fichte[22], Jacobi[23] and Bardili for support. His *Essay on a Critique of Logic from the Viewpoint of Language* was published in 1806. A further work on language, the *Foundation of a Synonomics for the General Use of Language in the Philosophical Sciences*, appeared in 1812. Reinhold died in Kiel on 10 November 1823.

II.

Reinhold's intellectual development reflected the development of European philosophy from the end of the medieval period. He was familiar with scholastic philosophy and the work of Descartes, Malebranche, Spinoza, Locke, Leibniz, and Wolff, all of which left traces in his own philosophical endeavours[24]. The major influence exercised on his outlook and thinking, of course, was the Critical philosophy of Immanuel Kant.

Jena was already established as a centre of Kantian philosophy before Reinhold took up his chair. Christian Gottfried Schütz had begun to lecture on Kant's philosophy in Jena as early as 1784. Schütz's newspaper, the *Allgemeine Literatur Zeitung*, did much to disseminate Kantian thinking. It was in the pages of this paper that Reinhold seems first to have encountered the thinking of Kant. In the winter semester of 1785 Carl Christian Erhard Schmid gave lectures on the *Critique of Pure Reason* in Jena. Schmid later

---

21 Goethe: *Werke*. 14 Vols. Hamburger Ausgabe. Ed. Erich Trunz (Munich: C.H. Beck, 1981), X, 440.

22 On Reinhold's relation to the philosophy of Fichte, see Ives Radrizzani: "Reinholds Bekehrung zur Wissenschaftslehre und das Studium von Fichtes *Grundlage des Naturrechts*", in *Die Philosophie Karl Leonhard Reinholds*. Ed. Martin Bondeli (Amsterdam: Rodopi, 2003), 241–57.

23 For a discussion of Reinhold's "conversion" to Jacobi, see George di Giovanni: "1799: The Year of Reinhold's Conversion to Jacobi", in *Die Philosophie Karl Leonhard Reinholds*, (ed. Bondeli), 259–82.

24 Cf. Schröpfer in Hinske et al. 1993, 101.

produced a dictionary of Kant's terms, first published in 1786[25]. Gottlieb Hufeland, a jurist, gave a Kantian twist to the study of jurisprudence[26]. In view of this emerging general interest in Kant's philosophy, the atmosphere was ripe for Reinhold's eight letters on the Kantian Philosophy. The *Letters* made Reinhold a leading exponent of Kant[27]. Kant, as already mentioned, declared himself impressed with Reinhold's work. The relative clarity of Reinhold's writing – more accessible than Kant's own – means that he can fairly be regarded as the first to make Kant's work more generally available to a philosophically minded public. Reinhold's son Ernst was correct to point out that the *Letters* also spoke to an audience beyond that of the small circle of professional philosophers who had dominated philosophy in Germany hitherto[28].

One of the notable students who studied under Reinhold was Friedrich von Hardenberg, subsequently known to the literary world under the name Novalis, who took up residence in Jena from 1790 to 1791. Novalis wrote to Reinhold in October 1791 that he could imagine an evening conversation between Reinhold and Schiller where he himself was not present, and felt sad. He wrote of his admiration for the work of Reinhold which retained for him an enduring "sublime enchantment"[29]. In a surviving fragment, Novalis noted that Kant grounded the possibility, Reinhold the actuality, and Fichte the necessity of philosophy[30].

Manfred Frank has written extensively about the work of the "Reinhold circle of students"[31], which included thinkers such as Baron Franz Paul von Herbert, Niethammer (a distant cousin and friend of the poet Hölderlin), the Danish poet Baggesen, Erhard and Forberg, as well as Novalis. These were all independent thinkers, however, and their admiration for Reinhold

---

25 *Wörterbuch zum leichteren Gebrauch der Kantischen Schriften* began life as a companion to Schmid's work on Kant's first *Critique* in 1786. A new expanded version appeared in 1788. A third edition was published in 1795, and a fourth in 1798. This fourth edition was reproduced in 1998 by the Wissenschaftliche Buchgesellschaft, Darmstadt as a companion volume to their edition of Kant's works.

26 The teaching of Kantian philosophy at Jena has been discussed in detail in Hinske et al. 1993.

27 Terry Pinkard: *Hegel: a Biography* (Cambridge: Cambridge University Press, 2000), 123ff., discusses the importance of Reinhold's work in the context of disputes and ideas that influenced Hegel.

28 Ernst Reinhold: *Karl Leonhard Reinholds Leben und litterarisches Wirken* (Jena: F. Frommann, 1825), 43. Quoted in Schröpfer 1993, 105.

29 "Ihre Werke immer einen unaussprechlichen Sinn und Geist hinreißenden über alles erhabenen Zauber für mich behalten [...]": *Novalis Schriften*. Ed. Richard Samuel with Hans-Joachim Mähl and Gerhard Schulz (Darmstadt: Wissenschaftliche Buchgesellschaft, 1965), vol. 4, 97.

30 *Novalis Schriften*, vol. 2, 143.

31 Frank 1997, 30ff. and passim.

did not prevent them from being critical. In a recent essay, Frank has called
these students "insubordinate"[32]. Hölderlin wrote to his brother on New
Year's Day 1799 that Kant was the "Moses of our nation". He described the
state of Germany, as he understood it, as one of "Erschlaffung" – a state of
torpor. The Germans, he claimed, were too fond of their own little worlds
and had become restricted to a limited domesticity. Kant, like Moses, had
given them the law, and led them into the free, solitary wilderness. There
was a widely shared view that Kant's work had shown the way, but that
Kant, perhaps like Moses in Hölderlin's image, had not himself reached the
Promised Land.

Reinhold held the view that Kant's work was still in need of completion.
In his teaching at Jena, Reinhold found himself having to think Kant's
premises through from the beginning again in an attempt to construct a
philosophy that would be both universally valid and universally acceptable.
He thought he had identified a major philosophical problem in the
transference of predicates that properly belonged to representation to things
themselves, and developed his theory of representation to deal with this.
His *New Theory* was offered as one of his courses in the winter semester
of 1789.

The work was read by Schleiermacher, with interest, but also with independence. In his unpublished essay "On Freedom" (1790–92) Schleiermacher
followed Reinhold in emphasizing the capacity of desire, understood
primarily as "drive". But he believed that the capacity of desire could not be
derived from the capacity for representation, because in that case practical
reason would not have the autonomous power to enact a representation[33].
Reinhold's concept of drives – the drive to form and the drive to matter –
may well have influenced Schiller in his *Aesthetic Letters*.

Kant seems to have remained grateful to Reinhold, even though he
did not finally endorse Reinhold's own work[34]. He nevertheless refused
to make direct statements against Reinhold. One response has been
recorded: Kant is reported to have shrugged his shoulders about Reinhold
in a general discussion of philosophers[35]. With Fichte, on the other hand,
there was no question of holding back: Kant was openly critical of Fichte's
work.

---

32 Manfred Frank: *Auswege aus dem deutschen Idealismus* (Frankfurt am Main: Suhrkamp,
     2007), 14.
33 Julia A Lamm: "The Early Philosophical Roots of Schleiermacher's Notion of *Gefühl*,
     1788–1794." *The Harvard Theological Review* 87 (1), (Jan 1994), 84.
34 Rudolf Malter (ed.): *Immanuel Kant in Rede und Gespräch* (Hamburg: Felix Meiner,
     1990), 432.
35 Malter 1990, 569.

Although Reinhold presented his thinking about Kant in the *New Theory* as a further exposition of the Critical philosophy, it is also clear with this work that Reinhold, in the words of Karl Ameriks, changed from being an expositor and disseminator of Kant's philosophy – a role he had faithfully adhered to in the *Letters* – to being its critic and its reviser. By purporting to ground Kant's philosophy on a principle of representation – one that Reinhold argued had largely been set out as such in the *Critique of Pure Reason* but not made clear and systematic – Reinhold accomplished much more than mere exposition of another philosophy: he became the first in a long line of post-Kantian thinkers to posit an allegedly more convincing, more comprehensive and more systematic ground for the Critical philosophy itself.

From this perspective it becomes possible to see that Reinhold, through his dissemination of Kantian thought and the transposition of this same thought, provided both a point of access to Kant's philosophy as well as a compelling problematic that served as a bridge for the idealistically oriented thinkers who were to follow him. This suggests his importance in any general assessment of this period in German philosophy. It also becomes possible to argue that Reinhold's particular understanding of Kant's Critical philosophy became a factor in the reception of Kant's thought in its own right. This is a point that has been made by Ameriks, who suggests that certain recent reactions to Kant indicate a general susceptibility towards the "old story of how the Kantian era, and everything in its long shadow, was marked by a confused obsession with representationalism and the project of securing for philosophy a strict scientific status of its own"[36]. In Ameriks's view, Reinhold contributed to a general distortion of Kant's legacy by saddling Kant's philosophy retrospectively with a notion of representation that was not properly germane to it. From this angle, Reinhold can be implicated in the "old story" of confused representationalism both through his expositions of Kantian thought as well as his own account of representation, whose assumptions about an underlying principle said to complete Kant's project became bound up with the project of the Critical philosophy itself. As Ameriks suggests, this old story must be left behind if the fate of our modern values is somehow thought to depend on it.

However much this assessment of the representationalist tradition and its problems has merit, it is also the case that Kant himself must be held responsible for some of the distortions and creative (mis-)readings his

---

36 Karl Ameriks: *Kant and the Fate of Autonomy. Problems in the Appropriation of the Critical Philosophy* (Cambridge: Cambridge University Press, 2000), 89.

philosophy inspired. Martin Heidegger examined one of the most problematic aspects of the *Critique of Pure Reason* in his *Kant and the Problem of Metaphysics* (1929)[37], a study that led him to assess the differences between the first and the second editions of the *Critique*. In this work, Heidegger found support in the "A" version of the *Critique* for a comprehensive theory of the imagination underlying the acknowledged duality of sensibility and understanding in Kant's conception of consciousness. The later "B" version of the *Critique*, by contrast, seems in Heidegger's view to have attenuated passages in the "A" version that had argued for the foundational significance of the transcendental imagination (Kant uses the term "Einbildungskraft"). Certain passages were even removed from the new edition altogether. Instead of the suggestive power of a faculty of the imagination under which both sensibility and the understanding were to be subsumed, the "B" version highlighted the key importance of the understanding and the aspect of spontaneity governing it. There was accordingly, in Heidegger's reading of Kant, no longer any recourse in the "B" version to a legitimating foundational principle lying beyond the understanding, or else no way to render either its existence or its functionality plain in philosophical language. Nevertheless, as Heidegger argued, the question of the existence of such a foundation was not removed entirely from the B version of the Critique, since the laying of a foundation itself was still central to Kant's purpose.

Whilst Heidegger's view of differences between the two versions of Kant's first *Critique* is not without controversy (and is certainly not the last word on the matter), it does indicate from a later perspective how Reinhold's attention might have been drawn to a notable shortcoming of the Critical philosophy. On the one hand, as Heidegger suggests, a careful reading of the first version of the *Critique* could not fail to identify the importance Kant attached to the need to find a legitimate, unifying ground for the dualisms that play a prominent role in Kant's argument: pre-eminently that between sensibility and understanding, but also the contrast between thing-in-itself and sensation, the apriori and the aposteriori, and indeed the duality of theory and practice[38]. Moreover, Reinhold's main study of Kant, which, as we have seen, took place in the period immediately before the appearance of the *Letters*, i.e. in 1785–6, was initially informed only by the first version of the *Critique* (and possibly also Kant's clarifications of it in the *Prolegomena to Any Future Metaphysics* published in 1783), which is to say, by the version in which the question of an underlying faculty with its seat in the imagination is brought into view. Even in the second edition

---

37   Martin Heidegger: *Kant and the Problem of Metaphysics*. Transl. and with an introduction
     by James S. Churchill (Bloomington and London: Indiana University Press, 1962).
38   Frank 1997, 63.

of the *Critique*, which Reinhold would have had to digest quickly, as its publication coincided with his assumption of responsibilities as professor of philosophy at the University of Jena (Reinhold mentions the interruption that occurred at this time to his study of Kant[39]), the question of some sort of foundational faculty could not (in Heidegger's view at least) entirely be dispensed with. In view of the expectation about the existence of such a faculty in the human mind that the *Critique of Pure Reason* raises in its earlier version and perhaps fails to dispel in the later version, it is not surprising that Reinhold's *New Theory* could link the *Critique of Pure Reason* to the general endeavour to secure philosophy once and for all to an unshakeable ground on which all previous schools of philosophy – each confirmed in its intrinsic value, yet at the same time purged of its manifest failings – would come together and be reconciled. This project would only succeed if the philosophical foundation to which Kant alludes could be made secure and fully evident. Reinhold believed himself to have uncovered this (as he saw it) Kantian foundation in the idea of a power of, or capacity for, representation, a capacity that would take the place of Kant's "far more complicated" notion of cognition (*Erkenntnis*)[40] and allow a more systematic laying out of the connections between sensibility, understanding and reason. Such a capacity for representation, moreover, would have one further redeeming feature, if the movement from the A to the B version of the *Critique* involving an attenuation of the notion of the transcendental imagination can be given credence: a capacity for representation, through the principle of representation per se (*bloße Vorstellung*), could link sensibility with the understanding without compromising the status of the latter, and indeed without involving the Critical philosophy in any occult speculation about a mysterious primordial force. This capacity for representation could thus also appear in line with Kant's revisions in the second edition of the *Critique*, which highlighted the role played by the understanding in consciousness. In the *New Theory*, therefore, Reinhold could look upon his work with some justification as continuing to provide a valuable service in the advancement of Kant's Critical philosophy, even if the question of whether he had introduced a crucial departure from it was now also raised into view.

The status of Reinhold's revisions of the Critical philosophy, as well as the merit of his attempt to put forward a "new theory", became the subject of debate among Reinhold's disciples as well as his critics soon after the appearance of the *New Theory* in 1789. This debate coursed through German philosophical circles in the 1790s and involved most of the significant

---

39   Cf. Foreword to the *New Theory*, 24 [58 in original edition].
40   These are Reinhold's words in the Foreword to the *New Theory*, 26 [65–66].

thinkers of the day, among them Schulze (also known under his pseudonym
Aenesidemus), Maimon, Diez, Fichte, Schelling, Novalis, Friedrich Schlegel
and the redoubtable Jacobi, whose provocative assertions about Lessing had
provided so much stimulation for Reinhold's reading of Kant in the first
place. The debate also involved Reinhold as an active participant, and led
him to issue clarifying restatements of his philosophy, as well as certain
modifications of it. The most significant among these modifications was
contained in the first volume of the *Beyträge zur Berichtigung bisheriger
Mißverständnisse der Philosophen* (*Contributions to the Correction of
Certain Misunderstandings in Philosophy*) published in 1790, in which an
increasing shift towards the subject as the enabling ground of the capacity
for representation can be identified. As Manfred Frank points out, it was
this first volume of the *Beyträge* with its further development of Reinhold's
now openly declared "elementary philosophy" that was to prove more
important than the *New Theory* for Reinhold's coevals, even if the *New
Theory* remains Reinhold's major work from today's perspective.

The first volume of the *Beyträge* was also important for Fichte, into whose
context with its pivotal contrast of the self and the non-self Reinhold's
philosophy seemed to be evolving. Reinhold was alive to this evolution
himself, abjuring his own theories in favour of Fichte's in 1797 when he no
longer felt able to defend his elementary philosophy satisfactorily against the
mounting chorus of detractors. A few years later he was to change course
again, abandoning Fichte and his own commitment to a single ground for
metaphysical philosophy in a turn toward Jacobi, whose unremitting focus
on the need to embrace religious truth through an act of faith alone finally
appeared too compelling to resist. By the beginning of the new century,
the cause of foundationalist philosophy in the tradition laid out for it by
Reinhold had been seriously weakened. The new creed followed by the
early Romantics instead favoured a more modest approach of "ceaseless
approximation" toward the goal of spiritual and moral truth[41].

IV.

Reinhold's *New Theory of the Human Capacity for Representation* is divided
into three books and a foreward, the last of which, published separately prior
to the *New Theory*, contains preliminary statements about the situation of
philosophy before the appearance of the *Critique of Pure Reason* and provides
an abbreviated intellectual biography of the author. While the first book sets

---

41 This is the position compellingly argued by Frank in his lectures on early Romanticism
    brought together under the title of "Unendliche Annäherung". See Frank 1997.

out the case for a new investigation of the capacity for representation, the second book expounds the actual theory of the capacity for representation, and the third book, the longest and the most complicated of the three, puts forward a theory of rational cognition, culminating in an idea of the absolute subject. In somewhat of a departure, the third book concludes with an introductory discussion outlining a theory of the capacity for desire. The connections between this theory and the capacity for representation forming the centrepiece of Reinhold's *New Theory* remain largely undeveloped. At the beginning of each of the three books of the *New Theory* stand quotes from Locke's *Essay Concerning Human Understanding*. This use of Locke is somewhat misleading as Locke's theories, while not discussed entirely without sympathy in Reinhold's work, nevertheless form part of an older representationalist backdrop that Reinhold certainly means to supersede. Both Locke and Leibniz, the other important old-style representationalist who features prominently in the *New Theory*, are referenced for their failure to complete Kant's Copernican turn toward evaluating the nature of the subject's representations, rather than with any admiration for their particular achievements.

Indeed, much is made throughout the *New Theory* of the cognitive problem that occurs when predicates are transferred through representation to objects without a proper warrant to do so – one of the key lessons that Reinhold draws from Kant. Kant had highlighted this problem in relation to the thing-in-itself, which, he contended, could not be brought within the subject's capacity for representation. Instead of these "noumena", which could never be directly apprehended or known, Kant limited subjective awareness to cognition of "phenomena" or "appearances" (*Erscheinungen*) and thus set out a bounded realm for all human cognition. The duality of noumenal and phenomenal awareness, which, as Kant conceived it, was necessarily imposed as a limit condition on human representation, also contained the seed of the problem of representation that Reinhold took over from Kant. Reinhold's response was not to follow the conceptually involved, longer path leading to what might be referred to as the "horizon of objectivity" outlined by Kant by way of a problem of judgment (the question posed at the beginning of the *Critique* of how synthetic apriori judgments are possible). Rather, Reinhold set out on a shorter route[42] to the question of objective knowledge by proposing to answer a related – but, for Kant, perhaps ultimately secondary – question: how cognition of objects in human subjects occurs on the basis of an underlying, "foundational"

---

42 See Ameriks's enlightening discussion of Reinhold's short argument for the unknowability
    of things in themselves: 2000, 125–136.

capacity for (or faculty of) representation. If this capacity contained within
it, or was, the basic enabling principle according to which cognition occurs,
Reinhold appears to have reasoned, then the long path to the question of
objectivity could be circumvented, and a more productive, more readily
comprehensible short path to knowledge of objects could then be traversed.
This more amenable shorter path to knowledge of objects would have the
added benefit, once it was fully derived from the principle of representation
on which it stood, of laying out a more systematic and complete account
of knowledge itself. Reinhold's mature philosophy, beginning with the *New
Theory*, therefore set itself the ambitious task of indicating nothing less than
the ground, as well as the nature, of systematic knowledge in general. It
was the promise of this path to knowledge in general that was to prove
so alluring for Reinhold's followers in the tradition of German idealism,
beginning with Fichte.

One further point about the *New Theory* can be made at the outset:
Reinhold does not repeat the basic problem dogging previous adherents
of representational thinking. Since he has made the Copernican turn with
Kant, he does not attempt to reduce representation to the question of the
representation of images[43], whether in line with the empirically based strategy
pursued by Locke, or the conceptually based strategy followed by Leibniz.
In an important sense, as Reinhold makes clear, representation is technically
"blind" to the input data it receives through the outer sense; there can be
no question of a direct relay of external images to the mind through the
operative power of representation. Rather, Reinhold establishes his account
of representation under assumptions that set out a triangulation of that
which is represented, that which represents ("the representing entity") and
the representation itself. This triangulation casts the question of cognition
of objects not merely as a question of receptivity – since it must be granted
that a measure of receptivity is clearly involved in representation – but also,
and in a sense more importantly, as a question of how images are actively
brought forth or "produced" (a term used throughout the *New Theory*)
from circumstances where no direct grasping of the essence of such images
is actually possible. Reinhold's approach proposes to make evident how the
process of delivering a representation under these circumstances is to be
comprehended. The triangulation of representing, on the side of the subject,
the represented, on the side of the object, and the representation (the unity
of representing and represented), which occurs at the first and deepest level
of human consciousness, promises a new account of the representational

---

43 Ameriks 2000, 128. Reinhold expands on the "prejudice that representations are images of
    things" on pp. 240–244 of the *New Theory* (pagination refers to Reinhold's original text).

process according to which each factor involved in cognition can be made explicit and the interplay of all factors involved in cognition – and thus also in the construction of rational knowledge – can be properly accounted for. While the blindness, technically speaking, of the capacity for representation to the images that are received could be taken to imply a certain idealism in regard to the objects of the outside world, and was in fact taken to imply as much by some later thinkers, Reinhold nevertheless upheld an underlying realism in relation to the objects of the outer world and did not doubt the existence of things-in-themselves[44]. Nevertheless, it was precisely the arguments made by Reinhold for the independence of the representative capacity that appear to have created problems for his attempts to maintain such realism.

While the failure of Reinhold's project to found all knowledge on a single principle of representation, the so-called "Satz des Bewusstseins" (or "article of consciousness") of his later philosophy, has been lamented with justification – Ameriks calls the final outcome of his thought a "shipwreck with spectators"[45] – it is also the case that a rich tradition in German thought was brought into being in the years immediately following the appearance of the *New Theory* and the later forms Reinhold was to give to this theory. As Manfred Frank has shown, Reinhold's contribution to this tradition, whose blossoming included the sublime poetry of Hölderlin, the literary-philosophical achievement of German Romanticism, and the comprehensively worked out philosophical systems of Fichte and Hegel, reveals a fertile posterity, not just a shipwreck. This alone argues for an ongoing assessment of the importance of Reinhold for us today.

Notes on the text and further reading

Two editions of the *Versuch einer neuen Theorie des menschlichen Vorstellungsvermögens* appeared in Reinhold's lifetime – in October 1789 and 1795. A reprint of the first edition was issued in 1963 by the Wissenschaftliche Buchgesellschaft in Darmstadt. The first volume of an annotated edition of the *Versuch*, edited by Ernst-Otto Onnasch, has recently appeared with the Felix Meiner Verlag[46]. Our translation follows the original text of 1789, which Onnasch's updated edition also faithfully

---

44 The argument defending such realism occurs, for example, on pp. 295–300 of the *New Theory* (pagination in Reinhold's original text).
45 Ameriks 2000, 159.
46 Karl Leonhard Reinhold: *Versuch einer neuen Theorie des menschlichen Vorstellungs-vermögens*. Hrsg., mit einer Einleitung und Anmerkungen von Ernst-Otto Onnasch, Teilband 1 (Hamburg: Felix Meiner Verlag, 2010).

adheres to. Where infelicities, discrepancies or errors not marked in the table of errata in the original edition needed to be taken account of, we have indicated these in our translation in a footnote. Numbers in square brackets in the translation indicate page numbers in the original 1789 text. All emphasis indicated in the text is Reinhold's own.

In matters of translation from the German to English, attention must first be drawn to our rendering of the title of the *New Theory*. While it is common to render Reinhold's title, as Ameriks has done, as "essay on a new theory of the human <u>faculty</u> of representation"[47], we have favoured the term "capacity" for two main reasons. For one thing, Reinhold repeatedly refers to the importance of ordinary language usage in making arguments for a proper understanding of terms. From this point of view, the common word "capacity" (for "Vermögen"), which suggests a potential to accomplish some action or task, would appear to avoid the unnecessary technical implications of the specialist term "faculty". Secondly, the term "faculty" suggests dimensions of a faculty psychology in the vein of the eighteenth century rationalist and Leibnizian Christian Wolff and other thinkers. Such a faculty psychology seems very far from Reinhold's true intentions in the *New Theory*.

Following distinctions Reinhold draws between the outer world and the mind's activity, further complicated by Reinhold's references to outer and inner "sense" which both relate to that mind, we have distinguished between the material of the inner "disposition" ("Beschaffenheit") and the "constitution" or qualities ("Beschaffenheit[en]") of the outside world. Aspects of the objective world are referenced as "attributes" ("Merkmale") or properties of the world within the mind itself. In all cases Reinhold is concerned to avoid an amalgamation of these properties animated by the mind with their finally unknowable actuality. His concern is to highlight the way cognition of objects renders, but also limits, what can be known of objects themselves.

The word "Gemüth" ("Gemüt" in modern German), which was often used as the German equivalent of "mens" in eighteenth and nineteenth century translations from Latin[48], in our view is rendered by the term "mind" in English mostly without difficulty. We have not found it necessary to express it in any other way.

Reinhold uses the adjective "bloß" in connection with areas of the mind and perception variously responsible for organizing and intuiting the appearances, among them the capacity for representation itself. In these cases Reinhold appears to indicate a pure functionality of that area or capacity relating to its form which we have rendered with the term

---

47   See e.g. *Reinhold: Letters on the Kantian Philosophy* (Ameriks [ed.]), xxxvii.
48   See, for instance, in Kant: *Opus Postumum*, Ak.-Ausg., 22:112. We are grateful to Alberto Vanzo for drawing our attention to this reference.

"per se". This term is distinguished from the general effects of the operation of the functionality relating to its content which Reinhold indicates with the term "überhaupt". We have rendered this latter with the term "in general". In rare cases both the functionality and its effects are used together.

A full list of technical terms and their translation can be found in the appendices at the end of this volume.

Finally, asterisks that appear in the text indicate Reinhold's own annotations. The notes of the editors are indicated by the use of Arabic numerals.

A helpful list of materials for scholars interested in Reinhold's philosophy may be found in *Reinhold: Letters on the Kantian Philosophy*, edited by Karl Ameriks (xxxix–xlii). Excellent introductions to the work of Reinhold are provided by the studies of Frederick Beiser, *The Fate of Reason: German Philosophy from Kant to Fichte* (Cambridge, Mass.: Harvard University Press, 1988), Manfred Frank, *"Unendliche Annäherung." Die Anfänge der philosophischen Frühromantik* (Frankfurt: Suhrkamp, 1997), Karl Ameriks, *Kant and the Fate of Autonomy: Problems in the Appropriation of the Critical Philosophy* (Cambridge: Cambridge University Press, 2000), and Dieter Henrich, *Between Kant and Hegel: Lectures on German Idealism* (Cambridge, Mass.: Harvard University Press, 2003). Helpful philosophical overviews are also given by Terry Pinkard: *German Philosophy 1760–1869* (Cambridge: Cambridge University Press, 2002) and Paul Franks, "All or Nothing: Systematicity and Nihilism in Jacobi, Reinhold, and Maimon", in *The Cambridge Companion to German Idealism*, ed. Karl Ameriks (Cambridge: Cambridge University Press, 2000). An important, detailed, and specialist discussion of Reinhold's philosophy can be found in Martin Bondeli, *Das Anfangsproblem bei Karl Leonhard Reinhold* (Frankfurt: Klostermann, 1995). Ernst-Otto Onnasch's notes on Reinhold's *New Theory* are also very helpful: Karl Leonhard Reinhold, *Versuch einer neuen Theorie des menschlichen Vorstellungsvermögens*, ed. with an introduction and notes by Ernst-Otto Onnasch, vol. 1 (Hamburg: Felix Meiner Verlag, 2010).

Faustino Fabbianelli has published a collection of the early reviews of Reinhold's treatise in the literary and philosophical journals of Reinhold's day – see his *Die zeitgenössischen Rezensionen der Elementarphilosophie K. L. Reinholds* (Hildesheim: Olms, 2003). Gerhard Fuchs's study *Karl Leonhard Reinhold – Illuminat und Philosoph* (Frankfurt: Peter Lang, 1994) provides interesting background material on Reinhold's life and career.

A further list of works relating to Reinhold can be found in the bibliography listed in the appendices. A chronology listing the publication of Reinhold's principal works of philosophy is also included.

Karl Leonhard Reinhold

Essay on a New Theory of The Human Capacity for Representation

Reinhold's Foreword to the Theory of Representation

On what has been Happening with the Kantian Philosophy[1]

The period in German philosophy directly following Leibniz and Wolff is not yet over, and so it is not surprising that its merits have been variously judged and that there is little agreement about whether it should be designated *eclectic* or alternatively as *empirical*; as if its imminent end is to be seen at the same time either as the end or as the beginning of the golden age of science. It may well seem stranger that opinions are just as divided about the *preceding* philosophy, [: 2] and that its very defenders and eulogists often fail to recognize the success even of its founder, through which he laid the foundations for the *current* philosophy. *Wolff*, by giving scientific form to the great discoveries of Leibniz, had set up a complete system of dogmatic metaphysics, and no dogmatist after him has been able to eliminate anything significant from this system or to add anything significant to it. The later eclectics began to diverge from this system when they adopted the rhapsodic instead of the scientific form in their discussion of metaphysics. Never before has a philosophical system found such swift and such universal acceptance as the Leibniz-Wolff system. It was accepted after only brief resistance[2] by the best minds of the nation and by the mediocre, and the majority of academic teachers vied with the best academics in declaring themselves in favour of a philosophy in which the most difficult and most important tasks of speculation have been solved with unprecedented thoroughness and clarity, and in which the interests of religion and morality were harmonized with the boldest claims [: 3] of reason. Yet for this very reason, and almost as

---

1   This preface is an edited version of the text that appeared first in Wieland's *Der teutsche Merkur* 1789, vol. 2, 3–37, 113–135. Manfred Kuehn calls the essay: *On the Destiny of the Kantian Philosophy till Now*. Dieter Henrich calls it "On the Destinies Kantian Philosophy Hitherto Had", 123. "Destinies" [*Schicksale*] figures also in the title of Christian Gottfried Schütz's lecture given in 1772: Über verschiedene widrige Schicksale der deutschen Philosophie. ["On various adverse destinies of German philosophy"]. In that lecture Schütz speaks of "Sectirerey", the sectarianism and diverse views of philosophy in the wake of Wolff's work. Cf. Schröpfer 1993, 14–15.

2   Reinhold is referring to the dispute between Wolff and the Pietists, especially August Hermann Francke (1663–1727), which raged in the 1720s in Halle and led to Wolff's dismissal.

swiftly, the essential principles of this universally popular philosophy lost the charm of novelty. Through such frequent use they gained the popularity of common maxims, and independent thinkers, while still following their lead, soon found it necessary to venture on to the path of observation, since Wolff had left them so little to do in the field of speculation. It was only natural that analytical acumen invested its energy in concrete empirical concepts[3] after it seemed complete in abstract notions, and that observation began when definition had no more to do. Some more recent writers thought they were enhancing the merits of observational philosophy by contrasting it as sharply as possible with the disparaged philosophy of Wolff, without taking into account that the problems the former sought to solve in nature had for the most part first been formulated or more closely *defined* by the very work they so decried; that the study of experience could not [: 4] succeed at all through common sense, however healthy, but only through reason guided by principles and trained in speculation, and that knowledge of facts acquired by groping around with no plan or by mere chance could only provide raw and mostly unusable materials unless disciplined by the scientific character of the systematic spirit. The philosophical world is filled with collectors because of the school of modern empiricists. Yet it was Wolff's work that trained the founders of actual *psychology* and *aesthetics*[4], and their efforts have far exceeded the most successful attempts of the English in these domains. The founders of purified theology and of reformed taste emerged from the school of Wolff. Philosophical theologians and philosophical aesthetic minds brought the light of philosophy to regions where it had never shone in Germany – from the mysteries of the most holy to the cabinets of ministers and princes, and to the toilet tables of ladies. A confluence of favourable conditions, which need not be enumerated here, seemed [: 5] to have completely broken down the unfortunate wall separating world from school, and Wolff's principles continued to operate without hindrance in this newly opened immeasurable field. At the same time, the *metaphysical dogmas* of the *Wolff school* based upon them either fell into oblivion when

---

3 "Empirical concept" is also Norman Kemp Smith's translation of the term "Erfahrungsbegriff" in Kant. The word occurs three times in Kant's *KrV*; twice Smith puts "empirical concept" [A224/B271; A487/B515]; the third time he puts: "it is this fundamental proposition which shows how in regard to what happens we are in a position to obtain in experience any concept whatsoever that is really determinate" where Kant had: "zeigt der Grundsatz, wie man allererst von dem, was geschieht, einen bestimmten Erfahrungsbegriff bekommen könne" [B357]. The term "empirical concept" is also used by Russell. An example he gives is "pebble".

4 The founder of Aesthetics was Alexander Gottlieb Baumgarten (q.v.). Wolff is regarded as the founder of "Psychologia empirica", and towards the middle of the eighteenth century psychology developed as a discipline in its own right, independent of metaphysics.

applied in new and multifarious ways to the empirical, or decayed because of the increasing spread of free thinking. Respect for strictly systematic discussion faded while examples of unfounded philosophical investigations couched in tasteful phrases multiplied among us. Philosophy was practised in prose and verse about every human, civic or domestic subject from the greatest to the most trivial. To incorporate the new achievements and bring them at least into some semblance of order new subjects multiplied: anthropology, history of mankind, philosophy of history, of language, of education, etc. were included in the ranks of sciences and newly won provinces of philosophy. [: 6]

What would *Leibniz*, *Wolff* or *Baumgarten* have said to anyone who had prophesied to them that a time would come when *metaphysics* would lose by the same amount that *philosophy* gained? We are actually now in such an era, and it is not going to be over for a long time. Of course the meaning of the word "philosophy" has changed a great deal during this time. The actual domain of this science became *less and less determinate* the more philosophers promulgated their achievements. The esteem and influence of the former queen of all sciences sank even lower as people began to attribute less *to her* and more to *experience*. It was to experience that the most essential principles were in the end attributed, the more these had gradually lost their scholarly character and had been dubbed maxims of good common sense. While positive theology and popular religion grew in morality and rationality through the gradual cleansing away of mythology, knowledge of our planet made extraordinary progress through physical geography and the study of lands and peoples, and empirical psychology [: 7] was enriched from all sides with highly important findings about the most obscure qualities of the human mind and heart, RATIONAL *theology*, *cosmology* and *psychology* were partly neglected, partly mistreated. Those elements of metaphysics which shortly before had been built on the unshakable ground of a universally accepted *ontology* for all time through what *Descartes* and *Leibniz* had done for the content, *Wolff* and *Baumgarten* for the form, and had seemed capable of defending religion and morality completely against superstition and unbelief, were now suddenly given up as untenable and unnecessary even by defenders of religion and morality. It cannot be held against most members of the philosophical public, who had their hands full with collecting and organizing facts, that they believed the most sacred interests of humanity were secured by their own efforts and common sense while they were endangered by metaphysics; even less, since metaphysics, in the hands of those few whose engaged in it out of a sense of duty, for professional reasons or from inclination, lost more and more of the *systematic* and *universal validity* through which alone it could [: 8] have justified its former claims. Metaphysics too was to be based on experience and *Leibniz* to be justified by *Locke*, or rather the theories of both were to be reconciled. The necessity and generality of the *ontological principles* became more suspect as the attempt to deduce them from experience was universally approved. The *principles* were now seen as *opinions*. They appeared in every new philosophical work disguised in a different *formula*. Every thinker sought to define them in his own way, built his own system and, in doing this, made use of fragments of older systems even when they contradicted each other, so long as they seemed to fit his own.

Gradually, all the great thinkers who had forged their own paths were conjured up. But the answer of each was *understood differently* by each of those who conjured him up*⁵ because there was no agreement about [: 9] the meaning of the points at issue, and this meaning was not determined by anything universally accepted. The philosophical essays which arose in this way, many of which would still have been highly esteemed twenty years ago, now found just as few critics as admirers, these being just as cold as small in number. The contradictions which encumbered each of the new doctrinal structures were hardly evident even to the minority of the small number of readers who still felt some interest in writings of this kind, given the increasingly widespread distaste for metaphysical enquiries, the unfamiliarity of philosophizing about representations without intuition, and the difficulty of finding one's way out of the labyrinths of so many opposed opinions, each of which was supported with equal acumen. Even those most acute readers could often not help being dazzled by the flights of genius and the glowing diction, most often however by the rhapsodic form of the expression which is a necessary consequence of imprecise concepts and inconsistent principles. But for writers who write with ease in this manner, and for readers who enjoy reading it, it is seen as the blessed fruit of a genuine philosophical spirit and [: 10] cultured taste.

As philosophy became *history* of philosophy in *text books*, it distanced itself more and more from the form of *strict science*. In *logic*, having *representations at all* was confused with *thinking*. Mostly, only empirical psychology was discussed, and the actual laws of thinking were everywhere mentioned only in passing, often disparagingly, in the category of old-fashioned hair-splitting. The space left for metaphysics was commonly filled with enumeration of the most famous metaphysical dogmas and the assessment of these on the basis of the so-called findings of common sense.

---

*   Compare, for example, what *Mendelssohn, Jacobi, Rehberg* and *Herder* have recently written about *Spinozism*.
5   This is a reference to the Pantheism dispute. An account of this is offered by Beiser 1987.

The basic truths of religion and morality continued to be demonstrated of course, but with proofs which hardly even the most ridiculous pedantic school master would still see as valid. One author puts up a whole host of arguments each of which he finds unassailable because the truth being discussed is not *allowed* to be questioned. Another, convinced that only one single proof could be valid, [: 11] contradicts all the others and thinks he has justified his own argument adequately; but unfortunately his work is found flawed and contradictory by his resentful colleagues. A third finally helps himself out of the embarrassment he feels when his skepticism collides with his official duties by presenting all the proofs so far known *historically* without declaring himself exclusively for one of them or for all of them together. No wonder that the broad road of the new *school philosophy* on which the leaders constantly get in each other's way is being more and more abandoned by those who think independently and who are not forced to tread it out of professional duty. Some of these thinkers have recently preferred to follow *Spinoza* in the opposite but much more consistent *dogmatism*, others *Pascal* in *supernaturalism*, and others again *Hume* in *dogmatic skepticism*. The great majority of *half thinkers*, not stupid enough to fail to notice how *metaphysics* is so *shaken* that it totters more and more, begins to doubt anything that cannot be tangibly grasped, and [: 12] boasts of its unphilosophical indifference, calling it *critical skepticism*, and leaving open any question that cannot be answered easily.

The absence of universally accepted principles was clearly evident in the publications of the philosophical world mentioned above and the need for these was becoming more and more urgent in the culture that had made such progress in other respects. In the mean time, the famous work of the philosopher of Königsberg appeared. Its goal is no less than eliminating that need for ever, and some believe it cannot possibly fail of this. Probably never before has any book, with one exception, caused such astonishment, been so admired, hated, criticized, and condemned for heresy and – misunderstood. For some years its very existence seemed to pass unnoticed,[6] and if it now occupies the general attention of the philosophical public it has gained this honor only very gradually and not so much because of itself, but rather because of reviews which praise or condemn it extravagantly. There have as yet been few writers of importance [: 13] who have declared themselves in favour of the *Kantian* system, a system which is distinguished from all former philosophies in that it must be accepted or rejected in its entirety. But these few writers have found in Kant's philosophy the complete and perfectly

---

6 This is also what Kant seems to have thought. However, see Manfred Kuehn; Norbert Hinske.

satisfying theory of the human cognitive capacity, the only possible source of universally accepted principles and the system of all systems founded in the nature of the human mind[7]. It was only natural that these and similar judgments which friends of the *Critique of Reason* could not prove to those who had not read or understood the work themselves were taken to be arrogantly presumptuous and ridiculously exaggerated. There was no lack of beardless and bearded scribblers who, partly to bring something to market, partly to have their profundity admired, thrust themselves forward as disciples of that "*Kant who grinds everything to dust*".[8] Their approach really did deserve the indignation and scorn which was heaped even on those who respected Kant's achievements thoughtfully because of everything they found to confirm their judgment. [: 14] A considerable number of philosophical minds, of which Germany is rightly proud, and among these most of the academic teachers, have declared themselves either opposed to the new system, or – and this is in fact the same thing – opposed to significant parts of it, and it was only natural that these men could only disparage the *Critique of Reason* through their objections and provisos all the more strongly the more sublimely high they would have ranked it had it sustained their examination. A not inconsiderable number in the baggage train of writers preferred to take sides against Kant in their treatment of the new fashion object, since they had rather more famous names[9] on their side and the certain prospect of not belonging among the parrots but rather to the refuters and instructors of the man whom even his most respected opponents were compelled to admire. Accordingly they repeated the attacks of their high allies, or imitated them rather with weapons borrowed from them which gained in *strong* emphasis what they lost in such hands of their former *clarity*, [: 15] as is the way with leaden wit.

The most common charge yet to be raised against the *Critique of Reason* accuses it of *incomprehensibility*.[10] This complaint is raised even

---

7   For a discussion of the early reception of Kant's *Critique*, see Manfred Kuehn 2006. Important contributions were made by Carl Christian Schmid, whose dictionary of Kantian terms was first published in 1788 in Jena. Johann Schulz published a commentary of Kant's work in 1784. Christian Gottfried Schütz, editor of the *Allgemeine Literatur-Zeitung* in Jena, published a substantial review of Kant's work in 1785, and it was this work that stimulated Reinhold into engaging with Kant's philosophy.

8   Reinhold uses the term "alles zermalmend" coined by Moses Mendelssohn in his *Morgenstunden oder Vorlesungen über das Daseyn Gottes*. The term achieved wide currency.

9   One of these "famous names" is Georg Heinrich Feder, Professor of Philosophy in Göttingen (q.v.).

10 This was something even some of Kant's supporters felt. Carl Christian Eberhard Schmid, who prepared the first Dictionary of Kantian terms, struggled to follow and prepared his lexicon to aid his own understanding. Cf. Schröpfer 1993, 48.

by those who think they have refuted the Kantian system, and who for that very reason ought rather to affirm that they had understood it. At the same time not one of the many opponents has yet stood up and maintained that he had grasped the meaning completely – none who was not compelled to confess, at least to himself, that he had found in several places insuperable obscurity. Most consider this obscurity to be the natural consequence of the apparent contradictions which they think they have found in the passages they do understand; while the adherents of the new system claim they have discovered the source of these contradictions in that very obscurity which is not supposed to be insuperable, at least for them, however difficult they confess it was to overcome it. Their answers to all the objections so far raised, like the explanations Mr *Kant* himself has made known about some of these contradictions, have no other content [: 16] than correcting the views of opponents about their misunderstanding of the *Critique of Reason*, although by these means they rather concede than refute the objection that a text which is misunderstood by so many acute minds and otherwise so competent judges *must be extremely obscure*.

This main complaint about a work which is so generally acknowledged to be important, at least in respect of what it promises, needs to be examined closely and it will become apparent in what follows that the complaint is intimately bound up with the situation I have described of the dominant so-called eclectic philosophy; that all of what has been happening with the new Kantian philosophy has occurred for reasons intrinsic to that eclectic philosophy; and that on this basis all the other accusations raised against Kant, about the restoration of scholastic hair-splitting, pointless neologisms, introduction of wretched skepticism, construction of a new idealism, collapse of the basic truths of religion and morality, can be explained with complete satisfaction. [: 17]

Assuming that the *Critique of Reason* had solved the great problem of discovering universally valid principles, would it not then already represent the only possible system of all speculative philosophy determined by the nature of our cognitive capacity and traced back to the very limits of all that is comprehensible? –

"Oh! then this system would have to be free of all difficulties, avoid all the false paths of speculation, refrain from substituting new puzzles for the old ones; it ought to be completely graspable, and utterly defeat all objections through an analysis that overcomes all hair-splitting pedantry; it ought to help the seeker after truth to avoid all involuntary errors. – How can the rest of us, whether or not we are familiar with it, expect such great things from a dogmatic system whose proofs are extremely *abstruse* and comprehensible only to the few, and whose results are far removed from the principles of familiar metaphysics and the simple doctrines of plain reason?" [*][11] [: 18]

It would serve no purpose if I were to oppose this unproven complaint with the equally unproven eulogies of those who think the *Critique of Reason* has actually fulfilled all the requirements discussed or even exceeded them. But neither do I need any prejudice in favour of the party to which I adhere to continue with my observations without taking those objections into account. It will suffice if my readers allow, as is reasonable to expect, that it is not *absolutely impossible* that the *Critique of Reason* has been misunderstood just as much by its supporters as by its opponents, however greater the number of the latter has been till now. It was not only the larger portion of *Newton's* learned contemporaries but even the better portion who found the theory of the great man that is now universally accepted so far removed [: 19] from the principles of physics known before as well as from the edicts of plain common sense, and found contradictions, puzzles and above all insuperable obscurity in his proofs, especially in the first decades after the publication of his new discoveries. Would people in France have sneered for nearly half a century with as much bitterness as our present POPULAR *philosophers* have been mocking the *followers of the Critique*, even if rather more subtly, at the *Newtonian* who prophesied to his contemporaries that the theory of attraction would be just as universally accepted and admired by their descendants as it had been rejected and decried a generation before? What would have been made in *Rome* of the assertion that *Newton* had found the means to establish the theory of the *motion of the earth*, a theory contradicted by daily *experience*, contradicting *holy writ*, and condemned by the apostolic throne, with such incontrovertible certainty that it would be supported and even taught from all philosophical podiums of this capital of orthodoxy with the prior knowledge and the approval of the supreme regent of faith? – [: 20]

"Newton's system owed this triumph to *mathematical evidence*, to which the *Kantian* system can make no claim."

Yet not even this mathematical evidence was able to prevent the almost general outrage of contemporary philosophers against Newton, an outrage so clearly similar to the current outrage against Kant. This evidence itself depended on proofs which were incomprehensible even for the majority

---

* I have taken this from the *Versuch über Gott, die Welt und die menschliche Seele*, ["Essay on God, the World and the Human Soul"] Berlin, Nikolai, 1788, and it could well be signed by most if not by all of the opponents of the Kantian system.

11 Reinhold paraphrases from Heinrich Corrodi's *Versuch über Gott, die Welt, und die menschliche Seele. Durch die gegenwärtigen philosophischen Streitigkeiten veranlaßt*, Berlin und Stettin 1788, 4th section: "Versuch einer Beurtheilung des Kantischen Angriffs auf die alte Metaphysik", 354–419.

of mathematicians at that time, or at least were declared by them to be so. What if the few who have yet understood the *Kantian* proofs saw their *logical* evidence which could rank in its persuasive power alongside the *mathematical*, which was perceived initially only by the few in Newton's work? – Is there now any philosopher still persuaded by the false pedantry of the four *syllogistic figures* and the sixteen concluding formulae? But [: 21] who cannot remember the time when these logical games were deemed important and indispensable for reasons based on the same logical evidence that now demonstrates the opposite? For the many famous supporters of those four syllogistic figures the current agreement about their nullity would have seemed just as impossible as the inevitable collapse of the *four metaphysical systems* (spiritualism, materialism, dogmatic skepticism and supernaturalism) must seem to current supporters of these opposed systems, and the peace achieved in the domain of speculative philosophy incomprehensible and inconsistent.

Assuming that the system of principles of philosophy proper found in the *Critique of Reason* were really *universally valid*, it would be consistent with the nature of the human mind that it would have to be found true by anyone who had *thoroughly* understood it; (an assumption about which I will only say here that it is not absolutely impossible), then I would assert: *first*, that [: 22] in the nature of such a system together with the current state of philosophy, *second*, that in the way this system is presented and *had to* be presented in the Kantian work, there are sound reasons why the *Critique of Reason* was *inevitably* misunderstood not only by the majority but even by the better modern philosophers. These reasons, as I hope to show, explain what has been happening with Kant's philosophy in a way that neither detracts from the honor of its begetter nor threatens the reputation of its worthy opponents.

If the new principles were to become truly *universally valid* and by their very nature *universally accepted* as well, they would have to treat every former philosophical sect with full justice, incorporating what was *true* in the basic principles of each system with the greatest determinacy, excluding the *false*, and by these means establishing a system which would allow every independent thinker to recognize what he has seen correctly from his perspective. [: 23] To develop the new principles to this end, some of the most paradoxical assertions would have to be sought out and supported, and on the other hand many of the most established cast into doubt or contradicted. It is only natural that the first attempt of this kind, however masterly, would have no success with those who have given shape to the current state of philosophy and to the others who have acquired from this the shape of their own philosophizing, in other words, that it would have to be misunderstood – and contradicted – by the *popular philosophers* who agree with each other and by the *metaphysicians* who are in dispute with one another.

To attain its sublime goal, the new attempt could only pursue a path which is precisely opposite to that which the great majority of the popular philosophers is accustomed to go on treading comfortably and without concern. Instead of the easy and amusing descent from the general to the particular, from the abstract to the concrete, [: 24] from principles accepted as established without investigation to facts, he would have to choose not only the more arduous and tedious ascent but also, if the work were to achieve something decisive for all time, continue this ascent to a height never before reached even by the most profound explorers. To reconcile the principles he was seeking with what is *true* in all former systems he would have to proceed from assertions that could not be doubted by any sect; that means, the *most general* principles yet demonstrated in philosophy would have to be for him the *particular*, from which he would have to climb to the more general, to the very *limit of the comprehensible*. How could the popular philosopher follow him without vertigo? –

What could possibly induce the popular philosopher to overcome the enormous difficulties with which an investigation of this kind must present him? He could not even dream that there might be some indispensable principles missing in philosophy. His philosophy [: 25] is built on *formulae* which have moved from the schools to common life because they have been used, sanctified and preserved in all the academies to prove *uncontested* basic practical truths, and are now taken back from ordinary life into the academies as examples of sound common sense. These are formulae which can only be doubted if one is prepared to surrender any claim to *Sensus communis*, and with it one's right to be called a philosopher. How fatuous it must seem to him if the attempt is made to examine the meaning of those formulae which he holds to be *inexplicable* because in his opinion they must be at the basis of every explanation, and *unprovable* because at the basis of every proof. Should he encounter results which are incompatible with these *truths* he holds to be *eternal*, or rather with his interpretation of these formulae, then this must in itself suffice for him as the complete refutation of the attempt. He must consider it the easiest thing in the world to present these established inconsistencies, supported only by his sophistry, to public scrutiny [: 26] in all their nakedness. He takes this to be his sacred duty since he is convinced that if these formulae are shaken the foundations of religion and morality are shaken too, and that this monstrous presumptuousness of *criticizing* understanding and reason must lead to an unprecedented plague of skepticism. He is strengthened in this opinion by the very fact that the noblest *criterion* for the correctness of the new attempt is precisely "that this adopts what is true in *each system*" and in this respect re-establishes and confirms the most characteristic discoveries made by dogmatic skepticism, materialism and supernaturalism from their one-sided perspectives. In the eyes of the popular philosopher this is the most certain sign that the new principles must be refuted. He is accustomed to thinking of these three systems as errors long since overcome, as unfortunate consequences of wretched deviation from sound common sense, of wandering in the abysmal land of chimeras. He considers the new philosophy responsible for the whole sum of heresies and mischief [: 27] which have in his opinion made each of those individual systems worthy of detestation.

The reception of our universally valid principles would have to be even less favorable, if that is possible, among those *metaphysicians*, or because most of them might protest against this designation, independent philosophers, who are engaged in the resolution of speculative problems. Until now, the *ontology* which has provided materialists, spiritualists, Spinozists and theists, fatalists and determinists with their basic principles and can for that very reason rely on the support of all of them, would have to be detached from its rank as the science of first grounds of knowledge and be shown and convicted in its most established basic principles as the source of a common misunderstanding of reason. How could this be made comprehensible in a single book to a man who is all the more vitally convinced about the principles of his way of thinking, the more time and effort it has cost him, [: 28] the more he has been able to support and embellish them with the thoroughness and wealth of his talent. His basic principles have maintained their fixity sufficiently for him because they have supported the whole edifice of his doctrine for such a long time. Their incontrovertibility cannot be suspect to him, the less they appear to him either when he surveys the completed edifice itself as its very foundations, or the more he is aware that they have gained through his own acumen and energy in the foundation *particular* determinations which would defend them against the usual objections to which the basic principles of his party is otherwise subject.

The more the practised thinker has done for metaphysics and the more it has done for him, the more impossible it will be for him to have this party appear alongside the new attempt before the court of his reason as a mere party. He has accommodated this court to his metaphysics, that is, to a judge before whom every party who appeals to his judicial authority must necessarily have lost [: 29] before any proper trial. For that reason all impartial examination of the new teaching is impossible for our philosopher and it is basically not much more than an empty formality if he sits in judgment on an argumentation which refutes his basic principles and protests against all partiality. For he cannot understand this argumentation and it becomes even more difficult for him to understand it the more he is convinced that anything that can be understood by anybody must surely be understandable to him. The reasons adduced by his opponent must seem inconsistent to him, because when traced back to what he considers established, to those principles which he applies without noticing all the time even when he ought and intended to abstract from them, really must acquire a quite different meaning from what they in fact have, and because he could only grasp this meaning undiluted and without falsification if he were capable of postponing his judgment about individual parts until he had surveyed the whole in which alone each part gains its actual meaning and determination. This survey however becomes impossible at the same moment [: 30] that prejudice introduces the wrong sense into even one single main principle. If anyone were to interpret the assertion "the basic truths of religion and morality cannot be conclusively demonstrated" to mean that *there are no universally valid grounds for them*; or the sentence "space and time considered in themselves are mere forms of intuition" to mean that *space and time are nothing but representations*; or "things outside us can only be cognized as appearances" to mean *things-in-themselves are themselves nothing but appearances*, and suchlike, he could only construe a system consisting of such main theses as completely fatuous, bizarre and not surprisingly even dangerous.

If the judge should burden a truly consistent system with one single inconsistent component in this way then it matters little how impartially, innocently and carefully he continues to work in the examination that follows; the understanding of the whole can only be virtually impossible.

Let it not be forgotten that the new universally valid principles are incompatible [: 31] with any metaphysics whether it is presented in its characteristic form or is veiled in beautiful images by a poetic imagination. At the same time, however, each metaphysical system would have to be evaluated on account of these principles in an unprecedented way and defended against the attacks of every metaphysical sect. The new attempt will accordingly have to persuade each avowed and secret metaphysician that his philosophy is only *half true*, the philosophy of his opponents however only *half false*, and as a consequence – no better than his own. Even if his reason is superior to all outraged self-love; will he, with the best will in the world, be able to renounce at once the long familiar way of thinking which he has acquired with such effort? So long as this influences his study of the new attempt, however, he will consider whatever is adduced there against the hidden error in his basic principles and whatever in favour of the hidden truth in the basic principles of his opponents as a disputing of the indisputable in his own. If he is [: 32] a *dogmatist* he will consider the new philosophy to be the attempt of a *skeptic* intended to undermine the certainty of all knowledge; if he is a *skeptic* – as the proud presumptuousness of introducing a new dominant dogmatism on the ruins of the formerly opposed dogmatic systems; if he is a *supernaturalist* – as a subtle trick intended to suppress the indispensability of historical documents of religion to establish naturalism without polemics; if he is a *naturalist* – as a new support for the collapsing philosophy of faith; if he is a *materialist* – for an idealist refutation of the reality of matter; if he is finally a *spiritualist* – as an irresponsible limitation of everything real to the world of bodies hidden under the name of the domain of experience.* Now when these judges give the philosophical public their verdicts, a substantial number will divide in its opinions about the new *strange work* into just [: 33] as many parties as it has found famous opponents, parties which are partly discouraged from reading the work themselves because of the influence of their leaders, and partly inevitably led to find in it what their leaders found. A smaller portion, noticing the contradictory aspects in the statements of equally competent judges, is wary of risking its time and understanding on a book from which not even professional philosophers can learn. But only the smallest portion is sufficiently sharp-sighted and just to regard the contradictions in the accusatory statements of the witnesses as a favorable indication of the innocence of the indicted new philosophy.

The introduction of universally valid principles would encounter the most violent and stubborn resistance in the *universities*. Most of our living contemporaries have never experienced an example of the reformation of philosophy which so affected the whole *discipline*. Otherwise it would be superfluous to note here that the philosophical guild has its orthodoxy just as much as the theological, just as much [: 34] its rut as the legal, just as much its empiricism as the medical, an evil which makes it difficult for every reformation in the same proportion as it makes it necessary. Anyone knowing the history of the *Cartesian* or the *Leibniz-Wolff* revolution even superficially will find it hard to name one contemporary university in which the new teachings were not initially rejected as unconditionally as they were subsequently adopted and advanced. The names Descartes, Leibniz, Wolff, which later served in the mouths of so many academic teachers instead of proofs, were never mentioned by his predecessor on that very same podium except when it was a matter of decrying some assertion as a baseless and dangerous novelty. Principles now universally recognized as cogent were broadly misunderstood and mistreated by the *anti-Cartesians* and *anti-Wolffians*, which must now seem incredible to anyone who has not had the opportunity or the leisure to be convinced [: 35] by the countless contradictory dissertations, diatribes, disputations, etc. which overwhelmed the philosophical world at that time but are now of course to be found stacked

---

* All actual verdicts pronounced in published documents against the *Critique of Reason* by its famous opponents.

in the corners of public libraries, having found their final destiny filling space
that would otherwise be empty. Even so, the achievements of Descartes,
Leibniz, and Wolff were actually the development and completion of a
system long prepared in the philosophical world rather than the introduction
of something completely new. The new discoveries and improvements of
those reformers served to the advantage of the one philosophical sect which
was by its very nature made to dominate in academies, not only because
it declared itself so decisively in favour of the basic truths of religion and
morality but also because it offered that form of persuasion which seems
most to satisfy human curiosity, or at least flatters human pride mostly; a
sect which is considered to be the only genuinely philosophical public by a
professor of philosophy who has so often formally and solemnly banished
the opposing dogmatism of materialists and Spinozists, dogmatic skepticism
and [: 36] supernaturalism from the domain of his science, and declared its
system to be the only true infallible philosophy. Now imagine a reformation
which threatens this sect with nothing less than complete downfall, which
can only be carried out given this downfall and which at the same time
cannot rely on the support of the other sects because it is preparing the same
fate for each of them, a reformation through which the system adopted
by professional philosophers is downgraded to a rank which in their eyes
has the status of a mere preliminary exercise of the human mind and of a
temporary makeshift; a reformation which for a teacher of metaphysics calls
into question even the existence of the old science through which he has
been earning merit and fame and makes it his duty to undertake the study
of a new science, whose possibility is so incomprehensible to him! – The
very idea of *such* a reformation must make me seem ludicrous to the bulk
of my readers, but nothing is more certain: [: 37] this idea, which seems so
bizarre, must cease to be a mere idea if speculative philosophy is to gain
principles which would establish their universal validity through becoming
universally acceptable.

Let us leave the passions of the academic teacher out of the discussion*;
let no ambition blind him with the false reflection that his well-founded
fame must collapse together with the system he has been practising; let no
secret envy prevent him from treating with justice a discovery which is not
his; let no jealousy over a younger colleague, who must in the nature of
things find it easier to adopt a completely new mode of thinking, spur him
to seek out nothing but weak aspects in this; and even then [: 38] the study

---

*   in which they seem to play a not inconsiderable role; e.g. when the selfsame famous man
      who believes he has pronounced the condemnation of a philosophical work when he
      declares he has not understood it becomes irritated when he is shown that he *really* has not
      understood it; when etc.

of the new philosophy will present him with difficulties based on its most uncontroversial merits and which very few in his position would be able to surmount. The more frequently and the better he has presented his former system orally and in print the more illuminating, the more familiar and precious it must be for him. He possesses a great skill in substantiating proofs of his system and refuting objections; for both have been the main occupation of his life; and since he is aware of having countered successfully all the objections of his opponents until now he is all the more inclined to suppose that nothing could be raised in objection unless involving a misunderstanding of his system which only few have come to know as exactly as he does. The more fields of philosophy he has been engaged in, the more his principles have justified their fruitfulness and harmony in his eyes, the more intimately they are intertwined with the total range of his ideas, the more, if I may put it this way, they have migrated into the very nature of his reason. I believe, [: 39] accordingly, that I am not asserting any paradox when I hold it established that the study, or rather the *understanding* of the new critical attempt, requires not only of most academic philosophers, but even of *some* of the most eminent more zeal, effort and time than of mere lovers of the science, even of many a talented young beginner. Where could older teachers find the zeal to engage in a new investigation of their system which has been complete for such a long time and has so proved itself, and to follow a leader of whom they have heard that he will refute their most cherished convictions? The efforts of so many younger ones is devoted to their overwhelming duties, the numerous lectures and writing tasks which must not be interrupted by any extraneous series of ideas. Many can only snatch rare moments of recuperation which they dedicate with prejudice and a lack of concentration to a study for which a whole year free of business would hardly suffice. Others may in the end spend all the zeal, all the effort [: 40] and all the time they can spare in a day in which they have only one lecture, and against their own will they will find it necessary to unravel in their lecture hour the fabric of new convictions they have labored to weave. The system they have to promulgate and prove from the podium is in contradiction with the new principles which must accordingly come off worst as soon as it is compared with the established doctrines of a system long accepted *before* it has been completely unfolded and thoroughly determined. Thus the tender seeds of the future tree of universally valid knowledge are crushed by the heavy grindstones of the old teaching structure.

Anyone following with a dispassionate mind the observations which I have only been able to suggest here rather than develop in detail may well agree with me in reaching the conclusion that the first attempt at establishing universally valid principles of all speculative philosophy, however successful, could only be misunderstood for a considerable period of time by the majority and [: 41] also by many of the better portion of the philosophical public. It is not my intention to assert that the *Critique of Pure Reason* does contain these principles because I can neither prove it here nor expect that I will be taken at my word. But it would really be inevitable that the *Critique of Pure Reason* would suffer this fate if it had first established universally valid principles. This fact is evident to the whole philosophical public.

Anyone who considers the lack of universally valid principles in speculative philosophy certain or even only probable is bound to agree with me without much scruple that this lack must have to do with a general misunderstanding common to all sects which has made it impossible for the most perspicacious and impartial researchers to agree on the premises which must underlie the solution of their problems. The *follower of Leibniz* refers in vain to a system of eternal truths present in the reason of each person [: 42], in vain the *follower of Locke* appeals to the testimony of experience subject to unalterable laws. Until now no oracle has been heard either from the temple of pure reason, accessible to so few, nor from the book of experience which lies open to all eyes to answer even the most important questions of most interest to all mankind in a generally comprehensible way or even in a way that satisfies the most practised thinkers. The philosophical world is divided into *four main parties* which have set up camp in a square around the truth, and those opposite each other perceived their object from opposite perspective, those adjacent to each other from different perspectives; the former have been engaged in constant battle, the latter fighting now on one side, now on the other. Thus, on the question of whether there is *knowledge* of an answer to the question of the existence of God, the theists and pantheists declared there is, the supernaturalists and dogmatic skeptics however that there is *no such knowledge*. The theists and supernaturalists, on the other hand, argue for the existence of a God different from nature [: 43] while the pantheists and dogmatic skeptics believe they have seen how groundless this assertion is. Sometimes the supernaturalist fought alongside the theist, whose camp is adjacent, against the pantheist, and sometimes he called on the dogmatic skeptic for aid against his former ally; thus each party did what it could to prolong the war in which they campaigned sometimes *for* the allies of their opponents and sometimes *against* their own. What if this battle, which was inevitable and essential given the gradual development of the human mind, stemmed at bottom simply from the one-sidedness of the perspective from which each party perceived the object they all have in common? If the truth, though only *one* side of it, is seen by each party, this one side only reveals itself to the extent that it is necessarily connected through contrast with the opposite side but not how it is at the same time consonant and necessarily connected with it. So long as each party declares the aspect of truth seen from their perspective to be the *whole truth* it must be *contradicted* by those opposite [: 44] who have their opposing whole truth clearly before their eyes. The truth as it appears to each sect is in part indisputable, but entails the very reason why no sect is suppressed by the others, and the one-sidedness in the perspective of each explains why none of them can gain a decisive victory over any of the others even under the most favorable external circumstances. Might it not be the case that because of some mistake common to each of them they have failed to meet each other in a single perspective from which all the separate and one-sided parties could be joined? What if it was reserved for the author of the *Critique of Pure Reason* to discover this misunderstanding and to do as much as lies in the powers of an individual to eliminate it?

This at least must be conceded. Given the goal he had in mind, he had to do precisely what he has actually done. He had to venture on a new path missed until now by every sect but intersecting with the characteristic paths of each of them. [: 45] As a consequence, as actually happened, each sect encountered the work sometimes on their own path and sometimes on that of their opponents. He had no choice but to declare that each former system is untenable. At the same time, he had to show the strengths of each sect, defending it against the others. Most significantly, he had to begin the great reformation of philosophy through an analysis that had never before been attempted, the analysis of the cognitive capacity itself.

The disputes of various schools have largely been about the *possibility of the cognition* of supersensory objects. For that reason, the attempt had to be made to determine the very possibility of cognition in general more closely, precisely and completely than had been done before. In this new determination, neither Leibniz's *innate truths* nor Locke's *objects* outside the mind could be presupposed as *uncontroversial objects of cognition*, and by no means as the basis for deriving the conditions or laws for the possibility of cognition, as has been the custom, (or the two together without indicating the particular contribution of each). The new definition could only be more successful [: 46] than the former if it assumed nothing but *uncontroversial* premises. In this respect it could not appeal to the reality of those innate supersensory truths which is denied by dogmatic skeptics, materialists, etc. Nor could it refer to the actuality of the objects of experience, denied by the idealists and with certain qualifications even by the spiritualists. Any attempt to redefine the nature and limits of the possibility of cognition would be doomed to failure if it assumed as uncontroversial any objects of cognition which are still subject to dispute in the philosophical world. It would presuppose what was to be proved, and would militate against the prospect of future agreement on principles. Instead of defining the nature and scope of the cognitive capacity on the basis of known objects, he had to investigate the possibility of cognition of objects from the *capacity for cognition per se*. [: 47]

Actually, the *Critique of Pure Reason* first established and explicated the concept of the cognitive capacity *per se*, and because of this explication the cognitive capacity appears in a form of whose very possibility nobody in the philosophical world had even dreamed; on the one hand, that is, independently both of experience and of innate basic truths, and on the other hand, however limited to the domain of experience in theoretical aspects, as much raised above this domain in practical respects. All puzzles which must be deemed insoluble until they are actually solved, and whose meaning can in fact only become comprehensible to many once they have been solved. Through an analysis still considered impossible by many of our most acute minds, this bold attempt intended to separate off with precision what in knowledge belongs to the mind per se from what belongs to things outside the mind, and by this means to distinguish completely the capacity of the mind per se from the capacity active in external sensation. There can be no doubt that such an analysis, [: 48] if it really succeeded, had to bring to light *how* the misunderstanding common till now to all systems of speculative philosophy is connected with the undefined concept of the cognitive capacity. It must be clear to every thinking mind that, before this was established, it was inevitable that there should be confusion between what belonged to the nature of the mind per se and what to the impression upon the mind from outside; predicates originally belonging to the one were inevitably attributed to the other. It is not surprising that what can arise in our minds in part by means of, in part not without, some impression from outside and to that extent belongs to external things, should sometimes be considered with *Leibniz* to be an original property of our mind, and sometimes however, what must be present in the mind prior to any impression and form the actual capacity of the mind should be attributed with *Locke* to the impression, and what is made known by this impression taken to be a property to be attributed to things independently of our capacity for representation?

If it is right about this misunderstanding, then by this means not only [: 49] is the old still continuing dispute among philosophers about the limits of the capacity for knowledge, the splitting of the sects about the great questions concerning the basic truths of religion and morality, and the lack of universally valid principles in speculative philosophy comprehensible; also even what has been happening with the *Critique of Reason*, its being misunderstood even by many of our most excellent philosophers, is explicable with very little effort. This general misunderstanding about the capacity for knowledge inevitably had decisive influence on the meaning of all formerly established basic principles, on the definition of all metaphysical notions, and on the meaning of all technical terms. The first man to have risen above all of that had to view and show the capacity for knowledge from a completely new perspective, and was obliged to put a completely new interpretation on the older formulae and expressions, rejecting several of the most common of them as unusable, and creating new ones in their place. However carefully he justified these necessary innovations, however cautiously he defined the sense of his new technical terms, [: 50] however complete his explications: all of this could only happen with words which had to have a completely different sense in the minds of his readers still affected by the old misunderstanding, and they could only lose this meaning once the misunderstanding had been eliminated, a meaning which lead even the most acute judges to stumble across passages in these explications that were sometimes completely incomprehensible and sometimes seemed inconsistent. The new meaning of the words, which could neither be avoided in the *Critique of Reason* nor defined by explanations of the individual terms, could only emerge through long lasting painstaking and repeated *comparison* of the individual pieces of the whole work; to a certain extent it had to be guessed and discovered by each reader; which was probably only possible through an uncommon application of time and effort, and over and above this was probably only possible for those who had either not adopted any metaphysical system or are dissatisfied with the one they have adopted. [: 51]

The author finds himself obliged here to say a few words about his own experience, through which he had the opportunity perhaps to penetrate to the actual meaning of the *Critique of Reason*, to become better acquainted with the danger of missing this meaning, and come to know this work better than most readers. He would have liked to spare himself the unpleasant task of speaking about himself if only he could have hoped to be able to explain sufficiently what he still has to say about the incomprehensibility of the Kantian system.

He believes that he possessed the knowledge necessary to embark on a metaphysical reading when he began to study this system in 1785. For ten years speculative philosophy had been his major study to which he subordinated his inclination to mathematics and aesthetics with a certain diligence. For three years he had given lectures according to the Leibnizian system, and [: 52] the writings of the great founder, as well as of his worthy opponent *Locke*, were by no means known to him only from the recent products of our fellow countrymen. In addition to this preparation of the mind, even if he has in this respect the advantage over the fewest of Kant's readers, there was an urgent need for him to find again the peace of mind which he had lost in the field of speculation and had sought in vain on all the paths known to him. Through his education *religion* was made not only the first but to a certain extent the only occupation of his early years. Trained *ascetically* as an *ascetic* he was engaged with what he called the work of his salvation, with all the youthful fervor of his temperament; and in this way, feelings which are probably not foreign to any human heart but which are fostered so unequally through the external circumstances of people became for him fixed and ineradicable inclinations. The philosophical critique of taste to which he applied himself from very early on to the benefit of his love of literature led him imperceptibly to the domain [: 53] of speculative philosophy, and he had hardly advanced more than a few steps in this before he felt with alarm the ground of his former contentment shaken. In vain he tried to withdraw behind the ramparts of asceticism and to avoid the struggle with alarming and alluring doubts that beset him from all sides. It had become impossible for him to believe blindly, as he had done, and he soon found himself forced to abandon himself to the enemies of his peace of mind for a time who promised to restore to him with interest what they had taken from him. Now metaphysics had become the major occupation of his solitary life with no other cares and no other business. Only after a period of several years during which he had taken up and then given up all four main systems one after the other did he reach the conclusion that metaphysics might well offer him a plan for coming to terms now with his head and now with his heart but had no single plan to offer which was capable of satisfying the earnest demands of both at the same time. The painful state of mind which was for him a very natural consequence of this conviction [: 54] and the desire to get rid of it at whatever cost were the first and strongest mainsprings of the zeal and effort with which he applied himself to the study of the *Critique of Pure Reason* once he thought he perceived in it, among other things, the attempt to make the grounds of knowledge of the basic truths of religion and morality independent of metaphysics. The perfect leisure which was afforded him during his stay in Weimar confirmed in him the decision not to give up until he had solved for himself all the puzzles which he encountered on almost every page of that profound work. The more he recalls the *enormous* difficulties he had to overcome in this labour, the problems which threatened to defeat him nearly as often as stimulating him, the more he is persuaded that he would not have been capable of the work without this leisure or without the need of his head and heart. In the first extremely attentive reading he saw nothing but isolated weak sparks of light glimmering out of the darkness, which had hardly disappeared entirely after the *fifth*. For more than a year [: 55] he refrained from almost all other reading, noted down those of the work's main theses he thought he had understood as well as those he really had not understood, and prepared more than one unsuccessful epitome of the whole thing. All he produced at the beginning in this way were fragments which seemed to him partly derived from other systems and partly completely incompatible.* But as he continued persistently on the one hand to gather new material from the work through repeated reading and on the other hand to arrange together what he had gathered, the fragments gradually fell into place in appropriate sections, obscurities which had seemed to him insurmountable and inconsistencies he had thought were obvious disappeared, and in the end the whole work stood before him in the full light of evidence which surprised him all the more, the less he [: 56] had considered them possible on the basis of his earlier experiences and basic principles in speculative philosophy.

Even if he were to indicate with the most conscientious impartiality through the driest narrative and in the most appropriate expressions what he found at the end of his investigations into the Kantian system and through it he would only have produced nothing but figures of speech and panegyric declamations of a sanguine enthusiast for most of his readers. He contents himself accordingly in acknowledging here: that all his philosophical doubts are answered for him through the newly obtained principles, decisive for ever even if unexpected, in a way that completely satisfies head and heart; and that for his own person he is completely convinced that one of the most general, remarkable and beneficial revolutions ever to have occurred in human concepts must be brought about by the *Critique of Reason*, a revolution which will not be held up by the numerous famous opponents but will be [: 57] fostered and accelerated far more emphatically than by all the efforts of his friends till now.

His own affairs were in order, and there awoke in him the desire to make some contribution so that something he felt so pleased to possess could be known and used by others as well. In his *Letters on the Kantian Philosophy* he sought to draw attention to the *Critique of Reason* primarily through those *results* which followed from it for the basic truths of religion and morality. He had realized soon enough that these results from the new principles could only be strictly proved for those who had themselves studied Kant's work and understood it completely. Since it was his wish rather to encourage this study and understanding than to assume it, he had no choice but to attempt to present these results independently of the Kantian premises, to link them with convictions already held, to make apparent their connection with the most essential scientific and moral needs of our age, their influence on the burial of old and as yet unresolved [: 58] quarrels in the philosophical world, and their congruence with what the greatest philosophical minds had thought about the great problems of speculative philosophy. He had in

---

*   It is accordingly easy for him to understand why certain opponents of the *Critique of Pure Reason* consider what they have understood to be *old* and declare what they feel they have not understood to be *inconsistent*.

this process none of the men from whom he is accustomed to be instructed, nor those who have stopped being instructed in anything. But in their place he had a clear picture of the estimable and large group of members of the public he could anticipate among readers of the *Teutscher Merkur*.

He had made hardly any progress in this work when he was called to the University of Jena and found it necessary to interrupt it for a time in order to think about the method which he would have to choose to lecture on the initial grounds of philosophy according to the new principles. In this occupation, which was virtually as demanding as the first study of Kant's work, he consulted the supporters and opponents of the Kantian philosophy known to him. He is still not clear *to which* of these [: 59] two he owes more clues and more illuminating insights for the solution of his difficult problem. Certainly he found that even the most acute opponents had more or less completely missed the sense of the *Critique of Reason*, and found no single objection in which the misunderstanding behind it was not clear, no refutation which did not have to do with assertions of which the author of the *Critique of Reason* could never have thought in earnest; and it was not a pleasant spectacle for him to see many a veteran he respected fighting in full armour against a shadow or pouncing with bitter scorn upon an inconsistency which was his own work. Certainly he observed on the other side most supporters of the *Critique of Reason* proceed with measures that could only rather spoil than further their cause, saw them producing assertions as if the matter were settled or presupposing assertions which their opponents could not possibly concede, and clothing their utterances in a language which could be comprehensible at the most to their fellow initiates; nor was it an edifying [: 60] spectacle for him when from time to time he came across a young lad joining battle against grown men in new armor that fitted him poorly, or behaving with arrogant pride over an insignificant advantage owed to his borrowed weapons. – But it was of the utmost importance for the author's intentions to attend to the voices of some of the most renowned representatives of the philosophical public on points of the new system which most required articulation, and on the other hand to be warned by many an example not to consider as clear to everyone a way of thinking which has only become familiar after considerable effort, and not to assume as settled principles which could only be settled by that which was to be proved by them. The more he compared the writings of the two parties, the more definitely he was persuaded that their dispute, as it had been conducted until then, could never be ended any more than the dispute between earlier dogmatic systems [: 61] themselves, and that this dispute would only become more involved and less comprehensible or tolerable to onlookers because it was conducted with completely opposed basic concepts and principles about questions which could only result in useless subtleties and more than scholastic niceties if there were no complete agreement about principles or the utmost sobriety of speculation. It became clear to him from countless examples that both parties associated very different or even opposite meanings even with those theses they believed themselves to be in agreement about, and that this difference in the way of thinking, not noticed by themselves, as well as the declared points of dispute in their feud could be traced back to the very same old and general misunderstanding of the cognitive capacity which is the basis for the lack of universally valid principles and all divisions in the philosophical world, a misunderstanding that was indeed uncovered in the *Critique of Pure Reason* but in the way it was developed there, and could only be developed, maintained its old influence even on the most [: 62] cautious reader of this work and could only make it extremely difficult for opponents to understand and for supporters to explain it.

These observations gave the following more precise sense to the problem whose solution occupied his mind entirely: "Finding an easier way to eliminate the old misunderstanding which could initially only be discovered through the rather more arduous complete analysis of the cognitive capacity, at least to the extent that this misunderstanding stands in the way of understanding and explaining the new theory of the cognitive capacity." The nature of that misunderstanding, which in the former way of thinking about *cognition* he is convinced consists in transferring predicates belonging to the *representation per se* of things to things themselves, made him think about the distinction between the concept of *cognition* developed in the *Critique of Reason* and the concept of *representation* simply presupposed in that work. [: 63] He was extremely surprised to find distinct features missed before now in the results produced in this way. These features, developed and systematically organized, produced a concept of representation itself, a concept which by its very nature was throughout safe from the former misunderstanding, and, established as a foundation for the Kantian theory of the cognitive capacity, seemed to ensure the same security for that theory itself. He read through the *Critique of Reason* with this consideration once more and was completely persuaded that he had really grasped the concept of representation which the famous author of that work had presupposed. But he believed he could see just as clearly that it was precisely the situation that that concept had to be *merely assumed* in the first presentation of the new theory of the cognitive capacity which explained why this theory had as yet been so little understood. He investigated again the opponents' most notable objections about which the friends of the Kantian system could least understand how [: 64] the meaning so clearly indicated in their opinion could possibly be missed, and he found that it was merely the *concept of representation* conceived differently by *Kant* and his critics which in all of these cases sustained the misunderstanding. To the extent that a complete articulation of this concept untainted by any misunderstanding was only possible by means of the *Critique of Reason* itself, no single reader of that Critique could probably think precisely *what* was presupposed about this concept in the work itself, and it was a matter of sheer chance if one reader should have conceived the concept of representation – which occurs in that work on every page – merely in an imprecise way, and consequently neither with the same nor with different features from *Kant*; (in which case he could imperceptibly reach the point in study of the whole work where he presupposed the same thing approximately as Kant himself) or whether another reader might have a precise concept but with completely different determinations from Kant's, in which case it had to be impossible for him not to find much said in the *Critique of Reason* [: 65] about cognition that was not incomprehensible or even inconsistent. Or how was it supposed to be possible to think in the same way about *cognition* unless thinking about *representation* was, if not unanimous, then at least not completely diverse. The more the author was convinced that the old and general misunderstanding had to be eliminated from the concept of representation if the *Critique of Reason* itself was to be secured against its consequences, the more he felt the need to develop the features of this concept he had discovered with all the care and caution of which he was capable.

From this arose an *Essay on a new theory of the human capacity for representation* in which the author was concerned solely with the concept of (*pure*) *representation per se*, which, given the smaller number of its features, was able to be dealt with fully more easily than the much more complex concept of cognition which required in Kant's critique for its full articulation sensibility, understanding [: 66] and reason. The basis on which the new theory could and had to be developed consists solely of CONSCIOUSNESS as it functions in all people according to basic laws, and what follows directly from that and is really conceded by all thinkers. The concept of representation had to be fully developed without any single assertion being used which could not be subscribed to by a philosopher of whatever sect on the basis of his former principles. In the whole treatise, accordingly, no thesis posited in the *Critique of Reason* could be accepted as proven or even only as probable, as little as any thesis of metaphysical dogma under whatever interpretation. In a word, the author had to seek to assure himself of the general validity of his theory by presupposing nothing at all as universally valid which is not really *universally accepted*. [: 67]

That the actual *premises* of a science are only discovered *after* the science itself is nothing new, but a necessary consequence of the analytic procedure prescribed by its very nature to the human mind in its progress. The theory of the capacity for representation which is intended to supply the premises for the theory of the cognitive capacity, whether this be the theory of the author or of somebody else, could only be discovered *after* that theory, although it must stand fast if it is to be worthy of the name independently of that theory and must be completely comprehensible even to those who have either not read Kant's writings or have not understood them. Since it draws that which is universally valid from the shadow in which it was placed partly by the hybrid light of metaphysical sophistries, partly by the clouds of dust raised in metaphysical disputes, the theory must also even be easy to understand and appear to the attentive reader to have the air of something long familiar. By means of this theory the essential results of the *Critique of Reason* must finally [: 68], independently of the profound observations with which they have been adduced in Kant's work, acquire full confirmation and a meaning of which the opponents of the Kantian philosophy may perhaps concede that they had not seen it in all their refutations.

Jena, 8ᵗʰ April 1789

Book One

Treatise on the Need for a New Investigation
of the Human Capacity for Representation

"It is ambition enough to be employed as an under-labourer in clearing the ground a little, and removing some of the rubbish, that lies in the way to knowledge."

Locke's Essay on Human Understanding, *Epist. to the Reader.*

[: 71]

§ I.

Philosophy has not yet established universally accepted grounds of knowledge for the basic truths of religion and morality nor universally accepted first principles of morality and natural law.

The *universally accepted* principle in philosophy is distinguished from the *universally valid* not only because it is, like the latter, found to be true by everyone who understands it, but is also really understood by every sound philosophizing mind. Any knowledge which is not universally accepted among philosophers can [: 72] of course be in itself universally valid. The principles with which Newton enriched science were an example of this from the time of their discovery. But they were only universally accepted after a relatively long period of misunderstanding and dispute. But any universally valid knowledge must at least contain within it the possibility of being universally accepted. Every philosopher who thinks he has solved some problem in his discipline, every producer of a new system or any reformer of an old one considers that the premises expressly or implicitly fundamental to it are universally valid and seeks the reason why they may not yet be universally accepted, though never in the premises themselves. Even if in this process he places too much faith in these premises, it is incontrovertible that the reason why a principle, correct in itself and properly presented, is not understood cannot possibly lie in the principle itself, but must rather lie in certain circumstances which are external to the writer and his art. In this category belong e.g. prejudices sustained by forms of government and dominant religions in all cultivated nations, even in those in which most philosophy is practised. Obstacles of this kind have on the whole been considered unalterable and their influence on philosophy taken to be so predominant that it has been thought necessary to give up all hope for universally accepted principles; and the advantage of the universally accepted has been held in low regard by most of the philosophical public. [: 73] Some take it to be a mere chimera; others however consider it an ambiguous quality just as compatible with error as with truth. I do not wish here to insist that the first charge is contradicted by the second or that the apparent or proven fact that there have been universally accepted errors in philosophy demonstrates the real possibility of the universally valid in general. I appeal only to the *fact*, universally acknowledged in the philosophical world, that there are not only universally valid principles in *mathematics* and in *natural sciences* but also in a science which is completely devoid of all material of intuition, i.e. in Logic, and these principles have become universally accepted. If it were established that certain other philosophical sciences, e.g. *Metaphysics*, had to do without this advantage for ever, then the sufficient reason for this necessary privation could not possibly be sought in external obstacles only; it would have to be sought in the sciences and in their universally valid principles themselves – or these sciences must have failed till now in establishing such principles.

Every philosopher who writes assumes something universally accepted at least among the class of readers for whom he is writing; for how could he otherwise hope to be understood? Even when he uses them to establish new universally valid principles about a certain material he must proceed from something he considers already universally accepted; and if [: 74] he fails to achieve his goal the fault was usually that he was mistaken in this latter opinion. The *dogmatic skeptic* who scorns the idea of the universally accepted in philosophy, contradicts himself when he publishes his mocking texts; the *supernaturalist*, who only allows the merit of the universally valid to revealed truths, and seeks the cause for their not being universally accepted in the inherited corruption of human nature, must take refuge in premises which the children of darkness and the children of light agree about, unless he can convert his opponents by a miracle or through burning at the stake. If finally *dogmatics* with however opposite principles, theists and atheists, spiritualists and materialists, fatalists and equilibrists march to war against each other, they must at least imagine that their weapons are forged from the indestructible steel of the universally valid. In a word, the universally valid is the only basis upon which the philosopher can hope to be able to ground the conviction of others about a universally valid principle.

I am not asserting anything universally accepted, even if it is accepted by a very considerable and respected part of the philosophical public, when I state: "*that it is the noblest goal of philosophy to give mankind universally valid explanations about the grounds of their duties and rights in this life and their expectation for the future life"*. This sublime goal is contested for philosophy [: 75] by more than one philosophical sect; it would have to be allowed to her however by every thinking mind if there had been success before in *establishing universally accepted grounds of knowledge for the basic truths of religion and morality and universally accepted first principles of morality and natural law.*

I cannot by any means engage in a discussion about whether philosophy will ever be able to provide this important service to mankind; I only regard the lack till now of the universally valid in respect to the highly important objects indicated as a generally known fact, which is perhaps for that very reason so little considered. It has always been the original sin of speculative philosophers that they neglected consideration of what they knew for certain to squabble about what cannot be known, and that they set the established aside as *old* in order to seek out the *new* in the unanswerable, incomprehensible, non-representable.

There is hardly need to point out that here by *religion* and *morality* is understood not a scientific system of theology and morality but the essential features of certain dispositions and activities of the will which are designated by this name. The convictions through which these dispositions and activities are first possible I call the *fundamental truths*; and the sufficient grounds for these convictions *grounds of knowledge* (not of objects but) [: 76] of the *fundamental truths of religion and morality.*

On the ground of knowledge of the noblest fundamental truth of religion

The great question whether there is a *God* and what is to be understood by this name that has been used and misused so much; it is an ancient and widely expressed opinion, respected by every well-meaning person of whatsoever sect, that this question is most closely connected with the most universal and sacred interests of mankind, and until the question is decided the reality of all natural and positive theology remains absolutely undecided; this main question has not only not been answered in a universally accepted way but philosophers are not even in agreement about the possibility that a universally accepted answer will in future be discovered, or even about the way in which anything universally accepted about this possibility could ever be established.

Philosophical reason has often been severely condemned for not being in accord with itself about this question, [: 77] while *common sense* has answered it affirmatively through the voice of all cultured nations with a notable unanimity. But has it ever been considered that the whole question has a different meaning for common sense than for philosophizing reason? For common sense it means: is there a God? But for reason on the other hand it means: is there any *ground of knowledge* for the existence of God which can be understood by every thinking mind and must be found true by any who have understood it? Common sense (*Sensus Communis*) is by no means conscious of the actual grounds which determine its statements, which are not so much results of quibbling *reason* as assumptions demanded by felt needs and effects of mainsprings found in the arrangement of the human mind. Mankind would have been ill served if it had owed its most indispensable convictions to reasoned grounds. What damage would have been done by many speculative philosophers to themselves and to others by their behaviours if they had not been required by an opposed and more strongly functioning conviction of their feeling to behave contrary to the strange principles of their speculation! And what benefit would religion and morality have been to the human race if their most beneficial consequences had not depended just as little on the philosophical cognition of their essence as the effects of light on our eyes depend on our opinions about its original nature? [: 78]

Those thinkers, usually warm rather than bright, who praise common sense at the expense of philosophizing reason forget on the other side almost always that with the ceaseless progress of the human mind clear but indistinct representations, partially mistaken because of heterogeneous features, must of necessity be resolved into more or less distinct concepts and explained. They forget too that for that class of people who have felt the need to give a strict account deduced from *distinct* concepts for any important conviction, such a conviction cannot and must not be the mere effect of unknown incentives. Such a conviction demands a philosophical *ground of knowledge* on whose truth or falsity, strength or weakness, purity or impropriety the conviction itself depends. This ground of knowledge in the short or long term must move from the philosophical world, where it is actually at home, into common life.

Philosophizing reason has *as yet decided nothing* about the ground of knowledge for the conviction of the existence of God (and in as much as philosophizing reason can only base its conviction of the ground of knowledge, it has reached no conclusion about the existence of God either). "Reached no conclusion?" I hear myself interrupted in a tone of surprise and displeasure by many teachers of *Natural Theology* whom I respect, "no decision? And what about [: 79] the astute *proofs** which have been

---

*   Among the proofs of reason, or as they are called by many of their supporters, *demonstrations*, I understand here and in what follows each ground of knowledge of the fundamental truth of religion used by speculative reason, which is intended to effect *more than belief* per se in the existence of God.

disputed in vain? With these proofs the wisest and best men of all ages and peoples have demonstrated the existence of God, from *Anaxagoras* down to the immortal *Moses Mendelssohn*?" – Vain attempts of reason misjudging its powers, is the answer of not just one philosopher – not the author of this book – but of a large number who might, properly considered, constitute *three quarters* of the philosophical public.

Unless *dogmatic theists* for example wish to claim exclusive possession of philosophizing reason, they must concede that those who possess this reason fall into *two main parties* over the question of the ground of knowledge for the existence of God: an *affirmative* and a *negative*. The latter party of course divides into two opposite parties of which *one* rejects any ground of knowledge of the existence of God because it considers the whole question of the existence of God unanswerable; the other party, however, because it believes it is obliged to answer the question negatively; the *first* party declares the concept of divinity *groundless*, the *other* as *contradictory* (*dogmatic skeptics* and *atheists*). [: 80] But unfortunately the affirmative main party has no advantage in this case over the negative ones, because it too falls into two equally opposed groups of which the *first* claims to have found the ground of knowledge for the existence of God *inside* the natural domain of reason while the *other* group claims it lies *outside*. The first party calls it a *proof of reason*, the other *revelation*, the first party disputes the *faith* of the others, the second the *knowledge* of the first (*dogmatic theists* and *supernaturalists*). The dispute which the two major parties (the affirmative and the negative) are compelled to conduct against each other is never likely to end without the mediation of a completely impartial third (which might persuade them for example *that they misunderstand each other mutually about the concept of a ground of knowledge*), and even less likely since the first half of the affirmative group makes common cause with the second half of the negative group, and the first half of that group makes common cause with the second half of the first group about certain assertions; the theist and the atheist, for example, make common cause against the supernaturalist over the assertion *that reason can and must reach a real conclusion on the question of the existence of God*. The supernaturalist and the dogmatic skeptic however join against the theist in the assertion *that nothing at all can be concluded about that question**. [: 81]

---

*   *Critical skepticism* which will be discussed in what follows can remove the necessity for a thinking mind to hold to one of these parties and to take the material up with the other three. Critical skepticism examines the *characteristic* assertion of each party and compares it with the assertions of the others. From this emerges:

a)   the assertion characteristic of *dogmatic skeptics* that the question of God's existence must remain absolutely unanswered is unanimously rejected by the other parties;

In our days I probably scarcely need to fear that I will be *chicaned* ([: 82] if I may be permitted to use this foreign word whose meaning cannot be given by any German word, perhaps to the honour of our fatherland) by philosophers about the existence of the *atheist party*. There were periods when theoretical atheism was considered to be a moral and political crime worthy of temporal and eternal fire, and in which [: 83] it was of course among the duties of conscience of a Christian philosopher to doubt the existence and even the mere possibility of atheism. In the thankless effort some recent famous writers have invested to preserve *Spinoza* from the *name* of an atheist I think it is possible to perceive not only traces of that unphilosophical age, but also of the forcing which in the *period of eclectic philosophy* one is required to apply to the meanings of words in order to defend oneself against the patently obvious consequences of the lack of universally accepted principles. – But let people think of *Spinoza* as they will. It is my present purpose to reach agreement with my readers about the meaning in which in my book the terms *theist* and *atheist* are taken. *Theist* means for me that philosopher who believes it is possible to prove a rational and free cause of the world,

---

b)   this is equally true of the characteristic assertion of the *supernaturalists* that the grounds for answering this question lie outside the domain of reason;

c)   and of the assertion by *dogmatic atheists* that the non-existence of God can be proven;

d)   and of the assertion of *dogmatic theists* that the existence of God can be proven.

The *antitheses* [Gegensätze] of these assertions about each of which *three parties* in the philosophical world are in agreement against a *single one* are then:

a)   the question of the existence of God can be satisfactorily answered. This is asserted against the skeptics by all the other parties;

b)   the question of the existence of God cannot be answered by revelation – against the supernaturalists by the other three;

c)   the question of God's existence cannot be answered negatively. Against the atheists by the others;

d)   the affirmative answer to the question of God's existence cannot be demonstrated. Against the dogmatic theists by the other three parties.

This unanimity of three parties against one other on the material of the major principles mentioned above has to my knowledge not been noticed before, despite its being so conspicuous given their complete disagreement in other respects. It must be remarkable to anyone who has himself ever in his life thought about religion and felt for religion. It must appear all the more remarkable when he considers that these principles are precisely the results which arise from the *Kantian* investigation of the cognitive capacity and constitute the conditions which the *Critique of Reason* demands for the only possible ground of knowledge of the existence of God, conditions which are only reconcilable in the *foundation of moral faith*.

This result of such careful reflection is easily understandable, but since it was announced in No. 231a of the Allgemeine Literatur-Zeitung it has been *misunderstood in multiple ways*. Thus for example a professor of philosophy was happy to mock it (from his *podium*) as a pretended proof for the existence of God, while another (in an *Anti-Critique*) as a ridiculous attempt to substantiate philosophical assertions by majority vote. For that reason it is probably not superfluous to declare (as I would otherwise have supposed at least in respect of the professional philosophers, especially of the *astute* ones) that that historical result is not intended to be either the first or the second.

essentially different from the world; an *atheist*, however, is any philosopher who believes he possesses proofs of the non-existence of such a being or of the opposite nature of such a cause. If he has reason to tremble at a particular name he may keep for himself the name of the particular sect to which he adheres and be called *Spinozist*, *pantheist*, or *deist*. I am using the term *atheist* here in as much as it means the opposite of a *theist*; and this is a meaning belonging to the term in *common* and in *philosophical* language use. I know that the term has other uses in philosophy; but I deserve at least to be excused if I hold to the most proper meaning. [: 84]

The *dogmatic theist*, who believes that the existence of God is completely demonstrated by proofs of reason, can at least not deny the fact that it is only proven for his party, not for the other three who unanimously reject these proofs of reason. I cannot of course discourse any longer with a man who replies to this: "O these skeptics, atheists, supernaturalists are long since refuted; just look at my compendium!" Such a man would save himself from much unpleasantness if he left my book unread. But I would ask any other person who does not think he has won over all the other parties in his *own person* to consider that each of the three other parties is just as convinced that the proofs of reason have long ago been refuted and their own system has gained in unshakeability and evidence through that attack. I would ask him to consider that each party from time to time establishes its system, only destroyed in the eyes of its opponents, with new adornments, and gains new important supporters from time to time. I would ask him to consider whether it might not at least be possible that the proofs of reason lack universal validity because they are only valid for a quarter of the philosophical world; whether they lack the power to convince because they have failed yet to convince three parts of four; whether it is not established because of the very existence and continuation of the three parties which reject all the proofs of reason that those proofs of reason are not irresistible demonstrations binding on all thinking minds. All the turns, discussions and amplifications these [: 85] proofs have been given at the hands of professional philosophers, of the whole venerable class of academic teachers throughout Europe, have not even achieved their universal acceptance by even the most enlightened, noblest searchers after truth.

I know there have been attempts to explain this fate of the proofs of reason now on the basis of the stubbornness, now on the basis of the ignorance of their opponents. But apart from the fact that one argument reveals a hideous lack of charity and the other a ridiculous arrogance, both are in respect of thoroughness so unphilosophical that one ought to think the time had at last arrived for leaving to them the antipodes of all philosophy. In the small circle of my own acquaintance I have met men of each party whom I esteem not only for their talents and insights but equally respect for their moral character. In fact these parties would long since have ceased if they had not been held up and propagated by adherents who were a match for each other. Each of them would otherwise have had to collapse either annihilated by the others or even by itself. The mass of every philosophical guild which can only be held together through respect and being led by others would have dissolved, left to its own devices, it would have been distributed among the other guilds at whose head it encountered the strongest and most famous leaders. [: 86]

For approximately the last twenty years great and minor writers in our fatherland have been campaigning with all sorts of weapons against *supernaturalism*, and have won considerable victories over it. It has become the laughing stock of the other sects in a way not entirely undeserved. At the same time it has never lacked among its adherents men of true genius and genuine philosophical spirit; and recently *Jacobis* and *Schlossers*[1] have stood up in its defence and have at least persuaded impartial observers that there has been no single and decisive defeat among all those victories.

In the same way it has been impossible up till the present to suppress dogmatic skepticism and atheism either through the interest of religion and morality which works against them, or through the positive laws of states, or through the intolerance of privileged philosophers and theologians.

Should the supporters of the proofs of reason argue in their own cause, as is to be expected, that the better philosophical minds are found on their side in numbers so great that those from all the other parties together would hardly constitute the fourth part of the philosophical public, it would above all depend on whether these greater numbers might not be explicable on grounds quite different from the depth of those proofs of reason. A teacher of philosophy employed and paid by the state primarily [: 87] for the explication and inculcation of the fundamental truths of religion and morality had for that very reason no choice but to declare himself persuaded of the existence of God. He had to adhere to the affirmative party and indeed to that section of it which builds its conviction on proofs of reason if he wanted to retain among his colleagues the name of a philosopher. Far from doubting whether the existence of God can be demonstrated at all, he employed all his acumen in actually demonstrating it and surpassing all the rest in the strictness and evidence of his demonstration.

However universally academic teachers have taken the path of demonstration they are disagreed about the question: what then is the actual incontrovertible demonstration? Some allow more than one proof, indeed a large number which should be capable of increase, while others firmly

---

1   Reinhold appears to be referring to Goethe's brother-in-law, who in 1776 had written against Basedow's education principles [Kuehn 2001, 227, 228].

insist that there is only one that can be genuine, excluding all the others; only they do not agree with each other about what this single genuine demonstration is. One offers the *ontological* proof as the only possible one, while another, arguing for the *physico-theological*, declares that argument to be a mere phantom of the brain. A third finally refutes both of them and seeks to establish the *cosmological* proof, which is disputed by the first two, as the universally valid. I need only refer to the compendia which have been appearing in Germany for thirty years to assert with full confidence [: 88] that there is not one single proof of reason which is not contested and rejected even by those who support the proofs of reason. Those to whom the proud claims of the dogmatic theist party have still not become suspect and those who are not afraid of the effort required to peruse a collection, even incomplete, of these compendia and to compare the demonstrations presented there with one another will soon be aware how these cancel each other so completely that not a trace of any is left behind. Also to preserve him from dogmatism or to cure him of it one might let a thoughtful young man journey to several academies to hear some of the most famous professors prove the existence of God.

Granted there is a considerable number of academic teachers of philosophy, but if one subtracts those who are in agreement with each other about the genuine proof of the existence of God, those who are not proving simply because they believe themselves called upon to prove, because they have learned proving from their teachers, because they would think it ignominious in a philosopher not to be able to prove; in a word, if one considers not the majority but the better part only, who prove as genuinely independent thinkers from the urging of their own genius; then would the number and the significance of these few be still greater than the number and significance of independent thinkers at the head of the other three parties? [: 89]

And what has philosophizing reason decided till now about the ground of knowledge for the existence of God by its noblest representatives?

The no less undisputed fact that the *second fundamental truth* of religion, namely the *conviction of a future life*, has shared the same fate as the *first* in the philosophical world needs no discussion here, since everything already said applies to it as well. All the more, however, what I understand by the *fundamental truth of morality* and its *ground of knowledge* seems to require a brief and exactly defined explanation.

On the ground of knowledge of the fundamental truth of morality

Morality is the *intended* accord of voluntary actions with the laws of reason. This very accord, leaving out the question of whether it was intended or not, is called *lawfulness* in general.

In as much as the accord is to depend on the volition of the actor, the actor must [: 90] have the capacity to implement the laws of reason despite the opposing demands of sensibility. This capacity is called *freedom*, since the actor in exercising this capacity is not acting under the constraint either of the laws of reason nor of the demands of sensibility. He is not compelled by the laws of reason to prefer the demands of sensibility if he wishes – nor is he compelled by the demands of sensibility to prefer the laws of reason if he wishes. (Since both are equally possible for him it depends entirely on him what he holds to.) He has the free choice either to *determine his decision* on the basis of reason or to *let it be determined* by the objects of sensibility.

Since man is aware of this capacity of choosing between two different laws (since he knows that he has it in his power to do good or evil) his consciousness of that freedom cannot be diminished through his certainty that the laws of reason are necessary. This necessity is insurmountable for reason itself, but it is not insurmountable for him, because he is not simply reason – just as the necessity of instinct is indeed inevitable for instinct itself but not for the being who has reason as well as instinct. It follows from the necessity of the law of reason that a human being has no other choice than between reason and sensibility, and that he *has to choose* between these two, but by no means that he has *no choice*, is not free. [: 91]

It is not my intention to investigate here whether or not it could still be called *moral* when the laws of reason are obeyed, however exactly, if this obedience were *enforced*; I am only arguing that the belief our will acts through compulsion, even if this is by the laws of reason, cannot possibly be compatible with the conviction maintaining the complete obligation and possibility of the law of morality. Such a belief would necessarily be accompanied by the consciousness that there are a number of cases in which the constraint of reason was defeated by the constraint of sensibility. Accordingly, a human being could only consider the law of morality binding for those cases (or, and this comes to the same thing) his own obedience possible only for those cases in which the constraint of reason was not outweighed by the stronger constraint of sensibility. He would then have to allow the lawfulness of his actions to depend on the strength of his sensibility which would be independent equally of his will and of himself; it would only be possible by chance in a few cases independent from himself. This is the reason why I have called the conviction of freedom the *fundamental truth of morality*.

I have even stronger grounds. I can only present these in what follows after I reach agreement with my readers about *universally valid principles*, that is, only *after* the *theory of the capacity for representation* is set out.

Even those who have never philosophized about freedom are as convinced of it as they are of their own existence. It is a fact for them, known from inner experience, and they are [: 92] conscious of it through their sense of self. They have it in their power at any moment to subject it to new tests. The reality of freedom is the strongest proof of its possibility. What to so many philosophers is incomprehensible in this possibility does not even occur to them, or concerns them as little as the incomprehensible in a thousand other cases in which they rightly believe themselves above all brooding about possibility because its existence is evident. Only in the philosophical world has the reality of freedom become a problem after attempts to reach agreement about its possibility have failed. There is no object about which even the most acute minds have written among a number of fine things so much that is quibbling, incomprehensible and unreadable. And there is probably no other question in philosophy which is harder to answer and at the same time more important to address.

Recent writers who are in other respects no less than skeptics have considered the question of the possibility of freedom to be absolutely unanswerable; and that attitude is the only way to explain *how* they see this question as superfluous and indifferent in respect of morality and have been able to assert audaciously – all doubts about the possibility of freedom are put to rest by the evidence of self-awareness, which bears incontrovertible witness to the actuality of freedom.

Surely it is impossible to deny that there are philosophers who for whatever reasons [: 93] are persuaded of the impossibility of freedom, and declare the evidence of self-awareness to be an illusion.

Philosophy must give account of the *ground of knowledge* for the conviction of freedom of the will, whether it is present in the sense of self or elsewhere. If freedom is an incomprehensible fact this incomprehensibility must at least be argued in a universally valid manner if it is not to be confused with impossibility, unless its impossibility is to be concluded from it. There has to be agreement that what may be incomprehensible is only the *cognizable*, not the *conceivable*, *metaphysical*, not the *logical* possibility of freedom. It may well be the case (for reasons that are easily understood) that it is not possible to comprehend how freedom is possible; it must nevertheless be completely understood and argued in a universally valid manner that it is not impossible; that it is not self-contradictory; that it belongs at least among thinkable things. It is only through a universally valid proof of this non-impossibility that the testimony of the sense of self (on the basis of which the reality of freedom can be supposed but from which its possibility can by no means be comprehended) can be secured against all brooding and doubts of speculation and be raised as a *philosophical ground of knowledge* for the fundamental truth of morality. Common sense can and must accept the non-impossibility of freedom with asking for proof; for common sense the testimony of the sense of self can and must be a completely valid ground of knowledge, independently of the proofs of reason. [: 94] Only philosophizing reason can and must require of itself proofs of *conceivability* before it can trust the evidence of a *mere feeling* which must remain suspect as long as there is no agreement about the *non-impossibility* of the testimony. Until that time there is no universally accepted ground of knowledge for freedom and in as much as philosophical conviction stands or falls with the ground of knowledge it is not established in the philosophical world until that time whether freedom exists or not.

Dogmatic philosophers have gone on believing that their proofs have rescued the testimony of the freedom of the sense of self from all objections, but they cannot possibly have the idea that *philosophizing reason* by *their efforts* has satisfactorily solved the great question of the freedom of the will while they have failed to persuade *the three parties which maintain the opposite* that their own claims to philosophizing reason are invalid. Also about the question whether there is any ground of knowledge for freedom the philosophical public divides into a negative and an affirmative main party which through their dispute with each other as well as through their internal divisions perpetuate the theatrical show of the four major sects and of their peculiar battle – a show which consists of as many acts as there have been problems facing speculative philosophy.

Dogmatic skeptics declare themselves against any ground of knowledge for freedom. They believe they are convinced of the *groundlessness* of the concept of freedom. There has been an attempt to deny [: 95] that this conviction necessarily follows from the principles of dogmatic skepticism in that this does allow subjective truth and consequently cannot withhold its approval from the evidence of self-awareness. Certainly the dogmatic skeptic concedes subjective truth, that is, the agreement of the representation with the object *insofar as this is conceived*. But he declares this subjective truth to be a possible illusion until such time as it is proved that the object *has* to be conceived in the way it occurs in the representation. He considers such a proof and the knowledge of the *objective truth* of freedom which depends on it to be impossible. Even if he cannot deny the *representation* of freedom he cannot consistently decide whether freedom is more than a mere representation, whether it is thinkable as something other than the representation, whether is it more than a mere fantasy. Insofar as he deems the thinkability of freedom as distinct from the mere representation unprovable he denies all philosophical ground of knowledge of freedom.

The *fatalist* goes even further. He finds the concept of freedom not only groundless but also contradictory; because he cannot conceive any act of will which is not determined by unavoidable absolute necessity. In this category belongs the *materialist*, for example, who subjects all operation and suffering of the mind to the *laws of motion*, and the *pantheist* who subjects all being and acting to the hypostasized necessity which [: 96] he views as the basic material of all reality.

The *affirmative* main party is hardly unified by the indefinite assertion that there is a ground of knowledge for freedom; its adherents are not in agreement with each other about whether this ground of knowledge is to be sought in natural reason or in supernatural revelation.

The *supernaturalist* considers all rational grounds for the thinkability of freedom to be illusions of the arrogance of misdirected reason. *Natural* freedom is for him exactly the opposite of what it means for the *dogmatic theist*. The latter thinks of it as a capacity for choosing the *best*, the former as a capacity for *choosing the worst* – the impotence of weakened reason which is self-indulgent or rather too easily given to sensibility, and which can only be reinstated as the freedom of the children of God through supernatural support, illumination from above, theological grace, ever since reason has become slave of sin. This freedom is only achievable through revelation and is given to the faithful with that light.

It is pointless for the supporters of *natural* freedom to declare this doctrine of *supernatural freedom* to be extremely unphilosophical. The older supernaturalists rejected the designation Philosopher as an insult, and some more recent supernaturalists believe they are transforming it into a title of honour by taking possession of it exclusively. The fact that [: 97] they refrain from all investigation into the *possibility* of freedom which is for them an *article of faith* creates for them the advantage that they are *in agreement with each other* about this possibility, while the good minds among them exercise their philosophical acumen to show what is unphilosophical in the weaknesses of the party which claims it can know freedom through grounds of reason.

Unfortunately, those who defend freedom on rational grounds, and these constitute the fourth party, are simply not in agreement about *what they are to understand by freedom*. The *determinist*, for example, finds freedom only in the dependence of the will on laws which are *known* through reason, and to that extent makes the will independent of the senses; the *equilibrist* on the other hand finds it in the complete independence of the will from reason and from sensibility. Both accuse the other side of fatalism; the first thinks it can show this in moral necessity, and necessary determination; the second group finds it in complete balance and blind volition. Against the *determinist* it is objected that his freedom is an empty word used to deceive himself and others; and his moral necessity is said to be a gentler name for irresistible compulsion. It makes no difference at all whether the will is compelled by sensibility or by reason if it is determined only by something that is not the will itself. In both cases [: 98] that by which it is determined is a law of nature independent of it. Reason, *the capacity to perceive the necessary connection of things in themselves*, is said to depend entirely on the necessary connection of things and the will to be dependent through reason on the same connection. To be determined by this necessary connection cannot possibly be called acting freely. To be determined by sensibility would be to be compelled by *individual* impressions of things, just as much as being determined by reason would be to be compelled by the *connection* of things. Why is the connection of things supposed to exercise less power over my will than the individual impression? Why should the one cancel my freedom while the other is supposed to constitute it? Etc. There might be no problem for the determinist in answering these questions, but whether the answers would be universally satisfying must remain open here. None of those so far offered at least has managed to satisfy other dogmatic supporters of natural freedom, and even less the adherents of the other three parties whose continuing existence testifies loudly enough that nothing universally accepted has been established in the philosophical world about the fundamental truth of morality any more than about the fundamental truth of religion. [: 99]

On the first principle of morality

If by *law of morality* is meant the guide-line determined by reason for certain human actions called voluntary (prescribed or just recognized?), philosophers are more or less agreed that there is a law of morality in this broad sense of the word, which each explains more narrowly in his own way. But if the term is understood to mean a law which is distinguished from all other possible laws by being able to be observed only insofar as it can be subordinated to no other purpose, a law which can only be satisfied by being obeyed for its own sake, a law that is compatible with no sanction which has the dependence of human will on pleasure or aversion as its basis, then one is understood only by very few, and is seen by the majority as a freakish enthusiast, and almost all will agree with each other that there is no moral law in this sense*.

As variously as the philosophical world has thought about the essence of the moral law, i.e. about its *ground of obligation*, there seems to be general understanding [: 100] that that *ground* cannot be thought as independent of pleasure and aversion and that what has been called moral law can either be the object of our will only *by means* of or *not without* the sanction of pleasure and aversion. But this very unanimity might well be suspect as a common misunderstanding if one examines as an impartial observer

---

*   At least all philosophers known to me except for *Kant* and all theologians except for – *Jesus Christ*.

the dispute of philosophers about the ground of moral obligation, or, and this comes to the same thing, about the question with which the moral law stands or falls, and in the end becomes aware that the very indispensability of pleasure and aversion to the obligation of the moral law is the dividing line which splits the philosophical world on the fundamental concept of morality itself *into two opposed parties* which, as long as this division remains, will never be able to become one.

The first of these parties claims that the ground of obligation in the moral law is found in the sensitivity of the mind to pleasure and aversion. This party considers that reason is only the *interpreter* or at most the *conceiver*[2] of the moral law, not its *legislator*, allowing this rank to the drive for pleasure. Some of these parties are of the opinion that this drive shares that rank at most with *things outside us* to the extent that these are more or less suited to satisfying the drive. The second party seeks the ground of obligation of the moral law in reason, and recognizes reason as the *legislating* [: 101] power, while the drive for pleasure is only the *executive power* in the government of the mind. It should perhaps not be held against this party when it declares the *theoretical virtue* of the first to be mere *prudence* and reserves the name *wisdom* exclusively for its own. But neither to be rejected completely are the grounds with which the first parties protest against all separation of the legislative and executive power in the determining ground of the will. At least the most admirable minds in this party have yet to be persuaded by any answer their opponents have offered to the question whether reason and its laws would have the capacity to determine the will without the intervention of pleasure and displeasure. And if they only gain this capacity through the drive for pleasure, whether then all the legislative force of the moral law does not depend on that? Without wanting or being able to decide between these two parties we must at present be content to elucidate the inner constitution of the parties and their relationship historically.

The moral law is *given* through the ground of its obligation, whatever constitutes this ground, and is only *cognizable* by means of that ground. To ask whether there is a ground of knowledge for the moral law must then mean asking whether there is a ground of obligation or even is there any moral law at all. In my opinion there is nothing more honorable for [: 102] mankind, nothing that can throw greater light on the holiness of the moral law and show the primacy of practical reason over theoretical more evidently than the remarkable fact that it was never a question in the philosophical world and could never be a question whether or not there is a moral law, but that this was always presupposed as present; and to

---

2 Concipistin

the question whether or not there is a ground of knowledge for the moral law no negative party has arisen, and that the really controversial question about the ground of obligation of the moral law never had the meaning whether or not there is such a ground, but only about *what constitutes it.**

The first major party, which seeks this ground in the susceptibility to pleasure and aversion, finds it either in an original and natural arrangement of this susceptibility or sees it as acquired and artificial, and divides on this matter into two very opposed parties.

Externally determined subjective ground of moral obligation

The drive for pleasure, the first of these two parties asserts, would if left to itself and its original [: 103] arrangement only follow the law of sensibility, as is actually the case with all other animals and with all peoples in proportion to their proximity to the original *state of nature*. If, as is the case at present, the drive for pleasure in cultured nations were to sanction in addition another law quite alien to it as the moral law is, then it must have received this direction which is not natural to it *from outside* through artificial education or compulsion, and the ground of obligation of the moral law as well as the distinction between virtue and vice which it determines would have been forced upon human nature rather than being characteristic and innate. It is claimed the moral law cannot possibly actually be a law of nature for human will, because if that were the case it would be followed by all or at least be acknowledged by all; no customs and positive laws could possibly be introduced even among the most cultivated nations which contradict the moral law; that which is a vice in one people could not be a virtue in another and vice versa etc.

But those who adhere to this view are not in agreement with each other either about whether to seek their *artificial* ground of moral obligation in education and custom (as for example *Montaigne*) or rather in bourgeois society (as for example *Mandeville*), or in both at the same time. The most acute commonly hold to the latter, [: 104] but in such a way that they subordinate education and custom to bourgeois society. They hold moral laws to be limitations on the sensual drive of individual human beings by means of the very same sensual drives of the whole of society. They believe that society is in a position, through its physical strength and sagacity which outweigh those of any individual member, to associate invented physical ills (punishments) with actions which disadvantage it, and invented

---

* Those individual outrageous writers who openly speak scornfully about all morality cannot be considered as a party any more than deformities and excrescences constitute a species.

benefits (e.g. *honour*) with actions that further its advantages, and in this way to produce with the aid of education and custom an artificial mode of representation, which one would be tempted to consider natural if the ceaseless contradiction between the demands of personal interest and society did not lead so conspicuously even in the most cultivated human beings to the distinction between what belongs characteristically to nature and what is enforced upon it through external circumstances.

Dogmatic skeptics commonly declare themselves in favour of this opinion when they want to be specific about the ground of moral obligation which they can, in accordance with their basic principles, only find under the conditions of subjective truth, *custom, education, experience*, etc.

Moreover, the party which supports the artificial ground of moral obligation is accused by all the other parties of annihilating all actual distinction between virtue [: 105] and vice, and asserts the moral law in name but denies it in fact. Mostly it is suspect to the second party which believes it has discovered the ground of moral obligation in the *natural* drive for pleasure in that it explains morality as an unnatural and violent state of man, since human nature only suffers violence through immorality, and the human being, on the *evidence of experience*, finds himself in a better situation to the same degree that he has become more moral. But they also hold up to their opponents with just as much confidence the evidence of experience through which, as they believe, they can demonstrate conclusively that among all cultivated nations, especially among those in which there is most discussion of morality, there is more vice than virtue; that the *wise man* and his happiness are a mere ideal; but the real friend of virtue is not only mostly impaired by the worst external fate but also finds his enjoyment of life destroyed by countless inner sufferings and the tormenting struggle with himself, and that, finally, vice is just as much an invented state as virtue, and its sad consequences alien to man in the same degree as he would be without having heard of a moral law, left to his own nature, free of the compulsion to which he is subject in bourgeois society. [: 106]

Without getting involved in the dispute of these parties I may be permitted to note here that *external experience* could be adduced by both of them with more or less equal right in support of their assertions, but that *inner* experience, which they do not address, also admits no assumption in good faith about whether or not the condition of morality is *natural*, and is only capable of persuading each of his own view.

Internally determined subjective ground of moral obligation

But even this second party, which derives morality from law of nature grounded on the original susceptibility for pleasure and displeasure, splits into two different and opposed parties, one of which is so far from acknowledging a drive for *pleasure in general* led by reason as the genuine ground of moral obligation that they believe they must explain this ground rather through a special *sense*, particular to the human, which they call the *moral* sense. The other party considers this sense absolutely superfluous, and endorses the familiar system of Epicurus, which is perhaps too disparaged by its opponents and too highly respected by its supporters.

Since the new Epicureans on the one hand are convinced that every pleasure, however intellectual its object may be, can only be enjoyed through *sensibility*; since on the other hand they view sensibility either as a mere [: 107] property of bodily organization or at least are not able to think it independently of bodily organization; they subordinate all *kinds* of pleasure to the *physical*, as the only possible *species*, and acknowledge the *state of the body* to be the only or the first and best source of all happiness and of all misery. Granted this, they declare the manner of acting determined in the moral law or *virtue* to be the only *means* to the necessary *end* of human will, namely *happiness*, or the greatest possible sum of pleasant sensations in the highest degree and for the longest duration. Since every means is only determined and made necessary by the end, they claim, the drive to happiness is the true and only ground present in human nature for moral obligation, especially since reason is nothing other than a modification of sensibility, the capacity of perceiving the connection of things.

Those who hold to this system, which especially *materialists* among others espouse, are accused by those who believe in the *moral sense* of having a theory which is nothing more than a more calculated system of selfishness and refined voluptuousness. Actual morality, which is completely incompatible with that theory, must certainly accept *pleasure* as the mainspring of the will, but a pleasure of a quite different type, which cannot be derived from the *physical*. They acknowledge that it cannot be denied that even the demands [: 108] of properly understood self-interest are fulfilled by observation of the moral law. But if self-interest is accepted as the ground of moral obligation, the observation of the moral law would in most if not absolutely all cases be impossible. Recognizing a duty on the basis of the consequences of an action would require a *calculation* to which even the most enlightened understanding would seldom be adequate, if ever at all; this calculation could only be avoided by a natural feeling which indicated the duty of some action through pleasure and the opposite through displeasure. This pleasure would have to be distinguished from all coarser and finer *sensory* feelings in that it would be no feeling of the improvement of our *own* state, that is, it would be completely *unselfish*. Two completely different basic drives in the human mind would accordingly have to be supposed one of which had as its end one's own, the other, however, the wellbeing of *others*. Happiness appropriate to human nature could consist only in the satisfaction of these two drives, a satisfaction which would only be possible to the extent that the selfish drive was subordinated to the unselfish drive and functioned in harmony with it.

This unselfish drive, replied the Epicurean, is nothing but the selfish drive itself, but modified by reason. All pleasure is the feeling of one's own improved state, [: 109] and I can only be interested in the improved state of another person to the extent that it grants me the same pleasure, that is, sensation of my own improved state. It is also possible to indicate with sufficient precision the paths on which the selfish drive reaches this refinement without by any means abandoning its former nature. On entry into bourgeois society, the individual puts his weal and woe largely into the hands of society. What is best for him depends on what is best for society. He can only guarantee his own enjoyment to the extent that he leaves the enjoyment of others undisturbed and he can ensure the increase of his own enjoyment no better than by fostering the enjoyment of others. To the same degree that he seems to forget himself he becomes more important to society as a whole and gains for himself claims to advantages which only society as a whole is powerful enough to grant him, advantages whose importance makes it easy to explain the sacrifice of many small benefits and the voluntary adoption of greater and uncertain ills. Should it happen that the man of virtue ceases to be aware of all selfish ends in the actions undertaken for the advantage of other people and that he begins to see virtue no longer as a mere means but as the end itself, then he loses nothing and he arrives on the same path as the miser who prefers his money to all other benefits which he could gain through the use of that money as a mere means. [: 110]

Internally determined objective ground of moral obligation

A third party thinks it has resolved this dispute. It claims to have found the ground of moral obligation in *reason*. This ground, they think, cannot lie either in an artificial or in a natural drive, it cannot be in physical or in moral feeling but only in that *object* which is the held up to the will not by sensibility but only through reason, and this object is called *perfection*. Reason, by its very nature, cannot approve of anything but the perfect. In as much as the will strives toward perfection, it acts according to the natural law of reason and not according to instinct, determined not by any selfish drive, but by the unselfish estimation of inner worth. It is a pity that the adherents of this party have not yet been able to reach agreement about what they mean by the concept of perfection[3].

---

3 Kant associates Christian Wolff and the Stoa in the table of Practical Material Principles of Determination taken as the Foundation of Morality, *Critique of Practical Reason*, A69.

Some understand it as nothing but that disposition of things in which these very same things become objects of pleasant sensations, the *unity* of the *manifold* in the object by means of which the object occupies our capacity for representation *lightly* and *strongly*, that is, *pleasantly*. Of course, this disposition insofar as it is supposed to be present in things does not depend on our sensibility, but neither does it depend on our reason. As perfection only, an abstraction, it can of course only be represented by *reason* [: 111], that is, be *conceived*; but in as much as it is supposed to arouse pleasure as the disposition of an object, as something concrete, it must be *sensed*, be represented by sensibility. The capacity of perfection granted to us is accordingly dependent on the *capacity for sensation* as much as on perfection itself. Striving for perfection would therefore basically be called drive for pleasure and those who support the principle of perfection would be involved in a squabble over words in the dispute with the Epicureans with whom they would be in agreement on the actual matter of dispute[4]. It would actually be quite incomprehensible how philosophers who allow perfection to every object insofar as it can grant pleasure, and in their writings at every opportunity call the *coarsely sensual* pleasure indistinct representation of the perfection of a body (for example, even the admirable *Moses Mendelssohn*) can at the same time make perfection an object exclusively belonging to reason, if one were not accustomed because of a thousand similar cases to seeing our more modern philosophers behaving so arbitrarily with the meanings of words.

To give the word *perfection* some meaning in which at least in the question about the ground of moral obligation, it should mean something dependent only on reason, others declare that perfection, which is supposed to be the basis for the moral law, to be agreement of the will with the laws of reason. Thus they accept the *consequence* [: 112] of moral obligation as its *ground*, and thus find themselves unawares in a vicious circle.

Others believe they are expressing it more adequately by explaining perfection as the agreement of all our inclinations and capabilities with

---

4 Kant also associates the Stoic principle of perfection with the Epicurean principle of
   happiness: "But the notion of perfection in a practical sense is the fitness or sufficiency of a
   thing for all sorts of purposes. This perfection, as a quality of man and consequently internal,
   is nothing but talent and, what strengthens or completes this, skill. Supreme perfection
   conceived as substance, that is God, and consequently external (considered practically), is
   the sufficiency of this being for all ends. Ends then must first be given, relatively to which
   only can the notion of perfection (whether internal in ourselves or external in God) be the
   determining principle of the will. But an end – being an object which must precede the
   determination of the will by a practical rule and contain the ground of the possibility of
   this determination, and therefore contain also the matter of the will taken as its determining
   principle – such an end is always empirical and, therefore, may serve for the Epicurean
   principle of happiness theory, but not for the pure rational principle of morality and duty"
   (*Critique of Practical Reason*, A70F, in Thomas Kingsmill Abbott's translation).

each other and with a common *purpose*, an agreement which can be made possible and necessary through *reason alone*. In the way they express themselves, they can indeed not even reach agreement about the *name* they want to give this purpose, whether it is to be called perfection, or greatest possible development of our capabilities, or the greatest possible effects of our powers, or the greatest possible wellbeing of the human race, and more of the same. But they are in agreement with each other (and without realizing it with their opponents too) that all these purposes are of interest to the will only through the pleasure they promise, and *consequently can be for the will nothing but the means to its supreme end – pleasure.*

Externally determined objective ground of moral obligation

The philosophizing *supernaturalist*, who also seeks the ground of moral obligation in perfection, although in perfection represented as *substance*, i.e. in divinity, smiles with compassion about these futile attempts of *blind heathens* to invent a morality [: 113] without God, a law with no legislator, and finds in the disagreement of the *naturalists* about the ground of the moral law the necessary result of the distorted attempts of reason left to its own devices. This supernaturalist finds it incomprehensible that the determination of a law on which the happiness of human beings or rather the worship of the divinity depends could be left to *human* reason, which can only acquire the use of its powers through observing this law; reason has shown only too well how completely inadequate it is for moral legislation already in the fact that even its noblest and most famous representatives have been unable to reach agreement amongst themselves about the ground of moral obligation. And even if in the end they could be in entire agreement with each other about what reason prescribes to human beings would still have to expect pleasure from the drive if this drive were to raise its prescriptions to real laws. For the supernaturalist therefore the will of the divinity is the only source of moral laws and the *dependence of the human on God* the only ground of obligation of those laws. It is fortunate if the supernaturalist thinks in a sufficiently philosophical way to allow the will of the divinity to be determined by *a reason* which, taking its limits into account, is only *human*. If he allows *divine reason* a completely different nature which is supposed to be partly incomprehensible and partly the opposite of human reason, then he must allow the divine *will* to set up *infallible* interpreters of his incomprehensible resolutions, [: 114] to command suppression of human reason, belief in contradictions, and to find delight in everything that is repugnant to human nature. The morality found in this way is still today the moral guide for more than half the Christian world.

But even the most enlightened supernaturalist must let the knot be cut by a miracle of supernatural grace if he means to determine human will through what he calls the ground of moral obligation, namely through the dependence on the divine, without the intervention of love, hope, fear and thus independently of the *drive to pleasure*.

Despite all the differences now discussed in opinions about the ground of moral obligation, or what comes to the same thing, about the essence of morality, there is at the same time in the philosophical world a fair amount of agreement that morality is a *science* in the strictest sense of the word, which takes second place in terms of evidence only to *mathematics*. Since it is accepted as established that every actual science must have a *first principle*, such a principle has been sought for morality – and there have been found just as many first principles deviating from each other as there have been discovered grounds of obligation. Each party promises [: 115] of its own that it corresponds to all the requirements of a first scientific principle, that it is the *only universal self-evident* principle not requiring a proof from the science it is supposed to ground, and has been refuting all the only universal and self-evident principles of all the other parties.

It is understandable enough *why* most academic teachers of moral philosophy have united over the principle that has the moral law determined by reason (apparently or really), does not subject it obviously to self-interest, and as *Kant* puts it somewhere: "it honours virtue by ascribing immediately to her the satisfaction and esteem we have for her, and does not, as it were, tell her to her face that what attaches us to her is not her beauty but only our advantage!"[5] "Recent philosophy", writes one of our most deserving academic teachers*, to which he should only have added: recent philosophy of the *German professors*, "has expressed the first principle of moral doctrine in this way: *We must make ourselves as perfect as possible*. The shortest way to persuade oneself of this basic truth is the one most have chosen, namely to derive it from the *nature of the will*. We can desire nothing, they say, which is not pleasing to us, or [: 116] what in intuition we represent to ourselves as good; and we can abhor nothing that does not displease us, or what in intuition we represent to ourselves as evil. If therefore (?) *that* is good by means of which our perfection is increased or our imperfection diminished then we must want our perfection and not want our imperfection. This makes a good point." – It does indeed make a good point, insofar as none of the four parties which diverge on the

---

5   Reinhold is quoting from the *Grundlegung der Metaphysik der Moral*, AA IV, 443.
*   Mr *Eberhard* in the paper "On the moral sense" published in his most recent miscellaneous writings, Halle, 1788, pp. 208 and 209.

subject of the ground of moral obligation would have qualms endorsing this whole chain of reasoning, while at the same time one party remains at liberty to deny the inner distinction between virtue and vice and the second party remains free to deny – the unselfishness of moral actions, and the third – the *natural* origin of the moral law. For everything in the argument discussed depends on what is meant by *good* and *evil*, *perfection* and *imperfection*, i.e. precisely on those points about which the four parties have not been able even yet to reach agreement. The famous writer understands by *our perfection*, as is apparent in what follows, *appropriate activity of our powers* and this, if the aim of this activity is *moral* – is this what is intended by the word *appropriate?* – is certainly a very noble meaning of the word. But unfortunately, until he reaches agreement with the three other parties on the concept of the appropriate, of that which is consistent with the nature of our will, which he presupposes, he cannot stop the formula *"make yourself as perfect as possible"*, [: 117] meaning for the *first* party the same as "behave in such a way that your self-interested drive is limited as little as possible by the constraint society puts upon it"; and for the *second* party, "make yourself as capable of enjoyment as possible", and for the *third* "do what the will of the divinity demands of you through his infallible interpreters, the *Bible*, or the *church*". – Without being able or wanting to declare myself for one of these parties here, I cannot refrain from confessing that any first principle of morality which does not establish the ground of moral obligation independently from the drive for pleasure seems to me only capable with a *moral* explanation of the sense of the word of that very meaning which it should ground, rather that presupposing.

On the first principle of natural law

Even greater, if that is possible, is the disagreement of philosophers about the fundamental concept of natural law. I think I can safely leave out an historical discussion of this, on the grounds that the various first principles of this science that have been posited before now can be summarized the very same major divisions as those in discussions of morality. Those who wish to become acquainted with the considerable number of these first principles one after the other can satisfy their curiosity on the subject of natural law from recent texts.* [: 118] In one of these** the résumé is offered after a very apposite examination of all first principles currently known "that natural law belongs either not at all or not with the scope and in the form it now has

---

*   I would suggest for this purpose the acute *Essay on the Basic Principle of Natural law*, Leipzig, Goschen, 1785 by one of our most admirable philosophical jurists, Professor *Hufeland*.

** In *Flatt's* miscellaneous essays, Ideas for the Revision of Natural law.

among the sciences". I believe that almost every reader who has not himself invented a new first principle would be persuaded by the writer's reasons.

There is no agreement even about the concept of *law* in general, sometimes natural law is confused with morality, sometimes it is considered completely independent of morality, sometimes it merges so precisely with morality that one believes it is necessary to renounce any precise determination of their limits.

The lack of a thoroughgoing determinate universally accepted first principle is expressed most conspicuously in the extremely awkward condition of natural law. This awkward state is seen in the lack of answers to the highly important questions about serfdom, death penalties, rights of princes etc. and in the still continuing indifference and contempt with which the subject is viewed and treated by most jurists. [: 119] This is of course terribly avenged by the barbarity in which positive jurisprudence on the whole has remained behind the other academic faculties and from which it can be raised up even after the unanimous avowal of our few philosophical jurists only by a completed natural law established on universally valid principles. From the time when *religious* prejudices lost their influence, *political* prejudices have become much more alarming, if not more numerous. *Worldly despotism* begins to whip humanity with scorpions as the *spiritual* despotism ceases to scourge with rods. Our unphilosophical law teachers seem to have taken over the role of orthodox *theologians* in this, in that they combat the documents of positive law with exactly the same spirit as the theologians fought against documents of positive theology. They believe in the wretched letter of laws in whose existence ignorance and superiority had at least as much a part to play as the striving of emerging reason and the obscure feeling of right in dark ages to uphold the palladium of mankind while the *despot* allows these laws to operate only to the extent that he finds in them a means to his final purpose of arbitrary power. When he overturns the most sacred treaties of nations, treats the goods of his subjects as his own property and sacrifices the lives of hundreds of thousands to his own ambition, his quest for territory or even for his amusement – in all of this he [: 120] need have no concern about *scandal* and *resistance* so long as the natural rights of mankind remain undecided even among those who teach, and those hundreds of thousands have little more advantage than the beasts on which they ride and which serve them as food except the wretched consciousness that they are destined to bear burdens for the benefit of the stronger and will, should the occasion arise, have themselves butchered.

§ II.

There is good reason to suppose that a lack of *universally valid principles* lies behind this lack of universally accepted ones, and this supposition leads to the *critical doubt*: whether philosophy is capable of establishing such universally valid grounds of knowledge and principles.

It does not at all follow from the fact that any knowledge is not universally accepted in the philosophical world that it *must* in itself lack universal validity. But it is at least thinkable that it *could* suffer from such a lack. In the present case there are good grounds for this supposition. Here it is not a matter of discussing *grounds for deciding* about questions which are posed out of mere curiosity or are treated by minds at leisure as a pastime or by acute minds in exercising their talents. It is not a matter of *first principles* of such sciences which are pursued only by certain classes of scholars and only for certain professional activities; [: 121] nor a matter of simple *subsidiary questions* about otherwise generally interesting objects, or of *corollaries* which may well belong in the domain of the essential sciences but are quite remote from their first elements and major principles, only graspable by a few who see more acutely. It is very easy to understand in all of these cases how certain propositions which must be found true by all who understand them are not understood by even the most honest and zealous enquirers and are accordingly not found to be true. But when these researchers are not in agreement with each other about the essential conditions of problems whose solution no philosopher who is not completely decrepit in mind or in heart can dismiss; when they even dispute with each other about the simple possibility of these conditions, it must be at least possible or even probable *that these conditions have not yet been grasped properly (in a universally valid way) in any of the currently adopted forms, in thought as well as in expression.* How could it happen that grounds of knowledge, on whose certainty, uncertainty, groundedness or falsity the expectation of a future life is meant to depend, that propositions by which the most essential of all sciences are meant to stand or fall, that the first principles of all our rights and duties, are rejected by three quarters of the philosophical public, if it was only a matter of understanding them to find them true, i.e. if they were really universally valid. [: 122]

Here, as was noted above, the distinction between philosophical grounds of knowledge and principles and the mainsprings of religious and moral conviction at work in common sense must be borne in mind. The question here is by no means whether the original arrangement of the human mind ensures that the essential knowledge of our rights and duties in this life and of the ground of our expectation of a future life generally speaking must always be maintained and brought to perfection, especially among civilized nations. Rather the question is: whether philosophizing reason has yet managed to achieve a clearly developed consciousness of this arrangement and has yet managed to reach some agreement about the *grounds* of that knowledge of our rights and duties, etc. The question is whether these grounds have yet been developed from clear, thoroughly determined concepts which are completely defined in their attributes and posited in propositions whose meaning could not be missed by any thinking mind otherwise familiar with the way language is used. The question is whether the *actual philosophical form* of that highly significant conviction has been discovered in grounds of knowledge and principles already present and clearly revealed.

"It would then be a matter of mere *formulae* even for the friends of recent philosophy", I hear one of our popular philosophers interrupt at this point with a scornful smile. Yes, sir, [: 123] indeed a matter of formulae; but truly not a matter of the formulae of popular philosophy enforced by the school of some dominant party or other on the manner of representation of the unschooled higher classes of the people and after they have become common currency there are adopted by the school of *empiricists* which arose later as expressions of common sense above all need of proof, and adopted because they have lost their former demonstrability because of the demise of the school in which they arose. – Not then about formulae whose truth is evident to anyone who has given up thinking about them, or, in the language of popular philosophy, brooding over them. But it is a matter of formulae which are the most apt expression of a thoroughly determined concept, secured against all misunderstanding; formulae capable of only one sense, and excluding all contradictory meanings arising from language use. How much depends on such formulae cannot be better recognized than by the mathematician. But how can a philosopher flatter himself he has established a universally valid assertion until he has found such a formula? His assertion is found true only if it is understood, and is only understood on the basis of the signs of his thought.

Any ground for any conviction whatsoever, however deeply and inwardly it is woven into the original fabric of the human mind, is for philosophizing reason [: 124] problematic until it is resolved by complete analysis into its last representable components and traced back to its actual source. It does not migrate into the domain of philosophy until it has become a clear concept, that is, a concept communicable to every thinking mind, and philosophy can only ensure its possession of it only by means of a universally comprehensible formula. As long as a formula, without doing violence to language use, permits more than *one* meaning it is not reliably a universally valid first principle; and neither is a series of such formulae taken together a reliable ground of knowledge. These formulae remain (even though they are the most suitable) expressions of undeveloped concepts in which either attributes that do not belong are involved or in which essential attributes are omitted. – Now should the so-called first principles so far established for morality and natural law, should the demonstrative grounds of knowledge for the fundamental truths of religion and of morality not belong to formulae of this kind, why should they not, however they are expressed, be capable of more than one interpretation without doing violence to the way language is used? Their defenders deny it of course. But since these defenders do not agree with each other and each of them adduces language usage to support *his* formula and *his* manner of proof, whoever belongs to no party can only suppose that there are in those principles and grounds of knowledge still undefined, [: 125] loose, undeveloped concepts which are not fixed by any language usage and cannot be ensured by any expression against ambiguity.

A readiness to deny universal validity to all parties but one's own and to see one's own party as the only genuinely philosophical public does not require any acumen. Whoever is convinced of the incontrovertible truth of his own thesis need only know that the thesis of another is the opposite of his own in order to consider that theirs is false and refuted by the grounds of his own thesis. That lady in the observatory who quarreled with a monk about a spot on the disc of the moon did not need to wrack her brains to persuade herself that her opponent, who thought he had seen two bell towers, was mistaken: she had seen in the very same place a pair of lovers caught in an embrace, and so they could not have been bell towers. The inmate of *Bedlam*, who pitied the insanity of his neighbour who thought he was *God the Father*, was no healthier in claiming he knew, being *God the Son*, how absurd and monstrous the presumptuousness of that wretched mortal was. I confess that I can hardly resist this really impolite comparison when I become aware of a mind, however sound it otherwise is, belonging to any party whatsoever, in dispute with other parties complaining about the obtuseness and stubbornness [: 126] of his opponents, and finding it incomprehensible that they have no intention of accepting such evident grounds as his and with a gesture of triumph boasting of having won the battle if they have left him the last word. The genuine philosophical mind respects those related to him in spirit no matter what sect they belong to; he knows that no thinking mind can assert some error without failing to support it upon some truth, which may be seen only from one side but is not for that reason at the same time completely false. Until he has found out what is the *truth* to which the major propositions of the other parties point, until he has found the point of common misunderstanding which prevents the parties from understanding in common that grounding characteristic of each party, as long as he supposes that his major proposition also, with all that it contains that is uncontroversial, carries with it something false that prevents other good minds from accepting his major proposition; as long as he views himself as a mere party, which can stand with the others not in a feud which is meant to annihilate all the others but in negotiation which treats all with justice.

It cannot occur to anyone who has not yet finished studying the great main questions of speculative philosophy and has only for the time being adopted the system he considers most probable and best in practice [: 127] to hold the universal validity of this temporary system to be established. But if the end result of his completed study proves to be the adoption of one of the currently established systems (*before* the *Critique of Reason*) which deals with the grounds of knowledge of the fundamental truths of religion and morality, or one of the so-called *first principles* of morality and natural law, then he will inevitably belong to one of the four major parties and will have to justify his conviction (at least for himself) against the objections of the other three parties. However solemnly he protests that he belongs to no party, no matter how carefully he seeks to differentiate his system from any yet adopted, no matter how unique and unsystematic the form he gives his conviction and disguises the metaphysical outline of this form through wit and the magic of fantasy, he will still have to base his answer to the question of *the existence of* God on the foundation either of dogmatic theism, of atheism, of supernaturalism or of skepticism. Either he has found that question answerable on rational grounds or not. If he has, he believes he *knows* the existence either of *a* God or of *no* God, and is either a theist or an atheist*. If he finds the question unanswerable on rational grounds [: 128] he either accepts grounds for the existence of God which lie outside the domain of reason, or absolutely none, and is consequently either a supernaturalist or a dogmatic skeptic.

A thinking mind not yet adhering to any of these parties and consequently not yet persuaded of the complete defeat of all of them with the exception of the one to which he belongs, must feel awkward given the necessity of belonging to one of these four major parties.** Whichever of the parties he declares himself to be in favour of he not only has the great bulk of the philosophical public *against* him but also three quarters of the high council of independent thinkers, and has principles to defend which are rejected in the philosophical world by a conspicuously determined majority among equally important voices. Even if this majority of voices is no refutation of the system he has adopted, it is obviously [: 129] a remarkable and alarming external ground against that system which he has to allow until he is persuaded by a complete study in which he will have to have interrogated every party that philosophizing reason has revealed itself only in one quarter

---

*   Or his imagination would have to have a power of creativity which has as yet been denied to the divinity himself, namely the capacity of reconciling the contradictory e.g. in the concept of a God who is at the same time *nature* and *non-nature*. In this case, however beautifully written the rhapsody, this product of imagination would make professional philosophers and also readers with healthy and at least not uncultured common sense miss the object for which language use has established the term *God*.

** The assistance offered by popular philosophy in this embarrassment will be discussed a few pages below.

of its representatives. Until then he must accept as possible that reason has at present made no decision about the great questions, in that it cannot possibly contradict itself; or that reason has been heard through what three parties are in agreement about against a single party. But *everything* in the four main systems is maintained by only *one single party* and is unanimously rejected by *three*. The universal validity of all systems established till now is denied by the verdict of philosophizing reason itself.

Anyone not believing himself in undisputed possession of universally valid grounds of knowledge and principles cannot at least infer their *possibility* from the *actuality* of such grounds and principles. Anyone on the other hand who recognizes this possibility on the basis of *inner* grounds so clearly that he is capable of giving himself and others a justification must for that very reason and by those very grounds have found these grounds of knowledge and principles. In that they would be *necessary* propositions their reality would have to follow immediately from their possibility *per se*. They would have [: 130] to occur in the determinate concept of their possibility as its components or this concept would be indeterminate and consequently quite inadequate for distinct knowledge. The conviction of the reality and of the possibility of universally valid principles is so completely inseparable that the one cannot possibly be conceived without the other. Anyone not yet convinced about the reality of universally valid grounds of knowledge for the fundamental truths of religion and morality and of universally valid first principles of morality and natural law cannot be persuaded of their possibility on the basis of inner grounds, but can only *doubt* them by being just as little persuaded of the opposite.

This doubt, which I call the *critical*, certainly arises in every impartial mind when observing closely the state of philosophy till now, and cannot be seen more clearly in its nature and in the beneficial influence it exercises on the development of philosophy than in distinguishing it precisely from, and contrasting it with, the two other modes of doubt: *dogmatic* and *unphilosophical*.

Dogmatic skepticism constitutes one of the four major parties of the philosophical world, which indeed through their disputes give occasion for that important doubt of critical skepticism. This kind bears the name "*dogmatic*" because it undertakes to demonstrate [: 131] that it will forever be necessary to doubt objective truth, i.e. the real correspondence of our representations with their objects*. The indemonstrability of objective truth

---

* The consistent dogmatic skeptic actually denies nothing but the demonstrability of objective truth; and in that sense not objective truth itself unless this term is understood as *knowledge* of objective truth. Objective truth itself is merely doubted but with a doubt that is unresolvable in its very ground.

is the *dogma* of this sect, and once it has been adopted can only subsist through an obvious but very common inconsistency in philosophical convictions in which necessity and generality are presupposed. Thus for example the necessity and generality of the moral law, and consequently the moral law itself, is just as indemonstrable without demonstrability of its objective truth. Critical skepticism doubts what the dogmatic regards as established; it seeks grounds of demonstrability of objective truth while the dogmatic skeptic believes he already possesses grounds of indemonstrability. The first kind of doubt demands and leads to investigation, the other declares this to be futile and superfluous and consequently makes it impossible however significant it may be.

Whatever may properly be objected to in dogmatic skepticism with regard to its grounds and its consequences (which, if dogmatic skepticism were to become general would be damaging for all philosophy), [: 132] it cannot be denied that this is a real philosophical system. The critical skeptic honours in dogmatic skepticism one of the four guilds into which the actual philosophical public had to be divided. These guilds have researched and discovered from their four partly opposed and partly differing perspectives that truth which the critical skeptic only doubts until he has found the common perspective unifying all the four one-sided views.

Of a quite different nature is the skepticism which I have called *unphilosophical*. It has nothing in common with *dogmatic* skepticism except in denying from time to time the demonstrability of objective truth, and has nothing in common with *critical* skepticism except doubting the philosophical grounds of all current systems. It protests against each of these although in fact it is perfectly compatible with them all in that it is a matter not concerning the systems themselves so much as their grounds to which he opposes no grounds except that something it cannot itself explain which it calls common sense. Skeptics of this kind who call themselves this do not accordingly constitute any separate party in the philosophical world, but rather a special group in that party with consists mostly of the rabble. They prove theism, atheism, supernaturalism and dogmatic skepticism through utterances of common sense and are only in agreement among themselves to the extent that [: 133] philosophizing reason, or as they call it, brooding metaphysics, is capable of producing nothing that cannot be refuted or at least doubted. On the other hand there is no appeal against common sense, which made all metaphysicalizing unnecessary.

This is that so celebrated and so zealously preached skepticism of *popular philosophy* which, since the Wolffian school ceased to dominate, has had such access to our academies and is proclaimed by its apostles to be the real benefit that has given our age the honorific title of the philosophical. The continuing controversies of the parties, increasing with every advance of the human mind, the works written by so many admirable profound minds in support of their systems and the overwhelming difficulty of understanding all these systems, let alone refuting them, the despair at ever being able to establish universally accepted principles; that striving in the culture spreading now through all classes to be read by a large public and in an age in which *factual knowledge, experience, observation* have become the slogans of this book-devouring public to save themselves and their readers from *thinking*, have, among other things, generated and brought up this skepticism of popular philosophy which denies outright the possibility of universally accepted principles in philosophy and in their place believes it has found a reliable oracle in sound common sense, whose utterances [: 134] justify them in its eyes because they are inexplicable and indemonstrable as the genuine principles of all explanation and demonstration. Whatever such a skeptic thinks he is easily able to understand is for him either such an utterance or at least deducible from one. Anything, by contrast, that seems to require more than normal effort of thought even if it is the proof of one of his own assertions is for him the object of doubt and is rejected as a brooding that contradicts sound common sense. Hence his hatred and contempt for metaphysics whenever this is more than a catechism of his popular philosophy and cannot simply be studied with the memory; hence his eternal declamation against hair-splitting, speculation and systems; and in this, for obvious reasons, he has on his side the great number of half-schooled and half-knowing who like to hear themselves called the great world.

One feels inclined to satire in imagining many an academic *metaphysician* of this kind, who enters his lecture room with his compendium under his arm or makes a public appearance with an expression intended to announce the important influence he believes he has in the cabinet of the queen of all sciences. The little Nabob of Natches occurs to me who appears every morning with his sceptre in his hand in front of his palace gate and in the force of his complete power shows the sun the path it is to follow in the course of the day. [: 135] One could wish to be a Juvenal when one considers the fate of metaphysics in the countless marketplaces of the sciences, called universities, where it is proclaimed by many of its sellers as the grandest wares, provided it is purchased at the stall of the person where alone it is to be found *unadulterated*, and not at the stall of his neighbour. Metaphysics, raised by such men to the rank of a general remedy, rewards those who manufacture and market it with the dignity of quacks. But it is just as difficult for me to resist this state of mind when I see the eagerness with which certain would-be Socrates in our time busily banishing metaphysics from philosophy in the name of common sense, popularizing everything scientific, and mocking everything that cannot be popularized as absurd or crying it down as dangerous. They compel philosophy down from the higher regions of speculation of course, in that they give her nothing more to do than demonstrating certain *dogmas privileged* by state and church under the pretext of common sense; and in this occupation they have enough leisure to ponder the different guises in which they hope to introduce their pupil, popularized philosophy, into the coteries of the elegant world and the workshops of artisans, on to the toilet tables of ladies and into the spinning rooms. It would be futile to ask these reformers to consider whether it might not be advisable to allow at least a certain kind [: 136] of philosophy to linger in the *higher regions* of speculation since it is only from there that one would be in a position to survey the whole domain of human knowledge and find out in any case the perspective from which everything correct found in a one-sided way by the individual parties could be encompassed. The attempt to make an end of the controversies of the parties or rather to destroy the misunderstanding of reason by which these controversies are sustained, seems to these men of the world an undertaking to which they would be showing too much honour if they were to put it in the *same* category as unifying the confessions of faith in the Holy Roman Empire. They regard those controversies as really over, ever since they came across the great idea of transferring verdicts about them to the court of common sense they set up themselves, and since this supreme court in matters of reason and faith has pronounced its verdict in favour of their compendiums, as could be seen from the stamp of popularity on these compendiums, so visibly impressed as a sign of their exclusive privilege. The fact that the three other parties protest against this verdict is of no significance in the eyes of the popular philosophers, in that the whole domain of actual philosophy has been cleansed by the aforesaid verdict of the three differing parties, which have been *declared unphilosophical*, [: 137] and is to be conceded to the famous founders of popular philosophy with their heirs and assigns for all time.

However *popular* these grounds may be in themselves they can be satisfactory only to those who do not know that this *very same path of appeal* to sound common sense has been taken by each of the other parties and that each of them points to a verdict from that court that is just as favorable to their cause. Indeed *supernaturalism* can boast with reason that it has an overwhelming number of votes which it owes to the sound common sense of the so-called *orthodox* of every Christian sect. What *atheism* and *dogmatic skepticism* lack in numbers of adherents they claim to make good through the importance of the votes with which sound common sense of the *elegant* and *grand world* declares its favour for the major doctrines of these systems since these have achieved a degree of popularity at the hands of the French radicals which might allow them to contest in this point too

the advantage of theism*. If these somewhat disconcerting facts are more
or less right, then popularized theism [: 138] which seemed to be secure
because it puts our ladies in a position to demonstrate the existence of God
without worrying their heads and because of all the charm it must have for
the *justified pride* of our philosophical age, might not after all be as secure
as our demagogues seem to think – because *leap to belief*, the *distaste for
all demonstration* and all school forms, and the *sense of freedom*, three
decisive merits of our age no less than that *pride*, must declare themselves in
favour of the popularized charms of supernaturalism, dogmatic skepticism
and atheism with the same emphasis and success.

Although I am inclined to consider the sound common sense of our
popular philosophers, which comes when called to the aid of every party, to
be the soul of that philosophy which is quite rightly acclaimed as suited to
adopting any forms and shape, I find it hard to believe that it is capable of
providing the peace between the various parties expected of it, because it is
compatible with every sect. It seems rather likely to make the controversy
livelier and more general since it strengthens the grounds of each party
through the weight of its esteem and the number of its adherents, through
its popularity. The tone at least which dominates in the texts of popular
philosophers has grown more bitter, more passionate, more combative in
the same degree that our philosophy has gained in popularity. It is no longer
just a matter of the *metaphysics* of one's opponent, [: 139] but of his mind,
and although it cannot be denied the popular way of arguing has much
advantage in emphasis and brevity over the metaphysical way, it would at
the same time be less suited to bringing the dispute closer to a decision
because the majority of the warriors on each side (especially given the high
esteem these days for sound common sense) would have to be more inclined
to give up his metaphysics rather than his sound common sense.

I may perhaps be forgiven for getting this off my chest briefly, in that
there is no more suitable place later in this work. It is not my fault if the
popular philosopher does not like the image in the mirror I have held up in
front of him. The spirit of his philosophy is hardly capable of any different
presentation. He has no system that analyses; no principles to be adduced
in some order or other; no whole which could be encompassed from some
sort of perspective. The syncretistic, badly conglomerated aggregate of
indeterminate ambiguous propositions of which he boasts under the name of
eclectic philosophy and which he seeks to defend by his eternal protestations
against hair-splitting and brooding from all examination can probably not

---

*   In the *capital of the elegant world* popularised dogmatic skepticism which has the advantage
    of much more convenience and security than atheism became the fashion at about the same
    time as its compatriot the redingote.

be presented by anyone who believes philosophy matters, and knows how to distinguish hair-splitting from thoroughness and brooding from thinking without scorn and distaste.

The characteristic doubt this unphilosophy raises against everything that demands reflection [: 140] destroys all study; and in the same way the doubt of the dogmatic skeptic must remain eternally unresolved given his argument; but critical doubt which arises from the philosophical comparison of the four current major systems makes a study of a completely different kind inevitable and bears with it the most urgent need for a resolution. While the dogmatic skeptic declares himself in favour of just one single party, the unphilosophical skeptic disputes and supports all four simultaneously; as a consequence *both* leave matters entirely where they were. The critical skeptic, however, rises above every party not to affirm one or all of them or to refute three or all of them but to learn from them all, and by means of the most precise comparison of their manners of representation to draw out what they share as well as what they dispute. Whether what they share can be offered, after closer observation, as evidence in whose light the more acute adherents of each party would be put in a position to see the contradictoriness of their former manners of representation which arises from one-sidedness and abolish it or, and this comes to the same thing, whether the matters of dispute among the parties could be decided by *universally valid* principles yet to be discovered, can be neither affirmed nor denied by the critical skeptic *before* that study. Yet he *doubts* it, but as mentioned, with a doubt which puts no obstacles in the path of study but rather means that such a study would be impossible without it. Because who seeks for [: 141] what he either believes he already has or can never be found?

§ III.

The interest of the sciences in our duties and rights in this world and the basis of our expectation of a future life, and consequently the highest interest of mankind, turns this critical doubt into the question: *How* are those universally valid grounds of knowledge and principles possible?

The author of the *Critique of Pure Reason* and the friends of his philosophy have been accused of basing the credibility of the fundamental truths of religion and morality solely on the interest which humanity must have in these fundamental truths. I cannot here get involved in a discussion about whether and to what extent the accusation against the critical philosophy is apt. Let me remind the reader simply that it is necessary to distinguish the universal and necessary interest of humanity insofar as this demands *study* and which is the matter here under discussion from that self same interest insofar as it is to make some *belief* necessary.

I certainly have the better part of my philosophizing contemporaries on my side when I hold the interest of morality (or what comes to the same thing the interest of humanity which can only not be misunderstood insofar as [: 142] this interest is determined by morality) as a compass without which one cannot venture with impunity on the ocean of human opinions in the study of philosophy, and when I maintain that principles which fight against that interest of humanity can be neither universally valid nor universally accepted. Even more certainly all philosophical parties (except dogmatic and unphilosophical skeptics, whose place is filled honorably by critical skeptics) will agree with me when I accept as established here that the discovery of universally valid principles (which guarantee their universal validity because they are indeed universally accepted) would raise the sciences of our duties and rights etc. into the ranks of actual sciences which they had until now only in name, and would create for them a dignity and influence which even their most ardent administrators have until now hardly believed possible – and that consequently this discovery could well be the most important gift that can be made by a human to mankind.

Let it not be forgotten that here it is a matter of *principles* only. Even those who view peace in the domain of speculative philosophy as a chimera and the dispute of philosophers necessarily endless at least concede that agreement about principles is necessary and possible among the disputants*, unless the whole dispute is thought to be [: 143] pointless and absurd, and through its persistence instead of eternal approximation to the truth rather ever increasing distance from it is thought to be brought about. Any dispute which is carried out only because of the lack of agreement about principles gradually falls away of its own accord with this lack, and it brings peace from the moment when it has found the happy turn through which the disputants have their attention drawn to the point of misunderstanding and are guided to agreement about principles. Let it not be a cause for concern that the end of the controversies among the four major parties or rather the end of the four parties themselves might impede the progress of the development of the human mind which has been fostered by these very controversies. These controversies were only indispensable and inevitable while the human mind had not yet risen to the knowledge of universally valid principles. As soon as it has reached some agreement about this it has ensured for itself by this very possession its future progress. It has the determination of its progress in its own control, without having to expect to make progress as before by chance discoveries and uncertain attempts alone. With the guidance of these principles it traverses the field of experience,

---

* Who will not subscribe to the old proverb: *Contra principia negantem non est disputandum.*

which is limitless but not bottomless, and this has enough to occupy it in a way appropriate for its own powers for a whole eternity. And it can promise itself all the more success, the less it splits time and energy with uncertain groping and futile disputing [: 144] of the field of speculation per se.

Whether and *what* morality and natural law would gain through universally valid first principles and religion and morality through universally valid grounds of knowledge can hardly be the question here; especially not for those who like me are persuaded that all our so-called systems of morality and natural law till now have only been scientific attempts, systematically ordered aggregates, more or less processed materials for future sciences and nothing like actual systems and already present sciences which could claim inner consistency, and universal conviction – and that in the end the fundamental truths of religion and morality have been till now only problems and disputes because of the lack of universally valid grounds of knowledge, and that the disputants have themselves failed to agree even about the concept of the object about which they are in dispute.

Without further discussion, then, I may state that the most important, necessary and, for that very reason, eternally operative interest which humanity takes in the sciences of morality and of natural law, in the fundamental truths of religion and morality make any indifference, any openness toward such questions, impossible, and may transform the doubt about whether universally valid first principles of those sciences [: 145] and universally valid grounds of knowledge of those fundamental truths are possible into the determinate question: *how are they possible?* I say: until the impossibility of such principles is demonstrated in a universally valid way that interest makes it the duty of every thinking mind to *investigate* their possibility and not *accept* it as established *before* any study.

Since nothing has yet been established in the philosophical world about real universal validity of found first principles and grounds of knowledge, their possibility cannot be inferred (at least for anybody not belonging to any party) from their reality but must be investigated in itself and shown first. It is then not a question whether these principles and grounds of knowledge are possible, but *how are they possible?*

And this problem is the point at which the two diametrically opposed ways which philosophical investigation into those important objects has followed until now *end* and lose themselves in each other, as it were, one which believed it possible to demonstrate the *actual possession* of those grounds of knowledge and principles, and the other, which held it to be *impossible*. Whoever wishes to work for the solution of this great problem must stop belonging for a time to the affirmative or to the negative party. He must be neither theist nor supernaturalist, neither dogmatic skeptic nor atheist; he must break with all current systems without however giving up hope that a system [: 146] may come about which will unify all that is useable and true contained in the current systems. By being located at a remarkable point missed until now by all philosophers except critical skeptics, knowing that every step backwards leads to one of the two sidetracks that lead further and further from the goal and disappear into the infinite void, the most sacred and important interest that humanity can have requires him to move forward along the path lying in front of him that has not been trodden before or, and this means the same thing, to make the attempt to solve that problem.

§ IV.

In order to be able to solve this problem one must first have found a universally valid answer to the question: What can be known at all? Or: What are the limits of the human cognitive capacity?

Anyone persuaded that the problem "*How are universally valid grounds of knowledge etc. possible*" is posed by the highest interest of mankind in respect of the present condition of philosophy must also accept that the conditions (data) which belong to its solution are given and can be found. Even those who are lacking in all conviction must, if his skepticism is critical, at least concede the non-impossibility of these conditions. [: 147]

Now these conditions cannot possibly lie outside the limits of cognizability, in the domain of blind faith, in the region of *hyperphysics*. For even if a critical examination were to turn out in favour of supernaturalism, the data at least which resulted in the indispensability of revelation would have to be contained inside the scope of the comprehensible.

Nor can these conditions themselves be found within the region of the cognizable insofar as this has been dealt with till now in speculative philosophy or in *metaphysics*. The critical skeptic has withdrawn from all affirmative or negative dogmatism, whether this is theism or supernaturalism, atheism or dogmatic skepticism. In the whole domain of metaphysics no space is thinkable for him which has not already been claimed by one of those four major parties. He has become tired of the apparent truths which contradict each other and are found on one and the same ground. And he has abandoned the field forever on which only *those kinds of truth* are to be found. His justified suspicion of metaphysics which keeps independent thinkers divided into parties or at least is incapable of preventing this or ending it, had brought him to that important problem: how could, how should he hope to solve it by metaphysics?

Since then the data for the solution of our problem may be found neither outside the whole region [: 148] of cognizability nor within it, as it has till now been worked, we have to seek them in areas of this region that have as yet not been worked and to that extent are unknown.

If one does not want to stray in this quest beyond the domain of the cognizable into the empty playground of imagination the limits of this domain must first be indicated precisely and determinately. In other words, a universally valid answer has to be found to the question: what is meant by the *cognitive capacity*, and how far does this capacity extend?*⁶

It is possible that the solution to this problem will provide a solution for the former problem. But this much is certain: that the first problem can never be solved until this one has been.

I am happy to concede that the task of *determining the limits of the human cognitive capacity in a universally valid way* must sound rather alarming to most of my readers. All the more pleasantly, I hope, they will be surprised by the ease with which they will encounter the solution itself, which is already half found if one has grasped just the meaning of the task properly and has reached an understanding about what is meant by cognitive capacity. [: 149]

I have discussed a possible objection which might be raised against the possibility of a completely satisfying solution to this task elsewhere;** and since this discussion belongs here and I cannot offer anything better, let it occur here again with a few modifications.

All the more significant things that have happened in our speculative philosophy had to have occurred before it was possible to think of posing that problem in its actual sense, let alone solve it. It could never have occurred to all those philosophers who thought they had already found the grounds of knowledge of the fundamental truths of religion and morality or the first principles of morality and of natural law to wonder whether it was possible for reason to establish universally valid grounds of knowledge and first principles – since they thought their reason was already in possession of such grounds of knowledge and principles. And if this question had been put to them by others they would have their apparent possessions to show instead of any answer. The atheists and the supernaturalists would have proceeded in the same way who *anticipated* that question by decisive answers although of a completely different kind. At the same time the philosophical world consisted largely until now of *dogmatics*, with the result that one might [: 150] perhaps count one skeptic for every hundred dogmatics. But this broad and so widely trodden path of dogmatism was not only inevitable before the posing and solution of our problem but even indispensable as a distant

---

*   Thus neither hyperphysics nor metaphysics, but critique.

6   In the first of his letters in the *Teutscher Merkur* Reinhold explains what he means by "hyperphysics": it is any supernatural theory of the supernatural. Kant writes that the transcendental dialectic is "a critique of understanding and reason in respect of their hyperphysical employment" (*Critique of Pure Reason*, A64f./B88 in Norman Kemp Smith's translation, 100–101).

**   In the first Letter on the Kantian Philosophy, Der Teutsche Merkur, August 1786.

preliminary to its solution. Without the zeal of the dogmatics, supported and enlivened by their sweet imagination of found truths, those numerous and partly admirable preliminary exercises of the human mind would never have come about, and to them reason owes the degree of development which is presupposed in greater enterprises. During this long period the merit of skepticism consisted in the main partly in forcing the dogmatics to sharpen their proofs, and partly in keeping them within bounds. But it never succeeded in tearing away from them their apparent knowledge. It had nothing better to offer them, and to the question what is *knowable* would have answered "*Nothing!*" or at the most "*I do not know*".

It sounds very metaphysical to ask the question what reason is capable of, and yet that question resounds at present in the voice of our age which is otherwise so little inclined to metaphysicizing. We have hardly any more theological battles than those which are expressly conducted for and against the capacity and right of reason to speak first in matters of religion. Through reason alone is the true knowledge of God real – through reason it is impossible are the slogans of the naturalists and the supernaturalists, and the real or apparent proofs of these [: 151] two assertions are the weapons with which they campaign against each other. Thus one strives, without having explicitly posed our problem, to establish *what reason is capable of*. There is an appeal to a certain extent from the attacked system to the capacity of reason or its lack and in this people hope to find uncontroversial premises for their disputed assertions. The lack of such premises is thus the difficulty which both parties come up against, and to that extent they are much closer to the actual point of the misunderstanding than they realize themselves. An obscure but lively feeling for this difficulty is expressed clearly enough in the despair which has become so visible in our times of having one's opinion prevail through proofs of reason and of being able to resolve one's doubts through rational grounds. This despair has caused many recently to support their shaky metaphysics with mysticism and cabbalism; many are led to attend to the invitations of secret societies which promised to answer through revelations and traditions the questions which seemed unanswerable through reason; many are forced to appeal from reason to sound common sense, feeling for truth, sense of intuition and whatever else the kangaroo courts are called.

Never before has it been so apparent that too much and too little has been attributed to reason than at present. The idolatry practised with it and the contempt directed toward it verge on the ridiculous; without [: 152] its being possible to conceal from oneself on the other hand that the exaggerated praise as well as the calumnies against reason have been at no time so skilfully refuted. Friends and enemies of reason, naturalists who tolerate no *belief*, spiritualists who tolerate no *knowledge* in religion accuse each other mutually of *misunderstanding reason*. Since both sides must justify their acquaintance with reason before their opponents, each is forced to discover, in addition to the proofs which had been satisfactory to that party, proofs which would be evident to the opponents. Each therefore has to go beyond his principles, considered till now to be first principles, to find features of reason not found before and to strive to found his knowledge of the capacity and authority of reason in universally valid ways – that is, for himself and for his opponents. None of the disputing parties can be satisfied with their current knowledge of reason any more than they can be with that of their opponents. None of them can leave things where they stood, and the need for a new investigation of the cognitive capacity would have to be acknowledged (even if there had been no critique of reason) as universally as the present general conviction that reason is misunderstood (by opponents).

Any impartial observer can see that there is a problem about what the cognitive capacity is capable of. It is as evident to such an observer in the host of unambiguous symptoms [: 153] as it is to the critical skeptic when comparing the philosophical systems. It would be no minor merit of our century if it were to clear up the old wretched misunderstanding of reason misjudging itself, a misunderstanding which however inevitable it has been for the human mind on the long and arduous path it had to take till it reached knowledge of its theoretical capacity, but which at the same time belongs among the greatest evils with which mankind could be afflicted; that misunderstanding of reason which in all sorts of guises has for millennia created damage, subjecting the cultivated nations to bloodshed and bloodless feuds of orthodoxy and heterodoxy, made unbelief and superstition necessary, wasted the energies of so many excellent minds with useless hair-splitting and squabbles, and seemed doomed to persevere in all these sad consequences; the merit of having drawn this misunderstanding from the obscurity of confused concepts, having reduced it to its simplest points, and thus having brought into consideration a problem whose solution gives hope for nothing less than universally valid First Principles of our rights and duties in this life and a universally valid ground for our expectation for the future life, the end of all philosophical and theological heresies, and, at least in the domain of speculative philosophy, promises an eternal peace the like of which no kindhearted cosmopolitan has dreamed. But how, if the solution of this problem is also reserved for our century as it draws to a close [: 154], if before it is completely past the majority of those good minds which occupy themselves in philosophy in Germany were united about universally valid principles, and if these philosophers were to cease from now on working against each other, without knowing or wishing to, were to begin (without any prior arrangement) to make the universally valid universally acceptable? – A more splendid crown could hardly be granted for the merits of our century; and Germany could inaugurate the activity of its sublime mission as *the future school of Europe* with no *more thorough* beginning.

1
What is meant by reason?

The question, what are the limits of the human cognitive capacity, cannot possibly be answered in a universally valid way before there is agreement about *what is meant by the cognitive capacity*.

"Oh, that agreement was reached long since", the popular philosopher objects, "every thinking mind, whether a philosopher or not, understands me when I simply name the cognitive capacity for him". [: 155] The famous writer who refuted the *Critique of Reason* in its two major elements by means of a text devoted to *space* and *causality*, Mr *Feder*, is quite correct to state in his popular and universally comprehensible textbook *Logic and Metaphysics* in the paragraph which deals with the cognitive capacity: "What it means *to represent something to oneself*, to cognize a thing, to think something, what *representations*, thoughts, concepts and ideas mean must be known to everyone by himself. Nothing more can be explained than this: if a word is not properly understood by someone, one chooses a different word which is intelligible to him in order to remind him of *things* through familiar terms which have to be known from one's own *sensations*. Of course it is possible to confuse concepts through obscure *artificial definitions* and give rise to disputes which one could have risen above." What sort of success have the obscure artificial definitions had which the *Critique of Reason* has provided for all these *things* so adequately known through sensation? As the *Kantians* themselves acknowledge and even assert, they were misunderstood by the most famous philosophers of our nation who have as yet declared themselves about Kantian philosophy, by a *Plattner**, Eberhard, Tiedemann, Reimarus, Feder, Meiners, Selle*** among others. [: 157] They have, as the famous philosopher *Meiners* narrates, in

---

* In the few respects addressed in the *Philosophical Aphorisms*, 1ˢᵗ Part, new edition, 1784;

** Reinhold gives references: in the Philosophical Magazine, the Hessische Beyträge, Über die Gründe der menschlichen Erkenntnis und der natürlichen Religion, Über Raum und Kausalität zur Prüfung der kantischen Philosophie, Grundriss der Seelenlehre (Preface), Grundsätze der reinen Philosophie. [These are in order of author.] Reinhold's footnote continues: "I believe I am justified in rejecting categorization as a Kantian, a term which sounds sectarian, as are all those who do not keep to the letter of the *Critique of Pure Reason*. At the same time I must endorse the assertion of the Kantians given here. I also believe that I am not compromising my sincere respect for those eminent philosophers I have named if I here publicly and loudly claim that I see all the scruples, doubts and objections they

their explanations and conclusions robbed hopeful youths of their peace of mind and probably more; even robbed one of them of his *understanding*, have caused Mr *Meiners* and as he supposes several of his peers *painful sensations*, etc.

As much as I would like to let our popular philosopher have his full say here I must at the same time ask him for the sake of other readers who are not popular philosophers to allow me first to present and prove my argument before he offers his objections to it.

I am showing that there has by no means been *any general agreement about the cognitive capacity*, and that the lack of universally valid principles in philosophy and all the ills and even in part the misunderstanding of the Kantian investigation of the cognitive capacity which are inseparable from that lack can be partly explained by the fact that our professional philosophers were quite happy to presuppose that their readers *must know for themselves what it means to represent a thing to oneself, to know a thing.*

Reason, as far as I know, has been reckoned by all philosophers until now as part of the *cognitive capacity*. Whether *sensibility* also belongs to it is far from being established among them. [: 158] Many exclude it from every function in actual cognition, many limit it to the so-called lower cognitive capacity etc., about which more to follow. First, then, on reason.

There is by no means agreement in the philosophical world about what is meant by reason. This can be concluded even on the basis of the dispute over the *capacity* of reason in matters of religion. The dispute can easily be traced back to the difference in conceptions which the disputing parties have of reason. The worst thing about this is that agreement is actually least where there is most feeling of agreement, in that where there is genuine agreement about certain features of the concept there is even less probability of suspecting any misunderstanding at all. Everyone, for example, who hears the term *Freedom of the Will* thinks with this word in common, even though one means merely the independence of the will from external compulsion, while another means independence from necessitation through sensory drives, and a third means independence from the laws of reason. This is even more the case with the word *reason*, since this word itself has more than *one* meaning in terms of language use.

---

have raised against Kantian philosophy as consequences of their mistaking the meaning of the *Critique of Reason*. Those readers who are not satisfied by the explanation of this strange phenomenon which I offered in the foreword have a free choice: whether they wish to consider that the opponents of the Kantian philosophy – among whom I count also Weishaupt, Flatt, Maass, Tittel, Stattler (in his Antikant which stretches over three volumes) among others, or that I, who have found the exact opposite of everything which these men found objectionable in the *Critique of Reason*, have not understood the philosopher from Königsberg.

I distinguish here *three* of these meanings: the *broader*: when the word *reason* indicates the capacity for cognition and representation in general, a property of the human being and distinguishing the human being from the animal; as a consequence [: 159] the more composite or artificial bodily organization characteristic of human beings, or disposition of the sensory tools is included in the concept; the *narrower* meaning, when one designates with the word reason that capacity for cognition which is commonly called *higher* to distinguish it from sensibility, the so-called lower capacity for cognition, and in which as a consequence the *understanding*, or the capacity for *judgment* is contained in the concept of reason; and finally the *narrowest* sense of the word reason, which comprehends only a part of the higher cognitive capacity, namely the *capacity to make inferences*, and thus is distinguished from the understanding.

I will keep to the last of these three meanings which is the most determinate of them all and about which, as far as I know, there is the most perfect agreement and which is believed really to indicate the actual essence of reason in contrast not only to sensibility but also to understanding in the capacity to make inferences.

What then is this *capacity to infer? Logic* gives us the answer in a nutshell: the capacity of the mind to perceive the agreement or non-agreement of two representations through comparison with a third representation. In syllogistics one may of course be satisfied with this answer, which indicates nothing more than a logical function of our capacity for representation with determining in what cases, with what kind of representations, this logical function, [: 160] this capacity to infer, may be used. Of what use to me is this answer, unless the discussion is of representations themselves in general? Is the agreement among representations produced by means of this logical function on that account also an agreement among the *objects* of those representations? Is it not possible that a syllogism, on the basis of its *form* (with respect to the logical function), is perfectly correct without being true in its content or capable of being applied to real objects? For example, a rich person may practise many acts of charity; now the king of *Eldorado* is rich, therefore he may practise many acts of charity. This syllogism is perfectly correct in its form. The conclusion follows from the premises, which are both as clearly true in themselves as is possible, and nothing is missing for the whole syllogism but the *actuality* of the subject under discussion.

Reason, insofar as it means nothing more than the capacity to infer, is capable of nothing but formal truth, forms of syllogism, setting up the structure of syllogisms; all of this can exist with all accordance with regularity alongside material untruth. Material truth, the relation of the representations linked in the syllogism to an object in reality, to something that is not mere representation, is by no means dependent on the form of the syllogism, and as a consequence cannot be obtained by the mere capacity to infer. By means of this capacity it could only be eternally [: 161] undecided whether or not there is a kingdom of Eldorado. It does not matter how many syllogisms one builds on top of others, one will not come one step closer to an answer to this question: as long as one sticks to the correctness of the form per se and leaves the correctness of the matter, the material, of the linked representations unestablished, the ground of objective validity found outside the form.

Where, then, does reason acquire the material necessary for the material truth of its functions, however correct these are formally – a material it cannot itself generate? If it is a question of sensory objects the answer is simple and comprehensible enough: from the world of the senses! Thus, for example, common and learned experience provides enough *data* from which it is possible to conclude that the country Eldorado does not exist. In this case, and in all similar cases in which so-called sensory objects correspond to representations, reason bases the material truth of its correct and empty forms of inference on a material which is provided and presented to it by its companion *sensibility*. It is not so simple to answer the question: how reason acquires the material it needs for the material truth of those inferences whose content has to do with representations which relate to *supersensory* objects. In the entire world of the senses, for example, there is no object and can be no object which the representation of the first cause or of the infinite thing would fit. In all experiences which are possible to our *mind* [: 162] only representations can occur, and never the *representing entity* itself, always only the effects of the representing subject, never the subject itself, which we are only capable of thinking as an unknown something, and can by no means intuit as a determinate substance even by means of the inner sense. Now if reason wishes to produce anything determinate about the nature of such subjects in which it is abandoned by the evidence of the senses, how does it reach supersensory material on which the material truth of its inferences depends?

"Through *divine revelation*", is the *supernaturalist's* answer, "which replaces the inability of reason, whether this is natural or the result of original sin". This answer can of course satisfy people whose faith is strong enough to have their conviction that the representation of the divinity produced in the human mind by a miracle is more than an empty representation (not just imaginary) produced by a second miracle, and to raise themselves in this way above the objection that a representation of the divinity would have to be present in the mind *before* any revelation if a person were to recognize such an extraordinary manifestation (miracle) as reliable, supernatural, *divine*, i.e. find it in accord with the proper concept of the divinity; in a word, that every historical revelation must presuppose reason's idea of divinity and could never give it. – But three parties in the philosophical world who protest against all supernaturalism, [: 163] indeed even a number of supernaturalists themselves, find this answer quite unsatisfactory and are in agreement amongst each other that the truth of conclusions relating to supersensory objects, if it were capable of a philosophical explanation, would have to be explicable *naturally*.

Thus it would have to be explicable from the characteristic essence, qualities of the nature of reason, how reason reaches the material of its supersensory representations since these representations belong properly and exclusively to reason. Since this is absolutely inexplicable however from its logical nature, i.e. since it means nothing more than the capacity to infer, reason would have to have another particular capacity apart from this to create the move from the material of supersensory representation to the material truth of its conclusions, which would constitute its nature together with the capacity to infer.

Since the capacity to infer is actually merely *logical*, we distinguish that other capacity by the name *metaphysical* reason.

The definition of reason which is believed to contain the narrowest sense of the word and with that the essence of reason, is therefore quite inadequate and so incomplete that it contains only *half* of the concept which is meant to have the essence of reason as its object.

Until *Kant*, the question was never raised in the philosophical world (in the sense just indicated): [: 164] does reason have a metaphysical capacity? At the same time it has been no less than established whether or not reason possesses such a capacity. Through the main theses of the major parties this capacity is either attributed to reason or denied to it, without any investigation of reason. The theists believed they had demonstrated the existence and nature of supersensory objects by means of their syllogisms, the atheists on the other hand that they had demonstrated their non-existence and impossibility. These two parties have made it impossible for themselves to investigate the question whether reason is capable of deciding about the existence or non-existence of supersensory objects because they have presupposed as already decided the answer to the question through the use they have made of a supposed metaphysical capacity. For what purpose would they pose the question whether or not reason is *capable* of knowing the existence or non-existence of supersensory objects when in their eyes reason has *actually* recognized this existence or non-existence. On the basis of the principles of the dogmatic skeptics and of the supernaturalists it is incontrovertible that reason cannot possess any metaphysical capacity. For what purpose would the *first* pose the question, who have already established that the agreement of human representations with their objects is impossible to demonstrate, whether these are sensory or supersensory? And for what purpose would the *second* pose the question, since they forestall the question though their confession of faith and have become accustomed to infer from the incapacity of reason, which they consider proven and never doubt, to the [: 165] indispensability of a supernatural surrogate.

Instead of beginning with the question whether or not reason has a metaphysical capacity and leaving the answer completely undecided before the matter is investigated, one half of the philosophical world asserts that it does and the other half has denied it, for reasons which could only have any weight because one group presupposed the reality and the other the non-reality of the metaphysical capacity.

Since the metaphysical capacity of reason is asserted by two major parties and denied by two, it is obvious that it is not established among philosophers whether or not there is such a capacity, whereas the logical capacity of reason is really universally valid, acknowledged by the most general accord, and as a consequence is universally accepted.

Until something universally valid is established about the metaphysical capacity of reason there is agreement only about one *half of the nature* of reason, it is only half understood if it is a question of reason in the strictest sense, and the parties of the philosophical world must set aside their dispute about the knowledge of supersensory objects until they have unified themselves about the metaphysical capacity of reason in a way that has never before been undertaken. [: 166]

It may now be seen that if the question of the problematic capacity of reason is to be answered decisively, and in a universally valid way accepted by all those who philosophize, there is need of a science – if there is to be such a science at all – which makes some discovery in the domain of reason that has *never yet been worked* through or known.

It may well be objected here that that question, whether or not reason has a metaphysical capacity, is nothing new, *Plato* and *Aristotle* among the ancients and *Leibniz* and *Locke* among the moderns, not to speak of several others, have only put it in different terms and really answered it in their admirable studies on the origin of human representations.

I consider the question which *Leibniz* and *Locke* (and the same thing applies to their ancient predecessors) had before them when they studied the origin of concepts a question which sooner matches the expression than the meaning of our question.

Leibniz and *Locke* were dogmatic theists and for that very reason the metaphysical capacity of reason was not at all problematic, being the most *established* thing in the world. For them it was not a matter of establishing for themselves whether reason has a metaphysical capacity or not; but rather to ask *in what* this capacity which they presupposed as real *consisted*. They accepted the dogma of their party as the basis of the doctrinal structure [: 167] dealing with the origin of representations, in that they proceeded from a supersensory knowledge taken as real and then studied not whether supersensory knowledge is possible at all, but rather how the human mind achieves supersensory knowledge.

If it is presupposed that reason has a metaphysical capacity and can therefore obtain for its supersensory representations real and not merely imaginary material, which is for us still an open question, then all possible cases are exhausted in *Leibniz's* and *Locke's* systems as to how reason can arrive at this material.

It can of course not produce such knowledge out of nothing, and so the knowledge must be *given* to it; and since it cannot be given to it either by the logical capacity to infer (through which only the form of inference is obtained) or *directly* by sensory impression, then it must either bring it when it enters the world or receive it only in this world; it must be given to it either directly in a set of innate representations (and, as some followers of Leibniz put it, in a system of innate truths) or at least *indirectly* in the material of sensory representations. In the first case, its metaphysical capacity consists in a material implanted in the soul for its inferences about the supersensory, and in the second case in the special faculty of deriving the supersensory from the sensory material. [: 168]

That innate material of supersensory representations implanted in the soul must be precisely distinguished even by its proponents from the supersensory objects themselves, which it is said only to represent in the mind. Otherwise representation and object would be one and the same thing, and therefore either the object would be a mere representation, a *thing of thought*, or the representation would be the object itself, our concept of the soul the soul, of the divinity the divinity itself. As it is, the material of a representation only has reality if there is some thing corresponding to it which is not the representation itself. How is the material of supersensory representations to be cognized? By means of the object outside the representation corresponding to it? – Impossible. Because this, given the presupposition, is supposed to be known only through the representation and its innate material. That is, by means of the real giving, the presence of that material itself, to which, if it is really given, an object must also necessarily correspond. But how is this real presence to be demonstrated? Perhaps in that it occurs in real representations, that is, really is represented? By no means. Because we have countless real representations to which no real object corresponds, and which as a consequence have a merely imaginary or artificial material.

It would be pointless to object here, "but such representations would not be *innate* and if it were established that any representation or even only its material were implanted in reason [: 169] and consequently were really *rational*, then it is already distinguished adequately from all deceptive and irrational representations *by that very means*". Certainly, if it is *established*. But that is precisely the question. And what would be the unmistakable universally acknowledged data by means of which it could be established that any representation or its material were really implanted in reason. Perhaps the generality and necessity of the representation; the unavoidable acknowledgment of an object corresponding to it; the evidence of knowledge? But then where does the dispute between the main parties come from about the question undecided amongst them: whether our representations of the *divinity, soul, freedom* are representations corresponding to proper actual objects – if the affirmative answer to this question was universally apparent and inevitably necessary for human reason?

Even several supporters of innate concepts have found themselves having to take refuge in experience, or what comes to the same thing, to sensory cognition; in order to account for how these innate representations which they held to be only dispositions, basic determinations of the mind, only possible representations, could reach the reality of actual representations. They believe they have made the whole matter comprehensible by supposing that the so-called mental ideas are woken, enlivened and developed* on occasion, and through the stimulus of sensory impressions. [: 170]

On the other hand a considerably larger number of recent philosophical writers have disassociated themselves from the *Platonic* or *Leibnizian* doctrine of innate concepts, and believe with Locke that they can, or rather must, explain the origin of representations of supersensory objects on the basis of the materials provided through sensibility, but processed and modified by reason. They believe that the mind could only reach by means of sense impressions any material whatsoever of its representations. And although it has not yet occurred to any of them as far as I know to call *God*, the *soul* or *freedom* objects of sensibility, they still assert that what sensibility is not directly capable of by its own means becomes possible for it through reason, which possesses a capacity of inferring the material of supersensory representations from *sensory* material, or rather is itself this capacity.

If the capacity for deriving the supersensory from the sensory were really present in reason, it would have to be different from the merely logical capacity; it would have to be the metaphysical capacity which, if the derivation were proper, would be sufficiently known not of course in its original nature founded in the arrangement of reason but at least from

---

* None of these words means any more than the others, and each one is placed in this hypothesis to fill the gap of a missing concept, not to denote any concept.

its effect, namely supersensory knowledge. [: 171] But it is precisely what is undecided, controversial and problematic about this effect that has caused that metaphysical capacity to remain undecided, controversial and problematic. Unfortunately we have no demonstration yet of the derivation of the supersensory from the sensory that is universally acknowledged even by professional metaphysicians and the most admirable minds among them. While *one* party in the philosophical world claims it has really undertaken this derivation (and notice that the members of this party are not in agreement with each other about the ways and means), the *second* major party does precisely the opposite and deduces the *non-being* of the supersensory from the sensory; the *third* party declares these two deductions to be equally baseless and a task inappropriate to the nature of the human mind and futile. The *fourth* party finally holds that deduction not only to be something impossible but also to be an incursion into divine rights in that it belongs only to the divinity to reveal the existence of supersensory objects. Anyone claiming therefore that his derivation of the supersensory from the sensory is established is asserting *the thing that is not*, and wants to impose upon us his little knowledge as the knowledge of the human mind, and is selling his readers or listeners an untruth, and of this anyone who is not looking through the metaphysical spectacles of that person but seeing with his own eyes can convince himself with a glance at what is really happening in the philosophical world. If the existence of the cause is to be concluded merely from the effect, then [: 172] the former remains unestablished until the latter is established. It is thus really not established whether there is a metaphysical capacity of reason, because it is not established whether a proper derivation of the supersensory from the sensory is possible.

If the question first to be established thus *whether there is a metaphysical capacity of reason* is not to be answered again on the basis of the controversial basic principles of the four major parties, and consequently not again treated on the old arena of metaphysics, it must be put in a sense that is completely new. It must not begin with the *reality* or *impossibility* of supersensory knowledge, but leave both of those to one side and concern itself with the capacity of *reason per se*. Accordingly, in answering it is necessary before all else to investigate not *how*, but *whether* a derivation of the supersensory from the sensory is possible or not; that is, whether it contains no contradiction, whether it does not contradict universally valid laws of the human capacity for representation. For in the case that such a contradiction could be demonstrated in a universally valid way it would be thereby decided that reason does not possess any metaphysical capacity.

Since reason in the derivation of the supersensory from the sensory would presuppose the *understanding*, the capacity to judge, the *understanding* will especially have to be investigated. It is the understanding which first [: 173] processes the raw materials received through sensibility and transmits them to reason. The judgments it makes establish *first* the material for syllogisms. It must therefore be shown what the understanding can do, what is possible through its processing of sensory material, in a word, the relationship of the *understanding* to sensibility must be precisely and definitely demonstrated.

Even the understanding, insofar as this term is understood to mean only the capacity to judge, can be nothing more than the logical capacity of generating judgments from a given material. The material which it needs for its operations cannot be created by it from nothing, but has to be *given* to it. If there is some error in the given of material, a judgment can be completely correct in its form and yet in its material quite false: e.g. *A golden mountain is something actual. The King of Eldorado is rich.* Even with the understanding, material truth does not depend on form per se but on the material given outside the form. Understanding can only operate with what is given to it, and can only operate with it insofar as it is given to it. In order to determine precisely *what* the understanding is capable of producing from the materials of sensibility there must be a prior investigation of what might actually be supplied to the understanding by sensibility and of *how* it is supplied by sensibility. That is, the relationship of the understanding to *sensibility* must be established. [: 174]

2

What is to be understood by sensibility?

Nothing in my opinion can be more obvious than the necessity of establishing, first, what is meant by sensibility and what is in general possible by means of the capacity which bears this name, before there can be any agreement about whether *sensibility can provide a material* from which the material of supersensory representations could be drawn by means of the operations of understanding and reason. Whatever contradicts the capacity for sensibility cannot be drawn from sensibility by any understanding or reason, not even that of the divinity himself. In order to show, however, what does or does not contradict sensibility one has to have thoroughly dealt with the essence, the nature of sensibility.

Until now, even less has been established in the philosophical world about sensibility than about understanding and reason. We will here consider only two major parties.

The *materialists* allow the validity of nothing but *sensory entities*, that is, they consider *sensory* representations to be the only ones to which real objects correspond. Everything real for them is a *body* or *property* or *disposition* of the body; and since understanding and reason can only judge and conclude about the existence and disposition of the world of bodies (apart from which for the materialists nothing is real) on the basis of the testimony [: 175] of sensibility, this testimony is for them the only basis of all knowledge of the real and of the possible. Further: since *corporality*, which constitutes the essence of all things which subsist in themselves according to this system, can only be known by means of the sensibility, sensibility is for them the source of knowledge not only of the disposition of certain things, but of the actual essence of all things, and even understanding and reason are to them nothing but modifications of sensibility, like sensibility a mere capacity for sensation with only this difference: that understanding and reason can sense nothing but *agreement* or *conflict* between the materials of sensibility.

The *spiritualists*, by contrast, maintain the very opposite about sensibility. I am not speaking here about individual spiritualist sects; not about the *idealists* who allow nothing real outside a mere world of ideas or minds, and deny to sensibility any capacity of providing a material to which a real object outside representation corresponds. I am not speaking of the *followers of Leibniz* who accept nothing other than simple substances in all of nature, deduce extension from a confused representation of the aggregates of those unextended substances, and consider sensibility basically as a mere limitation of the understanding. It does not matter how much they differ from each other in their particular opinions, they are still in agreement with each other about [: 176] this: that the *essence* of things is only cognizable to the understanding and to reason, that sensibility is not capable of showing even the essence of bodies, and that everything it may provide for us from these objects which are its own is nothing but contingent, mutable properties belonging to the mere surface.

The spiritualists are as little in agreement about where to place the capacity for sensory representations as about what they are to make of that capacity. Some assign its seat to the body, and consider it a mere capacity of bodily organization to receive impressions and to communicate these to the incorporeal soul. Others seek it in the soul and consider it to be a capacity of the soul to receive the impressions present in bodily organization; and finally still others locate it simultaneously in the soul and in the body and consider it to be the capacity of being affected by outer objects through the medium of bodily organization. The first see sensibility as nothing but the sensitivity of bodily organization and deny it completely to the soul, as a property which belongs solely to bodies and would contradict the nature of a simple entity. The second acknowledge it as a disposition of the soul but only as a contingent and transitory disposition which would be the mere result of the union of the soul with the body and can only persist as long as that union. The last group believe they have discovered in sensibility a mere limitation of the soul through the body by means of which it would be limited [: 177] to the intuition of common and low, deceptive objects as the entities of sense, while its power of thought is constituted for the *intuition* of higher and worthier objects.

The spiritualists thought and still think in such different ways about sensibility. The only point in which they agree amongst themselves consists in their belief* that the soul is capable of sensory representations *only by means of the organic body*. As a consequence, in their different ways, they make sensibility dependent on bodily organization. They believe they have thus rescued the incorporeality of the soul. But unfortunately the *materialists* not only concede to them that indispensability of bodily organization for sensory representations but prove it with even stronger grounds and conclude from these, in considering sensory representations to be the only ones to which real objects correspond, that not only is a capacity for representation impossible without bodily organization, but that any capacity for representation is only a property of a certain bodily organization.

All this is a natural consequence of the line of argument followed till now in investigating the cognitive capacity, *which is quite back to front*. Instead of trying to reach agreement first about what is meant by cognitive capacity and [: 178] cognizability and only then determining to what extent the subject of the cognitive capacity (the soul) is cognizable, the argument proceeded from the *subject*, supposed to be either a simple or a composite substance, in order to define the cognitive capacity from concepts of the subject which had been constructed. Thus both the materialists and the spiritualists included their *dogmas* among the *principles* for the investigation of sensibility. The word soul had for these parties a threefold sense in that it was sometimes understood as the mere cognitive capacity itself, sometimes however as the subject of this capacity only, and sometimes as both together. At the same time however, all these different meanings were confused whenever it was necessary to the advantage of their hypotheses. Thus it happened that they sometimes transferred what can only be true of the cognitive capacity to its subject, and sometimes what they believed they had proved about the latter to the former. Materialist and spiritualist were in agreement that *sensibility* belongs to the mind only through bodily organization. Since, however, the materialists thought they had discovered the subject of the mind in the organic body itself, they regarded what they had supposed to be true of the subject of the cognitive capacity to be true also of the cognitive capacity itself; the materialist believed it to be just as certain that sensibility constitutes the *actual essence* of the cognitive capacity as that it constitutes the essence of the soul. The spiritualist, on the other hand,

---

*   With the exception of certain idealists among them.

who had declared the subject of the cognitive capacity to be incorporeal, transferred [: 179] the simplicity of the subject to the cognitive capacity and asserted accordingly that this consisted in the *understanding* per se, the capacity for bringing unity to the multiplicity of representations or, as it was commonly expressed, for perceiving the connection of truths; and just as simplicity constitutes the essence of the subject, the understanding constitutes the *essence* of the cognitive capacity, of which sensibility is an attribute only by *chance*, only through the connection of that simple subject with the organic body.

In both cases two essentially different questions were confused. The question: in what does the cognitive capacity consist, was confused with the question: what is the subject of the cognitive capacity (of the understanding, of sensibility)? The first question is actually *logical* and is concerned with laws which constitute not the nature of the thing which a cognitive capacity has but the nature of cognitive capacity itself – the conditions under which knowledge is possible which, taken together, are called cognitive capacity and must be *given* in the cognitive capacity itself. The second question on the other hand is actually *metaphysical*; it is concerned with laws which are supposed to constitute the nature of a real thing – conditions under which a thing distinct from the cognitive capacity itself is to be possible, by which it can then only be established whether and to what extent it is cognizable if one has *already* investigated the cognitive capacity itself and [: 180] found its actual limits[7].

Through a muddling of concepts – the possibility of which our posterity may well find incomprehensible – essentially different objects of investigation have been confused till now: the representable cognitive capacity with its non-representable subject, understanding (capacity for unity in representations) with absolute unity (simplicity) of the representing subject; sensibility (capacity for the manifold in the representation) with the composition (extension) of bodily organization. In this way, what in itself is merely a logical law of cognition became a metaphysical property of the knowing substance; the logical law of the action of the understanding became the metaphysical disposition of the understanding subject; the logical law of sensibility became the metaphysical disposition of the non-understanding subject which is joined to the understanding subject. It was

---

7 Beiser 249: explicates the first question: What are the conditions of knowledge? – a strictly logical question about the truth conditions of our judgments; it is a question not about the laws under which something exists, but about the laws which govern the knowledge of what exists. The second question, what is the subject of knowledge, is a metaphysical question about the nature of the subject who has knowledge. It is not about the laws which govern the knowledge of reality but about those which govern something in reality itself.

not considered that the disputed knowledge of these problematic substances, of the simple and the composite, depended on the possibility of cognition in general; that a cognitive capacity must exist before any real knowledge and its conditions which together constitute the *possibility of cognition* must be given, and that for that reason the cognitive capacity cannot be derived from things accepted as really cognizable (objects of the cognitive capacity) but that rather the cognizability of things has to be derived from the cognitive capacity. [: 181] Precisely the opposite of what ought to have been done was done by deriving the nature of sensibility and of understanding from bodily organization and the soul, since these latter two, insofar as they are cognizable, ought to be objects of the cognitive capacity, in a word, their *cognizability*, should have been derived from the capacity for sensibility and for understanding.

In endeavouring to become acquainted with the *subject* of the cognitive (the substance of the soul), which is no more capable of knowing itself than the eye is of seeing itself, an acquaintance was neglected which is not only possible in itself but also necessary if philosophy is to avoid groping around haphazardly with concepts and be a secure and definite advance of the mind – and that is *acquaintance with the cognitive capacity*. The more there was agreement in the whole philosophical world about that part of the cognitive capacity which consists in the *logical capacity of understanding and reason*, the more there was an inclination to suppose that the cognitive capacity in general was known, or at least that there was agreement about it amongst themselves. It was only natural that there had to be agreement about the concepts of the *logical* capacity for understanding and reason sooner than about the concept of *sensibility*. Since understanding and reason must exercise their logical function for any knowledge, whether sensory or supersensory, anyone who [: 182] accepted even only one object as known, any knowledge in general, had to allow for the indispensability of understanding and reason; and the *agreement about this indispensability* could only lead to a universal common investigation of the functions which belong to the understanding and to reason in cognition in general. Since it was believed, however, that sensibility was only active in *sensory knowledge*, those philosophers who claimed knowledge of supersensory objects, and thus allowed a supersensory knowledge, inevitably came to the conclusion that sensibility is not essential for knowledge in general; had no* logical function in knowledge, and as a consequence did not constitute a part of the cognitive capacity. Others, on the other hand (the materialists),

---

* Logical in the strictest sense means only what belongs to *thinking*. I am using it here in a broader sense to mean everything which belongs to the manner of cognition determined in the nature of the cognitive capacity, every *law* of the cognitive capacity; in contrast to the laws of the objects of the cognitive capacity.

who considered sensory objects not only as the solely cognizable but even as the only possible (conceivable), not only had to allow for sensibility indispensability for any knowledge, but also had to elevate it to the status of the supreme condition of all thinking, the criterion of all possibility, and make it the whole cognitive capacity and representation and subordinate to it understanding and reason as mere modifications.

[: 183] Since sensibility was completely excluded by one party from the cognitive capacity but was taken as the cognitive capacity itself by the other, these two parties had made any way of investigating sensibility in its relation to the cognitive capacity impossible for themselves, and without the objections of the dogmatic skeptics aimed against the principles of both, this investigation might never have occurred.* The spiritualists and the materialists, left to their own devices in their dispute, would have moved further and further away from such an investigation, the longer their dispute lasted. The *zealots* on both sides [: 184] went further than allowing *no place* for sensibility in knowledge or granting it *everything* – the first, with *Plato*, declared sensibility to be an unfortunate obstacle to knowledge, necessarily a source of error, a mere limitation of the capacity for representation; the others declared with *Epicurus* that any representation was true insofar as it was confirmed by sense impression, and saw pure understanding as an absurdity and the notions characteristic of it as figments of scholarly imagination.

3

What is to be understood by cognitive capacity?

That there is no agreement about the answer to this question is evident from the huge variety I have shown in the meanings it has been customary to associate with the words *reason* and *sensibility*. Hardly even those who seemed to adopt sensibility and reason in their concept of the cognitive capacity, and divided the cognitive capacity into the *sensory* or *lower* and the *rational* or *higher*, found it necessary to wonder or to explain what they

---

* Even *Locke*, who has said so much that is excellent about the indispensability of sensibility in the human cognitive capacity and remained so faithful to his principles that he considers the existence of God indemonstrable because a spirit is not an object of sensibility (*Our senses not being able to discover them, we want the means of knowing their particular existences. We can no more know that there are finite spirits really existing by the Idea we have of such beings in our minds, than by the Ideas any one has of fairies or centaurs, we can come to know that things answering those Ideas do really exist. Essay concerning human understanding V.II. C.XI. § 12.*) Even Locke has not been consistent about the actual participation of sensibility in the cognitive capacity, indeed not even about its indispensability for knowledge in general, as will be clearly shown in what follows, and becomes partly apparent from his claim that the existence of God is *knowable*.

understood by knowing. I have not been able to locate a precise utterance about it either from the immortal *Leibniz* or from his worthy adherents *Wolff, Bilfinger, Baumgarten*. The latter begins his *Metaphysics* with the following definition: "Metaphysics is the science [: 185] of the first grounds of knowledge of human cognition", yet in the whole work, in which he is otherwise so generous with explanations, even in those parts where he is treating the cognitive capacity, he utters not one syllable about what he wants us to understand by this *capacity*. At the same time it would be extremely difficult, I dare say impossible, to infer the meaning from comparison of his individual pronouncements or from the context of the whole. Where, for example, he makes assertions about the distinction between *cognition through the senses* and *through understanding*, a distinction he finds in mere unclarity of the one and clarity of the other, or, as he expresses himself, in a *greater or lesser degree of knowledge*, he speaks in his utterance only of *representation*, which he confuses with *cognition*. At the same time, Baumgarten must have adopted a distinction between *knowledge* and representation. But what?

Locke by no means considered it superfluous to indicate what he understood by knowledge. "Knowledge", he says, "seems to me to be nothing but the perception of the connexion and agreement, or disagreement and repugnance of any [in the note in the margin he has '*two*'] of our Ideas"*. But it ought not to be surprising [: 186] that this concept of knowledge has found no currency in the philosophical world since it is extremely inadequate and imprecise and does not satisfy at all the conditions which Locke himself establishes as indispensable.

"Our knowledge", says the acute thinker, "is only real insofar as there is correspondence between our ideas and the reality of things (the objects)"**. This correspondence is of course essential in any knowledge, and any knowledge not real in this sense would be like a representation which represents nothing. At the same time it is precisely this essential condition through which knowledge becomes knowledge that is completely glossed over in Locke's explanation. It speaks only of agreement between ideas. But ideas (representations) are essentially different from their objects. *Locke* himself declares in what follows that with representations which he calls *simple* he is presupposing the agreement with what is not idea (representation). But this presupposition is precisely what was being investigated in the exposition of knowledge, since without the consciousness

---

*   V.II.B.IV. Ch.1, Of Knowledge in General.

**   Ch. IV. Of the reality of human knowledge [Essay Book IV, Ch 4: Of the Reality of our Knowledge (p. 563): "*Our Knowledge*, therefore is *real*, only so far as there is conformity between our *Ideas* and the reality of Things."]

that an object (something that is not merely representation) corresponds to a representation any knowledge [: 187] could not possibly be real, that is, would *not be knowledge*.

In Locke's exposition, too, knowledge is made the mere representation of logical functions of judgment and of syllogisms. As a consequence the cognitive capacity is confused with what otherwise is called understanding and reason. Actually Locke was compelled because of this confusion to give in what follows a mere description of *reason* in which the actual function of reason in knowledge in general is sometimes distinguished from, and sometimes confused with, its methodical procedure in discursive knowledge and scientific demonstration. Even in the excellent discussion of the misuse of the *syllogism*[8], in which he engages at this opportunity, it is evident enough that he has not completely distinguished the outer syllogistic form with which book-learning at that time still played its game with the sixteen forms of deduction, from the inner form of the syllogism itself, the particular mode of action of reason. It was only too easy for him to misjudge this after he had taken consciousness of the connection of several representations – a consciousness only possible through that mode of operation of reason – into his concept of knowledge. As a consequence, since he later had the task of speaking of reason in particular, he could not possibly adopt the syllogism as the general and characteristic activity reason has in cognition in general. He asserted, accordingly, that reason was the faculty which finds out the means and [: 188] rightly applies them to discover certainty and probability*.

I have sought in vain for an explicit explanation of *knowledge* in the work of many an adherent of the immortal Locke, in vain in the work of the acute eclectic *Plattner*[9], in vain among the professional *logicians*, e.g. the commendable *Reimarus*. In an attentive reading undertaken for this purpose I indeed found the word "*knowledge*" used sometimes to mean conviction, sometimes certainty, sometimes science etc., and found that the concept which they attached to it on various occasions referred sometimes to consciousness of the necessity of a judgment, sometimes to the thought necessity of a representation, sometimes to the relationship of a representation to an object. But I also found that the use they made of the word and of those concepts when there was discussion of knowledge of a representation,

---

8 Cf. John Locke: *An Essay Concerning Human Understanding*, Book IV, chapter 4, section 4: "From whence it follows that *simple* Ideas *are not fictions* of our Fancies, but the natural and regular productions of Things without us, really operating upon us; and so carry with them all the conformity which is intended; or which our state requires: For they represent to us Things under those appearances which they are fitted to produce in us."

* The faculty which finds out the means and rightly applies them to discover certainty, and probability, is that which we call reason. [Book IV, chapter 17, section 2: Wherein reasoning consists]

9 Sic. (I.e. not "Platner", the conventional spelling).

knowledge of a thing that was not supposed to be representation, was not consistent, was changed arbitrarily, in a word, that the most outstanding philosophical writers known to me were not in agreement with each other or even with themselves.

§ V.

It is absolutely impossible to reach agreement about the universally valid concept of the cognitive capacity [: 189] while there is different thinking about the nature of the *capacity for representation*.

Whatever concept of cognition one accepts, it presupposes a concept of representation. Not every representation is knowledge, but all cognition is representation. If therefore any essential attribute is omitted or something foreign to it or even contradictory is incorporated in it, then the concept of cognition in one of its major aspects (namely that of *representation*) is incorrect. And if two dispute together about how the cognitive capacity is to be understood, then one of them only has to have overlooked an essential attribute in his concept of representation or to have incorporated something foreign to it (without either noticing, as they are thinking expressly only of cognition and not of representation) and they will for ever remain in disagreement about the concept of cognition.

Suppose there were agreement about the following definition of cognition: it is the consciousness of the relation of a *representation* to a certain something different from it which is called *object*. This agreement would be as good as none – it would be a mere formula which each can understand in his own sense, if there is no agreement about the concept of *representation* and especially about that aspect *which distinguishes it from the concept of the object*. Without agreement [: 190] about this attribute any agreement about the distinction between cognition and representation per se would be impossible.

Everything cognizable must be representable, although it does not follow that everything representable is cognizable, because otherwise every representation would be a piece of knowledge[10]. Representability or the possibility of representation is determined solely by the capacity for representation. The latter must accordingly be investigated before all else.

Representation is the *only thing* about whose actuality *all* philosophers are in agreement. At least if there is anything at all about which there is agreement in the philosophical world it is representation; no idealist, no solipsist, no dogmatic skeptic can deny the existence of representation.

---

10   Here "Erkenntnis" seems to refer to knowledge, although it is mainly encountered in Reinhold's treatise in meanings relating it to "cognition".

Whoever concedes representation, however, must concede a capacity for representation, i.e. that without which no representation is conceivable. As soon as agreement has been reached about this, one has put oneself in possession of a universally valid principle from which must follow determination of the limits of the cognitive capacity and the possibility of universally accepted grounds of knowledge for the basic truths of religion and morality, as for universally accepted first principles of morality and of natural law if they are determinable at all. [: 191]

Although *representation* is accepted by all, and every philosopher has a concept of representation, this concept is not the same for all, not in all equally complete, equally pure, equally correct. There is even disagreement about its most essential attributes as can be concluded in part from the disagreement about cognition, and in part as I hope will be demonstrated in the following to everyone's satisfaction. Should this misunderstanding which lies behind the disagreement not be eliminated? There have been not so many studies which have been set themselves the task of investigating the concept of representation that one would be obliged to hope for less from some new attempt.

The concept of the capacity for representation brings with it this advantage, that it is very easy to exploit it in a universally valid way once its essential aspect is found, i.e. that with it an analysis can be undertaken in which there can be agreement that one has grasped *all* of its representable attributes and that there is none remaining which could be the seed or occasion of future misunderstandings because of an undeveloped and indeterminate concept. For if the investigation of the capacity for representation has been successful enough in discovering its essential, its major attribute, then one has found at the same time the attribute and criterion of *representability* from which the limit of [: 192] all further analysis can easily be determined by the *non-representable*. It can then be shown with little effort what and to what extent something that belongs to the concept of representation is *representable* or not.

Book Two

Theory of the Capacity for Representation in General

"Since the mind in all its thoughts and reasonings hath no other *immediate* objet[1] but its own *Ideas*, which it alone does or can contemplate, it is evident that our Knowledge is only conversant about them."

Locke's Essay B. IV. Ch. 1

[: 195]

§ VI.

The term *capacity for representation* encompasses in its wider sense everything that belongs first to the conditions of representation.

This paragraph is intended to express nothing other than the *wider meaning* of the term capacity for representation, i.e. the meaning about which *all* philosophical parties are in agreement to the extent that and for the reason that this meaning encompasses all the *particular* meanings of each party and each adherent, and fits every particular opinion about the capacity for representation. I am not presenting here the determinate concept, but only the determinable, and am drawing the widest possible line around the domain which is common to me and to all those who have some thought about the capacity for representation. [: 196] This domain accordingly includes those who by capacity for representation understand the *soul* itself, or the *representing force*, or even only the *capacity* for this force; it includes those who consider the capacity for representation to be a result of the capacity of bodily organization and of a simple intellectual substance, or as a capacity of bodily organization alone; those who see it as an incorporeal entity only; those who can only conceive representation in terms of the physical effect of things outside the soul and who as a consequence adopt in their concept of the capacity for representation the capacity of external things to have an effect on the soul – in a word, all

---

1 This is how it is spelt in Reinhold. The sentence in Locke is: "Since *the Mind*, in all its Thoughts and Reasonings, hath no other immediate Object but its own *Ideas*, which it alone does or can contemplate, it is evident, that our Knowledge is only conversant about them."

those who conceive the essential nature of whatever it is by means of which representation is possible in the *first place*.

Although it may seem to most of my readers established that at least in this wider sense the *organic body* and the so-called external and internal tools of sensation must be counted for the capacity for representation – which on the evidence of experience are the channels through which the *material* for representations of these objects is provided by objects *outside us* – there is no agreement about this in the philosophical world.

There are *idealists*, who declare the testimony of experience to be a deception, and *skeptics* who declare it unreliable. The first believe they know that there can be no bodies and that our organization itself is a *mere representation*; the others, however, hold that one cannot be completely persuaded [: 197] where our representations come from, in that even their agreement with objects is not established and must for ever remain unestablished.

The *materialists* who deny any distinction between the representing subject and organization are of course agreed among themselves about the indispensability of organization to representation, because they consider the capacity for representation to be nothing but a disposition, property, or force of certain organisms.

The *dualists* suppose an essential difference between the representing subject which they call soul and the organization which they call body, and they take the body as a *mere instrument* of the soul. But in this they are not in agreement with each other about whether this instrument is to be considered indispensable *for all* or only for a *certain kind* of representation, i.e. the so-called *sensory* representations. As a consequence, they disagree with each other about whether they should adopt organization into the concept of the capacity for representation in general or *only* into the concept of the capacity for sensory representations.

Those who undertake to prove the immortality of the soul from its nature find themselves, because of the susceptibility of the organic body to decay, required either to deny the indispensability of organization in general, or to attribute to the soul a finer body which persists after death. *Spiritualists* must adopt one of these views. They consider the capacity for representation to be a force of a non-corporeal [: 198] simple entity. Some consider that this force develops *no* representations through impression from outside but from its own predisposition, while others hold that this applies only to *supersensory* representations. Some claim that the capacity has no need of the body, which merely *impedes* it in its action, while others that it receives for the period of this life through the body the material which it processes into its representations.

Since it is *by no means established* in the philosophical world whether and to what extent organization belongs to the conditions of representation in general, and since the theory of the capacity for representation only allows as premises those that are *universally accepted*, the indispensability of organization for representation may here be neither asserted nor denied. That question must be left to one side for the time being, and absolutely must not be included in the concept of the capacity for representation which is to constitute the *foundation* of our theory and which in this respect may contain nothing except what thinking minds agree upon as soon as it is drawn to their attention.

That there really is such a concept of the capacity for representation is proved by the very dispute itself about whether organization belongs to the capacity or not. This question would be impossible if organization were such an essential component of the mere concept of the capacity for representation that the concept could not be thought without that attribute. All dispute would be impossible here if the parties were [: 199] not in agreement, even if implicitly, without their definite knowledge of it, about something which they call capacity for representation which they distinguish from that other something about which they are not in agreement, namely organization. They may seek the capacity for representation in mere organization alone, or in some simple substance distinct from organization alone, or in both together, but in each of these cases it is one and the same *capacity* which they derive from various sources; one and the same definite logical subject which they can only think by means of a predicate they endorse, because no subject can be determined except by means of a predicate, and they must endorse it in common if they want to establish among themselves whether or not another predicate (the indispensability of organization) must be linked with it or not. In order to find this common predicate, or the essential nature of such predicates, we must seek to determine more precisely the somewhat indeterminate concept, so ambiguous in its features, which we offered above.

There are *external* and *internal conditions* of representation. External conditions, which occur outside the representation per se, and must of necessity be *distinguished* from it, but at the same time are linked with it as necessary conditions. *Internal* conditions, which must occur in the representation per se, constitute essential components of it and cannot be distinguished from it without cancelling the representation per se. In the same way, for example, parents are *external* conditions while mind and body are *internal* conditions of a *human being*. But there is no need here [: 200] for an explanatory example, because the distinction between external and internal conditions of representation, as will soon be seen, belongs among the extremely few points about which all thinking minds are in agreement. The central attribute of the concept of representation, which is to give the *foundation* of my theory, is provided in the following paragraph.

§ VII.

There is agreement, necessitated by *consciousness*, that there belongs to representation a representing subject and a represented object which *both* must be *distinguished* from the *representation* to which they belong.

What *Cicero* said about "*lovers of wisdom*" is almost literally true: "No sick person has dreamed anything that some philosopher has not asserted while awake." Despite this, I doubt that it has occurred to any sophist of ancient or modern times to assume a representation with subject and object and to attempt to prevent the distinction between these three essentially distinct yet intimately connected things. He would have had to deny *consciousness*, or rather to have lost it. One is aware of oneself, of one's ego, only by means of the representation which one distinguishes from one's self, the *subject*, which can be denied no more than the representation per se; and one is only aware of one's *representation* by what is *represented* by it and what is distinguished from the representation per se, being able to deny it no more than the representation per se. [: 201]

Even though there may have been serious *solipsists*, i.e. philosophers who have denied the existence of all objects apart from their ego, even they would be forced by undeniable, irrefutable consciousness which defies all sophistries not only to distinguish their representing *ego* from its representations, but also a certain something which is *represented* by these, something that they with the rest of us call object, or must designate with the predicate of the *represented* if they intend to be understood by the rest of us. It may be the case that the solipsist sees this something as a representation. Then he must all the same distinguish this represented representation from the representation in which it is represented and allow that he has two different representations when he thinks the *object* of a representation and the *representation per se* of this object, and that the distinction cannot be cancelled at his behest.

Since it is not being claimed here either *that* or *how* objects are present *outside the mind*, but only that they must be distinguished from representations *per se*, I do not need to adduce arguments here against the *idealists* or against the *skeptics*. And since I am only arguing for the distinction occurring in *consciousness* itself without discussing the ground for it based outside consciousness, I do not become embroiled with any party whatever name it goes by. None of them asserts that what represents and what [: 202] is represented is *nothing*; or that the something that represents and the something that is represented are not to be distinguished from the *representation per se*.

Since, then, the representing subject and the represented object not only *can* be distinguished from the representation to which they pertain but *must* be so distinguished, they do not constitute components of the representation per se, and pertain simply to the *external conditions* of representation, and must be carefully excised from the concept of the *inner* conditions pertaining alone to representation *per se* – conditions which constitute representation per se.

Thus, we have managed to determine more closely the concept of the capacity for representation simply by removing what does not pertain to it, and have gained by these means the concept of the capacity for representation in its narrower sense, the concept of the *capacity for representation per se in general*. [: 202]

§ VIII.

The term *capacity for representation* encompasses in its narrower sense only that which belongs to the *inner* conditions of representation alone and in consequence excludes represented *objects* as well as the representing *subject*, as *external* conditions.

"To representation per se there pertains the representing *force* of the simple thinking substance", the *spiritualist* opines – "the representing force [: 203] of a certain organization", says the *materialist*; "the representing force is the simple result of the forces of the simple substance and of organization", the *dualist* interrupts me. Gentlemen! I have no desire in this paragraph to deny what any of them assert. I am seeking only to pause before insisting on any of their various opinions about the nature of the representing *force* until we have together attempted to reach agreement about the concept of the capacity for representation only. I have good reasons for avoiding the expression "*representing force*".[2] Here I am investigating the concept of the *capacity for representation*; and I am aware that by force, at least commonly, is meant the capacity taken together with its *subject*, the representing *substance*. People have tried long enough and commonly enough to know the capacity for representation by means of the representing force. Why should I not be granted the opportunity to determine the force by means of the capacity – by doing which, without producing a circular argument, I cannot by any means assimilate the *force* into the capacity. Every force manifests its active and passive *capacity* only in its effects, and there is no other way to know a force than by seeking to discover in the effects the means by which these were possible in the first place, that is, the *capacity* of the force. The representing force is only knowable through its effect: the *representation*. We intend, accordingly, to begin by investigating not the force but only what occurs in its effect, the *representation per se* itself. [: 204] Not the functioning subject *itself*, but only its capacity or, rather, features of its capacity can occur in its effect, the representation. If we are

---

2   This is presumably Wolff's *vis repraesentativa*.

successful in explicating this capacity per se on the basis of *representation* then we will know the force insofar as it is knowable.

With this determination of the concept of capacity for representation in the narrower sense of the term questions about the nature of the representing subjects or the soul, and about the objects represented, or things outside us, are excluded from our investigation which concerns representation *per se*. These questions have always crept into such an investigation and have distorted the aim of such a study. The distinction between *external* and *internal* conditions of representation through consciousness may have been suggested to philosophers, but they have tended to ignore it, and it has never occurred to them (it is even incomprehensible to most of them) that in investigating the capacity for representation per se there may be no discussion either of the representing subject or of the represented objects. The question of what constitutes the capacity for representation was confused with quite different questions: What constitutes the capacity for representation in us? How does the representing force function? Indeed in the fruitless attempt to answer these questions it was completely overlooked. *Representing*, one philosopher asserted, is the result of the functioning together of a simple substance (the soul) with an [: 205] organic body; the soul, accordingly, is no more capable of representation without the body than the body without the soul. *Thinking*, says another, can only be the effect of an incorporeal entity, and since there is thinking more or less in every representation, the capacity for representation is a capacity of the *spirit*. *Sensing*, replied a third, is only possible for an organic body; and since all representations can be derived from sensations, the capacity for representation is a capacity of a certain organization. By these means all investigations of the capacity for representation became more or less polemical, and the clouds of dust raised in the turmoil of battle usually hid the real object of the question from the eyes of the combatants. It was not yet established what is meant by *represent*, *sense*, *think*, and there was an attempt to explore the cause of representing, sensing, thinking. The investigation of the representing force was expected to provide information about what was to be understood by representation, and there was an attempt to learn what representation per se is on the basis of the representing subject and sometimes on the basis of the represented objects.

It does not require a deal of deep thought to become fully aware of the importance of the distinction we have established between the capacity for representation in the wider and narrower sense – in other words, the distinction between the capacity for representation in which the soul itself and the force of external objects affecting it and the *capacity for representation per se* [: 206] in which both are excluded. We know objects outside ourselves and even the representing thing in ourselves *only through the representations* we have of them and have to distinguish from them. Things represented outside ourselves and our soul are not themselves the representations we have of them, and our consciousness must make every effort to make it quite impossible to *substitute* what is *represented* for *representation per se* and this for the *representing entity* in us. As long as we do not know in a determinate way what pertains to representation insofar as it is *representation per se*, we can only continue to transfer what belongs solely to representation per se partly to the represented objects and partly to the representing subject; we can only continue to confuse the predicates which pertain to such different things as representation, the representing entity, and the represented, and consequently confuse things with representations and vice versa, which can only lead to misunderstanding, lack of universally valid principles and insoluble confusion of all philosophical notions. It will become more and more apparent in what follows how this has been the case. Into the investigation of the capacity for representation intruded problems which are alien to it of the representing entity or soul and of the objects outside the soul, even though one was compelled by consciousness to allow that all that could be known of these things was possible *only through the representations* we have of them and must distinguish from them. This distinction [: 207] was forgotten at precisely the moment when it ought most to have been kept in mind: in that this distinction alone could have prompted in the investigation of the capacity for representation the question what pertains to representation insofar as this is nothing but *representation per se*, and what must be distinguished in this aspect from the represented objects and from the representing subject. That is, in what does the capacity for representation per se, the capacity for representation in the narrower sense, consist? – The representing subject and its force and the accompanying effect of the represented objects which I am only capable of knowing through representations, i.e. the capacity for representation in the wider sense and what pertains to it, may consist in anything at all – the representing *force* may be a spirit or a body or a result of both. All of this is left to one side until the question is answered what is meant by the capacity for representation per se by means of which alone representation of the soul and of external things is possible.

Let me remind the *idealist* and the *dogmatic skeptic* here that I am neither asserting nor denying the distinction between body and soul or even the distinction between the representing subject and all so-called objects outside us when I make this distinction between representation, the representing entity and the represented which they have to grant me in virtue of their consciousness. Nor am I consequently establishing anything that these sects cannot concede to me as a consequence of their systems. [: 208] But here the empiricist might object that this means granting representations the reality which has been set aside for the question of *things*. This is not the case. My setting aside that question is not a dogmatic doubt and makes no claims about the distinction between body and soul or even the reality of things outside ourselves. I am refraining from all assertion until my readers and I have reached agreement about principles, when it will be shown that I ascribe ideal actuality to so-called *things* no more than I ascribe *real actuality* to *representations*, as the writer of the *Critique of Reason* has so often been accused of doing.

Spinoza abolishes the distinction between the representing entity and represented things in as much as he admits only a *single substance*. *Leibniz* and the *dualists* thought they *took cognizance* of this difference. The former attempted to explain it by assuming *different species* of a single genus of substances (namely of simple ones) – while the latter attempted to explain it through two *different genera* of substances. The dispute of these three different parties among each other as well as against the *dogmatic skeptics* who raise claims against the assertions of each of them is by no means settled. It will become apparent in what follows *how* this whole dispute must dissolve forever if one sets aside the controversy itself in investigating of the capacity for representation per se. And it will perhaps be completely understood [: 209] why it is necessary to reach agreement about the concept of representation *per se* if one intends to avoid misreasoning about *things* about which nothing can be established from *experience*.

Since we are at present engaged in the task of investigating the capacity for representation in the narrower sense, we must indicate in what the *inner* conditions of representation in general actually consist. What is it that must occur in every representation if it is to be a representation at all? What then belongs essentially to *representation per se*? Here it is above all crucially necessary that the concept of a representation per se be determined most precisely. Even the term *representation per se* can have more than *one* meaning.

§ IX.

The term *representation* encompasses in its wider sense sensation, thought, intuition, concept, idea, in a word everything which occurs *in our consciousness* as an immediate effect of sensing, thinking, intuiting, comprehending.

Given the unfortunate indeterminacy in which philosophers till now have left the important concept of representation, the term *representation* was used with no differentiation for everything that happens in the mind, for every active and passive function – indeed, many defined [: 210] representation simply as a *modification of the mind*. Yet representation is as distinct from representing as effect is from action, as consequence is from ground. This means that representation can never be the active or passive functioning of the mind in representing but only what arises from this active and passive functioning. Since the words *thinking, concept, idea* are never used for *actions* but always for *effects* of representing, this meaning in which the *thought*, the *concept* and the *idea* are subsumed under the common name representation is never *ambiguous*. It is however the case with *sensation* and *intuition*. Sensation sometimes means the mind being affected, the modification which an impression produces, the passive functioning of the mind when it occurs, and sometimes it means the representation that arises from this. Intuition, too, sometimes means the same as the *process of intuiting*, and sometimes the representation effected through that process. This ambiguity of the wider sense of the word representation, highly significant in its consequences, is avoided by never using it for any *active* or *passive* function of the capacity for representation but always only for the effect, the product of that modification which is called *representing*, and I intend to use it exclusively in what follows in the latter sense.

2.

Every *sensation*, every *thought*, every *intuition*, every *concept*, every *idea* is a representation; [: 211] but not every *representation* is sensation, thought, etc., or all of these together. Although the term *representation* which designates the whole genus can be used for each of these species, no denoting of a species per se can express the whole genus. Of course, to follow this rule one must be able to distinguish the *species* from the *genus* as well as one species *from the other*, and this in the case of *representations* has unfortunately not been the case before. Philosophy till now was in most cases far from making use of the *distinctions* between *sensation, concept* and *idea*, for example, to which language should have drawn attention through the very difference in the words. It usually* confused the meanings of these words while its officials tossed the blame for the slowness of their progress and the eternal disputes in their domain onto the *poverty of language*. Although careful designation of the different representations was so neglected, representations belonging to sensibility were called *sensations*, those however which were ascribed to the understanding and to reason were labelled *concepts* and *ideas*, there was at the same time agreement that not all representations [: 212] can without distinction be called sensations, concepts, ideas; but there was also agreement that all sensations, concepts and ideas can be called representations without distinction. I need accordingly have no concerns about objections to what I have set out in § IX.

---

* "Confused Ideas are such as render the use of words uncertain, and take away the benefit of distinct names." Locke [Book II, Ch. 29].

§ X.

To the extent that sensations, thoughts, intuitions, concepts, ideas are *representations* which are received through sensing, thinking, comprehending etc., the capacity to sense, think, comprehend etc. belong to the capacity for representation; in other words, the term capacity for representation encompasses in its narrower sense *sensibility, understanding* and *reason.*

Here it might be thought that I am adequately protected from misunderstanding and contradiction by language use which encompasses sensibility, understanding, and reason as essential components in the concept of the human capacity for representation or *mind.* But the common confusion of the representing subject with the capacity for representation, the soul with the mind, is so frequent, that I might draw upon myself harsh contradiction from a reader who holds the capacity for representation to be a *force* of the spirit and either denies outright any *sensibility* to this spirit or allows it only to the extent that it is joined with an organic body. It is not supererogatory then to remind readers that here there is absolutely no discussion of the *soul,* [: 213] about whose nature I have no desire, at least at present, to establish anything, but only of the *capacity for representation, wherever* this may come from and to *whatever* it may belong. Insofar as the capacity *to sense,* which is called *sensibility* in language use, belongs to this capacity sensibility constitutes one essential component of the concept of the capacity for representation.

Our empirical *psychology* has been so happily engaged with sensibility and our *logic* with understanding and reason that many a professional philosopher, who takes the term capacity for representation only in the *narrower* sense accepted formerly, and understands by it nothing but sensibility, understanding and reason, may find it ridiculously presumptuous of anyone to claim to offer something new, remarkable, even occasioning the reformation of philosophy. These men who utter *Nil Novi sub Sole* so frequently at any inopportune moment should at the same time reflect that despite all attempts so far the *science* of the capacity for representation has not made enough progress to bring agreement about *what* might be known by means of the mind, e.g. only sensory or also supersensory objects; they should accordingly not find it improbable to assume that what we know of the capacity for representation is by no means complete despite all our acquaintance with the *psychological* laws of sensibility and the *logical* ones of the understanding and reason. [: 214] There is actually a sense of the terms *representation* and *capacity for representation* which have not been thought of as yet either in *psychology* or in *logic,* and this sense has been left quite indeterminate in both, being reserved for the *general theory of the capacity for representation in general.*

§ XI.

The term *representation* encompasses in its narrowest sense only what sensation, thought, intuition, concept and idea have *in common*.

Representations of sensibility have in common with those of the understanding and reason, despite all the acknowledged difference, that in them something is *represented*. I call the concept, which I acquire by extracting this common attribute and thinking only of that, the concept of representation in the strictest sense, in the narrowest sense of the word. The term *representation* in this sense designates only the *content* of the concept of representation in general which has to be distinguished from its *scope*. This *scope* is *very large*; because it comprises everything that is called representation in the wider sense, sensation, thinking etc. That *content*, however, is *very small* because it excludes everything not belonging to the concept of representation in general, and as a consequence the aspects of sensibility, of the understanding and of reason by which the representations [: 215] of sensibility, understanding and reason are distinguished from one another. The term *representation in the strictest sense* designates, then, merely the *concept of the genus* of representation which, like every other concept of genus, subsumes all species *under* it without grasping any particular species in itself, taking it up in its content, or containing it among its essential aspects. This concept is a feature belonging to every particular species of representation, but no particular species of representation is a feature which is peculiar to it.

It should not be objected here that there can be no representation in the strict sense, since every actual representation must be either a sensation *or* a thought etc. This would mean as much as saying that one ought to reject the most precise meaning of the word *"human"* in which it designates neither a particular individual human being or a kind of human nor a class, but only the genus – the rational animal – on the grounds that the genus cannot exist outside the species and the species only in individuals. If genera cannot possibly and may not be confused with species and individuals without causing the greatest confusion in our concepts and without making an end of all our philosophizing, then *representation in general* must be distinguished precisely from *particular representations* as *species* and the full compass of those features belonging to it in that property be established with the greatest determinacy. For that reason I have chosen [: 216] the expression *representation in the narrowest sense* for the *concept of the genus* of representation because the concept of the genus shares the name *representation* with no other concept, while the term *representation* when it designates *species* belongs to *several*, namely to sensation, thinking, concept etc. And consequently it has a broader sense when it is used as the common designation of the species, that is, to designate more than one concept.

§ XII.

The term *capacity for representation* encompasses in its *narrowest* sense only that which belongs to the inner conditions of representation per se in the strictest sense, and consequently means neither sensibility nor understanding nor reason.

The capacity for representation encompasses only in a *narrower* sense (not in its narrowest sense) sensibility, understanding and reason, and consists accordingly neither of sensibility nor of understanding nor of reason alone, but of all three capacities together. If we could think the capacity for representation only in its *narrower* sense, then *every particular representation* would have to be the product of sensibility, understanding and reason *all together*. The capacity for representation could be manifest in certain representations, e.g. the sensations, not as sensibility without the cooperation of reason, and the capacity to infer would have to be accepted as indispensable to the most sensory representation. [: 217] This is not the case when the capacity for representation is thought in its *narrowest* sense, and sensibility, understanding and reason are not understood together, and one is not understood to the exclusion of the others, but rather simply we mean what is common to all these capacities. A capacity for representation is conceived which is manifest *either* as sensibility *or* as understanding *or* as reason or in all three simultaneously, but by its nature is capable of representations which are the result of all three capacities no more than being exclusively determined as sensations alone, concepts of the understanding alone, ideas of reason alone, but rather of all these three species of representation.

To facilitate an overview of the determinations offered for the concept of the capacity for representation, we will list the differences found between the three meanings of the term capacity for representation *one after the other*.

Broader sense

If one means by capacity for representation the entire compass of that which first belongs directly to the conditions of representation, there are contained within this compass the representing subject and the represented objects insofar as they contribute to the representation.

NOTE: In this broader sense alone the capacity for representation was adopted until now by those [: 218] who viewed it either as the force of a simple substance or of an organic body or as the result of a combination of both.

Narrower sense

If one means by capacity for representation the full compass of that which pertains only to the inner conditions of representation (only to representation *per se*) in the broader sense, then

1) the representing *subject* and the represented *object* are *excluded* from this full compass, which contains only the capacity for representation *per se*, and this is because both belong only to the external conditions which are distinguished from representation per se; but

2) sensibility, understanding and reason are contained, and this is so because they belong to the inner conditions of sensation, concept and idea which are encompassed by the term *representation in the broader sense.*

Narrowest sense

If one means by capacity for representation the full compass of that which *only* belongs to the inner conditions of *representation in the narrowest sense*, then there must be excluded from the full compass not only the representing subject and the represented *object* (as in the above) but also *sensibility, understanding* and *reason*, [: 219] and in this sense it contains only what belongs neither exclusively to representation of sensibility nor representation of understanding, nor representation of reason, but to representation in general, to representation κατ' εξοχηεν[3].

Thus we have the determinate *outline* of the concept of the capacity for representation κατ' εξοχηεν and in the strictest sense of the term. I say the mere outline, the mere delineation of the concept by which nothing is gained except the knowledge of *what does not belong in this concept.* However much is gained for philosophy already in this if such a delineation passes the test of universal validity (which I do not intend to assert about my own), and how this delineation rewards dry analysis, must be apparent to anyone who can recognize the misunderstandings and the damage arising from them and having to be sustained in philosophy if alien, superfluous, and contradictory features are adopted in an extremely important concept which lies at the basis of all other concepts or is at least associated with them all, as that of *representation.*

But this empty outline must be filled out; apart from the merely *negative* determinations of the concept of capacity for representation there must be *positive* ones, and since we now know what is excluded from this concept, it must be shown what [: 220] is actually contained in it. We know that its content can only consist of the inner conditions of representation per se, but we do not know *what* these *inner conditions* actually are. Once we have found these we have gained possession of the *positive concept* designated by the term capacity for representation in the narrowest sense. This concept must

---

3   Pre-eminently, par excellence

absolutely be determined in a *universally valid* way and set out if the concepts of sensibility, understanding, reason and of the cognitive capacity and its *limits* are to be determined more precisely than before, i.e. secured against the possibility of any ambiguity. How else can one indicate with certainty how representation of sensibility is distinguished from that of understanding or reason and what belongs to each species of representation, if it is not known what pertains to *representation* in general, to the *genus*, and what is to be understood by representation in general? How is it to be determined satisfactorily what can be represented by sensibility, understanding or reason until it is established what can be represented at all? And how is this last to be known, be set down in a universally valid way, until there is understanding and agreement about the conditions which pertain to every representation in general as representation, to representation *per se*.

§ XIII.

The full compass of that which pertains only to the inner conditions of representation in general, or [: 221] the capacity for representation in its narrowest sense, according to its disposition, cannot be derived from the representing subject, or the soul, nor from the represented objects, but only from the proper concept of *representation per se*.

If the capacity for representation were to be derived from the nature of the *soul*, one would have to mean by soul not the capacity for representation but its subject, the representing substance, insofar as this can be *represented* among the possible objects of our representations. This is also the case with reference to objects located outside our mind. The derivation of the whole capacity for representation or only of part of it could only be undertaken from these objects to the extent that these can be *represented*. It would then be necessary to derive either from *a particular* representation, i.e. the *soul*, or from *several particular* representations, i.e. the objects outside us, the conditions which pertain not to these *particular* representations (they are not under discussion here) but to *representation in general*. It is not possible to doubt that there are some conditions of certain particular representations which are not conditions of every representation, i.e. of representation in general. These two kinds of conditions would have to be distinguished from each other, and this is completely impossible unless the distinction between the particular representations [: 222] and *representation in general* is indicated. The determinate concept of representation per se is therefore the only possible source from which the conditions which constitute the concept of the capacity for representation can be drawn.

"But the representation is itself dependent on the representing subject and the represented object." Indeed, but only as on external conditions, which pertain to the capacity for representation but are not themselves that capacity. Here it is not a question of *how* representation *arises*, but *in what it consists*; it is not a matter of the *origin* but merely of the *nature* of the capacity for representation, not *where* the capacity for representation gets its components *from*, but what components it possesses; not how the capacity for representation can be explained *genetically*, but what is *meant* by capacity for representation. The difference between these two questions has been so generally overlooked that it cannot be emphasized often enough. The second question was always neglected, yet it is this question about which there should have been complete agreement if a satisfactory answer to the first, which engaged every mind, was to be possible.

The capacity for representation cannot possibly be derived from its cause (whether this lies in the subject, in the objects, or in both) while it is not known what is meant by it, i.e. before it is known not from its *effecting representation per se*. [: 223] At present the question to be answered is: in what does *representation* itself consist? Or: what can and must be thought in the *concept of representation*?

As we turn now to this important question we seem to stumble across an insurmountable obstacle blocking our further progress, and this consists in nothing less than the sheer impossibility of giving an actual *definition* of representation in the strictest sense. Attempting such an explanation would be the equivalent of proposing a concept of representation which was itself not a representation. A careful examination of all explanations of representation in whatever sense of the term offered by any philosophers whatsoever shows that the concept is not explained but presupposed as already known*.

But this completely established impossibility of a definition of representation can only continue to seem an obstacle to further study while there is the conviction that such a *definition* is *indispensable*. Since representation is that to which everything that is and can be object of consciousness [: 224] must relate, it is of everything that can occur in consciousness the most familiar but at the same time least explicable. It precedes all consciousness, and this is only possible because of it**, and since it must be *presupposed* in every explanation it is neither capable of or in need of an explanation. The *concept* of it on the other hand has indeed no *higher* concept over it from which it could be derived, because it is

---

*   Who for example can understand the old and mistaken definition discussed above in a different context that *representation is a modification of the mind* without meaning by mind the capacity for *representations*?

** And consciousness must be supposed as a *possibility* not in the theory of the capacity for representation, which is engaged with representation itself, but only after this has been studied, though in representation itself it is accepted in its undoubted *actuality*.

presupposed even in the concept of a *thing* in the broadest sense (i.e. of the *representable* or as it is usually expressed, the conceivable). For this very reason, however, the concept demands *discussion* all the more since its object admits no *explanation*. Since *representation* must be presupposed in every definition, it is only through the completely articulated and determinate concept of inexplicable representation that it is possible to prevent no more and no less of representation being presupposed than *must* absolutely be presupposed to avoid falsifying the representation which serves as a *premise* for all possible explanations. Since the concept of representation is presupposed in the concept of a *thing*, it is obvious that this important concept of thing which lies at the basis of all *metaphysics* could only remain ambiguous and vacillating [: 225] until the former concept was thoroughly determinate and established. It is also clear that philosophy ought to begin not, as was thought before, either with the most *singular* of things representable for us, our *representing self*, or with the *most general*, the thing in general, but with *representation*, and it is clear that the whole course of philosophy from its starting point went astray.

Both in the *clarity* and in the *inexplicability* of the concept of representation is found the reason for leaving this concept not only, as was inevitable, *undefined*, but also, as was improper, *undiscussed*. We have admirable essays about *thinking* and *sensing*, but to my knowledge not a single one investigating *representing in the strictest sense*, which is what thinking and sensing have in common. Whether those essays might have achieved considerably more than they did if this investigation had preceded them will become more apparent in what follows. At present only a few words about this, which might take us a good way along our path, however much they seem at first sight to move us away from it.

Certainly the distinction has been made between *thinking in the broader sense*, in which it was considered the equivalent of representing, and *thinking in the narrower sense,* in which it was the equivalent of *judging* and *inferring*, even if no use was made of the [: 226] distinction*. But that broader sense of the word *"think"* was usually an unfortunate game of thoughtlessness and of chance. Sometimes it was held to indicate what is *opposed* to *sensing*, sometimes as something by which one was meant to *include* sensing. In the first case, thinking was the equivalent of *producing* representations, the action of the representing force, in which the mind was held to behave only *actively*. In the second case, it was taken to mean *having representations*, and so was to be understood as not excluding sensing, the

---

* Even where the distinction should most have been considered, in logic, which was not restricted to the laws of thinking in the strictest sense but was extended to the psychological laws of representations in general.

passive behaviour of the mind. *Thinking* in the broadest sense of the word was used sometimes to mean *having* representations, sometimes to mean *producing* representations, sometimes for *receiving* them, and sometimes for *all of this together*. This unphilosophical use of the word "*thinking*" made the investigation of the capacity for representation more difficult on the one hand, but on the other hand it was also all the easier to use given the omission of this investigation. Whether and to what extent any *productive* action pertained to that same modification of the mind which was called *receiving* representations, and whether any *reception* pertained to what was called *producing* representations did not trouble most philosophers much at all. [: 227] They encompassed the indeterminate meaning of the expressions "*receiving representations*" and "*producing representations*" in the indeterminate expression "representing", and when necessary or convenient thought they had determined it closely enough sometimes with the word "*thinking*", sometimes with "*sensing*".

§ XIV.

Although no definition can be given of what representation *is in itself*, those properties must be able to be given through which it is *conceived* and which belong among the inner conditions of representation insofar as representation is not conceivable without these properties.

The impossibility of a *definition* does not entail the impossibility of a satisfactory *discussion*, as logicians know, and as is confirmed in science in a thousand obvious examples. Nobody knows what a *body* or *motion* etc. are in themselves, but it is known what is to be *thought* under these terms, what constitutes the *concept* of these intended objects, what is *essentially* subsumed and essentially omitted. It is not a matter for us here to establish what representation *is*, but only what must be thought under the concept of representation, which is possible and necessary. We are not investigating representation for its own sake but to reach agreement at last about the concept of *capacity for representation*, i.e. of what [: 228] pertains to the inner conditions of representation per se. But it is (not inexplicable representation per se, but) that without which representation per se cannot be conceived and which therefore is actually conceived in the concept of representation per se that pertains to the *inner conditions* of representation, insofar as they are conceivable. Despite the impossibility of a definition of representation, some discussion of the concept of representation is accordingly possible and this is perfectly adequate for giving us the insight we seek into the capacity for representation.

"But isn't every concept of representation itself a representation? And won't the promised discussion then drive us around in a *circle*?" The concept of representation (here one must add representation in the strictest sense, κατ' εξοχην) is certainly representation, but it is not itself representation in the strictest sense, κατ' εξοχην. It is a representation, but not representation, it is a representation which is a *concept*, and consequently belongs under one species of representation while its object, representation in the strictest sense, is the *genus*. Representation in this sense belongs to human beings and animals, but the *concept* of representation is the exclusive privilege of reason. How little danger there is here of a vicious circle will become more apparent in what follows.

If the discussion of this concept is to prevent any misunderstanding and even be [: 229] secure against any misunderstanding, and if it is to lay the ground for *universally acceptable* principles of philosophy, as is required of the general theory of the capacity for representation if it is to be worthy of the name, it must *deal completely* with the concept of representation, that is, *everything* representable in this concept *as far as* it is representable must be addressed. The analysis of what is representable in it must be pushed to the actual limit of representability, and this limit must be clearly determined and shown in a universally valid way. There is good reason to assert that *philosophy* has dealt fully with no single concept in actual understanding, and *could* not, since in each the formerly unexplicated concept of representation had to be presupposed. At the same time, the complete description of the concept of representation per se in general which I advanced earlier will be found not only not impossible but also not even very difficult if it is remembered: 1) that this concept, because of its *generality*, can include very few features. It is known from logic that the *content* of a concept becomes smaller as its *scope* widens. The concept of representation is presupposed even in the most general concept, that is, the concept of the representable, or of the thing. 2) That in completely describing this concept it is only permissible and possible to discuss essential features excluding everything contingent. 3) That these few essential features, as soon as they are found, [: 230] yield the criterion of representability in that whatever contradicts them cannot be representable; a criterion by means of which it is immediately possible to show what actually is representable of *representation* itself and what has to be *presupposed* of it as unrepresentable.

§ XV.

To every representation there belongs as an inner condition (as an essential component of representation per se) something which corresponds to the *represented* (the object distinguished by consciousness from the representation); and this I call the *material* of representation.

In calling everything that is represented and can be represented the *material* of a representation, an *ambiguity* crept in that is important in its consequences. This ambiguity was caused by the range of meanings of the word representation and must be eliminated here from the actual meaning of the expression *material of representation*. To be the *material of a representation* can mean two things, either *in* the representation per se as that which corresponds to the object distinct from it, or the object of a representation as distinct from the representation per se itself. For the reason that I am required by my consciousness to distinguish the *tree* I represent to myself from the representation per se of the tree, I am required to distinguish what *in* the representation per se corresponds to the tree by means of which [: 231] the representation of a tree is distinct from other representations, from the *tree* itself, from the intended object, which is not a representation. Only the former *is* the *actual material* of representation; it is not appropriate to call the latter material only in the broader sense and it should be called by its own proper name, *intended object*, in order to avoid the confusion of two essentially different concepts. Anyone wanting a clear idea of the distinction between the material and the object of representation could think of a tree at a distance that makes it impossible to be aware of its genus, species, its actual size and more detailed constitution. If the tree is approached gradually the representation will gain more material in proportion; the *material* of the representation will *alter*, increase, while the object in itself remains always the *same*.

The necessary consequence of the confusion of the *material* of a representation with the *object* was that the predicates appropriate to each were confused: that which belongs to the material *in* the representation and insofar as this is a component of the representation (belongs to representation per se) was attributed to the object outside the representation, and what is specific to this was attributed to the first, in effect cancelling the distinction between representation and object. The *material*, or what corresponds in the representation to the object distinct from the representation, is indeed determined by the latter whose place it takes (whose place it represents) [: 232] in the representation, but it has to undergo certain modifications in the representation through which it ceases to be mere material of a representation and becomes actual representation and in general a property of the representing entity. These modifications induced by the capacity for representation may not be transferred to the object to which they do not belong, if the philosopher is not to end up in an error even more absurd and alarming than that of the victim of jaundice who attributes to all objects the colour induced by his own visual apparatus. It will become sufficiently apparent in what follows what influence this error has had on the misunderstanding of the cognitive capacity which divided the philosophical world into disputing parties and kept them divided.

Every representation without exception must have some material in the meaning of this term already defined. Representation in general is inconceivable without material as any form of an *actual* thing without material. A representation without material would be a representation in which nothing is represented, a circle which is not round. The material is that component of representation from which its name (*repraesentatio*) actually derives, by means of which language designates something occurring in consciousness, and by its means something other outside consciousness is represented, held up to consciousness.

"But are there no *empty* representations?" Yes, there are, if by that is understood [: 233] representations whose material is determined by an object to which the predicate of reality is wrongly attributed because it is either not present anywhere or because it contains a contradiction in it. But even *these* representations, properly called *empty*, insofar as they are *actual representations*, actually have a material, something in them which corresponds to their object held to be actual and without which they would not be representations. *Empty* representation can never mean representation without any material, and of course this has not always been the case in philosophy.

A more serious ambiguity is found in the term "*representation per se*" and this could mislead many of my readers who might make the following objection to my assertion that *every representation must have some material*. "There are representations per se, that is, ones that have no objects. In representations, however, which have no objects there can be nothing present which could correspond to any object located outside the representation, so there are representations without material." The assertion that there are representations without objects can mean virtually that there are representations whose objects are nothing *actual* or to whose objects the predicate actuality can only be attributed in error, and then of course there is no objection to that assertion. But it would obviously be nonsense if this were taken to mean that there are representations which have no object at all occurring in consciousness, [: 234] because this would mean that there are representations in which nothing is represented, representations which are not representations. These monstrosities can then not be called representations *per se* any more than a circle *per se* could mean a circle that is not round. Actual representations, on the contrary, to which no *actual* object corresponds (in consequence however actually some object) and which are frequently discussed under the name of representations *per se* (representations whose actuality is grounded in the representing subject *alone*) would be far more aptly designated by the term *empty* representations so that the term *representation per se* could be reserved for representation distinguished by consciousness from its object and considered for itself alone, for which it is better suited.

A representation has *reality* (is not empty) if the predicate of reality belongs to its object, and this can only be investigated in the *theory of the cognitive capacity*. The theory of the capacity for representation per se in general would exceed its limits and miss its goal if it took as its object something pertaining to the external conditions of representation. It has done what is required of it once it has shown that a representation cannot be without material, that is, without something contained in it to which something called object corresponds that is distinct from the representation (whether or not it is *actual outside* consciousness). The following *axiom* is accordingly established:

[: 235] *That to which no material in a representation can correspond is absolutely not representable.*

§ XVI.

To representation in general there belongs as an inner condition (as an essential component of representation per se) something through which the pure material becomes a representation, and this something I call the *form of representation*.

In a statue, what makes its material more than simply material but a statue is the *form* of the statue. And thus I call what must be present in representation in general, and consequently in every representation without exception, the *form of representation*, without fearing that I am saying something my readers cannot understand. Material and form certainly constitute representation only when they are unified and cannot be separated one from the other without cancelling the representation per se. At the same time they are *essentially distinct* components of representation, and may not be confused for each other without causing a misunderstanding which can only have extremely significant consequences for philosophy, a misunderstanding which has actually occurred. The basic logical rule – everything belonging to an essential attribute of a thing is an attribute of the thing itself – can only not mislead if the concept of the thing under discussion is determined by distinguishing its attributes. Thus I can [: 236] assert without the danger of being misunderstood that a statue whose material is white Salzburg marble is marble and white, because I can presuppose that all those who hear this will only ascribe the predicate marble and white to the statue in respect of its material. But I cannot assert that the statue is from Salzburg if only the marble (the material) not the statue itself is from Salzburg. Rather, if I want to avoid being misunderstood I must explicitly indicate the distinction between material and form, and say the material of the statue is from Salzburg or the statue is of Salzburg marble. In the same way I cannot say that the statue was blasted by the stonemason from the cliff with explosives etc. Similarly

I may not assert of *representation in general* anything applying to it only in respect of its form or only in respect of its material if I cannot assume that my readers or hearers are following me in terms of this distinction between material and form. It is easily understood and will become clear enough in what follows that certain predicates apply to representation only in respect of its form, others only in respect of its material, and that confusion of these has had great influence on all speculative controversies in philosophy. The following remarks will aid in removing from the concept of the *form* of representation everything *alien* and *indeterminate* it must have for my readers.

1) I hope there is agreement with me that every representation (1) must consist of something [: 237] relating to the *object* distinguished from it in consciousness. I have called this the *material*, and it is this by means of which the represented (the object) belongs *to* the representation, and which belongs in the representation to the object; (2) of something which relates to the *subject* (the representing entity), equally distinguished from representation in consciousness. This is that *by means of which* the representation belongs to the mind, and *what* in the representation belongs to the mind; it can be nothing else but that by means of which the otherwise *material per se* of a representation is an *actual representation* – that is, the *form* of representation which the material could *only* acquire in the mind and *only* by means of the capacity for representation. While it remains to be established *in what* this form consists, it can only be the case that what in the representation is proper to the mind is sometimes assigned to the objects, and what belongs to the objects is attributed to the mind.

   "What makes the material of representation a representation is the soul, or the mind itself, and can accordingly not be called the *form* of representation."* *To make something a representation* can mean two things: [: 238] either it can be the cause of the representation, as distinct from the representation itself; or it can be the constitutive component occurring in the representation per se, the inner condition of the representation itself by means of which the material per se is *representation*. The *former* is the *representing force* (whatever this consists in), and it is not the place to discuss that here; the *latter*,

---

* It does not matter how sophistical and shallow this and other objections may sound to many readers; they are the natural consequence of the misunderstanding generally affecting *most* in their way of thinking about the capacity for representation. Even more acute and consistent thinkers who know how to avoid such objections or to respond to them may be helped by this resolution of them at least by making them familiar with a *new* way of thinking. In twenty years it will be possible to write a *briefer* theory of the capacity for representation.

however, is the form of representation in general, which is under discussion here, and which does indeed belong to the mind but not as accident or substance but as effect of the cause.

2) The present investigation is concerned with *representation in general*, the *general* form of all representations, the *genus* representation. The species of representations, e.g. sensation, concept, or idea, are distinguished from each other by means of their proper forms, which must be considered in the theories of *sensibility*, *understanding* and *reason*. Since they must be accepted and are required in all these theories as *representations*, the most productive explication it is possible to give of their individual properties, for example *Kant's*, can only be misunderstood while there is no agreement about what pertains to them in their common character as representations in general. [: 239]

3) The *form of representation* must be precisely distinguished from the *form of the represented*, or of the *intended object*; and although the discussion of this latter properly belongs in a theory of the *cognitive capacity*, it is important to note here an ambiguity in the expression *"form of the represented"* which could interfere with the proper concept of the *form of representation*. Otherwise it might be objected that since every representation must agree with its (actual or non-actual) object, the *represented*, the form of the representation, must depend on the *form of the represented*. My response is: in particular single representations (not in representation in general which has no determinate object) the particular nature or, if this is how it is to be called, the proper form of the material *per se* of the object which it represents in the representation must be determinate, and in this sense the objection to the assertion that the form of each single representation is dependent on the form of the *represented* would be nothing except that it ought to be called, instead of form of representation, form of the material of each single representation. The form of *representation* however cannot be given to the material determined by the object by the *represented*, the object, but only by the *representing subject*. The proper form of the *material per se*, which one could call the *objective* form to distinguish it from the form of *representation* which the material determined by the object must adopt *in* the mind [: 240], and which could appropriately be called *subjective* form, cannot *occur separately* from this latter in *consciousness* at all, that is, without the form of representation. The object of a *representation* only reaches consciousness through representation, i.e. only through the material corresponding to it ceasing to be material *per se* and taking on the form of representation. For that reason, nothing represented, no object, can be represented in its form independently of the form of representation,

as it is in itself, but occurs in consciousness only as modified by the form of representation. This remark however deserves further discussion, since it concerns one of the oldest, most general and deeply rooted prejudices which have been confusing the principles of all speculative philosophy till this moment. This is a prejudice which without being noticed affects even those who seek with the utmost caution to be free of it, and which has contributed largely to what has been happening to the *Critique of Reason*, the almost universal *misunderstanding*. I am speaking here of the prejudice *that representations are images of things*, that there must be *resemblance* between representations and *things in themselves*, and that the *truth*, or the agreement of our representations with the objects, must consist in this *resemblance*. It can be seen that this prejudice, if it really is a prejudice, could only falsify even the concept of *truth*, and have a decisive influence on the application of laws of *logic*. [: 241]

It is revealed as a *prejudice* even in its origin. This lies in the unmistakable *analogy* perceived between the nature of the *impressions* produced in our *organs* and the nature of the *objects* outside us, by means of which impressions are produced. It is an analogy which with the noblest organ, to which we owe the material of our most frequent and clearest sensory representations, namely the *eye*, consists in the actual resemblance of the image on the retina to the visible object. Already in ancient times an indeterminate analogy was supposed among philosophers between *seeing* and *representing*, and this was pushed further as it became necessary with the increasing cultivation of *empirical psychology* to borrow several terms from the operations of the eye for the newly discovered distinctions among the operations of the capacity for representation. The inner sense was thought of more and more as an *eye* of the mind, and the so-called representing force as its *force of vision*; and so much which could only apply to the eye and to *seeing* was transferred to the mind and *representing* which had formerly remained indeterminate, and was adopted into the concept of representation.

The indeterminacy of this important concept made possible only the confusion of the sensory *impression* with the sensory *representation*, and this could only lead to a second confusion of the undisputed similarity between *impression* and *object* with an obviously impossible resemblance between [: 242] *representation* and *object*.

The *impression* on the sensory apparatus is not a representation and its *form* not that of representation. As a simple impression it can no more be representation than the material it furnishes can be representation without the form of representation. The impression can do no more than furnish the susceptibility of the mind (whether the subject of that mind be spirit or body) with the *material* which then only in the mind acquires the form of representation and through that becomes representation. This representation holds up to consciousness the object to which it is related but only under the form which the material corresponding to the object has acquired in the mind and which cannot be separated from that form without cancelling the representation and with that the consciousness of the object.

From this it may be judged how proper it was to call the impressions present in the organs *material representations*.

None of our representations can be called in any sense an *image* of its object. Every *image* presupposes some resemblance to its original, and is only an image if such resemblance is found. If we were entitled to consider our representations images of things, there must then be some resemblance to be demonstrated between the representation and its object. But this is absolutely impossible. I can never compare the representation of the *rose* as *image* [: 243] with the rose itself as *original*. If I think of the rose as an *object* different from my representation of it, then I can only do this by relating the representation of the rose itself to something outside me which I only know by means of this relation and which is for me a mere subject = X independently of the representation in which all its predicates occur. I cannot therefore proceed from the alleged image to the original without making that image the original, that is, the image has no original for me; it is then not an image but is itself an original.

"It is conceded that the representation, insofar as it is an effect of the mind and is determined by the capacity for representation per se, has no resemblance to the things outside the representation. But it can and must have this resemblance in its content, since this is dependent on some object located outside the mind which determines it." If this content (the material of representation) is not to be confused with the object itself (that which occurs *in* the representation and constitutes it not to be confused with that which is distinct from it) then it must be conceded despite all the presupposed resemblance between the material per se and the object, that this material is not the object itself; and that only the material, not the *object in itself*, receives the form of representation. The material loses to that extent its resemblance to the object in itself when it takes on the form of representation. And since, in the relation of the representation to [: 244] object by which means alone this can be *represented*, the material per se, cannot be separated from the form of representation. Since not the material per se but the representation (material and form) makes present to consciousness in *respect* of the material the representable predicates attributed to the object, it does not matter how closely the content of a representation resembles the object, it will hold up no *image* of the object to consciousness. The representation will not be an *image* because that in it which could perhaps be called image is not held up to the subject of consciousness in its own form.

§ XVII.

In contradiction to the concept of a representation in general stands the representation of an object in its proper form independent of the form of the representation, or of the so-called *thing-in-itself*; i.e. no thing-in-itself is representable.

No representation is conceivable without material and form and these two are inseparable in the representation because they constitute representation only when unified. Only by means of this indivisible unification with at the same time an essential difference is the nature of a representation, i.e. the necessary relation of this to subject and object different from it, possible. That in the representation through which it relates to an object different from itself (the material) cannot possibly be the same thing [: 245] through which it relates to the subject, which is also distinct from it, the *form*. It relates to both in that it has something of *both* to show in itself which cannot possibly be the same thing as long as there is any possibility of distinguishing the representing subject and represented object from the representation. Since the material in it belongs to the object it would have to be related solely to the object and not be distinguishable from the object if it had not acquired the form of representation which is lacking in the object, by which it is differentiated from the object and which it owes not to the represented but to the representing entity. Although, on the one hand, consciousness and representation per se is possible only through this essential difference between material and form, this very same consciousness and representation are only possible, on the other hand, if material and form are inseparable. The representation can only be thought if the material ceases to be material per se and has acquired the form of representation, which cannot be detached from it without cancelling the *representation* and with it consciousness and even the distinction between subject and object. Accordingly, neither the material per se detached from the form nor the form per se detached from all material can be brought to consciousness, but both together in inseparable unity, and in distinguishing between object and subject in consciousness the form of representation is not separated from the material, but the *whole representation* is related through its form [: 246] to the subject, and the material is not separated from the form, but the *whole representation* is related to the object through the material. The object distinguished from the representation can accordingly only appear in consciousness, i.e. be *represented*, under the *form of representation*, which the corresponding material in the mind had to take on. Consequently it can by no means appear as *thing-in-itself*, i.e. under that form which would belong to it apart from all representation, would be denoted by the material per se of the representation and would have to be different from the form of the representation.

"But is the concept of the *thing-in-itself* posited here not arbitrary, in that a thing is understood by it whose form is different from the form of the representation. Why should the same form not belong to the thing-in-itself which this has in the representation per se?" Nothing is easier than to justify the concept of the *thing-it-itself* we have posited here. The form of the representation is that by which representation is distinguished from everything that is not representation. If, then, those who argue for the representability of the thing-in-itself concede that the thing-in-itself is not a representation, they must concede that the form of the representation does not belong to it. – "But, then, the same form belongs to it which it has in the representation?" – Do those who speak in this way really understand what they are saying? Their representable thing-in-itself is the object distinguished from its representation and this object is neither representation per se nor a component of representation per se and so does not [: 247] appear itself in representation but only through its *representative*, the material of representation. Suppose that this material, insofar as it is material per se, that is, insofar as it merely stands in for the object, has the same form belonging to the object, then for that very reason it cannot have in this aspect the form of representation per se. Indeed, its *objective* form must be essentially different from the *subjective* form of representation, because otherwise it would at the same time be material and non-material. However it must take on the form of representation, which differs from the material per se and does not belong to the object, if it is to be a representation and the object is to be represented by it. The form under which the *object* appears in consciousness through the material corresponding to it is, then, essentially different from the form which must belong to it outside the mind (in itself). This latter form by means of which it is thought as thing in itself is absolutely not representable in any other way *than by denying it the form of representation*.

And this leads to a response to the sophistical objection: "A representation of the thing in itself must all the same be possible since the concept determined here of the *thing in itself* is a representation which has the thing in itself as object." This objection is playing with *representation of a thing* in itself because of an ambiguity of this term. It improperly calls the *concept of the thing in itself in general* representation of the thing in itself (of a determinate thing). Certainly that concept is also a representation [: 248], but a representation whose object is not the thing in itself as some *thing*, but as the concept alone of understanding of an *object* in general.

This representation of a merely *logical* entity is confused in that objection with the representation of some *thing*. Those who advocate the representability of things in themselves believe it is only possible to accommodate and save for our understanding *a knowledge of things* by construing representation of the thing in itself as representation of some thing, representation of that object outside the mind to which the material and form of representation belong. What I am calling the concept of the thing in itself, the possibility and origin of which are to be explicated in the theory of the cognitive capacity, is the representation of an object *in general*, and this object is not a representation. It is not a representation of a *determinate, individual existent* thing. But what I call the *representation* of the *thing in itself*, whose impossibility I have demonstrated here, is representation of a determinate, individual, existing thing which is not a representation, but has at the same time the form of representation, a thing to which the same form is attributed outside the mind which it has assumed through the material of representation in the mind, and which consequently appears to the subject of consciousness not under a form proper to the mind, but presents itself to the mind in its own proper shape independently of the nature of the mind.

Things in themselves can no more be denied than representable objects themselves. They are the objects themselves insofar as [: 249] these are not representable. They are that something which must lie behind the material per se of a representation outside the representation, and because its substitute, the material, must take on the form of representation, and nothing pertaining to that something independently of this form is representable except the negation of the form of representation, that is, no other predicate can be attributed to it except that it is not a representation. All its positive predicates, insofar as they are representable, must have taken on the form of representation through the material corresponding to them in the representation, and this form cannot pertain to them in themselves. The thing in itself and its properties distinct from the form of representation are not only not impossible, but even something *indispensable* for representation, because no representation per se is conceivable without material and no material without something outside the representation which does not have the form of representation, that is, without the thing in itself. But in this respect the thing in itself is by no means *representable* as any thing, but only as a *concept* of a something that is not representable*. And the representation of this is not a representation of the actual thing as it is in itself, but a representation of a *subject* stripped of all its predicates, and this is not any thing but the most abstract among concepts. The necessary and

---

*   I am not saying that the thing in itself *is* (exists) as a mere concept, but it is only *representable* as a concept.

correct concept of the thing in itself is, then, representation of a *concept*, while the [: 250] impossible and improper *representation* of the thing in itself would be the representation of some thing from which, however, all representable predicates would have to be denied before one could attribute to it the name *thing in itself*. If the allegedly representable thing in itself is not conceived as a subject stripped of all *representable* predicates, if there is assigned to it one single predicate occurring in the representation apart from the empty title of a subject, then it ceases to be a thing in itself, it is no longer thought as thing in itself but represented by a material of representation – a material which has taken on the form of representation and consequently ceased to be proper only to the thing in itself. The following principle is accordingly certain:

That which cannot be represented under the form of representation is absolutely not representable.

And here was shown a new and highly important reason why I excluded the investigation of the representing *subject* and the represented *objects* so carefully from the investigation of the *capacity for representation*. All representation of what these objects are in themselves is impossible, and a completely determinate concept of what they are in a possible representation of them is only possible if they can be distinguished from representation per se, which is again impossible unless it is established in a universally valid way what pertains to representation per se insofar as it is nothing but representation per se. [: 251]

The *representing subject in itself*, independent of the *form* of the representation distinct from it under which it occurs in its own consciousness is accordingly for itself = X (which is to be distinguished from = 0). It is only representable to itself as an unknown something, as a subject without predicates. Only the great predicate of this subject, which is not representable in itself, by means of which it is actually representable, that is, the *capacity for representation*, is the object of our investigation.

The distinction between the representing subject and the represented objects was held even by those who thought they had acknowledged it to be knowable only by means of certain different *predicates* which pertain to both. *Subjects in themselves* were considered by all independent thinkers to be secrets of nature. I assert the very same thing, with only this difference: that I limit *representability* in general, and through it, *cognizability*, to *such predicates* which belong not to the *soul* and to the *things outside us in themselves*, i.e. independently of the *representation per se*, but only insofar as these predicates are representable. This does not mean that these predicates are not representations per se, because the *material* which corresponds to them in the representation certainly belongs to the *things in themselves*, but since this material must become *representation*, must acquire the form of representation in the mind if it is to reach our consciousness, and this *form* would only be [: 252] separable from it by nullifying the representation, this material can only hold those predicates up to consciousness insofar as they have taken on the form of representation. The *representable* predicates are then not predicates of the things in themselves, but predicates of things which have taken on the form of representation not belonging to the things in themselves. The impossibility of representing the soul and things outside us as *things in themselves* is not necessary for distinguishing their representable predicates from each other in our consciousness. Distinguishing between the subject and the objects of our representations occurs through the two-fold (subjective and objective) relating of the *whole representation* through its essentially different, but essentially unified, components which constitute the nature of representation. Because of this distinction grounded in consciousness and apparent to every thinking mind, it is not difficult, as will be shown in what follows, to distinguish the full compass of representable predicates which must be related to the representing subject and, taken together, constitute the *capacity for representation*, from the full compass of representable predicates which must be related to objects outside us which, taken together, constitute the domain of experience.

The improperly understood concept of the *thing in itself*, a natural consequence of failing to explicate the capacity for representation, can be regarded as the major site of the debility of philosophy till now. [: 253] From this emerge all dogmatism and all dogmatic skepticism. Both require the necessity of a representation of the thing in itself, and this is their common mistake, made possible through an improper concept of the thing in itself. The first believe they really are in possession of representations of things in themselves, and on these build their doctrinal structures about the *nature of things*, contradicting each other in the process. Others realize that it is impossible to represent the thing in itself, but since they are unable to explain the ground of this impossibility on the basis of the nature of the capacity for representation or of the proper concept of the *thing in itself*, they reach the conclusion that all knowledge is impossible. I can only offer hints here of what will be explicated later, of *how* every system of the dogmatics has arisen from transferring features of representation per se to the thing in itself, and from the confusion of the *inner condition* of representation per se with the inner condition of the thing in itself (the nature of things). Since there are two different inner conditions of representation of which one belongs to the *material* and the other to the *form* of representation, there had to arise three different opinions about the *essence of things*, according to whether the dogmatist based his investigations on one or the other or both (realized) conditions of representation per se, attributing these conditions to the thing in itself. It will be easily understood in the *theory of sensibility how* the *materialist* [: 254] created his doctrinal structure on a property belonging to sensory representation per se but which he transferred to the thing in itself. In the *theory of understanding* we will see *how* the *spiritualist* based his structure on a property belonging to the concept of understanding per se which he transferred to the thing in itself; and from these two theories *together how* the most consistent of all dogmatic theories, *Spinoza's*, could only come about because its great originator transferred the main properties of sensory representation and of the concept of understanding, *taken together*, to the thing in itself and from *space* and *objective unity* created his *unique extended substance*.

Kant demonstrated in the critique of reason with unequalled profundity and the greatest clarity that it is impossible to have *knowledge* of the thing in itself, and has shown that things could only be known under *the form of sensory representations*, or as he calls it, *appearances*. But those who echo him and those who refute him are still not in agreement about what the great thinker might have intended with this. So he is commonly declared by the dogmatic thinkers who profess to *know* things in themselves to be a *dogmatic* skeptic, and by dogmatic-skeptical thinkers who *do not know* things in themselves to be an *idealist*. If I should hope to be understood by my readers (a hope which I can only base on the fact that *my* problem is more easily solved than *Kant's*), then *Kant's* demonstration of the impossibility of [: 255] cognizing the thing in itself will begin to be understood by a shorter route. The thing in itself is not *representable*; how can it be *cognizable*?

The whole proof that it is impossible to represent the thing in itself would serve no purpose but to ground dogmatic skepticism if I did not manage to determine the inner conditions of representation more precisely than has happened before in this theory. If the warning not to transfer the predicates of representation to things in themselves is not to be futile, then the properties belonging to *representation per se* and distinguishing it from what is not representation must be indicated in a determinate way. As yet, we know of the properties belonging to representation only this much: that they consist in material and form, and that the form of representation may not be attributed to things in themselves. This form will however necessarily continue to be attributed to things in themselves until we know how it is distinguished from what in the representation belongs to things in themselves, i.e. to the material per se of representation. It is our task here to indicate the most general property by which the material of representation is distinguished from the *form*. This is shown here:

§ XVIII.

In every *representation* the material per se must be given and the *form* per se must be *produced*. [: 256]

Representation *arises in* and *with* consciousness. Consciousness is only possible through representation; to that extent a representation must be present if it is to be related to an object and a subject distinct from it. But representation similarly is not possible without consciousness because the nature of representation actually consists in that relationship of the subject and the object to each other by the medium of the material and form unified in the representation. A representation without any consciousness would have to be a representation which represents *nothing*, does *not* represent – is related neither to a subject nor to an object – i.e. not a representation, as will be shown in more detail in the discussion that follows the theory of the capacity for representation. Here I am only asking that it be conceded that every human representation has *arisen*, has not always been there, not always been present in our consciousness.

Representation is possible in consciousness only because in it a material appears under the form of representation, that is, there occur as a unity two different somethings of which one belongs to the subject which can be distinguished from the unity and the other to the object, also distinguished from it. Representation cannot accordingly arise from a single source given these two essentially different components which cannot have arisen in the same way, and could not possibly have a single origin. Only the form per se, i.e. that by which the representation is related to the subject, that in it [: 257] which belongs to the subject, can have *arisen* from the *capacity* of the subject. The material, by contrast, that by which the representation is related to its object, that which in it is proper to the object, cannot have arisen through the capacity of the subject, but must be *given* to it. If not only the *form* but also the *material* were produced in the mind all consciousness, all distinguishing of representation per se from subject and object would be impossible. This distinguishing is only conceivable if something is contained that did not arise from the action of the mind, i.e. is not merely the effect of its action but something that is presupposed in the action of the subject and is proper to the object. Representation cannot be related completely to the subject alone because and insofar as something occurs in it that has not arisen through an action of the mind but is the *given*; and the material being given and the production of the form with the given material must constitute together the actual production of each representation.

"But what if the representing subject represents itself, and consequently is simultaneously subject and object of its representation?" – Even *this* representation is only possible because the representing *subject* distinguishes itself insofar as it is subject of this representation from itself as *object*, and in one respect thinks itself as *representing* and in the other respect as *represented*, in both respects however as *distinguished* from the representation per se. [: 258] As *representing*, it can only conceive what in the representation is *effect* of its action; as *represented*, however, only what in the representation is not the effect of its action but *given* – or otherwise it must have produced itself in its representation and through its representation.

Now that I have demonstrated my thesis from the only valid premise in the theory of the capacity for representation, that is, *consciousness*, the following may be considered as confirmation and explanation of it.

Every *finite* representation, every representation that arises *in* and *with* consciousness, must be *generated*. Two kinds of things belong to each generation: something that only becomes actual by its means, is *produced*; and something which is not produced in the generation, but must be present as *given*. This is the *material*, the former the *form* of what is generated. The mind would have to create its representations, that is, produce them from nothing, if it had to produce their material. Not only the material but also the form, and consequently the *representation* itself, would have to be *given* if it were not its proper function to produce the form for the given material. In the latter case the representations would have to be present outside the mind before they were given to the mind, be representations before anything was represented by them; in a word, the mind would not be the *representing entity* if the form of representation for the given material were not [: 259] produced by the mind – then the mind as mind would have to be *nothing*; as it would have to be *infinite* if it were supposed to produce the material of its representations.

"But in many representations material is obviously something produced by the mind; e.g. in the representation of a judgment we have made, in any effect of our mind in general. In such representations at least the material and the form are produced by the mind." Not at all! In the first place, this kind of effect of the mind represented in the representation for which it provides the material, or rather the object, is not produced, but must be present before the representation, and the material corresponding to it, from which the representation arises, is as a consequence given in the same representation. In the second place, the effect itself, as it was produced in the mind, had to contain something given in which the action of the mind was manifest. For example, a judgment made occurs in the representation not as a mere effect of the mind but as an effect of the mind working with the material of a judgment, and this material must be given. In the third place, the *manner of acting*, as will be shown in what follows, is not by any means produced by the mind, but *given* to it, and only in this property is it possible material of particular representations.

Now we know what to make of those turns of phrase so common among philosophers: *to give the mind representations, to receive representations* [: 260], and *to produce representations*, even if this last expression sounds less remarkable since it does not exclude the necessity of a given material in the production of the representation so obviously as the expression *to give representation* – the production of the form, through which actually representation comes about from the material per se, which alone can be given. Representation cannot be given, nor received, nor produced; it must be generated.

A *confused* concept of representation lies at the basis not only of *Locke's* but also of *Leibniz's* doctrine of the origin of representations. Both fail to recognize the essential difference between material and form; and the *truth* that both these great men had in view with their opposite systems only becomes apparent in full light through the explication of that concept and forms a confluence in a single system. *Locke* had in mind the undisputed necessity of *givenness* in representation in general; but since he sometimes confused the material with the representation per se and sometimes with the object distinct from representation, he allowed his *simple representations* (ideas), by which he meant the last components from which all the other (composed) representations arose, to be given to the mind by the *objects* and declared that the mind, in respect of these simple representations (ideas) behaved absolutely [: 261] passively*. *Leibniz,* by contrast, had in mind the undisputed necessity of *production* in representation in general, and since he similarly sometimes confused the material with representation per se and sometimes with its objects, he had representation in general *produced* by the representing force. Since, however, he could only find it absurd that a finite force might produce its representations *from nothing*, just as absurd as thinking that they might be given to the force from outside and by objects distinct from it, he tried to find his way out of this impasse with the help of the ingenious hypothesis of *prestabilized harmony*.

We have now become acquainted with the essence of representation per se well enough to know that it consists of two essentially different components: material and form; and further we can indicate the proper features through which these two components are distinguished. By representation we now understand a *given* material upon which the form of representation is *produced*. On this basis the capacity of the cause of representation must be determined by means of a known effect, that is, the concept of the capacity for representation as it has been shown above.

"Then the capacity for representation is said to consist in part of that which pertains to the givenness of [: 262] the material, and consequently, if not by the creator of the material (the divinity), at least by the capacity of objects to give the subject by their effect on it the material for representations." Not at all! Unless one is prepared to transgress the limits indicated already for

---

* The mind is wholly passive in respect of its simple Ideas. Essay B.II. C.30.

the capacity for representation and acknowledged as correct, and so to move by philosophical inconsistency from the inner conditions of representation to the outer, from the question in what does the capacity for representation consist to the question of what it arises from at the very point when the first questions are being answered. What can be counted here in the capacity for representation is only that which pertains to the givenness of the material *insofar as* that is just an inner condition of representation per se. It is not my fault if the following brief discussion seems subtle; but it would be my fault if it remained incomprehensible to attentive readers who are used to thinking.

Material is only a component of representation per se to the extent that it *is* a given, not to the extent that something *gives* it – i.e. insofar as it occurs *in* the representation, not insofar as it is grounded on something different from the representation per se, whatever that may be. The being-given and the giving of the material must be distinguished from what is the given in the actual representation per se, and must be set aside from the concept of that as something that is not an *inner* condition of representation. The being-given and the giving of the material is thus (although quite unavoidable, nevertheless also) an *external* [: 263] condition and everything pertaining to it can only be counted towards the capacity for representation in the *broader* sense. Even the given of the material *in* the representation must be excluded with respect to its *actuality* which depends on the giving and whatever does the giving from the full compass of what is *merely only inner* condition of representation*. By contrast, what is the given *in* a representation, on the basis of its *possibility*, is an inner condition of representation, because representation per se is only possible (conceivable) if the given material *can* occur in the representation. That by means of which this possibility of being a given *in* representation can be thought, the *ground* by which being a given in representation becomes possible, is what pertains to the material of representation to the extent that it is just an inner condition of representation, and to that extent is a component of the *capacity for representation*. In this aspect it is called *susceptibility for the material of representation*, in a single term, *receptivity*.

The possibility and reality of the material *in itself* and the grounds of both do not belong [: 264] at all in the concept of the capacity for representation. All the more essential to this concept is the ground on which the possibility of the given material *in* representation can be understood: *receptivity*, which

---

* To the extent that no finite force can act completely independently of external conditions and none can create for itself the material of its functioning, the actuality of its products by no means depends upon it. Even the actuality of the representation is thus completely independent of the capacity for representation insofar as material pertains to it which must be given to the mind.

behaves in the capacity for representation as the *receiving* of material for *representing*. This receptivity pertains to the material of representation to the extent that this material is inner condition only, *just a component* of the representation, not to the extent that it is dependent on some external condition. It pertains to the material which belongs to the representation insofar as it is *received*, not insofar as something outside representation and the capacity for representation *does the giving*. What *does the giving* can never be the capacity for representation per se, because in the effect of the capacity for representation, the representation, the material can only occur as a given, never as produced. *Representing* means, then, to receive (not to *give*) a material for representation, and to inform it with the form of representation.

§ XIX.

The capacity for representation consists *first* of *receptivity*, or susceptibility to the material of a representation, and by this a merely passive capacity is understood.

It should hardly be necessary to recall here that by receptivity only *a passive* capacity of the mind is meant. As a consequence of the meaning of this term determined in the immediately foregoing, [: 265] this capacity signifies nothing but the ground of the is-able-to-be-given in representation – a ground present in the capacity for representation and constituting one of its components. In other words, the capacity for representation per se, insofar as it is not *itself active* in representing, requires something given, some effect from elsewhere and is consequently to that extent *passive*. But given the formerly indeterminate way of thinking about the mind when there was talk of a susceptibility of the so-called *soul*, and the term encompassed without distinction everything pertaining to the representation called *sensation* or to the so-called *receiving of the representation,* and consequently conscripted the *production* necessary for representation in general into the confused concept of susceptibility, it is not superfluous to draw attention here to the pure meaning of the word receptivity and to warn against the involvement of any feature of activity in the concept of receptivity.

This involvement was all the more inevitable since there has been no agreement about any determinate feature proper to the susceptibility of the capacity for representation and distinguishing the *passive* capacity from the *active*. It was occasionally conceded, when found necessary, that susceptibility must be an attribute of the mind, and even *spiritualists* could not completely avoid associating with their active *force* some passive capacity, [: 266] however little attention they paid to it in their *theories* about the nature of the *soul*. But they left unanswered the question of *what this passive capacity consists in.* Because of this lack of understanding of an essential basic capacity of the mind, it continued to be impossible for them to correct the *materialists*, who thought they had discovered the passive capacity of the mind in the organic body and were obliged to raise the body to the status of subject of the capacity for representation.

Materialists and spiritualists have only been concerned with the *site* and the *source* of the mind's susceptibility, without its occurring to them that it is necessary to begin with an investigation of what is meant by this susceptibility and what it *consists* in, insofar as it is indispensable to one of the inner conditions (the material) of representation per se. In a word, what particular role that capacity called susceptibility has in *representation per se*. The answer to this question would, as will be shown in what follows, have eliminated the whole misunderstanding which has divided materialists and spiritualists, and materialism and spiritualism themselves forever without obliging the former adherents of these sects to make an unfortunate choice between supernaturalism or dogmatic skepticism if they wanted to exchange their former systems for something better. [: 267]

§ XX.

The capacity for representation consists, *secondly*, of *spontaneity*, or the active capacity which produces the form of the representation for the given material.

Representation is only possible in consciousness if the material is given and the form produced (§ XVIII), and this *production* belongs absolutely to the inner condition (the form) of representation per se. I say the *production*. The material must arise *in* the representation through being a *given*, when the mind behaves passively, the form through *production*, when the mind behaves actively. Although the relating of the representation to its object is only possible if the material in the representation arises from being a given, when the representing entity behaves passively, the relating of the representation to the *representing entity* is only possible if the representing entity behaves actively with the arising of the form; that it produce the form; and this form, because it is the work of the representing entity, belongs just as exclusively to it as the material to the object by which it is given.

"But the representing subject belongs just like the represented object only to the *external* conditions of representation, and among these was counted even the *actuality* of the material in the representation per se, insofar as it depends on an external condition. Now the activity, the production of the form, depends on the subject, and consequently similarly [: 268] belongs among the external conditions." The activity of the mind has to be viewed from two very different perspectives. First, as it is grounded in the *representing entity*, and second as *representation* is grounded by it. Of course the activity must be counted among the external conditions of representation, to the extent that it is present in the subject as distinct from the representation per se and constitutes its nature either alone or connected with other properties, in a word, insofar as it is what is expressed generally by representing *force*. In this aspect the activity of the capacity for representation certainly lies outside the full compass of what belongs solely to the inner conditions of representation, and in that respect it cannot be discussed without risking the confusion of essentially different concepts when it is a question of the capacity for representation in the strictest sense. But although this activity, insofar as it is a property of the subject, can only be understood under the capacity for representation in the broader sense, it does constitute a component of the capacity for representation in the strictest sense to the extent that it is cause of the representation per se, or rather of its form. In this sense it is regarded not as a *force*, but as a *capacity*, insofar as this capacity is first manifest in a component of representation per se. It belongs to the inner conditions only to the extent that it belongs to the form of the representation per se as distinct from the representing subject [: 269]. In this respect the question is not about how this capacity which gives the form of representation arises or about its source. The question is rather what it consists in, what is its proper attribute. The answer to this *latter* question can therefore never be that this capacity is *simple* or *composite* but must be – this capacity is *productive* – is *activity*. It is distinguished from the capacity for material in the representation, the passive capacity, in that it cannot be other than active. What pertains to *one* of the inner conditions of representation per se is activity, as what pertains to the *other* is susceptibility. Both together constitute the capacity for representation per se, in whose concept the capacity to receive the material and to produce the form upon it are contained necessarily, just as the capacity for giving the material must remain excluded from it.

Every active capacity has *spontaneity*, insofar as it has the ground of its activity in itself, and that ground need not be sought in any other capacity. Thus spontaneity is an attribute even of a wound watch spring, in that the reason why it functions against the tension lies in the spring itself. The capacity for representation possesses spontaneity in the strictest sense to the extent that the ground of its *functioning* occurs in representation per se and need not be sought outside the capacity for representation. The production of the form must necessarily have its ground inside the [: 270] capacity for representation, just as the giving of the material must have its ground *outside*. The first must necessarily be an effect of spontaneity per se inside the mind, just as the second must be something functioning outside the mind. This spontaneity belongs to the *subject* only indirectly, i.e. only to the extent that this subject has a capacity for representation. It pertains directly to the capacity for representation, and through that to the subject whose predicate is the capacity for representation as a whole.

After all I have been saying about the capacity for representation I need not justify refusing to call the *activity*, insofar as it pertains to the capacity for representation in the strictest sense, *force*. The attribute of the substantial, of the subject subsisting in itself which is contained in the actual meaning of the word *force*, would immediately return us to the old arena of demonstrations and squabbles about the nature of the *soul* which we have been avoiding so carefully. It is important to recall (especially for experienced metaphysicians) as often and from as many angles as possible the danger of the unfortunate confusion of the representing subject and the capacity for representation. *Plattner*, for example in the new edition of his *Aphorisms*, continued to prove the simplicity of the representing subject and found it necessary to defend this view against the *Critique of Reason*, which he misunderstood. Having been warned not to confuse the *force* with the *capacity* he refuted this warning [: 271] by permitting himself this very confusion; and he thought he had demonstrated the simple nature of the *force* since he had demonstrated the *unity of consciousness* pertaining to the capacity for representation and grounded in it, a unity which could not possibly be the issue.

The concept of the spontaneity of the capacity for representation has suffered exactly the same fate as the concept of receptivity. Sometimes it was opposed to receptivity when it should have been considered in conjunction with it, and sometimes it was considered in conjunction with receptivity when it ought to have been separated. The *generation* of representation, the product of receptivity and spontaneity together, was usually attributed by spiritualists as solely the activity of the capacity for representation, or, as they called it, the *force*; while these philosophers held the unity *in* and the connection *between* representations, which is only the product of spontaneity (as will emerge in what follows), to be *given* by the material, and consequently inopportunely amalgamated receptivity and spontaneity. By materialists, however, spontaneity was completely ignored and the capacity for representation was viewed as only *receptivity*.

In what then do the receptivity and spontaneity, which constitute the capacity for representation, consist? Anyone wanting to seek the answer to this question in the representing subject would have again lost sight of the actual object of our investigation, the capacity for *representation per se*, [: 272] and would find himself beyond the limit of what pertains to representation per se and of what alone can be explicated in a universally valid way on the basis of consciousness, back on the old stamping ground of metaphysics. Through attempting *that sort* of answer he would not only prove that he had completely missed the point of our question, but would also have to undertake the unphilosophical labour of dreaming up a representation of the non-representable, because:

§ XXI.

Since receptivity and spontaneity of the capacity for representation are founded in the representing subject in itself, they are absolutely not representable.

The limit of representability, partly misconceived and partly ignored in philosophy till now, should be borne in mind especially when one approaches it as closely as we are in the present investigation*. There is the danger at every moment of [: 273] straying into the empty space of non-representability, and of wandering around in it with pointless hair-splitting. These limits must be determined especially for the *capacity for representation* itself, i.e. it must be shown what of the capacity for representation per se lies within the limit of representability, and what beyond if the representability of other things is to follow from the capacity for representation.

Any representation of the representing *subject in itself*, i.e. in its proper form as distinct from the form of the representation per se, is impossible (§ XVII). The representation of *receptivity* and *spontaneity* insofar as they are grounded in the subject in itself accordingly requires something impossible and is consequently impossible itself.

Representation of *receptivity* and *spontaneity* grounded in the subject is only possible to the extent that the subject itself is representable. Insofar as *receptivity* and *spontaneity* constitute the capacity for representation, they are the ground of *all* representability and consequently also of the representability of the *subject* itself. Of course insofar as each *subject* on the other hand is the *ground* of the predicate, while *receptivity* and *spontaneity*, taken together as the capacity for representation, are the *predicate* of the representing *subject*, the subject must be viewed as the ground of receptivity and spontaneity. But it remains *representable* for that reason *only* as the *logical* ground of the capacity for representation, i.e. as a subject which here yields only the *logical substratum* of the predicate. [: 274] When it is separated from its predicate it retains nothing but the empty concept of a subject in general. The subject *only* becomes *representable* by means of the

---

* The *law of contradiction*, which has been seen as determining this limit, presupposes a completely determined concept of *thinking* and of *representation* in general, if it is not to be misunderstood and misused. It will become apparent in what follows that this logical law, considered to be metaphysical, was completely misconceived.

predicate – the capacity for representation in relation to the *representing entity* – and only by means of the capacity for representation. The subject *distinct* from the capacity for representation can never be represented as the *real* ground of the capacity for representation.

Receptivity and *spontaneity*, insofar as they are present in the subject in itself as distinct from the representation, must behave in all reception of material and all production of form solely as the *receiver* and the *producer*. They must be *subject* in all representation and can to that extent never be *object*. The representing entity, *in as much as* it is the *subject* of all representing, can never be the *represented* any more than an eye is capable of seeing itself.

This is the actual reason for the futility of all past and any future attempts to come to terms with the nature of the soul when by this is meant not the capacity for representation per se but the substance – a futility which can only continue to seem paradoxical to the spiritualists and the materialists among my readers until an exposition of the representation of the *I* based on the nature of consciousness shows them that this representation cannot possibly be anything other than the representation of a *substance*. [: 275]

The question: in what do receptivity and spontaneity of the capacity for representation consist, to which the course of our investigation has led us, cannot be answered by any kind of observation of the representing subject. We must return, therefore, to the *representation per se* in which the *capacity* of the cause, which is operative here and with which we want to come to terms, is *manifest* as an effect.

At present we must discover from the concept of representation per se, as now determined, those features of *receptivity* and *spontaneity* by which these two capacities are distinguished from each other, in what their actual nature consists, and which in the strictest sense of the term can be called the *forms* of these capacities. By *form of receptivity* I mean then, in what follows, the nature of the susceptibility for material in the capacity for representation, and by *form of spontaneity* the nature of that activity determined in the capacity for representation by which the form per se is produced upon the form.

In that we now have the task of explicating these forms in which the nature of the capacity for representation we are seeking consists, and from which whatever belongs to the mind *alone* in every representation must become apparent from the features of the concept of representation per se, these features themselves seem to offer an insuperable obstacle, because: [: 276]

§ XXII.

The material per se and the form of the representation per se in general are absolutely not representable.

1.

What cannot be represented under the form of representation (the thing in itself) cannot possibly be the object of any possible representation. But the material in itself as material per se cannot be represented under the form of representation, because then it would have to be at the same time material in itself and material under the form of representation.

2.

What cannot correspond to material in a representation as distinct from the form is not a possible object of representation. But nothing apart from the form per se can correspond to the form of representation in any possible representation. So no material can correspond to it in the representation, i.e. it cannot be represented. Representation in general is only possible if what is *produced* in it is distinct from what is *given*, through which alone the representation can relate to an object. Insofar as the form per se merely means what is *produced*, no *given*, no material, can correspond to it in a representation.

In a word, whatever in *any* possible representation is material per se or form per se [: 277], cannot be the object of a possible representation, because it would have to be simultaneously material per se and not material per se, form per se and not form per se, if it were to be simultaneously material per se and object, form per se and object.

It is now established that the forms of receptivity and spontaneity which are being sought cannot be derived from the features pertaining in the concept of representation per se of *material per se* and *form per se* in themselves, of which no representation is possible.

But if there are in the concept of representation per se other representable features from which the natures of those forms can be derived, then we have lost nothing through the *non-representability* of the material per se or of the form per se, but have rather gained considerably in determining the limits of representability.

Here it is not a matter of representation of the form per se and the material per se in their own terms, but we only seek to know how these components, not representable in themselves, must be *distinguished* in the concept of representation so that we can determine from this distinction the distinction of the *forms* of receptivity and spontaneity, which is our only concern. Actually, we have already found predicates by which material and form in the concept of representation must be essentially distinct. For the material there is the predicate "*given*"; or rather, [: 278] since *giving* does not belong in the concept of representation, the predicate "*receiving*".

For the *form* there is the predicate *"produced"*. Even if what is *received* in the representation and what is *produced* cannot be represented singly and for themselves, we still know of them at least that both together constitute *representation* per se; and here all we want to know is what is to be understood by that receiving and producing pertaining to representation, how both are manifest in the representation, in a word, what forms of *receptivity* and *spontaneity* constitute the capacity for representation.

Since all material must be *given* to receptivity and this can only *receive* it, no representation arises from production alone, but there pertains to each in respect of its material an actual reception. Thus, there pertains to every representation an effect *on* receptivity in which this behaves only passively and by which the material of representation is given to it. I call the modification which arises in *receptivity* by this effect, *being affected*. Without this being affected representation in general cannot be conceived, otherwise one would have to conceive the incomprehensible representation of an entity to which the material of its representations may not be given because it creates it for itself. But this would not be representation in the actual sense of the word. Actually being affected pertains of course only to the actuality of the representation, [: 279] but the *determinate possibility* of being affected grounded in the capacity for representation and inseparable from it pertains to representation in general and is an essential component of the capacity for representation.

§ XXIII.

By receptivity of the capacity for representation the capacity for *being affected* must be understood.

The capacity for being affected only constitutes an essential component of the capacity for representation to the extent that it is *indispensable* for representation in general. As long as the indeterminate concept of representation continues to confuse all speculative philosophy, this essential capacity of the mind will only be misconceived. It is confused by *materialists* with the sensitivity of bodily organization, and by more than one *spiritualist* sect will be attributed to the *soul*, misconstrued as the capacity for representation – only in respect of the body that is made distinct from the representing substance united with it, which means that there is nothing left for the representing force than that *active* capacity that actually means to produce certain representations (the intellectual) by itself, without any assistance – representations arising out of susceptibility transferred to bodily organization. Only the prejudice that a material given by being affected and distinct from the form of representation per se is not necessary for representation in general [: 280], or rather the complete lack of a determinate concept of representation, could support such an unphilosophical way of thinking which could only be true if the capacity for representation could produce or create its *material*.

"But there can be a given material located *in the capacity for representation* itself; in which case certain representations at least would only arise if spontaneity were to give form to materials already present in the capacity for representation*". If one avoids mixing the capacity for representation with the representing *substance* and addresses only the *capacity per se*, nothing else can be conceived as given in it than that in which the capacity for representation per se consists, namely the manner of its receiving and activity, the forms of *receptivity* and *spontaneity*. Of course these can be represented, as will be seen in the following, i.e. yield objects of *particular* representations in which a material must correspond to them which, as will similarly be shown, cannot be given to the capacity for representation from outside. But this material *as material* is *only* given in those particular representations whose objects are those very forms. Insofar as these objects are present in the capacity for representation *per se*, they are not given [: 281] in an actual representation as its material. They are of course given to the representing subject which could not create its capacity per se *in* and *through* this *capacity*, but only as dispositions of this capacity not as material *in* an actual representation. They are only *given* in the *capacity* to the extent that they are present in it without being produced by the subject. When they are *represented*, however, it is not sufficient that they are given in the capacity per se, but the *material of representation* corresponding to them must be given by the effect upon susceptibility which behaves *indifferently* in respect of any possible material, an effect which determines for susceptibility a *certain* material which it cannot give itself, that is, by receptivity *being affected*.

It is now our task to investigate in what this capacity for receiving a material for representation through being affected consists and how it is distinguished from the active capacity by which the material receives the form per se of representation. We must seek to determine the proper forms of these two capacities if we want to be in a position to distinguish the *capacity for representation* from everything which can only be its object. Again, we have to seek our answer in the capacity for representation per se when we ask of what nature the material per se must be, to the extent that it is to be given through being affected, *in* the representation. My answer is: its nature in the representation must be *such* that by its means the distinction of representation per se [: 282] from the subject must be possible.

---

*   This is what followers of Leibniz had to state when they tried to give some apparent meaning to their innate representations.

Although the representation is related to the representing subject only by its form and only by its material to the represented object, although it only belongs to the subject through what the subject produces in it, and to the object through what is given by the object and received by the subject, the representation can *only* be distinguished from its subject, the representing entity, only by what corresponds in it to the object, the represented; i.e. by its material, upon the givenness of which depends the reality of the form in the representation, since this can only be produced upon the given. In the representation to be distinguished from the subject something must be able to be distinguished, and that which in it which permits such a distinction can only be the material, and everything in the representation that is material must permit of distinction, that is, be a *manifold*. Insofar as the material in a representation must be a manifold, the *form of representation*, as distinct from all material, i.e. manifold, can be nothing but *unity*. The *manifold* is then the essential mark belonging to the material, and *unity* to the *form in* every representation; they must constitute the nature of the material and the form if consciousness and representation are to be possible; and the following law of nature is established: [: 283]

§ XXIV.

If actual consciousness is to be possible then the material, the given, must be a *manifold* in the representation, and the form, that which is produced, a *unity*.

The given is distinguished in the representation by the manifold, the produced by unity. The given manifold becomes representation when unity is produced upon it; and the unity becomes form of representation when a manifold is given upon which it is produced. The mind, to which a representation can be related only in terms of its form, distinguishes the representation from the object by the unity which it has produced upon the *given* manifold by its action, and it distinguishes the representation from itself only by what it has not produced in it, that which is not unity, the given manifold.

Before this closer determination of the material and the form, we have emphasized and demonstrated that the material per se and the form per se of representation are not representable; and that they can only be held up to the subject of consciousness in their relation to each other in the representation which they constitute. This becomes even more apparent by the discovered form which the given and what is produced must have in representation. The unity can only be produced upon the manifold [: 284], and the given manifold can only become representation through the produced unity; and just as unity is not conceivable without reference to a manifold and the material per se, the manifold in itself, is not conceivable without reference to unity, so too the form, unity in itself with no reference to the manifold, is not representable.

Any cognition can be traced back to the distinguishing of objects of our representation. We know a determinate tulip in the flower bed only to the extent that we distinguish it from other species of flower and from other tulips in the same bed. All distinctions, however, which we perceive in objects, must occur in their representations and occur as *given* if they have their ground in the *objects* and are not to be arbitrary. Distinguishing is of course an action of the mind, but the diversity of objects which are not our product cannot be an effect of the mind, cannot be produced, it must be found and consequently given. The manifold can only be material of representation.

We are only conscious of a representation to the extent that something is represented by it, i.e. that it has an object, and as a consequence we can distinguish our representations from each other only by their objects, consequently only by their *material*, to the extent that something in them corresponds to these objects. The objects are only [: 285] distinct from one another to the extent that each of them contains several features, a *manifold*, to which material in the representation must correspond if it to be perceived in the objects. The material must therefore be a manifold.

"But aren't particular representations also distinguished by their forms? E.g. sensation from concept, and concept from idea?" Yes, when they are themselves represented, i.e. become objects in which the diversity of their forms, which is not produced by our mind but given to it, only occurs through the material corresponding to them in particular representations. To the extent that sensation, concept etc. are not themselves represented again but are nothing but representations, to the extent that they hold up to the mind an object distinct from them, they can only be distinguished by this object and what corresponds to that in them, the material.

§ XXV.

The *form of receptivity* consists in the manifold nature in general in as much as this manifold is the condition of the material in the representation determined and founded in the capacity for representation.

Consciousness and representation are only possible if what is given in representation is a manifold. Receptivity, the capacity to receive a material, must therefore be the capacity to receive a manifold; [: 286] and although the *actuality* of the material and thus of the given manifold depends on the *giving* of this material and thus on something outside the capacity for representation, the possibility of the manifold *in* the representation must be *determinately* present in the capacity for representation because receptivity cannot be conceived without being determined for the manifold, as capacity to receive the material of a representation, and can only be a component of the capacity for representation if it is not susceptibility in general but rather susceptibility for the manifold. The manifold of the material *in* the representation has its ground in the determinate possibility of representation and no capacity for representation can be conceived without conceiving by it the ground of the possibility of the manifold in the representation which constitutes the nature of its susceptibility, the *form* of *receptivity*.

This determinate manifold of the material possible in representation has been demonstrated here *only* as form of receptivity, and is only demonstrable in general in the theory of representation. We know it only as a disposition of the capacity for representation per se, and not as a property of the representing substance *in itself*, independently from its capacity for representation considered for itself. The soul, conceived as *substance*, is the object of a particular representation and consequently of a representation which contains a material corresponding to some object distinct from it which must be given in it, [: 287] and accordingly *presupposes* this very susceptibility and its determinate form as present in the capacity – a form which could only be given through and with the form of a particular representation if it were not to be attributed to the capacity for representation per se but to the represented substance of the soul as distinct from the capacity for representation per se. This form of susceptibility can therefore only be attributed to the representing subject to the extent that the capacity for representation per se can be attributed to the subject to whose nature that form pertains. The *materialist* would conclude too hastily in believing he had found a ground for *corporeality* of the soul in the form of susceptibility we have established, in that he would claim he had encountered the determinate manifold of the material possible in representation in the *extension* or composition of the representing subject, or with many a *spiritualist* would assert that that capacity for representation was limited by organization to the mere manifold of its material. He would again be confusing the questions about the nature of the mind and of the soul which we have so carefully distinguished: *in what* does the capacity for representation *consist*, and *whence does it arise*? That determinate manifold can only be a predicate of the capacity for representation per se and only subsist in the form of its susceptibility, because we have only found its necessity in the concept of representation per se and in the possibility of consciousness; and we are only acquainted with it as a mere component of the capacity for representation per se. [: 288] On the other hand, how it is present outside the capacity for representation and what it is in as much as something else different from the form of susceptibility must be conceived in it, in what property of the representing substance it is grounded, in a word, *from what it arises*, are questions which concern not the capacity for representation per se but an object which presupposes the capacity for representation if it is to be represented itself; they do not concern the capacity for representation per se, but objects distinct from that capacity; and there can only be questions about their properties after agreement has been reached in the theory of the cognitive capacity about the concept of *cognizability* and the *determining of the limits* of the cognitive capacity.

§ XXVI.

The *form of spontaneity* consists in the *binding* (synthesis) of the given manifold in general.

Since the form of representation, in as much as it is what is produced upon the material, cannot be anything but unity, the production of this form must consist in the producing of unity upon the manifold, in its binding and the way this activity of the capacity for representation functions, the *form* of spontaneity, must consist in the binding of the manifold in the representation in general, and this is called, to express it in a single term, *synthesis*. [: 289] The manifold only puts the given material into the position of being *material* in a representation without raising it to being an actual representation. Something different from the material per se must be added to this manifold if it is to become representation; this addition must be distinct from the entire manifold, and consequently be unity and be produced by the activity of the mind. This activity must therefore consist in the capacity of giving unity to the manifold. The unity then belongs only to the spontaneity of the mind and through this spontaneity alone is representation possible; it can never be given to the mind as material because everything that can be given to the mind as material is manifold. It is not produced by the mind from nothing, however, but from a manifold which must always only be given to the mind, and can never be produced by the mind.

Binding is the name not just for the action of binding but also for the effect of this action. In the latter sense the binding of the manifold is the same as unity of the manifold, or form per se of the representation; in the first sense, however, in which it means the same as *binding*, a closer definition of the term will avoid a possible ambiguity. In the concept of binding is conceived, *first*, a mere action in general (active modification), and *secondly*, the *form* of this action, that by means of which the action of binding is distinguished from other actions and because of which it is called *binding*. [: 290] The sentence "the form of spontaneity consists in binding" does not mean that it consists in the active *modification* which happens in the process of binding; but in *the form* of this active modification, in the manner of action; not in the action itself. The intention of this perhaps too subtly drawn distinction will soon become apparent if one considers that binding as mere action in general is dependent only on the acting *subject* or on the *force* which gives the binding the *actuality* of the action, but also only the mere actuality of the action not the *form* because of which the action is called binding. This form cannot be produced by the acting subject, but must itself be *given to it*, and is given to it in the *capacity per se* which the subject could not attribute to itself or create for itself. The form per se of representation, the unity of the manifold, is to the extent that it is *produced*, has achieved actuality, the *effect* of the representing subject and consequently produced by the force, the subject of the active capacity. But the *form of spontaneity*, the *manner of action* of spontaneity consisting in binding, in as much as it contains the ground for the product of spontaneity being *unity* and nothing but unity, is not produced by the spontaneity of the subject but given to the subject with and in it.

The capacity for representation is, on the basis of its forms themselves, no more determined by the *existence* of the representing subject in itself than the existence of this subject could be determined [: 291] by those forms themselves. Here I wish neither to deny nor to affirm that any conclusion can be properly drawn on the basis of the given form of the capacity for representation per se about the form of the representing subject as substance. I do not intend here to investigate from spontaneity's being able to produce nothing but unity whether it is justified to infer that it must exist only as unity, be nothing but unity, and be conceived not only as a single but also as a simple subject. Let it be enough for me to remind the *spiritualists* that in the theory of the capacity for representation it is a matter of the *form of the capacity* for the activity, not of the form of the force of the acting subject; it is a matter of the manner of acting of spontaneity, not of the manner of being of its subject; it is a matter of the nature manifest in the form per se of representation of the functioning, not of the nature of the subject as it functions in distinction from the representation. As thing in itself the substance of the soul absolutely cannot be represented – whether it can be represented as a thing under the form of representation can only be established after what pertains to the conditions of particular representations has been explicated, and in particular the representation of the substance has been determined from the nature of the cognitive capacity.

§ XXVII.

The forms of receptivity and spontaneity are *given* to the representing subject *in* and *with* the capacity for representation [: 292] and are *determinately* present in it *prior to* all representation.

The forms of receptivity and spontaneity are the essential dispositions of the capacity for representation per se. In as much as a capacity for representation is present in the representing subject, then the forms of receptivity and spontaneity must also be present in it. Now the capacity for representation must precede any actual representation, by which it is presupposed. Therefore the forms of receptivity and spontaneity must be determined in the representing subject before any representation. These forms then constitute the *nature* proper to the representing subject pertaining to it because of representation. There has been a substantial division in the philosophical world till this moment about the nature of the representing subject, because what was meant was the substantiality of the representing subject rather than the capacity for representation, which ought to have been investigated first in order to agree at last about substantiality. But the nature of the representing subject, insofar as this is a representing entity, the capacity for representation, was never sought in the only place it was to be found, in representation per se, in which as the effect the cause can be manifest; and so the proper features of the capacity for *representation per se* which constitute the nature of the *representing entity* were completely misconceived. Since, however, all objects of our representations [: 293] and consequently all *things outside us* can only be represented not as things in themselves but only under the form of representation, there occurred the illusion that matters not at all in common life but is confusing in all philosophy. This illusion leads us to believe that we represent to ourselves things in themselves under the form of representation. The illusion makes it inevitable that we confuse what is proper to the capacity for representation in our representations with what belongs to things outside us; and it was inevitable until the proper features of the capacity for representation per se were found through the discovery of the forms of receptivity and spontaneity, and this puts us in the position of being able to distinguish what belongs as a property to the representing subject from everything that belongs to the things outside us.

"This distinction is absolutely impossible, because in order to discover what in our representations is proper to the things outside us representation of what is proper would have to be possible. But the material given by external things is not separable in any consciousness from the form per se." – Certainly for this distinction representation of what is proper to things outside us is required, yet not representation of what is proper *in itself*, but its representation under the form of representation, is perfectly sufficient once the forms of receptivity and spontaneity are known. Once one has determinate representations of these forms what belongs to external things may only ever be represented under the [: 294] form of representation, but at the same time the essential distinction between what is form of receptivity and spontaneity and what it is not will occur in actual representations. Pure representation, that which has no object other than the forms of receptivity and spontaneity, will be able to be distinguished with sufficient determinacy from *non-pure* representations, which relate to other objects. In this case, everything depends on the representation of forms of receptivity and spontaneity isolated from everything which is not necessarily conceived in them, i.e. *pure*. If this happens, absolutely nothing is represented of them belonging to things distinct from the representing subject, things outside us. The material corresponding to the representations of the forms of receptivity and spontaneity must also be able to be distinguished from the material corresponding to the representations of things outside us with sufficient clarity. The representations of that form have no object located outside and distinct from the mind. Their material is therefore something to which nothing distinct from the capacity for representation per se corresponds. This material is given in its objects which are only dispositions of the capacity for representation to the representing subject in and with the capacity for representation and consequently before any representation, although only in its objects, i.e. only as form of the mind. If this material then becomes the *material* of representation in particular representations which have no other object but that form, then it is at least not given to the capacity for representation from outside, but [: 295] is a material given in that capacity before any representation, and determined through its object, but given in the representation through the action of the mind. We will therefore call it the *subjective* material in order to distinguish it from that which must be given to the mind absolutely only as material per se from outside, which we will call the *objective* material. This objective *material* is that which belongs to objects different not only from all representation but also from the representing subject, and which, to the extent that it occurs in our representations, contains the ground for distinguishing our subject from things outside us and the only possible ground for our conviction of the existence of things outside us. We want here above all to seek out certainty that such an objective material is indispensable for every capacity for representation in general.

Only an analysis of the concept of representation per se in general can achieve a pure, i.e. determinate representation of the forms of receptivity and spontaneity. But the concept of representation in general is only *abstracted* from particular representations and its object, representation in general, only *exists* as a genus in the species and through these only in particular representations. Now, representations of the forms of receptivity and spontaneity cannot be those particular representations from which the concept of representation in general is abstracted, because they are only found through the analysis of this concept and its objects are only [: 296] abstracted from this concept. Thus, the *concept* of representation in general must be abstracted from such particular representations which have objects distinct from the forms only of receptivity and spontaneity, from representations which have a *different* material from the kind to which the forms of receptivity and spontaneity correspond – in a word, from representations which must have an *objective* material.

Without a material distinct from the capacity for representation per se, distinct from what corresponds to the forms of receptivity and spontaneity in their representations, i.e. from the subjective material, and consequently given to the mind from outside, no representation in general could *become actual*. In the capacity for representation per se nothing is given to its subject apart from the determinate possibility of receiving a manifold and bestowing upon it, provided it is given, some unity through binding. These capacities can only be manifest according to their *actuality* in *actual* representations, and they can be manifest *initially* in such actual representations through which they are not themselves represented, of which they themselves are not the objects, but are things distinct from the mind and its nature. They can *only* be represented *once* they have revealed themselves in actual representations under the aspect of *forms per se* of activity and passivity of the mind, and this could only be possible with a material distinct from them themselves and given from outside. [: 297] Representations by means of which the representing subject achieves consciousness of the dispositions of his capacities cannot possibly be the representation of this capacity per se. The dispositions of the capacity for representation can only be known from the effect itself of the capacity for representation, in as much as this capacity is manifest through its effect. Now, in representation in general, the form of receptivity only occurs insofar as by means of it only the possibility of the material in the representation is determined, and the form of spontaneity only insofar as by means of it the unity of the given manifold is determined. Through them both no material is given for actual representation in general, but this must be given, if a representation in general is to become actual, by something distinct from the representing subject and its capacities.

§ XXVIII.

A material different from the forms of receptivity and spontaneity, not given to the subject in the capacity for representation but from outside, pertains to the *actuality* of representation in general, and this is called the *objective* material.

An objective material pertains to the actuality of representation in general. This does not mean that every representation must have objective material any more than the propositions that a representing entity pertains to representation in general, and that in every representation the representing entity is represented mean the same. [: 298] It is not being argued that objective material must occur in every representation as its content, but it is only argued that without it representation in general, and consequently also the forms of receptivity and spontaneity themselves, could not become actual, because in the capacity for representation per se only those of its forms are determinate which cannot be represented with a material distinct from them in an actual representation before they have occurred, any more than the form of the Medici Venus if it had not occurred with some material. But just as the form of this statue, once it has been realized with some material, can be conceived and investigated apart from this material, because it is given *with* the material but not *by* the material, and although unified with that material is still essentially distinct from it, so the forms of receptivity and spontaneity, after they have occurred upon a material distinct from them in actual representations can be represented even without this material with which they did indeed occur as a unit in those actual representations but by which they are not given, but are rather presupposed, by that material as conditions under which alone it can occur in a representation, and which must be present in the representing subject before it can be given at all. [: 299]

§ XXIX.

The *existence* of objects external to us is accordingly just as certain as the existence of a representation in general.

Since the material in a representation is that which corresponds to the object as distinct from the representation, representation which has an objective material given from outside must have an object located outside the mind. To the extent that objective material is necessary for the actuality of representation, so the existence of *things outside us* is proven on the basis of the existence of representation – a capacity for representation and a subject distinct from those things to which the capacity for representation per se belongs and which we call our *I*.

Only misconception till now of the capacity for representation per se could lead to and sustain sects in the philosophical world, and these either denied the thesis established in the present paragraph or doubted it. If the material of representations is confused with representations themselves, an *idealism* arises which virtually denies everything actual except the representations and the representing subject (or at the most several representing subjects). If, by contrast, the object distinct from the representation is confused with the material per se of representation, a *skepticism* then arises which doubts the agreement of the representations with their objects, and to that extent, also the existence [: 300] of things represented outside us. But given the universal indeterminacy in the concept of representation till now, did the *idealist* consider that the material per se of representation cannot itself be a representation and that the material not given in the capacity per se for representation, and consequently not having as its object the nature of the capacity per se, must necessarily relate to objects outside the representing subject? Has it been possible to show the *skeptic* before now that his requiring that *things in themselves* must *resemble* representations per se, or that the agreement of representations with their objects must consist in the *resemblance* between the two, makes no sense at all once he has amended his concept of representation and object?

All material in any representation whatsoever must be *given* through susceptibility *being affected*, and accordingly even the subjective material which is contained in the pure representations of the forms of receptivity and spontaneity. The action of affecting required for this cannot possibly happen through something outside the mind, but is only conceivable if spontaneity functions in accordance with those forms upon its own receptivity and by that means determines what was earlier determined as *form* per se in the capacity for representation per se before any actual representation as *material* in an actual particular representation. The material of pure representations [: 301] of the forms of receptivity and spontaneity is thus *determined* with respect to its object (from which it has its form as determinate material) in the capacity for representation per se, and thus in the mind before any representation – in respect to its *actual* presence in particular (pure) representations, through an action of the representing subject; while all *objective* material must be determined both in respect of its proper form, which it has as determinate material, and which is grounded in an object located outside the mind and distinct from the mind, and in respect of its presence in a representation, through the alien action on receptivity which gives it to the mind by means of affecting.

I call material, insofar as it is determined in the capacity for representation and thus also in the mind before any representation, *a priori material*. Insofar as it must be determined first in and with an actual representation by the mind being affected, *a posteriori material*, or *empirical* material. Material corresponding to the pure representations of the forms of receptivity and spontaneity alone can be called *a priori* material because, apart from these forms in the capacity for representation per se, nothing can be present, and because that material must be determined in the mind on the basis of its object before any representation. But it must not be forgotten here that this material is called *a priori* only with respect to its *being determined* in the *capacity* per se, not with respect to its subjectivity per se, and that one may not call [: 302] all subjective material *a priori* without distinction. Even subjective material must be called *a posteriori to the extent that* it is determined not by the capacity for representation per se, but by the action of the representing subject in particular representations. For example, the material which might be contained in the representation of a modification per se which spontaneity has brought about in receptivity, and consequently a material which might have nothing but the modification per se as its object, would be a subjective *a posteriori* material, because it would be determined on the basis of its *object* not in the capacity per se before any representation but only with and in the representation through the action of the representing subject. *How* representations having an *a priori* material contained in the mind achieve actuality, however, cannot be determined in the theory of the capacity for representation in general.

With respect to the material given either *a priori* or *a posteriori*, I call representations whose content it constitutes either *a priori* or *a posteriori*, *pure* or *empirical* representations.

§ XXX.

All representations which contain an objective material are *a posteriori* or empirical representations.

All objective material is *a posteriori* because it is not at all determined in the capacity for representation per se and consequently not before all representation in the mind, but is determined by something [: 303] distinct from the representing entity, and only then in the mind when the mind is affected and is only determined *in* the mind on the basis of its disposition (as material) *in* the mind because the mind is affected from outside in such and such a way and not otherwise. It is therefore nothing that might arise only then through the mere affect from outside and consequently not only with and in the representation if the capacity for representation with its forms (the *a priori* material) were presupposed in the mind. All material of every possible representation (whether this be *a priori* or *a posteriori*) is indeed, insofar as it cannot be produced by the mind but must be given to it, determined in its ground before any representation. But not all material can be conceived as prior to all representation in the mind, only that to which no other object corresponds outside the *mere nature* of the capacity for representation (the form of receptivity and spontaneity). The objective material is indeed prior to any representation but only determined in its ground as distinct from the mind. To the extent that it is to occur in the mind, it must be determined not only with respect to its actual presence in the representation, but also with respect to its proper form corresponding to the object by being only affected from outside, and consequently only in and with the representation per se, i.e. *a posteriori*, while the material corresponding to the pure representations of the forms of receptivity and spontaneity [: 304] is determined in the mind *a priori* by its objects which are not present outside the mind.

§ XXXI.

Representations of the forms per se of receptivity and spontaneity contain a material determined *a priori* in the capacity for representation and are accordingly *a priori representations*.

We have been warned sufficiently not to jump from the proposition we have posited and demonstrated, that without objective material (and consequently without the so-called objects of outer experience) no representation in general can become actual, to the conclusion that there is no other material of representation in general but the objective and that all representations arise from *outer* experience. This was not what was meant by Locke, to whom adherents of this view appeal, when he derived the *material* of all representation from experience*. He does not exclude *inner experience* (the givenness of a material in the mind itself), but rather indicates this inner experience at every opportunity as a particular source of representations, which of course he does not distinguish sufficiently from the *material*. "The impressions then [: 305] that are made on our sense by outward objects that are extrinsical to the mind; and its *own operations* about these impressions, reflected on by itself, as *proper* objects to be contemplated by it, are, I conceive, the original of all knowledge"**4. If a material corresponding to an object distinct from the mind is given to the mind, there arises *representation* but not the *mind* itself, not the determinate susceptibility which must be present if the material is received by the mind; not the manner of acting which must be given in a determined way in the mind if the form of representation is to be bestowed upon the material; not those forms necessarily determined before any external material in the mind, which, once they are represented, cannot be represented as objects of particular representations in the mind by any material given from outside, and can be related to nothing located outside the mind.

---

*   Whence has the mind all the *materials* of reason and Knowledge? To this I answer in one word: From *Experience*. In this all our Knowledge is founded, and from that it ultimately derives itself. Essay B II. Ch. 1.

**   He had expressed it earlier in this way: *External* objects furnish the mind with Ideas of sensory qualities, and the mind furnishes the understanding with Ideas *of its own operations*.

4   The quotation in the main body of the text is from Essay Book II Chapter 1, 24. The text cited by Reinhold in his footnote is from the Essay Book II Chapter 1, 5. Reinhold does not give the reference to either. His own translation of Locke might be rendered back into English as follows: "Those impressions which occur upon our senses through objects which are present outside the mind and the proper actions of the mind which arise from the inner force proper to the mind and which become objects themselves of its observations through reflection are, as I have already said, the primary sources of all knowledge."

A priori representation must not be confused with *a priori* material, which merely constitutes its content, if we are to avoid confusion and misunderstanding. Only *a priori* material, not *a priori* representation, is present in the mind before [: 306] any representation and given to it in the capacity per se. *A priori representation* cannot be *given* to the mind but must be *generated* by it and can no more precede *a posteriori* material than the *a priori* but presupposes both – the *a priori* material with respect to its object and the *a posteriori* with respect to its necessity for the actuality of a representation (from which the forms of receptivity and spontaneity can be abstracted). One can view the *a priori* representations as *anatomical preparations* of the human mind. Just like actual anatomical features they merely have an artificial existence to the extent that, on the basis of their objects, they are rendered separate merely for the benefit of science from the whole, from the *a posteriori* representation in which alone the forms of receptivity and spontaneity are manifest in their natural determination. Their objects are of course present in it before any analysis of *a posteriori* representation through the capacity for representation, but only as subjective determinations of an objective material given from outside without which they could not have achieved actuality *in such a representation* any more than, for example, the nervous system without bones, muscles and the other parts of the human body, although they are not given by that objective material any more than the nervous system is given by the bones, muscles, etc., but after they have achieved actuality with objective material in *a posteriori* representations can be examined as well as the nervous system [: 307] in isolation from muscles, etc.

The forms of receptivity and spontaneity are not *representations*, but, to the extent that they are given in the mind, dispositions of the capacity for representation; to the extent that they are manifest in representation per se in general they are features of representation in general and indeed *necessary* and *general* features of it.

§ XXXII.

A priori representations, to the extent that *necessary* and *general* features of representation in general are represented, are necessary and general and in this respect representations independent of any *experience*.

The material of *a priori* representations represents in consciousness *necessary* features of representation in general, that is, such features without which no representation in general can be conceived. Without the determinate susceptibility and indeed without susceptibility determined for the manifold, no material is possible *in* the representation, and without the unity produced by binding of the manifold, no form of representation is possible, and as a consequence, without both conditions being present in the capacity for representation and indeed constituting it, no representation in general is possible. *Multiplicity of the given* and *produced unity must* accordingly [: 308] occur in every representation*. And the representations of these necessary features are on the basis of their objects absolutely necessary. This *necessity* could not be asserted of them if they were not given to the mind merely by susceptibility being affected only in and with the representation and not determined before any representation in the capacity for representation per se, that is, if they were abstracted from *experience* alone. If it could only be asserted of the forms of receptivity and spontaneity that the mind had manifested itself in its former representations on their basis but did not have to manifest itself on that basis, it could not have manifested itself in any other way. Nothing actual can be known as necessary if it cannot be known through its possibility determined before its actuality as the *only possible*.

The material of *a priori* representations represents *general* attributes, i.e. belonging to all actual and possible representations without exception. Since representation in general cannot be conceived without the forms of receptivity and spontaneity, these forms are determined and apportioned before all actual representation by the nature of the capacity for representation [: 309], and through this acquire a generality which reaches further than any possible evidence of experience since this evidence can only be corroborated when extended to actual cases that have occurred, not to all possible cases. Without the *priority* of the forms of receptivity and spontaneity their generality would no more be comprehensible or demonstrable than their possibility on the basis of experience, whether this is internal or external.

They are accordingly *independent of experience*. And this would be demonstrable already from their necessity and generality, although we have no desire at present to demonstrate them on that basis. To derive a representation from experience can however only mean to derive it from some external or internal impression, the affecting of receptivity by the affecting thing. The material corresponding to *a priori* representations must of course be given in these representations by receptivity being affected and be determined as material *of the* representations in which it is the material, and to that extent *a priori* representations are dependent on (inner) experience. But this affect determines of the material nothing but its actuality in those representations, not its proper disposition, that which distinguishes it as determinate material, that which in it corresponds to its objects. This can only be determined in and with its objects, the forms of receptivity and spontaneity, and is therefore *determined* [: 310] not by the functioning

---

* *Occur* as subjective determinations not as *material* of every representation, for which reason they are not represented in every representation.

of spontaneity, but before that, in the capacity for representation as its disposition. Just as neither receptivity can determine its manner of being affected nor spontaneity its manner of affecting, both presuppose them as given in their capacity, with every affecting or being affected. The forms of receptivity and spontaneity are then objects by means of which receptivity's being affected from without and from within and consequently all external and internal experience is alone possible. Their pure representations on the basis of their objects absolutely do not depend upon experience, but as actual representations they do depend on *inner* experience, with respect to being affected through spontaneity which is necessary for their occurrence as *a priori* representations, and on *outer experience* with respect to the objective material which is necessary for *a posteriori* representations which must have preceded them (see § XXVIII).

The acute *Plattner* said something extremely apposite (§ 82 of the earlier edition[5] of his *Aphorisms*) about the way in which the systems of *Leibniz* and *Locke* could be made to concur about the *origin of representations**. "*Locke* concedes basic determinations [: 311] in the soul, and these make the soul capable of *sensing* necessary truths." (This ought to be put as "become conscious of the necessity of certain judgments")[6]. "*Leibniz* wants ideas, but without images. Perhaps Leibniz's ideas without images are nothing other than Locke's basic determinations." I subscribe willingly to this supposition, which is for me more than a supposition. The two great men mentioned have seen truth reliably only from different perspectives. It is just as certain that *each of them only* saw this *truth* from different *perspectives* and consequently in a *one-sided way*. Leibniz insisted that those basic determinations present *a priori* in the mind were *representations* because he did not adequately distinguish the material from the form in representation in general and called everything that happens in the mind representation. Locke, by contrast, insisted that knowledge of those basic determinations depended absolutely on experience, being affected from outside and from inside, because he did not adequately distinguish the material in the representation from the objects as distinct from the representation, and therefore could not conceive how the material of the representations of those basic determinations could be present in the mind

---

5   Reinhold's abbreviation: "ä.A."

*   But omitted in the new edition from the treatise *On the controversy about innate concepts*, we do not know why.

6   Di Giovanni 2005, 47 translates this as "fundamental dispositions". Leibniz, in the *Nouveaux Essais sur l'entendement humain*: "Now the soul contains existence, substance, unity, identity, cause, perception, reasoning, and a quantity of other notions which the senses could not afford. This is in agreement with your friend the author of the *Essay* [Locke], who finds the source of a good part of our ideas in the reflection of the mind upon its own nature."

in a determinate way before any representation and consequently before his objects occurring in actual representations, i.e. before those basic determinations had affected receptivity. These two philosophers could not reach agreement about the undisputed truth which each had in mind since [: 312] they had not clarified their concept of representation. In representation in general there is something independent of any experience, and this is what *Leibniz* claimed, and something dependent upon it, as *Locke* claimed, but how could they have reached agreement about what the dependent consists in or what the independent consists in when both neglected to investigate what pertained to *representation per se in general*, about which they had no determinate concept. From the concept of representation and of the capacity for representation which I have been explicating and have now determined it emerges quite clearly: *That there are neither innate representations, nor that all representations without distinction presuppose experience in the sense that the material of all representations would have to be determined simply by being affected in general, and even by being affected from outside.*

Just as the nature of the capacity for representation in general can only be discovered through the thoroughgoing determination of the concept of representation per se in general, the *sensory* capacity for representation, and that of the *understanding* and of *reason, sensibility, understanding* and *reason,* can only be known from representations per se of sensibility, understanding and reason. In the theories of the particular capacities for representation we will accordingly be required to [: 313] determine the meanings of the words sensation, thought, intuition, concept and idea in the *strictest sense.* However, since all these terms are used to mean representation in general in certain respects, these respects must be shown in the theory of the capacity for representation in general and the grounds and limits of that use of language must be explicated by a list of determinations of the broader senses of those words.

§ XXXIII.

To the extent that there must occur in representation in general the affecting of receptivity, being affected in general however (the modification in which the mind is passive) is called *sensation,* representation in general is called *sensation* in the broader sense of the term.

The part played by *being affected* in representation was not completely misunderstood in the unexplicated concept of representation in general; but the sensual philosophers for whom all representation were just sensations, gave it too large a part, and the *rationalist philosophers* who regarded being affected as merely occasional cause of the representation produced by the *force* of the soul, made it too small. [: 314]

To the extent that capacity for sensing (for being affected) is called sensibility in the broader sense of the word, *sensibility* belongs to the capacity for representation in general; and *sensibility* in this sense does not reduce man to animal but it must rather be common to him and to the highest of all created minds.

§ XXXIV.

To the extent that an action of spontaneity must occur in representation in general, the action of the mind is *thinking* and its effect called *thought* in the broader sense, representation in general is called *thought* in the broader sense.

The part played by spontaneity in representation was not completely misunderstood in the unexplicated concept of representation in general, but the *rationalist philosophers* made it too large, and the *sensual philosophers* too small – the first held the whole capacity for representation, insofar as it is grounded in the subject, to consist of pure activity, the second however saw its activity consisting in a mere *reaction* to the impression.

Insofar as the active capacity is distinguished from the passively operating capacity denoted by the name of *sensibility*, [: 315] it is called the *intellectual capacity*, or the understanding in the broader sense; and this must be present in every capacity for representation, even in that of the beasts. The material of every representation is *sensed*, the form is *thought*.

§ XXXV.

To the extent that representation in general on the basis of its material must contain a manifold, and by means of this manifold in it the object is represented to the subject, it is called *intuition* in the broader sense.

The eye intuits when, affected by the shape of a visible object, it makes that figure present to the mind. In a similar way the object, or rather that part of the object which is given to the mind through being affected and by means of this, is made present by means of the manifold in the representation affecting the receptivity and corresponding to the object.

§ XXXVI.

To the extent that representation in general on the basis of its form contains in itself a manifold that is *comprehended* (brought together, brought to a unity), [: 316] it is called *concept* in the broader sense.

The word "*concept*" characterizes that modification in the mind by means of which a representation arises through the form, [and is] so definite that one can tell from the very look of it that it belongs among the most conspicuous examples of the many illuminating hints, neglected by philosophers till now, which the human spirit has given about the true *nature* of its *function*[7]. But none of the different words defined by language use to mean representation in general (to the extent that this is seen from varying perspectives) was more misused, especially by followers of *Leibniz*, than the word "*concept*". It was used by them without any qualification to mean representation in general, as is only to be expected of philosophers who were used to seeing representing as the simple action of a *force*, and representation as *effect* of that force.

§ XXXVII.

To the extent that the representation in general is as representation per se different from and not present outside the representing entity, [: 317] the representation is called *idea* in the broader sense.

The word "idea" is so frequently used without qualification to mean representation in general that I will probably not lack readers who might declare this definition of its broader sense arbitrary. But they should consider that there are for the philosopher no words that mean the same (*synonyms*), and that the actual sense in which the word "*idea*" is determined by language use to designate representation in general, despite all the negligence that this sense has experienced even by our best writers, has persisted up till the present day and is revealed clearly enough in several instances. The word "*idea*" is preferred when one is opposing pure representation to *things* and means to indicate something merely present in the mind: "That is only an idea:" – "to realize an idea", "The world of ideas, etc". In the end the *broader* sense of the word "*idea*" which I have here introduced will be secured against all scruples by means of the *narrower* sense to be defined in what follows (and with every word the broader sense must be compatible with the narrower).

Thus, language usage, which permits the use of the words *sensation*, *thought*, *intuition*, *concept* and *idea* to mean representation in general [: 318] and indeed is sometimes required to, is accordingly justified on the one hand, but on the other hand contained within limits which may not be transgressed if confusion of concepts and ambiguity of expression are to be avoided. If, for example, the word "idea" in its broader sense is used to designate representation *per se* in general, it cannot be used of a sensory representation, e.g. the colour red, without doing violence to the philosophical use of language.

[: 321]

---

7   "Gedankenzeichen": Reinhold is discussing the connection between the noun "Begriff" (concept) and the participle "begriffen" which contains the root idea of "greifen": to hold, seize, grasp.

Book Three

General Theory of Cognition

"The extent of our Knowledge comes not only short of the reality of things, but even of the extent of our own Ideas; though our Knowledge be limited to our Ideas, and cannot exceed them either in extent or perfection."

Locke's Essay Vol. IV. Ch. 3

§ XXXVIII.

Consciousness in general consists of the relatedness of the representation per se to the object and subject and is inseparable from every representation in general.

In proceeding from the concept developed above of *representation per se* to what is not contained in the concept as an internal condition of representation per se but yet is necessarily linked with it as an external condition of representation, one arrives at the *object* and *subject* as distinct from representation. Representation stands in a necessary relation with the former through its material, and with the latter through its form. Just as material per se and form per se taken together [: 322] constitute the internal conditions of representation per se, so the relation of representation per se to the object and to the subject taken together constitute the internal conditions *of consciousness*. One can call the representation per se, the object and the subject – the *content*. Their relation one to another and the manner in which they occur together in consciousness and constitute it is called the *form of consciousness*. Here it is my task to explicate only the *form* of consciousness.

All previous philosophizing about *consciousness in general* has been just as scanty and just as askew as it has been about representation in general. "What consciousness means is self-explanatory, everyone knows without being told, we learn about consciousness from our own sense of self." These were the excuses our *empiricists* used to simplify their thinking about consciousness or to save themselves from it altogether. Out of a timid concern to avoid hair-splitting and ponderous rumination others closed their mind's eye in investigating this important topic, in order to become better acquainted with it through groping it with their emotions.

Even the very few who have really thought about consciousness failed to go beyond certain *species* of consciousness whose peculiarities they could only indicate in a very vague and imprecise manner, since they had overlooked consciousness in general in their investigations. Even the otherwise acute eye of a *Plattner*, for example, failed to penetrate through to consciousness in general. Everything this philosopher says in the first paragraphs of his *Aphorisms* [: 323] about consciousness of *existence* and of *personality* is rich in psychological insights about these two species of consciousness but fails to answer the question: in what does consciousness consist? Rather it presupposes that the question has already been answered. But since this answer could only be the fruit of an earlier investigation which had not yet been undertaken, it is only natural that Mr *Plattner*, like so many others, assumed a very improper concept of consciousness.

In the universal confusion about the concept of representation per se usual till now nothing contradictory was found when any modification of the mind was labelled a representation. Consciousness was declared in consequence to be representation, the representation of a representation. Or, if the nature of consciousness was more deeply penetrated, it was claimed to be the representation of the relation of a representation to the representing subject.

Yet consciousness in general is so different from representation in general that it is not possible for any species of consciousness as consciousness to be representation. Representation *pertains* to every consciousness but it is also more than representation, for the subject and object are distinguished from representation in consciousness. However, to call the relation of representation per se to object and subject representation would be an unphilosophical confusion in language usage, which has used this word [: 324] to define what in consciousness is related to the subject and object. Not only is the double relatedness of representation not itself representation, but is not even *represented* in consciousness in general, of which it is the form. The *representing* of this relatedness is not itself the relatedness, not consciousness, but a representing of consciousness, and the representation of this relatedness is not consciousness but representation of consciousness which, related to consciousness as object and to the subject, provides the consciousness of consciousness. Consciousness can even less be representation of the mutual relation between the subject in itself and the form per se of representation, the object in itself and the material per se of representation, since none of these four things can be represented.

Representation, accordingly, cannot be meant by consciousness. Representation is merely that modification of the mind through which representation per se is related to the object and to the subject: a double action of the subject through which representation is assigned in respect of its material to the object and in respect of its form to the subject – an action of spontaneity on account of which the representation is *bound* with the subject and with the object, both of which are distinct from it. This binding, the proper mode of action of spontaneity, is also manifest in consciousness as a separating, a distinguishing, in that the representation is separated from consciousness. In being bound with the object it is separated from the subject, [: 325] and in being bound with the subject it is separated from the object.

That *which* is conscious is called the subject of consciousness, that *of which* one is conscious the object of consciousness. Through relating the representation to the object the subject is conscious of *something*, through relating it to the subject it knows *it is* conscious of something. This *something* is in every consciousness the *object of consciousness*, but at the same time it is also the *object* of the *representation per se*, which, together with the object and the subject, constitutes the content of consciousness. The subject and object are in one and the same consciousness so essentially distinct from each other that neither can be substituted for the other without cancelling the difference between the double relating of the representation, and with this, consciousness itself. That which in consciousness is its subject, accordingly, cannot in that same consciousness be an object of consciousness and nor of representation either, which is to say, the subject of consciousness cannot be represented as the subject per se of consciousness.

The consciousness of representation, the consciousness of the representing entity (self-consciousness), and the consciousness of something represented are related to consciousness in general in the same way as a species to a genus. They are distinguished from one another merely through their objects. And what belongs to each of them is consciousness in general. 1) *Consciousness of representation* has representation itself as its object[1], and this representation must be represented, that is, must become the object of another representation [: 326] distinguished from it, a new representation whose double relatedness thereupon constitutes the consciousness of representation. With this type of consciousness a representation of a representation occurs that has usually been broadened to the point where it is considered to comprise consciousness in general. 2) *Consciousness of the representing entity* in general, self-consciousness, has as its object the representing entity itself, that is, must become the object of a representation per se distinguished from it as subject

---

1 In this section Reinhold appears to use the term "Gegenstand" to indicate a physical object, literally a thing "standing against" (or in the direction of) one's gaze, and "Objekt" to indicate a represented object or an object of representation – perhaps ultimately a grammatical function. Since English lacks a suitable synonym for the term object, we use "object" in both meanings in the translation.

and object – a representation that by virtue of being so related carries out an activity of self-consciousness indicated by the word *I*. 3) The consciousness of the object has as its object an object distinguished from representation represented together with an attribute distinguished from representation per se, that is to say, consciousness in this aspect must become the object of a special representation (distinguished from it on account of the way in which the object first appeared in consciousness) whose double relation constitutes consciousness of the object. This consciousness of the object must be carefully distinguished from *consciousness in general*. Notwithstanding that one becomes conscious in every act of consciousness, and therefore, in consciousness in general, only of the object of representation per se, it is not the case that each object of each act of consciousness is an object represented as something different from its representation per se or an object thought on the basis of a particular representation of this difference, i.e. not every act of consciousness is consciousness of the object κατ' εξοχην, although one must indeed become conscious in every act of consciousness in general of an object [: 327] which can just as well also be a representation, and a representing, as it is the *object* distinguished from both (the object in its strictest sense).

With these three genera of consciousness (to be further explained in the following) what is common to all of them and constitutes consciousness in general, and what also allows one to speak of consciousness, is the relatedness of the representation in general to its object and subject – something we therefore must take to be the actual nature of consciousness in general.

Such consciousness in general is inseparable from representation in general, and therefore one is entitled to say that *there are no representations without consciousness*. Representation per se, i.e. that manifold thing given to receptivity and brought to unity through the activity of spontaneity, is called representation for the sole reason and extent that *something is represented* as a result of its action. *Something* is represented only insofar as this product of affected receptivity and active spontaneity is related to what corresponds to its *material*, i.e. the object, and to which its form pertains, i.e. the *subject*. The material in representation per se takes on its proper function as representative of the object initially only when it makes the object present to the subject through the relation of the representation to both. The representation per se is by no means consciousness itself; it only represents something in consciousness, and [: 328] it is *only in* consciousness that something is represented. For something can only *be represented* when it is bound to this *something*, and something represents only when it is bound to the representing *subject*. Quite apart from this connection (this real relation between object and subject), representation is called representation per se only insofar as it is something distinct from subject and object in which nevertheless the possibility of a double relation by which something is actually represented is determinately apparent. Insofar as it is distinguished from object and subject such a thing can be investigated according to the theory of the capacity for representation as representation in general; insofar as it is more than representation per se in its relation to the object and subject it can be investigated according the theory of cognition.

I do not wish here to repeat the reasons Locke has advanced successfully to reject representations without consciousness – among them a few reasons, admittedly, that might even go too far in what they demonstrate. But I admit that I am as little able to follow him in conceiving of a representation entirely without consciousness as I would a hungry man without the sensation of hunger. I can only have a representation when something is represented to me, or, better put, when *I* represent *something* to myself, i.e. when *I* (the representing subject) relate a representation (the product of an effect on me from outside and of my counter-action) to something (the object) and refer this something through that product to me. A representation which *I do not* have and which represents *nothing to me* is not a representation. [: 329]

The reasons why the possibility and reality of representations without consciousness have been put forward all issue from the indeterminate concepts of representation in general and from the improper concept of a representing *force* that has accompanied them. "Force", say, for example, the followers of *Leibniz*, "can never be without effect and the effect of the representing force is a representation. Now, the soul is frequently not attended by consciousness and thus it must also possess representations without consciousness." But in this notion of *force*, as shown on many occasions previously, the subject of the capacity for representation is confused with the substance of this subject. The *activity* of the representing subject (in which its substance may be taken to exist in all cases) together with *susceptibility* constitute the essence of the capacity for representation (not the essence of the substance that represents). The activity of the capacity for representation, however, *which cannot act independently of susceptibility*, is expressed at the first moment when susceptibility is affected.

If, as has often been the case until now, all that occurs in one's mind is called representation without further discrimination, there are indeed many more representations *without* consciousness than *with* it. Everything occurring in one's mind prior to a representation and everything following it has been called representation. As if the preparations for a piece of work and the consequences of it could be called the work itself? Or must the preparations and effects of representation be called representations for the reason that they are only partly represented? But, then, is what is capable of being represented [: 330] represented (the object of a representation) and for that reason is it to be considered a representation? Is the process of being affected, the binding of the manifold in representation in general, in judgment, in the syllogism, a representation because it can also be represented? Well, in that case it is not the mind but representation which generates representations from representations.

Mr Plattner, who expressly maintains representations without consciousness, does not see any inconsistency here, for he even professes, in the manner of *Leibniz*, "that representations without consciousness are on the one hand effects and on the other causes of conscious representations". In § 36 he is of the opinion that "representations without consciousness appear to run counter to common experience". But then in § 49 he professes the belief "that the very first sensory ideas (representations) of the new born child are without consciousness", and in § 59 "the consciousness of a person often disappears at moments of deep contemplation". With respect to this latter I even contend that one's consciousness of *existence* could also disappear. Yet on the basis of the reasons given above I can neither call the affections of a child, where there is a professed lack of consciousness, nor the exertions of the scholar who loses himself in speculations and hence is also considered to lack consciousness, a *representing*, without muddying the sense of such an important word. A real representation arises in the affectedness of the child and in the exertion of thought of the thinker only when the material given to [: 331] the receptivity of the one is grasped and the material sought by the other for a new representation is found and the representation per se of both is related to its object.

Finally, according to the way of philosophizing current till now, representations without consciousness could only mount up on a large scale because *consciousness in general*, which had never been investigated, was frequently confused with *clear*, indeed also with *distinct*, consciousness. There are representations without clear consciousness. If it is not established on what basis clear consciousness is distinguished from consciousness in general, then nothing is more natural than to look upon the lack of clear consciousness as a lack of consciousness in general. A prominent reason why this confusion really did commonly occur lies with the circumstance that consciousness was either considered to be nothing more than representation per se of representation, or at very least the representation of representation was considered to be an essential component of *every* act of consciousness – and this, as will soon become apparent, can only be maintained about clear consciousness.

§ XXXIX.

Consciousness in general is *clear* insofar as it is consciousness of representation.

The *three* types of consciousness in general are consciousness of representation, of the subject, and of the object. We therefore wish to [: 332] seek the clarity of consciousness in general in the clarity of these three types. The *consciousness of representation* is clear insofar as the mind is conscious of no other object than its own representation. The consciousness of the subject (*self-consciousness*) is clear insofar as the mind is still conscious outside itself of the representation on the basis of which it represents itself. The consciousness of the *object* is clear insofar as the mind outside the consciousness of the object is still conscious of the representation per se. In all these cases clarity of consciousness in general consists solely in the *consciousness of representation*. Now, as each act of consciousness consists in the relation of representation per se to the object and subject, then in the case of clear consciousness in general, whose object is always a representation, this representation must be represented by a representation distinct from it (as object). In the case of clear consciousness, therefore, representation of representation necessarily occurs. This is the reason why – with that type of consciousness called *clear consciousness of the object* – the distinction between representation per se and the object is made not just by the mind (for this occurs with every act of consciousness in general); the representation per se distinguished from the object is also represented, and with this type of consciousness one therefore not only distinguishes the representation of the object, but one also represents both in particular representations.

In as much as a representation becomes the object of consciousness and consequently is itself represented, [: 333] i.e. must correspond to a representation as an object in general differing from it, to this extent its *relatedness* to the object – through which it held up something of what was distinct from it, its object, to the mind – falls away, and nothing more of it remains than the affectedness of receptivity and the product of spontaneity, i.e. what in itself is the *modification of the mind*. It represents nothing more to the mind but is, itself, now represented. It is no longer related to its object and *to this extent* ceases to be a real representation, and is merely the modification in the mind which bears the name of representation per se, if only in regard to the possibility of making the object present through itself. The consciousness of representation per se is therefore in the strictest sense consciousness of the modification of mind that occurs in a representation.

§ XL.

Consciousness in general is *distinct* in as much as it is consciousness of the representing subject, of the representing entity, i.e. insofar as it is *self-consciousness*.

Consciousness *of representation* is distinct in as much as the mind, in addition to the representation, is also conscious of itself as the representing entity – the consciousness of the *object* insofar as the mind, in addition to the object, is also conscious of itself – and *self-consciousness* is distinct insofar as the mind is not conscious of any other object than itself. [: 334] In all these cases in which all types of consciousness are encountered, distinctness of consciousness in general occurs in *self-consciousness*.

With self-consciousness, the representing subject is represented as the *representing entity*, that is, the representing entity becomes the *object* of a representation that, with respect to its material, relates to it as *object*, but with respect to its form relates to it as *subject*. The object of this consciousness is thus the representing subject but only in its capacity to function as the *representing entity*. The subject per se, distinguished from the predicate of the representing entity, is in this act of consciousness still only *its subject* and in consequence it is represented to this subject, yet the subject *in itself* cannot be represented, it cannot become its own *object*. Everything that can pertain to the subject and thereby which itself can become an *object* is just *this representing*. On account of the capacity to function in this way it is called the representing entity.

The representing subject can thus become the object of one of its representations only insofar as it can represent itself as *representing*. This is possible, however, only insofar as *representing* per se has the capacity to represent itself, i.e. insofar as it can *represent* to itself the attributes through which representing per se distinguishes itself from all that which is not representation, and insofar as it can represent to itself what is proper to representation per se: the predicates of the pure capacity for representation, the forms of receptivity and spontaneity. The possibility of self-consciousness thus depends on the possibility for representations of [: 335] those two forms whose material is determined in the mind *a priori*.

However, self-consciousness does not merely contain the representation of the *representing entity*, but also the representation of the representing entity *that* represents in that same entity, i.e. in self-consciousness the object of consciousness is represented as identical with the subject. How, with this difference between object and subject essential to consciousness, is this *identity* possible? I think it is possible in the following way. The *material* of representation per se whose object is the representing entity can and must be seen in two respects: *first*, insofar as it is *a priori* determined (according to its proper constitution) in its objects, the forms of receptivity and spontaneity in the *capacity for representation*; and, *secondly*, insofar as it must be determined in the representation whose content it constitutes through the *affectedness* of receptivity which forms part of every representation. This affectedness takes place in a representation that represents forms present in the mind *a priori* where *nothing outside* the capacity for representation is rendered, but only what occurs through the activity of the capacity for representation itself. Now, in as much as the material for representing the representing entity in the forms of receptivity and spontaneity is determined in the mind *a priori*, and in as much as it is *given* to this mind and is not produced by it, the mind becomes an *object* to itself through this *given* (the material). However, insofar as this material, determined *a priori* in the capacity for representation, [: 336] is determined as actual material in a particular representation through a spontaneous *action* (the actuality of this material *in* the representation is produced by the action of the subject), the representation also represents – of the representing represented object – the subject in its aspect as object. It represents that subject, I say, to which the material of representation singularly belongs both insofar as it is determined *a priori* in the *capacity for representation* and insofar as it is determined *a posteriori* in the *actual representation*.

And here I believe myself to have supplied the basic principles of the actual origin of the significant representation of the *I*. The *I* is taken to be the representing subject insofar as it is the *object of consciousness*. The path from the indistinct consciousness of an object, from which all consciousness proceeds, to distinct self-consciousness is traversed via the *clear* consciousness of a *representation* that must first be represented in its difference from the object before the representing entity can be represented in its difference from the representation. The mind must have first represented *representing per se* to itself before it can conceive itself under the terms of the predicate of the *representing entity*. The mind is distinguished as the thing receiving the material and producing the form of representation, i.e. the form of what this receiving and producing is manifest and from which the predicates are taken and in whose terms alone it can become *object* to itself – predicates only given to it in its capacity for representation *per se* and [: 337] which can only be represented *a priori*. The following paragraph, therefore, does not require any further proof.

§ XLI.

Representation of the I and self-consciousness is only possible through the *a priori* representations of the forms of receptivity and spontaneity.

None of my readers would presume to bridle at this point with the following objection: "Self-consciousness can hardly have been possible, according to this statement, *before* my theory that first provided for the representations." Still, some of our most famous philosophers have brought forward objections that are even less to be expected against many far less obvious statements of the author of the *Critique of Reason*. I therefore ask readers who might oppose this crucial point whether they would consider possible any individual's representation without the particular attribute of *substance* it contains and which, among other attributes, it represents? Still, philosophers right up to the present day engage in a dispute about how this attribute, which no ordinary human being nor philosopher can do without even in regard to their most trivial representations, is to be understood. Thus, beams of light had the fundamental element of colour even before *Newton* identified this quality in them in his theory of light. Or can any of my readers ascertain how the subject of a mind can represent itself as the *representing entity* without [: 338] representations possessed by something which, as representation, belongs to the representation per se, something proper to the subject of the representation distinguished from what lies outside it?

Since the subject cannot represent itself as pure subject, but only as object, and since there is no other predicate than that of the *representing entity*, it is readily understood that the subject must remain forever incomprehensible to itself insofar as it is said to be some other distinct *representing*, as substance, beyond the logical substratum of the predicate. The *I* is a natural mystery to itself insofar as it is thought in the properties that constitute it as a substance as being something more than the representing entity per se. Yet it thereby becomes more intelligible to itself, to its *capacity for representation* as *predicate* – a capacity containing the key to the entire cognition of the I and all that can be perceived outside it, but a capacity that, until now, has remained almost completely misunderstood.

Insofar as the *Theory of Reason* will show that every pure representation is *a priori* possible only through reason, it will be readily comprehended that and why the representation of the *I* on which the consciousness of *personality* depends is an exclusive characteristic of rational beings.

Until now the *distinct* consciousness explained here, as well as *clear* consciousness, have been confounded with *consciousness in general*, and where one did not encounter the former one did not wish to acknowledge the latter. One denied the difference between the representation [: 339] of object and subject as long as object and subject were not *represented* in particular representations, and therefore one denied consciousness in all these cases. As if that distinction did not actually occur in the mind without always being *represented*? As if the distinction did not have to precede all its representations? As if every act of consciousness had to be clear, every act of consciousness distinct, in order to deserve the name of consciousness? At the same time one knew well and often repeated that many things occurred in the mind of which one had no representation. Even the appointed teachers of philosophy were in the habit of looking upon the soul as a *substance* in which each modification must be called a representation. And in this significant misuse of the word one was far less predisposed to discover confusion the less one was concerned about the concept of representation per se. If one asked "what is a representation?" one got the answer "a modification in the mind". What is the mind? "A representing substance." What is the representing substance? "A singular representing entity?" And one came back again to representation where the *first* response was summoned anew. Without the salutary intercession of the *materialists* and the *skeptics* who from time to time drew to attention the fact that something different from the unknown *representing force* inheres in a representation, the *scholastic philosophers* would never have escaped the unphilosophical circle in which their knowledge of the capacity for representation so uncomfortably turned. However, since one got involved with the [: 340] materialists and skeptics – far from wanting to learn anything – only to the extent that one believed oneself compelled to *refute* them, nothing on the whole ever changed, and one defended right up to the present moment one's notion of the representing *substance* while maintaining its unrepresentable substantiality and its representations without consciousness – representations that represent nothing, or representations that, while representing, represent nothing to the mind, therefore which represent no object at all!!

§ XLII.

Consciousness of the object is called *cognition in general* insofar as the representation is thereby related to a determinate object.

All cognition is a representing, but not all representing is cognition. Only the process by which the representation is *related* to a determinate object can be called cognition. I say *is related*, I do not say *relates*. Each representation relates, according to its content, to a particular object determined by this content, but it is not always related to it *insofar as it is determined*. This can only occur with consciousness of the object, and cognition without consciousness to this extent is impossible.

The difference already indicated above between consciousness in general (as genus) and consciousness of the object (a type of consciousness) must be considered here in detail. [: 341] With consciousness in general the object is also distinguished from the representation per se. But the action of *this* distinguishing consisting in the binding of representation with the *subject* is not itself a representation. With consciousness of the object the object is not only distinguished from representation per se it is also *represented as* being distinct from it. With consciousness in general the representation is related to the object not yet represented, yet is nevertheless represented through this process. With consciousness of the object the representation is related to the object as object, which for that very reason must be represented beforehand, that is, must already have become an object before it could be represented in this capacity. I call the object that is distinguished from representation per se and represented (conceived of) as object the *determinate* object *in consciousness*, and I call the relatedness of the representation to the determinate object in consciousness *cognition** in general.

The expression *determinate object* has brought such tiresome confusion as could only be dispelled through the determinate concept of [: 342] representation per se. The *determinate object* can be called, first, the *thing in itself*, insofar as it is beyond all representation and becomes what it is neither through affectedness in the process of representation nor an action of the mind in consciousness but subsists quite independently of the capacity for representation in itself on account of its qualities and characteristics. Since the representation of the thing in itself is impossible, all representation of the determinate thing in itself is impossible, notwithstanding that, until now, it has been taken to be actual cognition. The *determinate object*, secondly, is called the determinate object in consciousness, and I have used the term in this sense in my explanation of cognition. I distinguish this meaning, which I call the *narrower* meaning of the term from a further dimension of meaning in which this term, *thirdly*, indicates *the* object determined by affectedness in representation per se.

The word *object*, like all words indicating general concepts, was originally a metaphorical expression derived from the analogy between representing and seeing. The expression actually means that which stands against (opposite) the eye in the process of seeing; that which is held before the eye and must put itself before the eye when the eye is called upon to see something: the *thing thrown before* [*Vorwurf*], the *objectum*. If the concept of representation is to be rendered correctly, it must cease being a metaphor and consequently be purified of those original concepts that had accompanied it. It then signifies something different from the representation per se to which the [: 343] *material* in the representation corresponds and to which the representation is related in view of its material. Now, as the material of a representation can only occur through the process of being affected in representation, nothing can be represented (i.e. as the object of a representation) which does not correspond to a material through being thus affected, and each object must be *determined* insofar as it *is affected* in the representation corresponding to it. This determination of the object depends, *first*, on its being affected through receptivity, on the action of being affected in view of the *objective* material of the *things outside us*, and

---

*   The consciousness of the object is called cognition only with respect to the relatedness of the representation to the *object*. With respect to the relation to the subject, cognition is called consciousness. The clear or distinct consciousness of the object is therefore to be distinguished from the clarity and distinctness of cognition.

in view of the subjective material of the action of spontaneity to the extent that the object is received through such receptivity. It depends, *secondly*, on the *disposition* of the material in representation, or the manner *in which* receptivity is affected. This is determined in relation to the objective material through the constitution of the things outside us, but in relation to the subjective material through the disposition of the capacity for representation, that is, the forms of receptivity and spontaneity. Now, to the extent that the material of representation is determined in relation to one of these two types of material or to both types at once, each representation must have a material insofar as each representation – in a further meaning of the term – can be called a representation of a determinate object.

The representation in which the object is determined *solely* on the basis of the material corresponding to it becomes the representation of the determinate object in the *narrower* meaning of the term when it [: 344] is related to the object that is *determinately represented*. This object, insofar as it is object, i.e. insofar as it is the represented thing distinguished from representation per se, in turn becomes the object of consciousness. Only in this sense can it be called the determinate object in consciousness, the object of which, as the object *represented*, one is conscious. With this consciousness a particular representation must be present on the basis of which the object is being represented as represented, i.e. which does not immediately relate to the object, but relates to it to the extent that it is already represented (through another representation).

This representation of the object in which the object is represented (*conceived*) as the represented thing presupposes another representation in which the object is *first* represented and which relates to it *immediately* – and not to the extent that it is already represented (in another representation) (through which it is *intuited*). A representation also related to the object that is distinguished from the representation per se but not represented as being different. For the representation per se from which the represented object is to be distinguished must already be present in the mind beforehand if the representation of the represented thing is to be possible. It must, as the representation per se of the object, lie at the basis of the representation of the determinate object distinguished from it. In this representation the object must be determined *solely* through the *given material* in the absence of which no representation can arise and no representation can be related to an object. It must relate *immediately* and be immediately related to the object [: 345] because it does not relate to the object through any other representation, but, on the contrary, relates to *the object* only on the basis of its given material – material that, through representation, was able to become the *represented*. It must also relate immediately to the object because the object is represented in consciousness not to the extent that the object is distinguished from the representation, but rather, to the contrary, through such representation. This representation must therefore have *immediately arisen through the manner in which receptivity has been affected*, so that the spontaneous element in it, through its action on what is *given*, contributes the very form of representation. Since in this representation the object must be determined solely through the material, the representation itself can only arise on account of the determination of the material in representation, that is, through the manner in which receptivity is affected. For a material can be distinguished from another material in the representation only by receptivity's affecting the one in one way, the other in another way, that is, through the varying disposition of its affectedness.

§ XLIII.

To cognition in general belongs, *first*, a particular type of representation that occurs through the manner in which receptivity is affected, that relates immediately to the object, and that is called *intuition* in its narrower meaning.

Intuition in the narrower meaning relates to representation in general as type relates [: 346] to species. Every intuition is a representation, but not every representation is an intuition. In the concept of representation per se in general there is the determination that an affectedness belongs to every representation in view of its material, but what does not hold is that every representation *shall arise* immediately through the manner of its affectedness, as with the concept of *intuition*. In the concept of representation in general there is the determination that every representation must relate to the object, but not immediately relate, as intuition relates to the object. This is all that need be said for the time being of the type of representation called intuition that is essential to cognition.

With intuition the object is not represented (conceived) as being different from representation. For that reason every act of consciousness in general can rightly be called *unclear* insofar as no representation occurs other than an intuition. For with such mere *intuiting* nothing is represented as object and only the representation that immediately relates to the object and itself cannot be represented again occurs, in which case no clear consciousness (§ XXXIX) takes place. With intuition per se one is not *especially* conscious of the representation, nor of the object. Through this process the object is represented insofar as it is determined in the material of representation, but not that object insofar as it is determined (conceived) as represented in consciousness. With an intuition one is conscious of the object, but not insofar as it is an object distinguished from the representation. To the latter [: 347] belongs, in addition to the intuition, a representation distinct from the intuition.

This representation must take as its object the object distinguished from intuition per se insofar as that object is already *represented*. It can therefore not *have arisen* immediately through affectedness, nor from the given material, but from the *intuition*. Its immediate material is not the given itself; it is the given that has received the form of representation. It can only arise by the action of *spontaneity* binding the manifold made present, i.e. represented, through intuition, thereby generating a new representation that receives a represented manifold according to its material – a manifold that has received through its form a *unity of the represented thing*, i.e. *objective unity*. This representation is called the *concept* in the narrower meaning because it combines the represented manifold (the attributes of the object) in a unity of the represented (unity of the object) that is different from the binding with the material per se (the unity of the representation). Now, the concept does not relate immediately to the object as intuition but only by means of material not only given on account of its affectedness but also represented. It relates via the attributes of the object represented through intuition and thus also through a representation distinct from the object itself, i.e. *the intuition*. From this we can see how the concept of the representation [: 348] of the determinate object in the narrower meaning is brought about. It is a representation encompassing the manifold in a particular unity distinguished from the unity of representation per se appropriate to intuition – the manifold through which the object was determined through its being affected in another representation and which has taken the form of the representation in this representation, i.e. *the represented manifold*.

§ XLIV.

To cognition in general pertains, *secondly*, a particular type of representation that comes into being through an action of spontaneity, relates only indirectly through another representation to the object, and can be called *concept* in the narrower sense.

The concept, too, is only a type of representation, as species. Every concept is a representation, but not every representation is a concept.

The *concept* and the *intuition*, whose nature will be illuminated in more detail in what follows, must occur in *a single* act of consciousness if cognition is to occur. They constitute cognition, the consciousness of the determinate object, and are consequently the *internal conditions* of cognition in general. If consciousness of the determinate object is present, the object, *first*, must be determined in representation per se, and, *secondly*, in consciousness. *In representation per se*, by way of [: 349] the given material on account of its affectedness – material that has received the form per se of representation through spontaneity – a representation comes into being which does not relate to another representation but immediately relates to the object and is called *intuition*. *Without* this representation nothing would be present in consciousness that relates to something which is *not a representation*, that relates to the object. But even *through* this representation by itself the object would be represented (intuited), but not represented (conceived) as determinate. Therefore, in addition to this representation, there must be yet another – a second – kind of representation in which the object is represented in its difference from the first, and represented as determinate, as the thing represented: a *concept*. The material of this representation is not the raw material, the material of intuition, but material raised to the level of a representation through the action of spontaneity, or it is the representation itself, which in view of the manifold, the represented thing, the attributes of the object, is raised to the level of a new representation through a binding of these attributes – a representation which encompasses the represented manifold and, through these means, relates to the object determined through these its attributes.

§ XLV.

The *cognitive capacity in general* consists of the capacity for *intuitions* and *concepts*.

We have discovered here a clear difference between the *capacity for representation in general* [: 350] and the capacity for representation insofar as it is the *cognitive capacity*. Just as we have come to know the capacity for representation in its two essential components through the *forms of receptivity* and of *spontaneity* determined in its nature, so we will now become acquainted with the cognitive capacity through the form of its components that are a part of its nature once we have succeeded in adumbrating this form from the effects of its capacities concerned with cognition and from its *intuitions* and *concepts*.

Nothing can be more intelligible to readers who have understood my meaning so far than the fact *that*, and *for what reasons*, the cognitive capacity has been as good as completely misunderstood till now. Admittedly one has generally acknowledged till now that the understanding (the capacity for concepts in their more restricted sense) is important for cognition. Yet since one left the concept of representation without proper explication, and was thus also *obliged to* leave the concept of the *concept in general* undetermined, it was also not possible to make clear in what the activity of the understanding involved with cognition actually consisted. One therefore confounded the *understanding* with the *cognitive capacity* and ascribed cognition without discrimination to the cognitive capacity, with the result that one had even less prospect of finding something sensible there since one had completely mistaken the essential difference between intuition and concept and ascribed to the understanding both intuitions as well as concepts. The mistake was even less avoidable since in each moment of cognition two different representations [: 351] occur that are bound in an act of consciousness. This binding of two representations is an action of the understanding that can be called judgment in an extended sense. In the immediately following discussion dealing with the *capacity for intuitions* we will become acquainted with a particular capacity for representation quite distinct from the understanding yet, along with the understanding, a capacity indispensable for cognition in general that has been given the name of *sensibility* in the most proper meaning of the term.

Theory of Sensibility

§ XLVI.

The *fundamental concept of sensibility* has necessarily been mistaken until now insofar as one assumed it to contain certain attributes that, ostensible or real, cannot be assigned to the capacity for representation per se but to its subject (as substance).

As varied as the questions here are – how must the representing substance be constituted if it is to be capable of *sensory* representations? how must the capacity for representation itself be constituted if it is to be capable of sensory representations? from what does the sensibility of the capacity for representation *arise* and in what does it *consist*? – such questions have [: 352] been thoroughly confused and mixed up until now. Just as, for example, the difference between the *I* and its bodily organization obliged one to consider the I to be a substance quite different from this bodily organization and a substance existing in its own right, one also believed oneself justified on the basis of ordinary experience in establishing that the *five tools* of sensory organization make up an equal number of channels through which the representing subject is provided with the material of representations of things outside us. One believed oneself justified, too, in allowing the susceptibility of the representing subject to depend without any clear distinction on such organization. One soon had a ready answer to the question: in what does sensibility consist? "It consists in the capacity to be affected by means of the organs of sense", or "in the limiting of the representing force through the bodily organization accompanying the representing force", and each of these answers put the organizing body more or less under the aegis of explanations arising from sensibility, that is, under attributes of the concept of sensibility. Thereby, however, the question posed was by no means answered but rather a quite different one was answered, namely the question: how is sensibility present in the representing *subject*? – A question, if any answer is possible at all, which could only be answered if another quite different question is answered first: how is one obliged to think under the conditions of sensibility? For how can one speak of one or two substances or one spirit on its own or in connection with a body constituting the subject of *sensibility* if one has not reached agreement with oneself or with one's opponents [: 353] about what one understands *sensibility* to be.

"Every schoolboy", I hear one of our popular philosophers interrupt, "knows what he understands sensibility to be, and philosophers are supposed not to be in agreement about this?" – Yes, every schoolboy indeed, and perhaps also every popular philosopher as long as he only has schoolboys in front of him. Yet if one has him take his place on the battlefield against the wretched *materialists*, he will soon have forgotten that he wished to take *sensibility* to be nothing more than what the world takes it to be. He will soon enough reveal to every attentive observer not confined to the ranks of popular philosophers that the spiritualist no less than the materialist fails to have a conception of the sensory capacity for representation common to all human beings. For the one will include in his concept of sensibility, along with the attribute of organization, a non-corporeal substance, while the other will admit only bodily organization itself, and it will soon become apparent that both parties in conflict with one another think as differently about the one thing they have agreed not to contest, about the concept of sensibility *per se*, as they do about the actual point of contention (the nature of the soul), which they have absorbed into their shared premises without being aware of it.

In the philosophical world one is only in agreement about the meaning of the word *sensibility* as long as one finds oneself compelled to provide an explanation of it, in the same way as one would have to explain the meaning [: 354] of the words *force, nature, God,* etc. Now, with the expanded concept of sensibility, as long as an attribute occurs about which the philosophical world is not in agreement, and as long as the representing substance and the organic body are included among the attributes of this concept, one can count on the fact that the materialists and spiritualists – I will not say are at peace with one another – do not even properly know what they are at odds about. They have essentially dissimilar concepts of the nature of the representing subject, to the extent that this is a substance, since the materialist considers it to be a *compound* substance and the spiritualist holds it to be a *simple* substance. As soon as they conceive sensibility as the disposition of the representing substance, and not as the disposition per se of the capacity for representation, one can say they conceive of sensibility in essentially different ways. And yet, with the word sensibility, they would have to conceive of precisely the same thing if they seek to converse intelligibly about the question of how the subject of sensibility must be constituted, that is, if they desire to know about what it is they are actually debating.

There must therefore be a concept of sensibility that remains the same whether one seeks to locate the subject of sensibility in the body, or in a mind, or in mind and body together, and this is the concept of the sensory capacity for representation per se. This concept is *falsely rendered*, as soon as one includes the *subject* of sensibility among the attributes of sensibility, for then the concept immediately ceases to be a concept of the *capacity per se*. [: 355] The determination of the proper attributes of the concept is rendered impossible at the moment when one urges a foreign attribute upon it. Yes, even the question "what is the subject of the predicate sensibility?" ceases to have meaning as soon as the subject sought is included under the attributes of the predicate. The question, "Is the mind alone, or mind and body together, or the body alone the subject of sensibility?" becomes nonsensical when one takes sensibility to mean a capacity of the body alone, as the materialists do, or a mind connected to a body, as the spiritualists do, or even a mind alone, as the idealists do.

Meanwhile, as long as the proper attributes of the sensory capacity for representation per se were not found, nothing was more natural than this persistent confounding of the capacity's disposition with the disposition of its substance. For one already had to have particular attributes in mind if one wanted to think in definite terms about sensibility. One took them, therefore, where one believed them to be found. They were forced upon every thinking mind by this thinking mind's believing to know (without investigating the capacity for representation) about its own representing subjectivity partly through experience and partly from its own metaphysical system. They were, therefore, nothing other than the supposed attributes of substance, or of substances which represent. And by thinking that one had already found the attributes of the sensory capacity for representation *in these attributes of substance*, the search for and the discovery of the actual attributes [: 356] of the capacity for representation per se was hindered just as much as lack of acquaintance with the truth encourages dependence on falsity.

By declaring, however, that I consider the organic body and every constitutive aspect that accompanies it not to be an attribute of the sensory capacity for representation per se, I also declare the subject of the capacity for representation to be just as little mind as body, and believe myself thereby to be supporting spiritualism no more than I refute materialism.

I restrict my claim in this respect to the sensory capacity for representation per se, and wish to see the attribute of bodily organization not pertaining to this capacity removed – the subject of the capacity for representation may be purely mind, purely body, or mind and body together.

In the same way that we have expounded the concept of the capacity for representation per se from the concept of representation in general after removing those heterogeneous attributes not pertaining to it, we are now in a position to determine the concept of the sensory capacity for representation per se from the concept of sensory representation per se after this concept has been purged of those attributes of bodily organization confusing it.

§ XLVII.

Representation per se is called *sensory* to the extent that it immediately arises from the manner in which its receptivity is affected. [: 357]

According to this explanation, the material of sensory representation is immediately given through its being affected, and consequently is not already represented, as with the concept, through another representation. The form of this representation therefore can only consist in binding the given, insofar as it is given, whilst the form of a concept consists in binding the represented and is consequently already bound with a representation. In *sensory representation* spontaneity is less activated than in the *concept*. In the concept spontaneity generates a new representation from one already present, a new representation owing its occurrence immediately to a pure act of spontaneity; in sensory representation, however, it produces only the form per se of a given material of representation which owes its occurrence immediately to the affectedness per se of receptivity. In sensory representation it binds the material per se through which only a *single* representation is unified. In the concept it binds the already represented manifold and gives unity through this to *two representations*. I call spontaneity, insofar as it actively generates itself in this sensory representation, the *first* degree of spontaneity, and its action, which consists in its coincidence with the given, *apprehension*.

In sensory representation the capacity for representation behaves more *passively* than *actively*. Here spontaneity has no part to play whatsoever (as with the concept, whose material, intuition, spontaneity works upon) and the producing of form here is [: 358] not any unforced action, but an opposing action wrung from its action on receptivity. This representation thus arises more through passivity than through a working of the mind.

This remark is quite old in the philosophical world but, despite its rectitude, has led to numerous philosophical prejudices. By mistaking the action of the capacity for representation for the *understanding*, assuming activity only where one believed the understanding to be operative, one ascribed to the understanding those representations in which its power of judgment could be demonstrated, by linking with it those attributes belonging to an object – the *distinct* attributes – and consequently separating out those not belonging to it. And thus all that remained to sensibility were the *indistinct* attributes that the understanding had not worked upon, which were then often called, without further discrimination, *confusions*. One thus believed oneself to have characterized *sensibility* and *understanding* quite correctly when one declared the former to be the capacity for unclear and the latter for clear representations. Through the indeterminate nature of the concept of representation in general one was prevented from recognizing that all representations, the clear as well as the unclear ones, in as much as they assume a given material, depended on that capacity which is passive with respect to its behaviour and active with respect to its form, and that this passive capacity, receptivity, is not a restriction of activity, is not a confusing incapacity, but an essential part of the capacity for representation [: 359] without which even representation's spontaneity would be inconceivable. In the following one will see which confusions necessarily resulted from philosophy's failure to provide a proper explanation of sensibility.

§ XLVIII.

Sensory representation is called *sensation* in the narrower sense, insofar as it is related to the subject, and *intuition*, insofar as it is related to the object.

Insofar as sensory representation is related to the subject, it is nothing more than a modification in the state of the subject resulting from the affectedness of receptivity and the reaction of spontaneity, a modification in relation to which the subject behaves more in a passive than an active manner – which is what one denotes with the word *sensation* in its actual meaning. One has often, but in each case quite incorrectly, declared sensation to be consciousness of a modification in the physical state. Sensation is the modification of the state itself, not the consciousness of such a modification. The latter presupposes representation of the modification of state, and is thus consciousness of sensation, *clear* consciousness. Admittedly consciousness is a part of each sensation in its stricter sense – a consciousness in which sensation consists in the sensory representation *related* to the subject. Yet consciousness of sensation does not any more belong to a sensation than does consciousness of representation to a representation. Sensory representation is a [: 360] modification per se of state only insofar as it is related to the subject. This relatedness as *sensation* is thus essential to it. Now insofar as the relatedness of a representation per se to the subject is impossible without relatedness of the same to the object, and insofar as the relatedness of sensory representation to the object is called *intuition*, no sensation is possible without intuition and no intuition without sensation.

The *relatedness* of sensory representation to the object – one of two *actions* of which consciousness is composed – turns sensory representation into *intuition*. Therefore, those who have mistaken the activity of the mind for the understanding have conceded to the understanding the capacity for intuition. However, not activity per se any more than susceptibility per se, but both together, are activated in the process of intuiting, although the *former* far more than the latter since the mind in intuition behaves more in a passive than an active manner. The understanding, the capacity for concepts, thinks, and is not able to intuit anything; this can be accorded solely to the sensory capacity for representation but admittedly only as long as the concept of representation remained indistinct and was not able to be distinguished with sufficient precision from the understanding.

In the *relatedness* of sensory representation to the object, which is of direct importance for intuition, we can find part of the reason for the *optical deception* of the mind by which we believe ourselves to be representing *things in themselves*. The representation immediately [: 361] arising through what corresponds to the object, through its material, immediately containing what accords with the object, what relates immediately to it, is *assigned* in the process of intuiting to the object made present to the mind only through the representation and not of itself. Intuition in this way is confused with the object, and this is all the more the case since with *intuition per se* – an activity on which concepts and all discursive cognition must be based–the object is *in no way* represented as *distinct from intuition*. Thus, when no thorough investigation is first undertaken of what must be distinguished from representation *per se*, to the extent that it can be distinguished from objects, and which is exclusively assigned to intuition as *representation per se*, *all* predicates discovered through analysis of their particular intuitions, e.g. the body, cannot fail to be conflated without distinction with the objects per se (e.g. that which corresponds to the intuition of the body outside the mind).

One agreed hitherto to call representations of individual things intuitions and to distinguish them from the representations of *genus* (several things possessing common *attributes*) without being required to concede to sensibility through this distinction its special claim on the intuitions since one assigned representations of genus to the understanding. Yet notwithstanding that every representation of an isolated attribute must arise from direct representation of the object through action of the understanding and not [: 362] from its being immediately affected, a direct representation of the object can only occur from the direct circumstances of its affectedness, from an impression on receptivity, by the object's being held before the mind, just as it is determined solely through that which belongs to it immediately, i.e. through the material of representation, without the understanding having ordered, connected, and separated the individual attributes which constitute the content of intuition.

Direct occurrence through the manner of being affected is the common character of sensation, intuition, and sensory representation in general, and the capacity for representation possesses sensibility to the extent that it possesses the determinate capacity to achieve representations through the manner in which receptivity is affected.

§ XLIX.

The capacity to achieve representations through the manner in which receptivity is affected is called *sensibility* in the narrower sense.

I say in the narrower sense in order to distinguish from receptivity this more closely defined capacity of *sensory representations* – to the extent that receptivity belongs to the capacity for representation in general and to the extent that it is understood as a capacity that behaves in a passive manner in regard to representing in general and therefore can be called *sensibility in a broader sense*. Receptivity [: 363] in general is understood to be an essential component of the capacity for representation in general. Sensibility in the narrower sense is understood as an essential component of the capacity for cognition. Receptivity is the determinate susceptibility for the material ingredients of representation in general. Sensibility in the narrower sense is the determinate capacity for those representations that occur immediately through the manner of their being affected.

In this explanation sensibility appears as a particular disposition of the capacity for representation – a disposition that is assigned to this capacity insofar as it can generate representations occurring immediately through the manner of affectedness. Sensibility is thus assigned to the representing subject to the extent that this subject has a particular *capacity for representation*, not to the extent that this capacity has an organic body or is itself organic body. Whether and how sensibility *arises* through bodily organization is neither affirmed nor denied here. On the other hand it is maintained that sensibility consists in a particular capacity of the representing subject, which is to say in a particular disposition of its capacity for representation, and this in consequence negates the fact that it *consists* in a *bodily organization* that is no capacity for representation per se, without determining whether the capacity for representation belongs to its organization or whether it belongs to one of the entities distinguished from it[2].

---

2   Our translation here assumes a typographical error in the original.

"But are not certain changes in bodily organization essential to every sensory representation?" It cannot be denied that certain representations [: 364], and particularly those whose material is provided through the so-called five senses, depend on changes, and in regard to bodily organization on the disposition of organization, and that these representations are the first to attain reality in our mind and that all objective material occurs in them. But as indispensable as they may be to sensory empirical representations, and, to the extent that sensory empirical representations must precede all others, to the reality of each representation in general, they nevertheless belong only to the *external* conditions of sensory representations not to the *internal* conditions, that is, to those conditions which are components of mere sensory representation in general. They by no means constitute the sensory capacity for representation. Bodily organization itself can only become an object of our representations by an intuition's being related to it, i.e. a representation occurring through the manner of its affectedness, and consequently organization presupposes the sensibility of the capacity for representation. Modifications in organization insofar as they are representable also presuppose a sensibility in the capacity for representation that consequently cannot possibly *be* the capacity for these modifications. To the extent that they are not representable, their connection with what may occur in the representing subject *per se*, which is equally not representable, cannot possibly be given. The materialists and the spiritualists, in as much as they include an organic body and its changes in the basic concept of sensibility, explain sensibility [: 365] by means of something that itself presupposes sensibility by making objects that are only representable on the basis of sensibility the internal condition of sensory representation per se. They may themselves care to judge whether they achieve anything more by this than when they prefer to derive the visibility of objects from the objects rather than from the eye.

The receptivity of the capacity for representation must be affected by two very different aspects: from *without*, i.e. through something distinct from the mere capacity for representation, and from *within* through its own spontaneity.

§ L.

To the extent that sensory representation emerges through the manner in which receptivity is affected from without, it is called, in its relation to the subject, *external sensation*, and, in its relation to the object, *external intuition*; the determinate capacity of receptivity to be affected from without is called the *external sense*.

This external sense belonging to the mind was usually confused with the sensitivity or susceptibility of bodily organization. One would have to have a representation of the representing subject *in itself* and as *substance* if it was to be identified: *how* the external sense was present in this sense, i.e. *whether* and to *what extent* it arose from bodily organization and its disposition, and whether the representing subject [: 366] without bodily organization would have any external sense. Yet in order to know that one was not entitled to conceive the sensitivity of bodily organization under the rubric of the external sense, one only needed to have a determinate concept of the *capacity for representation*, which, abstracted entirely from the subject, contained the *form* per se of the capacity for representation, and spoke solely in terms of what it contained and not about where it came from. The external sense, that is, the determinate susceptibility for the objective material, must *precede* organization and its sensitivity in the mind to the extent that these can be sensed and intuited. I know from experience that all material corresponding to representations of objects existing outside me are modified by the so-called *five tools of sensation*, yet I am also aware of these five tools of sensation as objects which I distinguish from myself as representing subject in clear consciousness of them, and must count them among the objects external to me. The affectedness of these tools of sensation, to the extent that I can represent it, must be distinguished from the affectedness of receptivity belonging to pure representation. It consequently assumes the receptivity of the capacity for representation as present *a priori* in the mind. Thus the receptivity of the five tools of sensation belongs to my sensory capacity for representation not as a component present in this capacity *a priori* but as a *modification* of this presupposing the external sense to be given determinately. In other words, the five tools of sensation belong to the mind's external sense merely as five *empirical* [: 367] *modifications* known only from experience and given only through an external impression *in* representation. They belong not to the form of sensory representation in general, but only to the determinations of the *material* of certain sensory representations of things outside us. They can be represented only on the basis of representations *a posteriori* in which a material corresponding to them is given to the capacity for representation from the outside.

All material given through and to the organic body is given to the mind from the outside and is related to an object found outside the mind, of which the bodily organization of this object is constituted insofar as that organization is able to represent it. Representation arising through the manner of being affected and mediated by a modified impression according to the disposition of the tools of sensation, insofar as it is referred to the subject, is nothing but a modification of the mind brought about by the organs of sense, *external* sensation, and, to the extent that it is related to its object, *external* intuition. With representations of so-called visual sense, this is convincing enough where the object corresponding to the material received through a modification of a sense organ is represented determinately as existing outside us. With representations of the more confused and less refined senses – with sensations of sexual desire aroused by an indeterminate object, for example – it is certainly the case that no object distinguished by a modification in the mind is put before the mind through a modification of an organ of sense. [: 368] The organ itself in which the objective basis of a modification is encountered, at least in *distinct* consciousness, is an object represented outside the mind. Now if the sensitivity of every representation in general consisted of modifications in bodily organization there would be nothing other than external representations, that is, sensory representations related to something outside the mind, and there could not be any sensory representations, which, in distinct consciousness of them, are not related to any thing external to the mind; there would not be *internal* sensations and *internal* intuitions.

§ LI.

To the extent that sensory representation occurs through the manner in which receptivity is affected from within, it is called *internal sensation* in relation to the subject and *internal intuition* in relation to the object. The determinate capacity of receptivity to be affected from within is called the *internal sense*.

By spontaneity's binding with that part of the manifold given to receptivity from without (i.e. giving it the form of representation), receptivity affected from without is also affected from *within* through spontaneity with each representation of the external sense. Every external sensation is called external only in consideration of its material given from without, yet at the same time – to the extent that receptivity has also had to be affected from within in apprehending this material [: 369] by which that material becomes something belonging to the mind – it is called *internal sensation*.

There are also internal sensations *per se*, that is, sensations that have arisen in a direct way merely by receptivity's being affected by spontaneity. The distinct *consciousness* of *sensation* is essentially different from the clear consciousness of a *thought* or a concept. In regard to the latter, the mind represents itself through the predication of the representable form of spontaneity by binding with the manifold, by *thinking*. In regard to the former, on the other hand, it represents itself through the predication of the representable form of receptivity by receiving the manifold, by *sensation*, by representing the manner, the *form* of receiving (the form of receptivity) as something proper to its own capacity in a representation *a priori*. This, however, is only possible through the process by which spontaneity, the form of receptivity determined in the capacity per se, is determined as the pure material of representation in a representation corresponding to this through an affecting of receptivity in accordance with that form. The representation occurring through this affectedness is the *internal sensation per se* in consideration of its relation to the subject and the *internal intuition* in consideration of the object (the form of receptivity).

The internal sense is present with the external sense in *one and the same* receptivity, but as a capacity essentially distinct from the external sense. The *external* sense is the determinate susceptibility for impressions of objects [: 370] that are outside the representing subject; the *internal* sense is the determinate susceptibility for impressions belonging to the spontaneity of the representing subject. The material given to the external sense relates to objects outside the representing subject; the material given to the internal sense, by contrast, relates partly to modifications per se in the representing subject and partly (in representation *a priori*) to forms of the capacity for representation, and consequently to the proper disposition of the representing subject to the extent that it is a representing entity.

Since sensibility consists essentially of the internal and external senses, yet bodily organization and the five senses, to the extent that these provide representations, belong to the capacity for representation only as empirical modifications of the *external* sense, so every definition deprives sensibility in general, which bodily organization brings under the attributes of sensibility, of one essential half of its capacity, namely the internal sense, and is as a result too restricted for the basic concept of sensibility.

A consequence of this incorrect definition of sensibility was that one usually confounded the *internal sense* with *consciousness* and accorded representations belonging to it partly to the *external sense* and partly to the *understanding*. The latter was particularly so in the case of the *spiritualists* who ascribed distinct representations without discrimination to the understanding and held the understanding to be the capacity to have real intuitions of a sensory nature appropriate to *things in themselves* ([: 371] representations modified by bodily organization according to their system).

It is generally difficult to say what an entire philosophical sect has posited even in regard to those basic pronouncements it seeks to defend in opposition to other sects. For mostly the agreement of individual proponents of a sect consists rather in common expressions and formulae that each proponent takes their own way than in universally determined basic concepts and statements. Many spiritualists, therefore, will contradict me when I maintain that their sect reduces sensory representations to those relying on bodily organization. They will refer me perhaps to *Baumgarten's metaphysics*, in which, in the new edition of Mr *Eberhard*, one finds quoted on page 182: "I have a *capacity to feel*, that is, a *sense* which is either an *internal* one, the capacity for internal sensations or for representations of the present state of my soul, or an external one, the capacity for *external* sensations or for representations of the present state of my body." – And Baumgarten, you say, is said to allow no difference between the internal and external sense and to have reduced the full compass of sensibility to the internal sense? – Everything here will depend on what Baumgarten takes the capacity *to feel*, takes *sense* to be, and that is admittedly quite difficult to make out. Does he take *sense* to be *sensibility*, the capacity for sensory [: 372] representations? In this way he can allow *sense*, and consequently the internal and external sense, to be nothing more than the capacity for *indistinct* or *confused* representations, for thus are sensory representations defined by him in § 383. He must then assume that without which he is unable to conceive of indistinct representations to be an essential component of his so-called sense. Now, in § 376 he says: "It can be seen from the position of my *body* in this world why I represent some things more dimly, some more clearly, still others distinctly." Since he takes the *understanding* to be the capacity for *distinct* concepts, this passage can actually have no other meaning than that the basis of indistinctness is found in the *position of the body* obstructing the understanding in certain cases from carrying out its functions and producing distinct concepts, and that the basis of distinctness is found in other cases in the *understanding* which, from the position of the body, is not so obstructed. – Or does Baumgarten take what he calls the capacity for sensation or sense not to be sensibility? Certainly he often takes it to be more than just sensibility. Thus he says, for example, "the representations of my present state *or sensations* are representations of the present state of the world, and they are *activated* by the power of the soul through which it represents the world according to the position of the body." And here *sense* (the capacity to have sensations) and *soul* would be made one and the same thing, and representation of my state (internal sensation) [: 373] would be both representation of the state of the world (or, as it is called above, of the body) and external sensation!!! *Bilfinger*, certainly a no less incisive and successful commentator on the great *Leibniz*, speaks of the capacity to have sensations in more definite terms. For him this capacity is: "A capacity of the soul to represent the things *outside it* as existing outside the soul according to those modifications which are caused by these things in a certain part of the organic body"*. If one now considers that both Bilfinger and Baumgarten** and who else besides confuse internal

---

*   *Potentia animae repräsentandi res ut extra se positas secundum mutations, quas in certa corporis parte organica faciunt. V. Dilucidationes De Deo Mundo et Anima § 252.*

**   These are the internal sensations [sensatio interna *conscientiae* strictius dicta] Baumgarten § 369.

sense with the *consciousness* that indeed cannot be taken to be any mere component of the capacity to be affected, one can only ascribe this to the inconsistency of spiritualists so common in our philosophy until now – even if they either do not deny the representing subject completely all ability to be affected (as they might have been able to do under the protection of the hypothesis of *pre-established harmony*) or if they take this capacity to be something more than *external sense* per se.

Our more recent spiritualists of whom the largest part already acknowledges the hyper-hypothetical system of pre-determined harmony [: 374] to be what it really is, have admittedly contented themselves with an even laxer justification of the concept of *sensibility*. Yet in this regard they are still thoroughly in agreement about the fact that they declare the external sense to be the capacity to be affected through the mediation of the sense organs and the internal sense to be consciousness. Since it is their view, therefore, that sensibility is limited to the external sense and its modifications, they have no alternative other than to allow the material of representations that cannot be given to the external sense to be received by the understanding, and in this way to follow *Aristotle* in ascribing to the understanding a *passive capacity*. Now to the extent that they consider understanding and sensibility to be a capacity to which the content of representations must be *given*, they are obliged to allow the way in which understanding is given to be different from the way in which sensibility is given. They therefore hold to the view, still under the sway of *Leibniz's* thinking, that objects are given to the understanding in exactly the same way in which the understanding encounters them according to analysis of their attributes undertaken beforehand, that is, in distinct representation, but that precisely these objects of sensibility occur in complete confusion about their attributes, that is, they would be given in the same way in which they occur in indistinct representation – a representation they call the *sensory*. In both types of representation they mean to possess the representation of one and the same *thing in itself*, only with the difference that they believe themselves able to cognize through the understanding the thing in itself as it is *constituted in itself*, yet cognize through sensibility [: 375] how it *appears* through the *medium* of bodily organization (which is alien to the soul).

For such a violation sensibility would exact sufficient revenge from the *materialists* if the basic conception of sensibility postulated by this sect were correct. Whilst the spiritualists consider sensibility to be a modification per se (resulting from bodily organization) of a disembodied representing force confounded with the understanding, the materialists declare the understanding to be a modification per se of sensibility and sensibility to be a sensitivity belonging to animal organization which, in the more complete bodily organization of human beings, also expresses itself as understanding. It must be admitted that the main article of the materialists' philosophical faith, "that the essence of all things consists in their *embodiment*", is not an inconsiderable factor in the type of explanation offered of sensibility and of the capacity for representation in general. Their entire system is certainly no less than this a quite natural consequence of the indeterminate concept of sensibility they uphold and of the indispensability of the bodily organization for the capacity for representation, and must forever collapse merely as a result of the correct application of that concept.

From these remarks about sensibility the following results: 1) that those proper attributes of sensibility that hitherto have been entirely mistaken and on account of which the basic concept of sensibility had to be investigated in greater detail in § XLIX do not come from any disposition of the representing *subject*, whether this be [: 376] mind or body or mind and body together, but, on the contrary, are found in the disposition per se of the capacity for representation per se and constitute sensibility only as it is determined in the capacity for representation. 2) That on the basis of these attributes sensibility would have to stand out very clearly both from the receptivity of the capacity for representation in general and also from the understanding. 3) That from these attributes it must be determined how sensibility in general as a type encompasses the external and internal sense as genera of sense within itself and how both these genera are distinguished from each another in the sensory capacity for representation. According to these conditions, then, the attributes in question signify nothing other than the manner *in which* sensibility is a priori determined in the capacity for representation per se as *internal* and *external* sense. They must contain *in the* capacity for representation, or rather in its receptivity, the particular manner in which this receptivity has to be affected if representations of internal and external sense are to be possible.

I say the particular type of affectedness *in the* capacity for representation and distinguish this from the particular manner of affectedness in *things in themselves outside* the capacity for representation according to the manner in which these things affect receptivity through the objective material. Through this type of affectedness whose basis lies in the constitution of things outside us, however, nothing is determined in sensory representations but the material through which they correspond to certain things outside the mind – not [: 377] their form as sensory representations per se nor as representations of the external sense. This latter can only be determined by becoming sensory representations in general and sensory representations of the external sense, i.e. in the sensory capacity for representation, to the extent that the possibility of being affected from without is determinately present in this capacity.

The *sensibility* of the capacity for representation must be distinguished from the receptivity per se of the capacity for representation by sensibility's encompassing the determinate possibility of being affected from without and within in regard to its sensory representations, whereas receptivity contains nothing but the determinate possibility of affectedness in general in regard to representation in general. Just as I called that attribute proper to receptivity the form of receptivity because it demonstrates the *manner* in which the susceptibility of the mind in general must be affected, so I will call those attributes proper to sensibility the *forms* of *external* and *internal sense* because they must indicate the way in which susceptibility has to be affected in the context of sensory representations which either belong to the external or to the internal sense or both together. We can therefore establish the following without further amplification:

§ LII.

If representation per se of the external and internal sense is to be possible, the proper attributes of sensibility of the capacity for representation per se consist [: 378] in the determinate manner *a priori* in which receptivity must be affected or in the *forms* of *external* and *internal sense.*

The form of receptivity consists in the manifold nature of the material in general determined *a priori*, or in the susceptibility of the capacity for representation determined only for a manifold in general. The forms of external and internal sense must therefore consist in the determinate manifold of external and internal material, in the determinate susceptibility for a manifold given from without and within, and in the manner determined in the mind in which the manifold must be given from without and within if sensory representation is to be possible.

§ LIII.

The *a priori* determined form of external sense consists in the determinate possibility of *externality* in representation occurring with receptivity, and external sense consists in the capacity to achieve representations by way of a manifold, to the extent that this is given as a manifold per se in parts encountered externally.

The receptivity of the capacity for representation consists of a twofold, and consequently also diverse, susceptibility whose difference is based on the [: 379] nature of the mind, of the susceptibility for an objective material without which no representation of an object outside us and not even the reality of representation in general is possible, and of the susceptibility for a subjective material which can only be given through the affectedness of the spontaneity of the mind in representation. The one is susceptibility for affectedness from without through the action of an object distinct from the representing subject. The other is susceptibility for affectedness from within through an action of the representing subject. Now, since every action of spontaneity consists in *binding*, susceptibility for affectedness from within must be susceptibility for a manifold in general to the extent that the manifold is given through spontaneity, i.e. *bound*. Consequently, susceptibility for affectedness from without must be susceptibility for affectedness for a manifold to the extent that the manifold can be given to susceptibility as a manifold in its externally encountered parts without the involvement of spontaneity, and therefore without being bound. The receptivity of external sense can thus be found in the determinate possibility of being affected by a manifold in parts externally encountered, insofar as this is a manifold per se, and external sense itself is the capacity to achieve representations through a manifold given externally. The representation per se of external sense then arises through the manner of affectedness determined in the mind, on account of which objective [: 380] material can be determined as a material, i.e. with respect to its manifold nature in representation per se only as a manifold encountered externally. The *form of external sense*, i.e. that in which the *external sensibility* of the capacity for representation is found, is nothing other than the possibility of the externality of the manifold *in* representation determinately present in receptivity and prior to every representation.

§ LIV.

The *a priori* determined form of the representation of external sense consists in the unity of the manifold encountered externally, which, to the extent that it is related with the representation to the object, is called the *form of external intuition*.

A representation is sensory in as much as it occurs through the manner of its affectedness, and it is a *sensory-external* representation, in as much as it occurs through the manner of an affectedness that consists in the external givenness of the manifold determined *a priori*. Just as material in general can only occur in representation as an *a priori* determinate manifold in general, so the material of the representation of external sense only occurs in the same representation as an *a priori* determinate manifold encountered externally. The form of material per se as material determined in the receptivity of the capacity for representation in general is the manifold in general; the form of external material per se as external material determined in sensory receptivity [: 381] is the externality of the manifold per se in general. Just as the form of every representation in general determined by the capacity for representation in general (receptivity and spontaneity taken together) is the unity of the manifold, so the form of representation determined by the capacity for representation along with its external sense is the unity of the manifold encountered externally. To the extent that the representation is related to an object and called intuition, this unity is then called the *form of intuition*.

§ LV.

The *a priori* determined form of internal sense consists in the determinate possibility of the *succession* of the manifold in representation arising through receptivity, and internal sense consists in the capacity to achieve representations through a manifold, in as much as this is given in bound, successive parts.

The susceptibility of external sense as receptivity in general can only be affected under the terms of the form of the manifold, – as susceptibility of internal sense. However, it can only be affected through a spontaneity whose action consists in being bound. The manifold can thus only affect internal sense insofar as it is grasped *in its manifold nature* through synthesis, that is, through successive apprehension of the parts of the manifold or, what amounts to the same thing, insofar as it must grasp [: 382] *every part* of the manifold through spontaneity in the process of binding. With the affectedness of internal susceptibility, the binding of the manifold must proceed *within* receptivity, and such binding must be affected through the action of synthesis in order to achieve its manifold (the material)[3]. The manifold can be given to it only insofar as spontaneity – in an action determined through the manifold nature of what is to be grasped – gives successive unity to the manifold through an affectivity of receptivity corresponding to each part of it.

§ LVI.

The *a priori* determined form of the representation of internal sense consists in the unity of the successively given manifold, which, in as much as it is related together with the representation to the object, is called the form of internal *intuition*.

Since the discussion of this paragraph was obliged to repeat § LIV, I will not continue the same discussion here.

It is essential to the representation of internal sense that the object of representation is not anything found outside the mind but is either a

---

3   There appears to be at least one (grammatical or typesetting) error in the original in this
    sentence.

modification of the mind per se or an element in the disposition of the capacity for representation. To this end a distinction is necessary in the mind between the reception of material given from without, through which representations are related to things outside the mind, and [: 383] reception of material given from within, through which representations are related to something in the mind. The way the mind is affected from without must be essentially different from the way it is affected from within, or the way it affects itself. In as much as receptivity is affected from without, it behaves merely in a passive manner, it binds nothing; material in its manifold nature based merely on the nature of receptivity is given to it. Its determinate capacity to be affected from without must therefore consist in the determinate externality of the non-successive, and consequently *simultaneously*, given manifold (in regard to internal susceptibility). In as much as it is affected from within and receives its determinate manifold through an action of spontaneity, it is only receptive to the manifold insofar as things are given to it through apprehension by way of its parts and consequently *not* in a simultaneous manner, but successively. The attribute of being given *simultaneously* is only accorded to objective material insofar as the material is not given through internal affection occurring successively.

§ LVII.

In as much as affectedness *from within* also belongs in essence to the representation of external sense, the unity of the successively given manifold is the *general form* of every sensory representation and consequently also of every intuition in general, and *sensibility in general* consists in the *a priori* determined capacity [: 384] to achieve representations through a manifold successively given to receptivity.

The material given from without can only become a representation insofar as its manifold is bound by receptivity, and, consequently, receptivity affected from without is also affected from within through a synthesis of spontaneity. The manifold thereby given from without is taken up into internal sense and becomes a representation bound by the receptivity of the capacity for representation, i.e. becomes a representation per se. The representation of *external* sense must therefore also consist of a successively given, spontaneously bound manifold to the extent that it simultaneously belongs to the internal sense, and the form of the representation of internal sense is thus at the same time the *general form* of all sensory representations, the *immediate* form of representations of internal sense and the *indirect* form of representations of external sense. The *a priori* determined way in which receptivity from within must be affected, or the successive givenness of the manifold determined in the mind, is also the form of sensibility in

general, i.e. not only of the internal but also of the external sense by means
of the internal, and is the direct form of internal sense and through this the
indirect form of external sense.

The characteristic attribute of sensory representation in general, the
characteristic rendered determinate *a priori* of every representation insofar
as it is said to be sensory, consists of the occurrence of a representation
through the successively given nature of the manifold. [: 385] Each sensory
representation insofar as it is related to the subject and called sensation
is also affectedness of receptivity through spontaneity per se in internal
sensation per se; it is affectedness from without in external sensation
through something distinct from the capacity for representation. In the case
of the latter, the affectedness from without must always be accompanied by
affectedness from within – the action of a contrary effect on receptivity – if
sensation is to occur, i.e. a representation modifies the mind and is not just
any mere impression on receptivity.

§ LVIII.

The representations of the *a priori* determined forms of sensory representation of external and internal intuition are *representations a priori*.

The material of all representations *a posteriori*, (of all empirical
representations), presupposes in the capacity for representation – insofar
as it is said to be objective, to be given from without, and to correspond
to objects outside the mind – the determinate susceptibility for a manifold
given externally, and, in as much as it is said to be determined through
the action of spontaneity in receptivity, a determinate susceptibility for a
successively given manifold. What is presupposed of all empirical material
for the possibility of representation as it is present in the capacity for
representation, however, [: 386] cannot be given to the mind in and through
the empirical material and the affectedness from without. Thus, when
something is represented, it is determined through material determined
in representation through the action of spontaneity *only according to its
actuality*, but which, according to its proper *disposition*, is determined prior
to all representation in the mind through the object present in the capacity
for representation (the object of external and internal affectedness), i.e. it is
represented by a representation *a priori*.

It is solely through the representing subject and the capacity for representation per se of this subject that what belongs to sensory representation
(and not to a sensory representation of this or that particular object
determined by an objective material) can be present in representation.
One would be obliged to cancel the distinction between the mind and
objects represented as existing outside the mind and thereby the *distinct*

consciousness of these objects if one wanted to derive from objects outside us what pertains to the representation per se and consequently what comes into representation through the capacity for representation. For the possibility of distinguishing in the mind so-called outside things has its ground in the circumstance that something in the representation of outside things belongs properly to the mind and to outside things – something which the mind represents to itself in distinct consciousness by representing as the representing entity the predicates of the forms of external and internal sense [: 387] and by representing through the predicates of objective material (that has assumed the form of sensory representation) what is distinguished from the representing entity and from things existing outside it. In the consciousness by which both the *I* and the *outside thing* is represented, the mind must represent in particular that *part of the object* which is *affected*, the external and internal sense, and represent it simply as its own property, in order to distinguish it from that *by which* it is *affected*, namely the outside thing, which is represented in a particular representation. If the forms of sensibility, therefore, were not determined *a priori*, and the representations of the same were not representations *a priori*, such distinct consciousness would not be possible.

"If both forms of sensibility are nothing but dispositions in the capacity for representation per se required to be present in the mind *a priori* before the commencement of experience, it is not evident why many other qualities of sensory representation per se, e.g. smells, colours, sounds, etc. are also not enabled by the disposition per se of the mind and represented *a priori*." This objection, often put to the author of the *Critique of Reason*, betrays an ambiguity in the conception of a *capacity*. One frequently takes a capacity to be nothing more than an *indeterminate* possibility (non-impossibility per se). In this way of understanding, an *a priori* capacity exists in my mind to attain an intuitive representation of the Emperor of China. [: 388] It must be admitted to whomever wants to call this indeterminate possibility a *capacity for representation* that we have as many capacities for representation as there are individual sensory representations. The *determinate* possibility, however, which makes up the capacity of a subject, is either determined through the disposition of the subject itself or through something distinct from the subject, i.e. is either an *original* capacity in the subject or a *derived* capacity. Now, the capacity for representation that alone is proper to the representing subject if clear consciousness of outside things is to be possible cannot possibly come from a derived ability not determined in the subject and determined only through something outside it. How should a representation in regard to its material be at all able to be related to something distinct from the mind, to a thing outside the mind, if all that is material in this representation does not pertain to the thing outside the mind and all that is immaterial but which is a part of the form of a representation as representation does not pertain to the mind, and consequently would not be determined through the material but in the form of the capacity for representation and would not be accorded its material given from without through the mind first of all? Thus, everything pertaining only to the form of *representation per se*, be it sensory or not, must be based on the disposition of the mind, determined *a priori* in the capacity for representation, and the determinate possibility in the subject to represent therefore constitutes the actual capacity for representation. But *only* everything [: 389] pertaining to the form per se of representation per se. For not everything proper to the material given from without and given to the capacity for representation through this material pertains to the representing subject whose predicate is the capacity for representation per se. Its possibility is not determinately present in the capacity for representation per se, but is only determined in the capacity for representation from without presupposed in it and can consequently only constitute a derived, empirical capacity, as, e.g. the capacity to attain representations through the eye, ear, etc. The predicates constituting the original capacity for representations, of which there are the derived and the empirical, are sufficiently distinguished through the attributes of *necessity* and *generality* that alone are proper to them.

§ LIX.

The material of representation of *space per se* is determined through the form of the external sense in the mind, and space per se insofar as it can be represented is nothing other than the *a priori* determinate *form of external intuition*.

I distinguish the representation of space *per se* from the representations of *full* and *empty* space. The latter are mixed and derived representations, the former is the pure and original representation of space. The representations of empty as well as full space contain attributes which are by no means essential to space per se, for space [: 390] must remain space no matter if it be full or empty. – "But is not at least one of these attributes essential to it? Is not space empty precisely because it is not full and not empty precisely because it is full?" – Emptiness admittedly follows of necessity from not being full and fullness from not being empty, but neither follows from space per se, in the same way that to be learned and not learned does not follow merely from being human, regardless of the fact that one of these two predicates must be assigned to every human being. The essential attribute of space is that it is immutable. Now, fullness or emptiness in regard to space is something very mutable; they are thus a merely contingent attribute of the concept of space per se. The representation of full space has space, *and* alongside space the fullness of space, as its object. The representation of *empty* space has space and emptiness of space as its object, which arises from the fact that one can remove in thought from space what fills it. Consequently, apart from the attribute of space per se, the representation of empty space has the attribute of the negation of fullness – an attribute that by no means is a part of the concept of space per se. It has to be said that it is not just the *common* type of representation that confuses empty space with space per se. *Famous* philosophers, too, have almost always been guilty of this confusion in their appraisal of the *Kantian theory of space*, and, by discussing the empirical origin of the representation of *empty* space, have believed themselves to have demonstrated the empirical origin of the representation of space *per se*. [: 391]

Representations of full and empty space are in no way *original* representations of space, i.e., representations relating immediately to space per se on its own as object and arising from material per se that corresponds to space as an object distinct from the representation of it. For both the predicate of full and empty space presupposes the representation of space as the subject of these predicates. One must not confuse the *original* representation of space per se determined above with the *empirically original representation* of space in general, that is with that representation in which space first occurs under the attributes of empirical representations in consciousness. Every representation *a priori* must precede an empirical representation in which the object of the former has proved itself to be, in regard to an objective material, the form of the representation per se. The empirically original representation of space is apparently that of *full* space from which gradually the representation of *empty* space resulted, from where again as a result of further analysis what is common to both, the representation of space *per se*, finally ascended to consciousness. This undeniably empirical origin of the representation of space caused the objections against the priority of the material of this representation, which, in all kinds of ways, defended the statement, never attacked by Kant, that the *actual* representation of space has an empirical origin. However, the empirical derivation of space can indicate the origin of its representation only insofar as the material [: 392] of the representation is presupposed as *given*. From *where* it is given cannot be identified through experience – an experience in which this material must be encountered as already given. Whence does the *material* come from which the representation of space arises – what is given in the representation per se of space to which the object distinguished from it corresponds? Is it a part of the objective or the subjective material? Is it determined in the mind *a priori*, or *a posteriori*? – These questions can only be answered on the basis of the determinate concept of the capacity for representation.

In regard to the representation of *space per se* I now maintain: that the *material* proper to it is determined according to the disposition of the material through the form of external sense *a priori* in the mind. For through this form, consisting in the determinate way of its being affected through an externally given manifold, the form of all objective material in the mind is determined. This is a form under which the objective material – the externality of its relation to the manifold – is alone able to occur as material in a representation of external sense. Now, no material can correspond to *space per se* in representation other than the *manifold in general under the form per se of externality*. For in regard to space per se: 1) only a manifold *in general* can be thought, not this or that particular manifold, nothing which corresponds to a determinate impression, no thing *in* space; 2) the externality of the manifold essential to *space per se* as object must be determined in the representation of space only *of* and [: 393] *through* the material because it alone is a form per se of the manifold per se, that is, of the material. Now, by spontaneity's producing unity with the form of the representation in the manifold in general determined under the form of externality, a representation arises immediately related to its object: *intuition of space per se*.

The *represented* space per se is thus none other than the *form of external intuition* itself, and every attribute of space per se must be derived from the form of external intuition and its direct representation. The form of external intuition consists, *first*, of the determinate form, which the *objective* material, i.e. the material given through affectedness from without, must assume in general in the representation per se of external sense in the *externality of the manifold. Secondly*, it consists of the *unity* through which this form of the material per se becomes the form of representation per se. These two components of the *form of external intuition* are the essential attributes of space per se in the externality per se of the manifold in general, and consist of a bound, connected, single externality. From the form of representation of external sense it is therefore completely evident why space consists of nothing but *bound* parts of which each must be conceived *again as space*, as a manifold existing externally – the *continuity* of space and its *infinite divisibility*. [: 394] – From here we can also comprehend the *succession* of parts in space and their *simultaneity* – a necessary consequence of the difference between the form of external and internal intuition. The latter consists of *succession alone*, the former *not* of succession but of *simultaneity*.

An actual *intuition* is the representation arising immediately from the material corresponding to the form of external intuition, for it arises immediately from the (*a priori*) determined manner of being affected in that its material itself is nothing other than the manner of affectedness from *without*. Now, in as much as each intuition is representation of an *individual* object and there is only a single form of external intuition, the proper characteristic of space – that it is only a *single* space and all diverse spaces are only part of one and the same space – is sufficiently explained.

Just as space per se can only be represented through an *intuition*, so the parts of space are represented only through *concepts*. Since nothing about an object can be distinguished through intuition per se, no particular part of space insofar as it is intuited per se is distinguished. Parts of space must be determined either through the material given in space or through the action per se of spontaneity. Insofar as they are to be *represented* as parts of space, in both cases they presuppose *concepts*, i.e. representations distinct from intuition [: 395] that relate only indirectly, i.e. through intuition, to space.

The indirect representation of the form of external intuition or of space per se is representation of *external sense*, which is to say, it is *external intuition*. It comes about through the determinate way of being affected from without, and although its material is determined not by an affectedness on account of an object outside us, but according to the *disposition* of affectedness in the capacity for representation per se according to its actuality, that is, according to the action of spontaneity in representation that affects its own receptivity in accordance with the form of external sense, this material itself is none other than the *manifold* corresponding to the form under which objects *outside us* are intuited. Representation of the form of external intuition is representation of the most general attribute assigned to all objects insofar as they can be intuited outside us. The form of external intuition is the condition determined in the mind under which alone objective material can occur *in* a representation and an object outside us *is capable of* being represented through it. Intuition of this form is admittedly not related to any actual objective material, however it *is* related to the possible objective material in the mind and through this material to *possible* objects outside us. Space per se therefore contains nothing actual existing outside us and to this extent is a mere *nullity*, compared to things existing in it [: 396] and external to the form of the intuition of them. Nevertheless, it ultimately encompasses the possibility of the actual and the *extended within* it. If one were to take extension from space it would remain space, but taking space from extension is impossible. The form of external intuition is necessarily related to objects outside us on account of the objective material that it turns into a representation, and space relates in this way necessarily to what is extended with the result that it cannot be conceived otherwise than with the possibility of extension. Representation of space is the intuiting representation of the possibility of extension.

The apparent paradox accompanying the statement that the representation of the form of external intuition, and thus the representation of an object that is not present outside the mind, is itself an external intuition, dissolves completely when one considers that this form present in the mind is precisely that *which* or *through which* the mind refers to things outside itself prior to every representation. If this form is represented, something relating in the mind to something outside the mind is represented. The form of external intuition has a double relation: namely, to the mind, insofar as it is based on the disposition of receptivity of the capacity for representation, and to something outside the mind, to the extent that it is the form that all objective material (given from without) must take in the mind. [: 397] It is thereby, as it were, the medium of communication between the mind and things outside the mind. The objective material obtained from these things and the form of external intuition obtained by the mind in representation constituting it makes up – when unified and related to the object – every (empirical) intuition of things outside us. The represented form per se of external intuition must therefore refer in the same direction as that of the representation whose form it is: to *something outside us*, and precisely for that reason it must also be represented as something existing outside us *in which* everything existing outside us must occur. For this reason it is completely intelligible why space – regardless of whether we consider it a substance or a contingent effect of a substance or a relation between several bodies (for space must also be thought where there is no body), and no matter that we cannot possibly locate it in the sequence of actual things and the elements of their constitution and notwithstanding that we are unable to consider it a mere *nullity*, indeed, in spite of all objections we might make through speculation – why space forces itself upon us, as it were, as something outside us lacking all the properties of real things.

Finally, we can say, requiring no further proof, that the form of external intuition is not any object existing outside our mind. Its representation is therefore also not any representation of an object existing outside us, but the intuition of the form that *all* objects [: 398] outside us must take through the objective material corresponding to them in representation, insofar as they are said to be *intuitable*. Representation of this form per se is representation of the manifold per se unified under the form of externality, which consequently is a *limited* externality, neither determined through an objective material in an empirical intuition nor through the understanding in a concept. Therefore, no determinate limit of the manifold existing externally can occur in the intuition of this form per se, and so it is evident why and to what extent space per se is *infinite*.

§ LX.

The direct representation of the form of external intuition or space per se is *intuition a priori*; space, to this extent, is a *necessary* object for us and through it *extension* is a *general* attribute of all intuitable objects outside us.

In view of what has been said in the *theory of the capacity for representation in general* about *representations a priori* and in the previous paragraphs about representation of the form of external intuition or space per se, the statement that this representation is intuition *a priori*, in as much as it is related immediately to its object, needs neither proof nor further discussion. Yet the fate of the *Critique of Reason* up till now [: 399] – so lamentably misunderstood on this point, admittedly following a different route of miscomprehension – necessitates an explicit, although otherwise superfluous, explanation, namely that I am *not* calling *space* itself intuition *a priori*, but only *representation* of it, and that I also call this intuition *a priori* not in the sense that it precedes *empirical* intuition nor that it is not drawn from *empirical* intuition of full space or *abstract* intuition of empty space, but only insofar as its material, which does not correspond to any object other than the form of external intuition, is determined according to its constitution only through a form of external sense that cannot be given on the basis of an empirical impression but must be present in the mind as a condition of external affectedness *a priori*.

As the object of a representation *a priori*, space is a *necessary object* for our mind. Since the determinate possibility of being affected by something existing outside us necessarily pertains to our capacity for representation and thus constitutes a necessary component of this capacity and is the external sense inseparable from our receptivity, and since the form of external intuition thereby determined is the form all objective material must assume if representation of things outside us is to be possible, for this reason such a form is just as necessary to our mind as the possibility of representing outside things. Space per se is thus inseparable from our mind. Therefore, we are certainly able [: 400] to remove all objects from space in thought, but not to dispense with space itself, and we must forever represent space when we want to represent things outside us, and, finally, we are not even able to have a representation of what is *present outside us* without invoking the assistance of space in the process.

Along with the aspect of necessity space, as an object or a representation *a priori*, has the additional aspect of *generality*. It has generality to the extent that space is the *a priori* determinate form of every external empirical intuition and thus is a *general attribute* of every intuitable *thing outside us* – a thing to which it is related simultaneously with the representation. Thus, all things outside us are not only present in space but must also *fill* and be extended as part of space. The material corresponding in representation to the object outside us given as a result of being affected from without can only become a representation on the basis of the form of external intuition which the material assumes in the mind, and, in its indivisible unification with this form, is only related to its object, as a result of which the material can only be represented in terms of this form, and consequently only as something which *fills* and *extends space*.

As an object of representation *a priori* space is *dependent on experience* to the extent that experience consists in the givenness of a material *a posteriori*. For space is the condition which must be determined in the mind if the objective material, which cannot be given otherwise than *a posteriori*, occurs in the mind [: 401] and is to become a representation. *In this respect* representation of space is independent of experience, namely, in regard to its material determined *a priori* in the mind, although in regard to its origin as a real representation it depends on the givenness of an objective material in an empirical representation. For without this latter the external *a priori* determined form would not have any instigation to determine the form of external intuition of this material, and this intuition would be as little able to represent form per se as any other form that has not occurred in concreto in a material, no matter whether this form is given with or through the material. – Nothing is therefore more readily comprehended than how all preceding attempts to derive space from experience without this restriction necessarily had to founder, and why one section of philosophers who consider space per se as something real and independent of things was obliged to acknowledge this standpoint to be a necessary, infinite and independent – nonsense, whereas the other group, which looked upon space as a relation per se between things, could neither explain why space must be thought as something infinite, nor why it is also there when things are not, and how it happened that the properties of space per se would *necessarily* have to be assigned to things that fill space.

From the *necessity* of a space that depends on the determinations of the mind there results the otherwise inexplicable *apodictic certainty* [: 402] *of geometry* which is nothing but a science of the necessary properties of space not demonstrated through concepts per se but concepts relating immediately to intuitions. If the substratum of geometry – space per se – is necessary, each of its properties must be necessary. Space, however, can only be represented as necessary in my consciousness in as much as it is a condition of actuality. Since space per se as the form of my external intuition is not any object existing outside me, I know that the attribute of space called e.g. a *triangle* and all properties of this triangle which must be ascribed to space in my representation, i.e. to space and the triangle *in itself*, that all possible triangles which my imagination can sketch in advance and all real triangles that occur to me in the world of the senses, all *must* have the same properties – something I could not will if the substratum of the triangle were only known to me from an experience whose testimony does not extend further than the given cases.

§ LXI.

Through the form of internal sense the material of representation of *time per se* in the mind is determined *a priori,* and time per se, insofar as it can be represented, is nothing but the *a priori* determined form of internal intuition. [: 403]

Here as well I distinguish *full* and *empty* time from *time per se,* which can only be the object of the pure (unmixed) and original representation of time (original on account of its material per se and thus relating immediately to time). The essence of time can consist neither in fullness nor in emptiness. Both together are predicates of time that in no way constitute the concept of time as subject, but only presuppose this. In terms of time per se neither the succession of real things is indicated nor the succession of our representations nor the order of planetary movements nor something else through which anything that fills time as a component of time itself as its internal condition and the essential content of the concept of time *per se.* I admit, indeed I contend according to my theory, that representation of time per se must arise *not in the absence of* the empirical representation of full time but only in *accordance with* it, and to the extent that the abstract must occur in the concrete in respect of the gradual development of our concepts, only *through* this. But I also maintain that the material that corresponds to time per se in the representation of it in no way is given through affectedness from without (which I consider indispensable for the reality of the representation of time per se), but, on the contrary, is determined according to its disposition and its proper form through the form per se of internal sense *a priori* in the mind.

The form of all material in general is determined on the basis of the form of internal sense consisting in the determinate manner of being affected through a successively given [: 404] manifold, a form under which that material alone can occur as material in a representation of internal sense – namely the succession of the manifold. Now, no material can correspond to time per se in its representation other than *the manifold in general under the form per se of succession.* For in relation to time per se 1) only a manifold in general can be thought, not this or that particular manifold, not something in time, and nothing which would correspond to a determinate impression. 2) The succession of the manifold essential in thought to time per se as object must be determined in its representation per se solely of and through the material, because the succession of the manifold is a form per se of the manifold per se, i.e. of the material itself. Now, by spontaneity's producing *unity* with the form of representation from the manifold in general determined under the form of succession, a representation occurs that is related immediately to its object (that to which its material corresponds).

Represented time per se is therefore nothing other than the form of *internal intuition* itself, and every attribute of time per se must be derived from the form of internal intuition and its immediate representation. The form of internal intuition consists, *first*, of the determinate form that every material given to internal receptivity as the material of internal intuition in representation per se must assume [: 405] in the succession of the manifold; *secondly*, of the unity through which this form of material per se becomes the form of representation per se. These two components of the form of internal intuition are the essential attributes of *time per se*, which consists in the succession per se of the manifold in general in a *bound*, connected and single succession. It can be easily seen from the form of internal intuition, therefore, why time per se consists of nothing but bound parts of which each must be thought again as time, as a successively occurring manifold: the *continuity* of time as well as its *infinite divisibility*. From this it can also be seen why nothing can happen in time per se *simultaneously*. Simultaneity presupposes the form of *externality* of space per se and can only be thought on the basis of the *binding* of time and space[4].

The representation consisting immediately of the material corresponding to the form per se of internal intuition is an actual intuition, for it immediately arises from the (*a priori* determined) manner of being affected since its material is itself nothing but the manner of affectedness from *within*. Now, in as much as each intuition is a representation of an individual object and there is only one *single* form of internal intuition, the idiosyncratic aspect of time – that it is only one single time and all the various times are only parts of one and the same time – can be satisfactorily explained. [: 406]

Just as time per se can only be represented through an intuition, the parts of time are only represented through concepts. They must be determined either through the material grasped in time or through the action per se of spontaneity. In both cases, in as much as they are to be represented as parts of time, they presuppose *concepts*, i.e. representations variously stemming from intuition that are related only on the basis of intuition to time.

The immediate representation of the form of internal sense is itself a representation of internal sense and thus is *internal intuition*. It occurs through the determinate manner of being affected from within, and although its material does not consist in a manifold given from without and taken up into internal sense, but, on the contrary, is determined according to its disposition in the capacity for representation per se in line with its actuality in representation per se through the spontaneity affected in relation to its receptivity following the form of internal sense, nevertheless this material is a real and determinate manifold in the mind that has its determinate object in the form under whose terms *a thing* can be intuited in ourselves *a*

---

4 Our translation of this sentence ignores typographical errors in the original.

posteriori, but in such manner that everything which can be intuited *in us a posteriori*, namely *change* within ourselves, can only be intuited within us ourselves and only as an object of *internal* intuition. The representation of the form of internal sense is to this extent representation of the most general attribute that must be accorded to everything *a posteriori* within us as existing within us. Everything [: 407] that can be represented as existing in the representing subject is either the *a priori* represented form of the capacity for representation per se, under whose terms the form of internal sense also belongs, or real representation itself, to the extent that it can be represented as a thing existing *a posteriori* in the mind, which latter can only occur according to the form of internal intuition, i.e. in time per se. Thus, representations must also be represented under the general predicate of *full* time within us, as modifications within us.

The form of internal intuition is the condition determined in the mind under whose terms alone a manifold (as subjective material) occurs in a representation, and through this manifold an empirical object, i.e. a modification in the mind, can be represented within us. The intuition of this form per se is thus related not to any real affectedness, but indeed to all possible affectedness from within, and through this to possible modification within us. *Time per se* contains, therefore, no real modification, and is only a nullity when compared with the changes occurring in full time and separated from the form of its intuition. Nevertheless, in the final instance, it grasps the possibility of reality within itself, i.e. of change within itself. If one removed change from time it would still remain time per se, but if one then removed time from change, change would not be possible. The form of internal intuition [: 408] is related to change within us as a representable object necessarily by means of the internal affectedness according to which it becomes intuitable, and time is thus so necessarily related to change that it cannot be conceived other than in terms of the possibility of change. Representation of time is the intuiting representation of the possibility of change.

Intuition of the form per se of internal sense is intuition of a manifold per se in general insofar as this is unified under the form of succession. The manifold in general occurring in this intuition can for this very reason neither be determined through an empirical material nor through the action of spontaneity, and consequently cannot be *limited*. No limitation of succession can occur in the intuition of time per se, and thus it is evident how and to what extent time per se is *infinite*.

§ LXII.

The immediate representation of the form of internal intuition or of time per se is *intuition a priori*; time per se is to this extent a *necessary* object for us and through it *change within us* is the general attribute of all our representations in as much as they are objects of internal sense.

This paragraph will present no difficulties after what has been said before if one guards [: 409], for instance, against confusing time with the representation of time per se. The *material* of the representation of time is determined according to its *disposition a priori* immediately in the mind – not the representation of time or time itself. Time is not the form of internal *sense*, but the form of internal *intuition*, and arises merely out of the form of internal sense (succession per se), to the extent that it has received through spontaneity the form of representation, the unity of the manifold.

As an object of a representation *a priori* time is a *necessary* object for our mind. Since the determinate possibility of being affected by spontaneity is necessarily part of our capacity for representation and constitutes an essential component of it and is the internal sense that is inseparable from our receptivity, and since the form of internal intuition determined through this sense is the form that every material must take insofar as internal sense is said to be affected by it, such form is as essential to our mind as the possibility of representation in general and particularly the possibility of internal intuition. Time is therefore inseparable from our mind. It is for that reason that we can remove every object from time in our mind but not time itself, that when we represent our own representations to ourselves as something really occurring we must also represent time, and that we can have no representation of any presentness *within ourselves* without the assistance of time and without thinking of what *arises* within us. [: 410]

As an object of a representation *a priori* time acquires the attribute, along with necessity, of *generality*, insofar as it is a general and immediate attribute of objects within us and of every *change* within us as an *a priori* determined form of each empirical, internal intuition. From this it can be seen why everything that is an object of a representation of internal sense, of a representation that has arisen through the manner of affectedness from within, must not only be present in time but also fill a part of time, a part of the manifold corresponding to time, i.e. be *change*.

As an object of a representation *a priori* time per se is dependent on experience, to the extent that experience consists in the givenness of a material *a posteriori*. For it is the condition that must be determinately present in the mind if the material *a posteriori* is to be grasped into internal sense and a representation is to arise. *In this respect* the representation of time is also dependent upon experience, although with respect to its origin as a particular representation it depends on the givenness of an objective material as well as of affectedness through spontaneity. – Every attempt to derive the representation of time from experience that neglects the circumstance that the constitution of the material corresponding to time per se in representation must be determined *a priori* in the mind must necessarily fail and deny time either its *necessity* or turn it into an independent and eternal nonsensical thing. [: 411]

§ LXIII.

Time is the *general form of all intuitions* in general, and therefore it is an essential attribute of objects insofar as they are intuitable.

The form of internal intuition is the general form of every intuition in general insofar as the material of all sensory representation can be bound by spontaneity simply in terms of the form of internal sense in receptivity or, which amounts to the same thing, can be taken up under the form of a successive manifold into internal sense. Time is therefore also a form of external intuition, but only indirectly by means of an internal sense that must be affected in external intuition, and time must be related along with the sensory representation of external sense to the object (existing outside us) and so occurs under the attributes of this object. Every intuitable object must therefore be intuited *in time*.

However, time cannot be any *immediate* attribute of objects outside us, of objects in space. The manifold corresponding to the object outside us in as much as the object must be thought through the understanding as something existing for itself can only be intuited according to the form of external sense in space per se, a space in which it alone is able to be given, and the time of this space can only be maintained indirectly and, indeed, only as a negative characteristic, that is to say, the object, in as much as [: 412] it is thought of as existing *outside us*, can only be intuited as something that does not fill time per se and does not run continuously with it, but that *endures in space*, just as enduring qualities can be assigned to it in space alone, and consequently not in terms of the form of succession, but as *simultaneous* parts.

"Yet in the objects *outside us changes* also occur, and of these objects attributes are apparent which only become real in time and thus are apparent proof of the fact that time is also something outside us and should not be thought of as the form per se of our intuitions." I answer: *for one thing* these changes are in no way intuited in time per se, but in space *and* in time taken together, and their most general predicate is *motion*, change in space and in time. If the time in which these changes are intuited were not the form per se of our intuition there would also not be space. *For another thing*, such changes to the objects distinct from our representations can only be *represented* insofar as they occur in representation per se and are related with and through this to the object. Change outside us can only be represented through a change within us; the representation of this thus depends on the form determined in the capacity for representation

under which alone change *within us* can occur, that is to say, it depends on
the susceptibility [: 413] for a successively given manifold determined in
receptivity, on *time per se* determined in our mind.

All succession in receptivity is possible in receptivity only insofar as it is
internal sense in the same way that all externality is possible only insofar
as it is external sense. All actual succession can be determined in receptivity
only through the spontaneity of the capacity for representation, just as all
real externality can be determined only through an outside impression. For,
in as much as the manifold is given to receptivity *successively*, it can only be
given in *bound* parts, only by way of synthesis, only through the action of
a grasping, apprehending spontaneity. Succession represented through the
process of intuition of movement occurring together with externality can
occur in representation per se only insofar as spontaneity grasps something
given successively at the same time as the objective material, i.e. according
to the form of internal sense. – "What, then, would the difference between
change within us and outside us consist of, if both were attributable to
the work of spontaneity?" – It would consist of the fact that both are the
work of spontaneity in different ways. Change within us is entirely the work
of spontaneity as representation per se of internal sense. This is not the
case with respect to change outside us that in no way can be considered a
representation per se. Spontaneity certainly affects internal sense according
to the form proper to it, yet not through itself, but, on the contrary, is
determined toward this action on the basis of that by which external sense is
affected. I will attempt [: 414] to illuminate this obscure area of the human
mind by giving a few pointers.

The affectedness that occurs in the mind under the form of the successively
given manifold is related simply either to the representing subject or to a
represented object, a thing outside us. The former occurs with representation
of internal sense, the latter with representation of motion. In both cases the
possibility of succession determined in the capacity for representation per
se, and the *grasping* of the manifold insofar as it is a part of succession in
representation, must be the work of spontaneity and consequently occurs
only in *internal sense*. In the former case, real succession is the work of an
action of spontaneity per se and is thus also called change *within us* and is
the form of each actual sensory representation insofar as this is related to
the subject and is sensation. In the latter case, real succession is the effect
not of spontaneity per se alone, but of a successively grasping spontaneity
determined by an action of something outside us, and is called a change
in us in consideration of this determination from without, and is also the
material of the representation of actual motion. In as much as the action of
grasping material successively is the effect per se of spontaneity, it occurs
with every sensory representation and consequently also with external

intuition, but it is not represented and not immediately related to the object with its objective material. [: 415] It is therefore represented only under the form of objective material, only in space alone, and consequently in terms of the simultaneity of its attributes and of what is durable. If the reason why a manifold is grasped successively in representation is determined in representation from without, receptivity is affected from without but not according to the form per se of external sense alone, and if in respect of the objective material something according to the form of internal sense is given, that is to say, given in such a manner that it can be grasped in space but not in space per se, then spontaneity is determined not through itself but through affectedness from without to grasping in succession, and this determination to grasping whereby the mind behaves more passively than actively and to which the mind was determined through an object distinct from itself is simultaneously related with the objective material to the thing outside us, and is represented as a change within us insofar as it exists in space and in consequence exists outside us. It would certainly be inconsistent to wish to characterize time per se, the form of internal sense, as the form in which changes outside us occur since space and time in their essential connection are the form of motion and change outside us. But it would also be just as inconsistent to attribute time per se, the form per se of the existence of the succession of the manifold in general (of the material per se of a representation) to *things in themselves*, since it can only be related through itself, and consequently [: 416] only through the form of external intuition to things outside us.

If we remain true to the conception of what the *theory of the capacity for representation in general* has established of the *thing in itself*, we are so little likely to contradict the statement that time per se is a form per se of intuition that we must rather affirm it. For if all representation of a thing in itself is impossible, not a single representable predicate can accompany the *thing in itself*, and consequently neither can space nor time nor anything else apart from the general predicate of a subject per se without any of its predicates. And even through this it does not yet become a thing in itself, but is conceived as a predicate grounded in our understanding. Represented space per se and represented time per se can thus not possibly be attributed to the thing in itself. Even the material corresponding to them in their pure representations cannot be any objective material given through affectedness from without belonging to things in themselves, since such material can only be given *according to its disposition* through the essential form determined *a priori* in the mind under which receptivity from without and from within must be affected. Such material, following what is presupposed of every objective material in view of the nature of the capacity for representation per se in the mind, cannot be given through this objective material. [: 417]

§ LXIV.

The relatedness of an empirical representation to its determinate object is called cognition *a posteriori*, of a representation *a priori* cognition *a priori*. Of all objects (distinct from the capacity for representation per se) only cognition *a posteriori* or empirical cognition is possible.

Every representation is *empirical* to the extent that its material is not determined in the capacity for representation per se, but through affectedness in the mind. All objects distinct from the capacity for representation per se can only be known empirically, for in the capacity for representation per se nothing is determinately present but the form per se of this. The objects of *internal* sense distinct from the capacity for representation per se are changes within us, or the representations themselves, to the extent that they are sensations, and as internal sensations through affectedness by spontaneity alone are determined simultaneously as *external* sensations through affectedness *from without*. The objects of *external* sense distinct from the capacity for representation per se, by contrast, are the *objects outside us* to which a given material must correspond through affectedness from without. Of both types of objects distinct from our capacity for representation only empirical representations and thus also only *empirical cognitions* are possible. Our cognition *a priori* is restricted solely to the capacity for representation and to cognition per se itself, capacities in which [: 418] the forms of receptivity and spontaneity, the forms of sensibility and – as will be shown more clearly in the following – also of understanding and reason, must be determined as objects of representation *a priori* prior to any affectedness.

§ LXV.

The object of an empirical intuition, in as much as it can be represented only in terms of those forms of intuition determined *a priori* in the mind and consequently that are proper to the mind and not the *thing in itself*, is called an *appearance*. Thus only *appearances* are cognizable empirically.

The essential difference between the meaning of the word appearance [*Erscheinung*] established here and what one normally conceives under the term *seeming* [*Schein*] cannot be dealt with here.

Intuition is an essential component of all cognition, and empirical intuition is an essential component of all empirical cognition. In regard to sensory representation the form of sensory representation, which belongs to the mind *a priori* and which cannot be separated from the material in consciousness determined *a posteriori*, must be related to the object if intuition is to arise and the object is to be intuited. The object is therefore not intuited as it is in itself but as it appears in terms of the form belonging to it intuited in the mind. – The object appears and is to this extent an appearance. And since the object is only able to be cognized [: 419] insofar as an intuition of it is possible, it can only be cognized as an *appearance*.

§ LXVI.

Space and *time* are essential conditions of every appearance but not of things in themselves, and essential attributes of all that is cognizable distinct from our capacity for representation but not of all conceivable things, and they are the limits of our cognitive capacity but not of the nature of things in themselves.

An appearance is the object of empirical intuition. Empirical intuition is only possible through the form of intuition determined in the mind, i.e. through space per se and time per se, thus an appearance is possible with respect to what is subjective about it (what must pertain to the mind alone) only through time and space – an external appearance on the basis of space and time, an internal appearance on the basis of time only. But precisely for this reason space and time cannot be conditions of the thing in itself, that is, of what corresponds to the material per se of a representation alone, external representation, and must therefore in essence be distinct from every representation. No objective material pertaining to the things in themselves outside us can correspond to space per se and time per se in the representation of them because they must be determined in the mind prior to all objective material as conditions of possible ways to receive this material.

Space per se and time per se are essential attributes of everything *cognizable*. To the extent that the predicate of space [: 420] contradicts an object, it cannot possibly be perceived as an object distinct from the capacity for representation per se and our representations, or, which amounts to the same thing: if an object distinct from our capacity for representation per se and our representations is to be cognized, a material must correspond to it under the form of external intuition in representation and consequently must itself be represented in terms of the predicate of full space or extension. Our *representations* themselves, however, can only be perceived as something *real within us* insofar as full time can be predicated of them and insofar as they are *changes* within us. Space and time are only attributes of the empirically cognizable in as much as the empirically cognizable is cognizable. To wish to make them into attributes of things in themselves would not only be to represent the unrepresentable, but also to dispense with the distinction between the mind and things outside the mind, a distinction which can actually consist only in the circumstance that the forms of the capacity for representation and of cognition are not the forms of things in themselves, just as clear consciousness of the objects outside us is only possible by virtue of the fact that the mind is able to distinguish what is proper to it (through intuitions *a priori*) from what is proper to the things outside us (through empirical intuitions).

The actual *limits of our cognitive capacity* are given as universally valid on the basis of the conditions and attributes of *cognizability* found in space per se and time per se. [: 421] We have the capacity to distinguish in precise terms the region of cognizable things from that of the uncognizable. We therefore know, for example, that the soul (as *substance*), insofar as it is not the (*a priori* cognizable) capacity for representation per se but the subject of this capacity, is not cognizable at all because all objects distinct from the capacity for representation per se that are not said to be representations per se, if they are to be cognizable, must be represented in space, i.e. *outside us*. But the region of cognizability not extending beyond sensibility is not yet the region of the conceivable, much less of the things in themselves not representable to us, both of which must be carefully distinguished.

The region of the *conceivable* can only be distinguished in a precise way once the nature of *thought* is given. For this, the following investigation of the *understanding*, or of the second essential component of the cognitive capacity, shall prepare the way.

[: 422]

Theory of the Understanding

§ LXVII.

Representation arising directly through the manner in which spontaneity is active is called the *concept in the narrower sense*, and the capacity to succeed to representations through the manner in which spontaneity is active is called the *understanding in the narrower sense*.

We have called representation in general, in as much as a binding of the manifold must make it occur, the *concept*, and spontaneity, insofar as it is engaged in the process of this general action of binding, the *understanding in the narrower sense*. A concept, in this meaning, can also be called an intuition to the extent that is a *type* of representation in general and cannot occur without a binding of the manifold. On the other hand an intuition is a representation arising directly through the manner of its being affected and indirectly though the action of spontaneity insofar as an affectedness of receptivity binds what is given and only insofar as it is given, i.e. according to the manner of its affectedness. The indirect reason for a representation's occurrence here lies in affectedness per se and the constitution of the same. –

However, [: 423] we have already become acquainted above (p. 347) with a different type of representation indispensable for all cognition and intuition possessing a quite opposite constitution – a representation, namely, not immediately affected at all in the manner of receptivity but, on the contrary, acting directly the way spontaneity acts, i.e. it arises through binding. The material of this representation is not raw material – the given immediately affected by affectedness – but a material that has already received the form of a representation, is already representation and consequently has been processed by spontaneity already. Through another binding of this already bound manifold a new representation now occurs that grasps not a givenness resulting directly from affectedness, but an already represented manifold – the *concept* in the narrower sense. The immediate reason for the occurrence of this representation does not lie in affectedness but in the action of spontaneity in its proper mode of action, in a binding through which a new unity is produced in the represented manifold – a unity of the represented. Spontaneity acts here to a far higher degree. Its action is not any contrary effect per se, is no immediate consequence of being acted upon. It is not enforced through any affectedness. It is the action of the *understanding in the narrower sense* which I call *thought* in the same sense.

In every concept in general two bound representations must occur: one from which [: 424] the concept has arisen, and the concept itself. The first representation takes the place of the object itself and to this extent is called the subject, or the object. The second representation is representation of the represented through the first and is called the *predicate*, or the attribute of the object. The concept is a representation that is related through its attribute to the object. To relate an attribute to an object, to bind a predicate (positively or negatively) with a subject means *to judge* in an extended sense, and the product of an action called judgment is a representation which consists of two bound representations arising through binding – a concept. Language usage determines the word *understanding* in the narrower sense in the meaning of the capacity to judge, and thus confirms our explanation defining the understanding in the narrower sense as the capacity to succeed to representations through the action of spontaneity.

However, in the following it will be shown that not every representation from which a new representation arises through the action of spontaneity can be an intuition, and that spontaneity through its mode of action produces, also from concepts, a new type of representation we will call an *idea*. If, therefore, the concept in the narrower sense means every representation that arises through the mode of action of spontaneity, it is also the case that the concept in this meaning is a species containing the idea or the representation arising through spontaneity from concepts, and the concept or the representation produced from intuition through spontaneity contains the concept in the narrowest sense as *types* within itself. The meaning of the word *understanding* must accordingly be explained in more detail.

§ LXVIII.

The representation which arises from an *intuition* through the action of *spontaneity* is called the *concept*, and the capacity of spontaneity to produce concepts from intuitions through its action is called *understanding in the narrowest sense*.

Ordinary language often uses the word *understanding* in a sense that includes *reason*, but far more frequently uses it in its most appropriate sense to mean a capacity distinct from *reason*. Far less strictly, then, *understanding* in language usage tends to mean the capacity to think insofar as to think encompasses both *judging* and *inferring*. In the strictest sense, however, it means the capacity to make actual *judgments*. I say to make *actual judgments*, for inferring is also not infrequently called to judge, partly because a or syllogism consists of nothing but bound judgments, and partly because the result of the syllogism – the binding of the predicate with the subject – is a judgment in its final statement differing from other judgments in that the predicate of the [: 426] major premises was able to be related to the subject by means of another predicate, whereas with judgments in the strict sense the predicate is immediately related to the subject. A judgment is distinguished from a syllogism as a direct judgment is distinguished from an indirect one; and if the capacity to make inferences, to judge by indirect means, is *rational*, actual understanding can only consist in the capacity to judge by direct means. A direct judgment means an *intuiting* judgment (*Iudicium intuitivum*) not in the sense that it consists in an *intuition* per se, for in intuiting per se no judging is carried out, but because in such a judgment the predicate is related to an intuition per se, to a representation that immediately relates to the object not distinguished from it by a representation in consciousness, and whose place it consequently takes in the judgment. In the case of an intuiting judgment, the subject is not thought but intuited, and the predicate is consequently not related to what is thought through an attribute of indirect representation, but, on the contrary, is related to what is immediately represented, to the object itself. The predicate therefore can only be a representation that has arisen from intuition per se through the action of spontaneity – a concept in the narrowest sense.

When one considers that every material of a representation – even that which is determined according to its disposition in the capacity for representation per se and corresponds to no other object than the forms per se of the capacity for representation – must arise and be given through an affectedness in real representation [: 427], it becomes more obvious why an intuition must precede every actual concept, i.e. a representation in which the material per se is given through affectedness, and that actual understanding is the capacity that mediates between sensibility and reason, a mediation whose materials are delivered to it by sensibility and which prepares sensibility for processing by reason. Sensibility provides *intuitions*, i.e. representations that immediately relate to an object; the understanding provides *concepts*, i.e. representations that relate to the object through an attribute; reason provides *ideas*, i.e. representations that relate to objects through an attribute of the attribute (the mediating concept). If one calls the real element in a representation the *reality* of the representation, and the real in a representation through the operation of the capacity for representation *subjective* reality, and that which is real by affectedness through the means of the objective material *objective reality*, then, with respect to objective reality, the *first* level is attributed to *outer intuition* relating the real object independent of our mind immediately to what is not representation and not mind; the *second* level is attributed to the *concept*, i.e. a representation relating immediately not to the thing itself but only to an intuition; and the *third* level, finally, to the *idea*, which relates through an attribute of the concept to intuition, in other words, directly to the concept, and consequently has neither a thing nor an intuition as its *nearest* object but only a concept. In regard to subjective reality [: 428] this order is reversed, and one can take the following as axiomatic: *the greater the subjective reality of our representations, the more restricted their objective reality, and vice versa.*

The more spontaneity is involved in a representation, the more subjective reality there is in a representation; the less the involvement of spontaneity and the greater the share of affectedness from without, the more the representation has objective reality. The latter is the case with *outer empirical intuition*. The reason for the subjective reality of a representation actually lies in the *action* of spontaneity, just as the reason for the objective reality of a representation lies in the *action of the thing outside us*. But since representation can only be intuited in time and only in terms of the form of *change within us*, and since the thing outside us can only be *intuited* in space and only under the form of *extension* and consequently can only be *cognized* in terms of these forms, so it is that *change* within us and *extension* – essential attributes of the subjectively and objectively real, or the actual, to the extent that it is empirically cognizable, the latter for everything that is within us, the former for everything that is outside us as something *real* in the strictest sense and distinct from our capacity for representation per se – so it is that change within us and extension are cognized. This has been suspected for a long time in the philosophical world, yet a mistaken concept of the *thing in itself* prevented philosophers from reaching agreement among themselves. For the *materialists*, *extension* since time immemorial has been the essential quality of what is real, exists for itself and has duration in space, but this meant [: 429] they were not able to acknowledge the existence of representations. For the *spiritualists*, by contrast, *change within us*, representation, was the first criterion of all actuality (the *Cogito; ergo sum*). Change for them was the immediate attribute of everything real and only through this could one make inferences *indirectly* about the actuality outside the representing entity. Leibniz, the greatest of the spiritualists and the philosopher who completed this thought system, held representation to be such an exclusive feature of the real that he turned everything real existing for itself, all *substances* – from the *divine* to the elements of matter – into representing subjects (monads), and declared *extension* to be a mere illusion. Spinoza, on the other hand, made both *representation* and *extension* into essential and necessary properties of what exists for itself, substance, apparently because he looked upon representation and extension, not without justification, as being essential features of the properly *actual*.

§ LXIX.

The unity produced by the binding of the manifold represented by intuition is called *objective unity*, and is the most general form according to which the object (of an intuition) is *thought* and the most general attribute of all cognizable objects, to the extent that they are able to be thought.

In language usage the word *object* κατ' εξοχηεν means the full compass of [: 430] properties and things constituting it that are thought together and are attributes of one and the same representation: a whole made up of interconnected determinations, an *individual*. The *binding* of the attributes thus constitutes the essence of what is thought under the word object – an object which would cease to be a full compass and an individual if this binding were removed from it.

I call the unity produced through the binding of the manifold in intuition *objective unity*, partly in order to distinguish it from the unity of representation per se belonging to sensory representation, intuition itself, and partly because it is really a unity of the represented, i.e. of the object. What is combined within it is that which is represented by sensory representation, that which is contained in the sensory representation, the intuition and the manifold that is related to the object.

I call *objective unity* the form under which the *object* is thought in order to distinguish it from the form under which the object is intuited, the form of intuition per se, of the unity of the *given* manifold consisting of the binding of the manifold that is not yet represented and has not yet received the form of representation but is material per se. The representation per se of the *represented* object, intuition per se, arises through the binding of this material per se. It is *not yet distinguished* from representation per se. On the other hand, the representation of what is distinct from the representation per se, the *concept* of the object, arises through the binding of what is represented in intuition [: 431].

I call *objective unity* the form under which the object is thought. The object is thought to the extent that it is represented by a representation distinct from intuition (i.e. of the sensory representation immediately related to it). It is intuited through sensory representation, that is to say, represented under a form which it receives through the material corresponding to it and through the form of intuition in the mind. It is thought through the concept, i.e. represented under the form given to it by the understanding, as a unity distinct from representation per se in which the attributes occurring in intuition are combined by a particular action of the mind.

Objective unity is the form of the object in general insofar as it is conceivable. That to which intuition is related with respect to its material, and consequently only occurs through the manifold corresponding to it in representation, becomes an *object* in consciousness only when and insofar as this manifold is bound in a unity distinct from representation per se. The binding of the manifold occurring in intuition is the reason for the origin of the representation of the object as object, and in this aspect is nothing other than the unity of the represented manifold. [: 432]

This unity is therefore the proper *attribute* of the *conceivable* object in general, and consequently of all objects insofar as they are conceivable as objects. It is the predicate which must accompany *what is intuited* if this is to be *thought* as object, something which is only possible through the fact that, as a predicate, objective unity as the subject in consciousness is bound to what is intuited. An *object in general* can only be thought by assigning to something that is not representation, yet is nevertheless representable, the predicate of objective unity, the unity of the manifold represented in a representation.

Since this unity is produced by spontaneity to the extent that it is called understanding, and since it is produced by the mind and consequently cannot be given with the objective material by a thing outside affecting us, it cannot possibly pertain to the *thing in itself* insofar as it is the thing in itself. It is therefore also only the form of the object insofar as it is conceivable, not the form of the *thing in itself*, something usually confused till now with the *conceivable* thing (the intelligible thing) to the detriment of philosophy. Even the understanding is not capable of conceiving the object as the *thing in itself* but is only able to conceive it under a form which is determined *a priori* according to its nature as the representation (the concept) proper to it, i.e. as the objective unity produced through the binding of its intuited attributes. But anyone having a different understanding of these matters (something not possible even for philosophers according to the manner of doing philosophy till now) [: 433] will be content with the form of the object insofar as it can be thought, with the conceivable form, without wishing to conceive the form of the object to the extent that this cannot be conceived, the inconceivable thing. The *thing in itself* is that which is outside us that is appropriate to the material per se of our representation without its form; something to which, therefore, no form of our representation – neither an intuition nor a concept – may be related and that consequently cannot be intuited nor thought. If anyone takes the thing in itself to be nothing but objective unity itself (as is universally the case when one really wishes to think something), the thing in itself will be conceivable but not as a thing distinct from its representation and independent of its faculty of represention but, on the contrary, as a mere concept that can only be more than this when it relates to an intuition in which a material is determined through its being affected. What this material outside representation corresponds to is called, with some justification, the object, but it can only be represented as something different from intuition when the form in the sole terms of which an object is conceivable, objective unity, is related to it – not therefore as the *thing in itself*, but as the thing conceived under the most general form of a concept: For

§ LXX

The unity of the represented manifold, or objective unity, is the most general [: 434] and, according to the nature of the understanding, the *a priori* determinate form of the *concept in general*, and representation of objective unity is representation – the *concept a priori*.

The concept is the representation arising out of an intuition through the mode of action of spontaneity. Its form as a concept must thus consist in the unity of the intuited manifold, just as its form as representation in general consists in the unity of the manifold in general, and just as the form of intuition in general consists in the unity of the successively grasped and given manifold. As unity in general, this form of the concept is based (in the process of binding) on the mode of action of spontaneity in general. As unity of the intuited manifold it is based on the *understanding* or on the capacity of spontaneity through which unity is able to bind the material – not in the first degree of its mode of action (in its initial potential), but is able to bind material that has already become a representation, and thus is able to produce from this material a unity of a higher type, *a unity of the understanding*.

To the extent that the form of the concept is determined through the mode of action per se of spontaneity called the understanding before any real representation takes place, the representation of this form is a representation to which no *a posteriori* determined material corresponds, i.e. a representation *a priori*. This, however, is a representation that occurs not immediately from the *a priori* determined manner of its affectedness, but from the *a priori* determined mode of action of spontaneity. Consequently, it is not [: 435] an intuition but a concept *a priori*. In truth the representation of the form of the concept does not immediately relate to its object (for no manifold can correspond in representation to the unity), but only through the means of the represented form of intuition whose manifold is bound through the understanding, i.e. is *thought*. The form of the concept cannot be intuited but, on the contrary, only thought; its representation is thus not an intuition but a *concept* per se.

From this the necessity and generality appropriate to objective unity as the object of a concept *a priori* becomes apparent.

Nothing is more easily comprehended than how the objective unity of the *spiritualists* was turned into *simplicity* of substance, since they viewed this necessary and general attribute of all conceivable objects as a property of things, just as the materialists believed themselves to have discovered in extension the necessary and general attributes of all intuitable objects outside us, the essential property of what is more than representation per se, i.e. the essential property of things in themselves.

§ LXXI.

To gather the manifold of an intuition into an objective unity means *to judge*; to produce objective unity from an intuition, means to *judge synthetically*, to bind the thereby produced objective unity to [: 436] an intuition, means to *judge analytically*.

A judgment is understood as the action of the understanding through which two representations are bound*, of which the one is called *subject*, the other, which is bound to the subject, the *predicate*. This binding must happen directly between the predicate and subject, that is, the predicate may not be bound to the subject by means of another predicate if the judgment is not to be a rational inference but a proper judgment. The subject with which a predicate is to be bound through a judgment per se may not be *thought prior* to this binding (i.e. not through a particular attribute) but must be immediately represented, i.e. *intuited*. The representation that is the subject of an actual judgment must be an *intuition*. The predicate which

---

* Negative judgments, too, occur through a binding of the negative attributes. In general the understanding separates into smaller elements only through the process of binding elements of the manifold that belong together.

is an attribute of the subject must, on the other hand, have arisen from intuition and be a representation relating not immediately to the object but only by means of intuition – i.e. is a concept. It was believed that the origin of the predicate had been well enough explained by ascribing to a confusedly grasped understanding a special capacity to separate into smaller elements, to abstract, independent of the capacity to bind. Through this capacity [: 437] the understanding separated an intuition, the total representation, into its attributes, the partial representations which, as predicates binding with the total representation to the subject, was then called to *judge*. However the following also had to be conceded: the representation of the predicate would occur – prior to the judgment through whose process the representation is connected with the subject – only on the basis of another judgment through which, as something distinctly represented, it would be separated from the subject. Consequently, abstraction would not precede every judgment but, on the contrary, would itself be a type of judgment and, according to this explanation, the representation of the predicate would also arise from a judgment, not the judgment arising from a preceding representation of the predicate. And how? If the predicate is elicited from intuition through analysis, must it not have been present in intuition through the activity of binding? Does not precisely the separation into smaller elements presuppose, therefore, a prior activity of binding, does not analysis presuppose synthesis?

The representation which in judging is called the predicate is a concept, and, as such, originally arises from an intuition – not through separation into smaller elements but through the binding of the manifold represented in the intuition, in the same way that that most general of predicates, objective unity, or the attribute of conceivable objects in general, only occurs through the binding of the manifold in general represented in the represented form of intuition in general. Through precisely this action by which the thing represented through intuition is bound and the unity of the represented occurs in consciousness, [: 438] the unity of the represented is represented as separate from the representation per se, the concept separate from the intuition, and the predicate separate from the subject. If the action by which the predicate is represented as distinct from the subject is called judging, so it is the case that intuition's combining of the manifold into an objective unity is called to *judge*.

Through intuition's combination of the manifold into an objective unity (intuition's) binding of a subject to a predicate (the concept) is determined, i.e. a judgment is made. This combination can happen in *two* ways. Either by producing objective unity only through an intuition, or binding the thereby produced objective unity to the intuition. In the former case, the attribute of the object is produced only from an intuition, the predicate is separated from the subject through what is produced from it, and through the combination of the represented manifold a representation of the determinate object distinct from the intuition is produced. In the latter case, the attribute distinguished from the intuition is bound again to the intuition. I call the first action of the understanding a *synthetic* judgment because the action through which the predicate is produced from the subject or through which the representation of the object distinct from the intuition is produced consists in *synthesis* as such, the binding of the intuited manifold, and I call the second action of the understanding an *analytical* [: 439] judgment, because the binding of the already generated predicate to the subject presupposes the separation of the predicate from the subject effected through the process of production. Both synthetic and the analytical judgment have in common the fact that they are judgments, actions of the understanding, by which the relation of a concept to an intuition is determined, but they are distinguished from each other by the fact that the determination of the relation of the two, in the case of synthesis, occurs in the production of the relating representation, and, in the case of analysis, in the binding of the relating representation to the intuition, and by the fact that the latter binds the same predicate to the subject generated out of the subject by the former through the combination of the intuited manifold.

Every analysis must be preceded by a synthesis and every analytical judgment must be based on a preceding synthetic judgment. If through an analytical judgment a given predicate and subject grasped under an objective unity are to be produced, these have to have been grasped previously in an objective unity. If in cognition the representation is to be related to the determinate object through an analytical judgment, the object has to have been determined previously through a synthetic judgment. If the connection of two representations is to be made conscious, this connection has to have happened previously, and what understanding represents as bound it must have bound previously. [: 440]

The most general form of all analytical and synthetic judgments consists in intuition's combination of the manifold in objective unity, and precisely this combination is at the same time the most general form of representation by way of a concept. The form of synthetic judgment is the form of the action by which a concept is generated, and the form of analytical judgment is the form of action by which *representation* occurs through the means of an already generated concept. To generate a concept, to judge *synthetically*, means to *generate* objective unity through intuition's combination of the manifold. – To *represent* through a concept, to judge *analytically*, means to have a representation that relates through an attribute (objective unity) to the object (the intuition). The most general form of the concept as a product of the understanding is thus determined through the most general form of judgment as the action of the understanding that has the same form for analytical and synthetic judgments, only with the difference that analytical judgment is only possible through a preceding synthetic judgment, not through this or that judgment, and consequently that all precise determinations of analytical judgment pertaining to the understanding must have been preceded by synthetic judgment. It is therefore sufficiently clear that what is to be represented as bound according to laws of the understanding must be bound according to laws of the understanding.

§ LXXII.

Through the particular forms of judgments determined according to the nature of the understanding [: 441] are certain modifications of an objective unity determined *a priori* as those particular forms under which objects must be thought, and these determinate forms of conceivable objects are called *categories*.

I call a *modification of objective unity* the more precisely determined manner in which the represented manifold is bound in a unity. Through the nature of the understanding not only must the binding of the represented manifold be determined, but also the manner of its being bound, not only the general class per se of objective unity, but also the types of these, not only the possibility and the form of judgment in general, but also the forms of particular ways of judging, not only the possibility and the form of the concept in general, but also the possibility and the forms of particular types of concepts. The understanding goes beyond the most general form of judgments and concepts contained within it; it must lie within the nature of the understanding to determine everything that forms part of every type of judgment and concept insofar as these depend on the action of spontaneity.

The modifications of the most general form of judgment determined by the nature of the understanding or the combination in objective unity are particular logical forms of judgment, and just as the most general form of the conception of objects results from the most general form of judgment [: 442], so just as many particular forms in which to conceive objects determined in the nature of the understanding or just as many attributes of objects in general dependent on the understanding result from the particular logical forms of judgment. We must thus seek out the logical forms of judgment.

Regardless of the fact that the forms on which all analysis is based have to occur initially in synthetic judgment, they can only be recognized *in consciousness* in analytical judgments. For representations of *determinate* objects only occur in *cognition* (in the *consciousness* of determinate objects). Nevertheless, these objects are obliged to occur not as the understanding will determine, but as it has already determined, and not as its concepts have generated out of intuition, but in the way they are already generated and related to intuitions. Cognition is the relatedness of the representation to the determinate object as a relatedness by which the object has already been rendered determinately conscious. The type of judgment that the predicate (or the determinate concept) in cognition relates to the subject (the *object* occurring in intuition), therefore, is an *analytical* judgment – a judgment through which the already *generated* concept is bound to intuition. In analytical judgments occurring in actual cognition in consciousness, and in its various forms, the forms of synthetic judgment not distinct from them must be brought to light [: 443], or the forms of judgment insofar as they are originally determined in the nature of the understanding.

In the case of analytical judgments, an (already synthetically generated) *predicate* and a *subject* – in consequence: two representations – occur whose previously synthetically determined relation to objective unity is determined in *consciousness*, and one can explain the difference between analytical and synthetic judgments through the fact that the same attribute in analytical judgment is bound to the object *in consciousness* which was generated *prior to consciousness* through synthetic judgment by means of intuition's combination of the manifold.

We intend to call, on the one hand, the predicate and subject inhering in each judgment the *logical material*, and, on the other hand, the *synthetically determined relation* of this to objective unity, i.e. the manner in which the represented manifold is combined into objective unity, the *logical form of judgment*. The various relations which the logical material and the logical form of judgment can have to objective unity must depend on the possibility of combination in objective unity – an activity determined in the nature of the understanding –, or what amounts to the same thing, the various types of relation are only possible through just as many ways of combination proper to the understanding or just as many types of *functions* of the understanding in judgment. [: 444]

Through these relations the various *logical forms* of judgment must be given and fully accounted for. We shall investigate the possible relations of logical material and form to objective unity in the following.

The logical material of judgment is composed, *first*, of the subject, and this subject relates to the *objective unity* of the predicate or to the attribute either as *unity* or as *multiplicity**, or as *multiplicity* and *unity* together. In the first case *one* subject, in the second *several*, and in the third case *all* subjects are combined into the objective unity of the predicate, and the predicate is operative either in regard to *one* subject, *many* or *all* subjects, and judgment is either a *single*, a *particular* or a *general* judgment.

---

*   *Multiplicity* here refers to the *manifold* in general to the extent that it is opposed to *unity*.

The logical material consists, *secondly*, of the *predicate*, and this relates to the objective unity of the subject or to the *object* as *unity* or as *multiplicity* or as *unity* and *multiplicity together*. In the first case, the predicate is taken up into the objective unity of the subject, in the second case it is excluded from this, and in the third case, by the predicate's being taken up into the unity of the subject, something of the subject is excluded and something in the subject is *posited* through the predicate, or something of the subject [: 445] is *taken*, or *both posited* and *taken*, and judgment is either *affirmatory*, *negatory* or *infinite* (*indefinitum*).

The logical form of judgment consists of the process of combination into objective unity, and is determined, *first*, with respect to what is combined, *secondly*, with respect to combination itself, that is to say, with respect to the predicate and the subject to the extent that *both*, *taken together*, relate to the unity of the object, and with respect to the subject's combination (the process of thinking) insofar as *combination* is related to it.

In the *first* respect the subject and the predicate, combined into objective unity, relate by way of *unity*, or of *multiplicity*, or *unity* and *multiplicity* together.

If the subject and predicate, combined to make an objective unity, relate by way of unity, they constitute together only a *single* object; the predicate is connected to the subject *internally* as the *attribute* with the *object*, and the judgment is *categorical*.

If the subject and predicate, combined to make an objective unity, relate by way of multiplicity, they constitute together two connected objects; the predicate is connected with the subject *externally*, and consequently with its ground, and judgment is hypothetical. [: 446]

If, finally, subject and predicate are combined to constitute objective unity by way of *multiplicity* and *unity together*, they then constitute, when taken together, one object made up of several objects, i.e. a *community*, and the predicate is connected to the subject internally and externally as an element that with its other part together constitute a system. Then if the one part, with which, taken together, it bears the attribute of the whole, removes from itself its other part, the judgment is disjunctive.

In the *second* respect, the relation of the combining entity to the combination is determined in objective unity. Since the combining and representing I is representable as a subject of the understanding only through the consciousness of combination, or through the relatedness of combination to the subject, then the relation between the combination and the combining entity, insofar as this is representable, can consist only of the relation of the combination to the relatedness of combination to the subject, or, which amounts to the same thing, only of the relation between consciousness and combination.

Now, consciousness relates to combination either as a *unity* or *multiplicity* or as *unity* and *multiplicity together*.

In the first case, combination is connected *internally* with consciousness and occurs in consciousness itself; it is combined in actuality and the judgment is assertory. [: 447]

In the second case, combination is connected with consciousness *externally* and does not occur in consciousness, but, on the contrary, is represented as something distinct from consciousness, occurring in consciousness not as an action but as a mode of action, not as a real action, but as a merely possible action, and the judgment is *problematic*.

In the third case, combination is connected both *internally* and *externally* with consciousness, and representation per se of the combination is inseparable from the actual activity of combination which is carried out in consciousness for precisely that reason. The actual action of combination is determined in consciousness through its possibility, and the judgment is apodictic.

With every judgment, therefore, several types of relation must be determined through the nature of the understanding, and there are an equal number of possible *inner* relations grounded in judgments: 1) the relation of the subject to objective unity, or the *quantity* of the judgment; 2) the relation of the predicate to objective unity or the *quality* of the judgment; 3) the relation of the subject and predicate together to objective unity, or the *relation* of judgment; 4) finally, the relation of objective unity determined in all three respects, or of judgment itself, to consciousness, or the *mode* of judgment. [: 448]

Quantity, quality, relation, and *modality* are thus logical modifications of *every* judgment in general determined by the nature of the understanding. However, since three different subordinate modifications are possible for each of these, it emerges that there are *twelve particular forms* of judgment, of which four – *one* from each of the four types of modification containing *three* forms each – must be accorded to every judgment.

I call these forms of judgment original forms of judgment because they attach to each judgment on its own and constitute its inner nature, whereas all other constitutive elements of the judgments attaching only to a particular judgment when compared to another judgment are merely *external* relations and *derived* forms, e.g. the *enunciationes Identicae, compositae, comparativae, exceptivae, exclusivae,* etc. – forms first identified by Kant in his table of the *original forms of judgment*, although not derived in a determinate manner by him and so criticized by several opponents of the critical philosophy, but quite clearly without justification.

The *representations* of all twelve forms of judgment consist 1) of the representations *a priori* established in the theory of the capacity for representation in general, i.e. of the *manifold* (or multiplicity in an extended sense) and the *unity of the manifold*; 2) in the various types of binding of the manifold. – Their entire content can only be determined in the *capacity for representation, to the extent that this capacity has understanding,* and consequently can only be determined *a priori.* [: 449]

In the same way as the general form of judgment acts with respect to the general form of the concepts, or to the form in which objects are thought, so the particular forms of judgment also act with respect to the particular forms of the concepts, or to the forms in which objects are thought – the *categories*:

A priori determined mode of the understanding

In the form of judgments	*In the categories*
I.	
Quantity	
Singular	*Unity*
Particular	*Multiplicity*
General judgments	*Universality* of objects
II.	
Quality	
Affirmatory	*Reality*
Negatory	*Negation*
Indeterminate judgments	*Limitation* of objects
III.	
Relation	
Categorical	*Substantiality*
Hypothetical	*Causality*
Disjunctive judgments	*Concurrence* of objects
[: 450]	
IV.	
Modality	
Assertory	*Actuality*
Problematic	*Possibility*
Apodictic judgments	*Necessity* of objects

In the same way as the forms of judgments are divided into *two main classes* – in one of which the relation between the *logical material* (the subject and predicate) and objective unity, and in the other of which the relation between the *logical form* of judgments and objective unity is determined – so the *categories* determined through the forms of judgment consist of two corresponding main classes, one of which can be called with good justification the *mathematical*, and the other the *dynamic*. The former concerns only those predicates that are determinable in intuition and to this extent are mathematical – either, on the grounds of *quantity*, in regard to how *many times* a subject is determined as objective unity with respect to a predicate, or, on the grounds of *quality*, in regard to whether the predicate in the objective unity of the subject is posited positively, negatively or through limitation. The dynamic, by contrast, concerns only those predicates that attach to objects on grounds relating to their existence, and which are determined not in the material of judgment but in the form itself, not in intuition, but in the concept per se – in combination, the physical exertion of the mind. [: 451]

The mathematical categories

1) An object is accorded the attribute of *quantity* insofar as its relation as *subject* to the object of a *predicate* is determined. If the subject acts as a *unity*, the object acquires the predicate of *quantitative* unity which must be distinguished from *objective* unity. If it acts with multiplicity, the object acquires the predicate of *quantitative multiplicity* which must be carefully distinguished from the manifold in general as the form of the material. If it acts as a unity and with multiplicity at the same time, the object acquires the predicate of *quantitative universality* which demands to be distinguished with no less care from *totality* in general, about which we will say more in due course. The *unity of the predicate* is just as important an attribute in the concept of magnitude as the *multiplicity* of the subject, and, in accordance with it, magnitude is thought of as multiplicity of the same, of that which has *one* and *the same* predicate, and numerical unity is conceived as unity of the same. Quantity can *only* be thought as a *particular magnitude on the basis of all three* categories subordinate to it, and every determinate magnitude has quantitative unity, multiplicity, and universality.

2) An object is accorded the attribute of *quality* insofar as the relation of its predicate to the objective unity accruing to it as subject is determined. If the predicate acts toward the objective unity of the subject as a unity, it is something which through the process of combination – through which the objective unity of the subject [: 452] occurs – is taken up into the full compass of the manifold, i.e. is posited *positively* in the subject, and the object is thereby accorded the predicate of *actuality*. If the predicate acts toward the objective unity of the subject with multiplicity, it is something which through the combination – through which objective unity occurs – is excluded from the full compass of the manifold, i.e. is posited *negatively* in the subject, and to this extent the object acquires the attribute of *negation*. If, finally, it acts simultaneously as a unity and with multiplicity toward the objective unity of the subject, it is

something which through combination – through which objective unity occurs – is taken up in the full compass of the manifold in such a way that excludes the activity of taking up; the positive attribute is at the same time negatively posited in the subject, and the the object acquires the attribute of limitation. Multiplicity, i.e. the manifold of what is combined in the subject (qualitative multiplicity), is just as essential to the concept of *quality* as the unity of each of these predicates (qualitative unity). The quality of an object, as the sum-total of positive and negative attributes combined, of the *quantitatively multiple*, and each of these attributes (*a* quality of the object), are accordingly thought either as a positive or negative, i.e. *qualitative* unity, or as both together. The *determinate quality* of the object itself (not quality in general) can only be thought through all three categories subordinate to the concept of quality: reality, negation, and limitation. [: 453]

The dynamic categories

3) An object acquires the attribute of *relation* insofar as the relation it has as subject to (communitarian) objective unity, together with a certain predicate, is *mutually* determined.

    If subject and predicate together act toward objective unity as a unity, they are connected *internally* in objective unity. In that case they are not part of *one* object but themselves together consititute just the *one* object – an object in which the subject must be thought as the object itself, the predicate as something *in the* subject, an attribute. Through this determination with respect to the predicate, the subject is accorded the status of subject in the strictest sense, namely, of a subject that is not the predicate and not an attribute of the object but is the object itself, and the predicate, with respect to the same subject, is determined as the predicate in the strictest sense, i.e. as something which through its being connected as predicate with its counterpart (the subject) has objective unity and is present in an object. The object acquires the attribute of that which exists in itself, substance, with respect to what is subjective about it, and with respect to what is predicative about it, the attribute of contingency.

    If subject and predicate together act toward objective unity with multiplicity, they are connected *externally* in objective unity, and the predicate, in that case, does not consititute with the subject *one* object, but a particular object that [: 454] can be thought as an object only through being *connected externally* with the subject. The subject through this determination is accorded the status of an object that, when posited, posits an object other than that connected to it – an object which, although itself being an object, still depends on that object and is determined through it. In this respect the one is called the *ground*, the other the *effect*, and the object, insofar as it is determined as the ground of another, acquires the predicate of *ground*, just as the other, which is thought determinately as the consequence, acquires the predicate of *effect*.

If subject and predicate taken together act toward objective unity as a unity and with multiplicity, they are connected in the objective unity *externally* and *internally* and constitute a single object consisting of two objects. Through this determination the subject obtains completely the same status as the predicate, which without any further distinction can also obtain the position of the subject, and both together are accorded the status of an object consisting of several objects which, thought as predicates, are connected *internally* with one another, and which, as subjects, are connected *externally* with one another, exclude and *mutually* determine one another. The object, in this respect, acquires the predicate of *community*, but the attributes of the predicate acquire the predicate of its constituent elements, and their mutual relation to objective unity acquires the predicate of *concurrence*.

4) An object acquires the attribute of *modality* insofar as its relation [: 455] as objective unity (as object) to the consciousness of the representing entity is determined.

If, with respect to consciousness, the action of combination – that through which the object is thought as objective unity – the process of combination in consciousness does not occur as something distinct from consciousness and is not represented in consciousness but carried forward to it, in that case a process of combination leading to objective unity actually occurs and the object acquires the predicate of *actuality*.

If the action of combination with respect to consciousness involves multiplicity, the process of combination occurs as something distinct from consciousness, that is, is merely represented and not carried forward. The combination in that case is not taken forward into objective unity, but only its form is thought, and the object acquires the predicate of *possibility* (of the *merely conceivable*, but not thought).

If the action of combination with respect to consciousness involves both unity and multiplicity, the process of combination, by being represented in consciousness, is also taken forward to consciousness. The object, by being represented as conceivable, is actually thought. Its possibility contains the ground of its actuality, and in this respect it acquires the predicate of *necessity*.

The predicates of *modality* determine nothing of the object but its *relation* [: 456] *to consciousness*, whereas the predicates of *quantity*, *quality*, and *relation* are further determinations of objective unity itself and to this extent must be thought as *internal* predicates of the object. I leave it to others to assess with what justification these predicates have been ascribed to *things in themselves.*

"So would the actuality of an object merely depend on the actuality of what is thought of the object, consequently, on thought per se? And would this not be a clear and crude idealism?" – The actuality of the object, insofar as it *merely thought* and is nothing but objective unity, indeed depends only on the real activity of combination, on thought, and here we are only speaking of predicates determined through the form of thought and whose actuality, consequently, depends on the fact that it is really being thought, that the form of thought is really expressing itself. But it is only the actuality of the *conceived* object which depends on thought per se; the actuality of the object (not just thought through a concept but intuited) depends on the *affectedness* through a given material. – Of the actuality of the thing in itself, however, nothing more is possible than a contradictory representation, a mere figment. The expression *actual*, which is derived from the verb *to effect* [*wirken*], indicates everything that is the product of an *effect* in representation. All *reality*, all actuality in our representations, must be the product of an *effect*. – The subjective effect: an effect governed by spontaneity; the *objective effect*, an effect of things outside us [: 457] on our receptivity. To the extent that an object is merely thought, its representation – the representation of objective unity – is a product per se of the understanding. A representation that has *subjective* reality and the actuality accompanying the object is merely a *logical* actuality that depends on the effect of spontaneity. However, in as much as the conceived object is also intuited, as objective unity relates to a manifold given from without through an affectedness producing it, representation has objective reality, and the actuality accompanying its intuited object is not merely a logical actuality but a *real* actuality depending on an effect of the thing outside us that has affected our receptivity, regardless of whether it can be thought as *actuality* only by thought – the activity of combination of that which is given in intuition through an outside effect.

The three – as yet only positively determined – predicates of *modality* can also be determined *negatively.* If the predicate through whose combination objective unity is generated is not combined with the subject, it acquires to this extent the predicate of the unreal. If the predicate through whose combination with the subject objective unity occurs cannot be combined with the subject, the subject is thought as something unthinkable, and to this extent acquires [: 458] the predicate of *impossibility.* If, finally, the predicate is combined with the subject in objective unity in such a way that this combination is determined not through its representation per se, real thought, but through conceivability, through actuality, the subject acquires the predicate of the *contingent*.

Both *dynamic* classes of the categories have *correlates*, that is, they consist in each case of two concepts relating to each other: *substance* and *accidence*, *cause* and *effect*, *systematic whole* and *parts*, *actuality* and *unreality*, *possibility* and *impossibility*, *necessity* and *contingency*. The mathematical, by contrast, have no correlates, and the reason for that is that they consist of the one-sided relation either of the subject or the predicate on their own to objective unity, whereas the former, the dynamic, consist of the relation of subject taken together into *objective* unity and the predicate – something which, with respect to objective unity, must be *mutually* determined through *relation*, or with respect to *consciousness*, through a positive or negative combination as positive or negative *modality*.

The categories are thus originally nothing other than determinate forms of combination into objective unity, a determinate mode of action of the understanding, and insofar as the nature of understanding consists in a mode of action of the understanding, they are proper attributes of the nature of the understanding insofar as it is comprehensible. Now [: 459] if anyone wishes to inquire further how the understanding comes to its particular mode of action they would be pursuing a fruitless endeavour. The action of the understanding deduced in the categories which I have developed in application to the most simple *representable* elements is the limit of all that is comprehensible and even representable by the understanding – a limit one cannot transgress without losing oneself in the limitless region of the unrepresentable. The understanding which must be presupposed in every explanation cannot itself be explained, and its mode of action through which thinking is determined, once acknowledged, cannot be determined by thought in any way according to its external grounds.

The attempt to derive the mode of action of the understanding from the represented objects conceived as *things in themselves* was admittedly unavoidable in view of the general failure of the concept of the capacity for representation till now. However, this attempt to proceed with the mistaken concept of the *thing in itself* must now fall away of its own accord. Since the representation of the object as object is an effect of the understanding, the action through which this effect is produced, if it were determined through the conceived object, would have to be an effect of its effect (of the object insofar as it is thought as object). Since, of the things outside us, the representation itself cannot be given to us, but only the material of representation, the representation of the determinate object can also not be given, but only its raw material, the empirical [: 460] manifold per se, which must be unified and represented only in the mind before it can be combined into a unity of the *represented* through the understanding. Now, what this combining per se consists in or, rather, the determinate manner of this combining per se, pertains to combination, i.e. spontaneity, which thereby is accorded its status as *understanding*. Whether and to what extent is the mode of action proper to spontaneity grounded in the things in themselves? Or how does it connect at all with them? These are questions no-one will raise who understands their meaning and who knows the limits of representability.

§ LXXIII.

The pure representations of the categories are representations, *concepts a priori* – representations of *necessary* and *general* attributes of the objects determined by the understanding.

The categories themselves are not representations and are therefore also not concepts, but they are *forms* of concepts and, insofar as they are representable, are objects of representations that cannot be represented immediately by intuition but only through concepts whose representations are concepts. In actuality, the forms of objective unity can only be represented, i.e. thought, through their relation to a represented manifold. Now, in as much as the forms [: 461] of objective unity are determined through the action of the understanding, the categories are objects which are determined prior to representation in the mind per se – objects to which no material determined through affectedness in its representations corresponds but only the mode of action of spontaneity conceived *a priori*, i.e. that mode of action of spontaneity related to a representation *a priori* (the represented manifold in general). The categories are represented in *pure* form when they are represented through their given affectedness and from the forms of intuition separately from every empirical element in space per se and time per se. As objects of these pure representations they are determined *a priori* through the understanding per se and the capacity for representation in general independent of sensibility, although they relate to intuitions and consequently also must be determined through sensibility if they are to become attributes not merely of conceivable, but also of cognizable (i.e. conceivable and intuitable) objects – as will be shown in more detail below. One can call with some justification the pure representations of the categories the *core concepts* of pure understanding, provided that this term is understood not to encompass innate representations but concepts immediately derived from pure understanding, although they cannot occur prior to experience in consciousness.

Through objective unity the object is thought as *object in general*, and the *categories* as *determinate objects*. Every judgment must have quantity, quality, relation, and modality [: 462], that is, no actual action of the understanding is possible that has not had to be determined through the action of the understanding from these four points of view. Thus, no concept of a determinate object generated through a synthetic judgment occurring in any other form than from these four points of view is possible. Every determinately conceived object, to the extent that it is thought determinately, must be thought through the attributes of quantity, quality, relation, and modality. The categories must accompany all determinate objects because these are only *able* to be determined through them, i.e. the categories are *necessary* and *general* attributes of determinate objects.

By an illuminating account of the *necessity* and *generality* of the most general predicates of cognizable objects which nonetheless remained unproven in regard to every other derivation of the categories, the *Critique of Reason*, which demonstrated the origin of the categories in pure understanding initially and only by following its own path, was meant to have been secure against the objection *that it removed the certainty of human knowledge*. How would the certainty of our knowledge otherwise be found than in consciousness of the necessity of certain judgments? And how should this necessity be demonstrated more convincingly than by showing that it has its ground in the nature of the understanding? Or is a judgment not deemed necessary when it is necessary according to its form under which the understanding itself is able to make a judgment? Is the attribute of an object necessary and general [: 463] when it is nothing other than the form under which a determinate object alone can be thought? Is not every necessity provable only as a condition of the real, but is it also really proven when it is established as a condition of the real? If a single represented object is to be made conscious really and determinately, then so must the necessity and generality of the categories be made conscious for through them alone actual representation of the determinate object is possible. From where, by contrast, would necessity and generality come if the categories were determined *a posteriori* through an affectedness per se, as if, as empirical attributes, they pertained to things in themselves? Could their necessity be explained in any other way than through *custom*, and their generality be considered to reach *further than the number* of cases that had taken place in experience?

§ LXXIV.

In relation to the faculty of understanding in general the categories pertain to the understanding in the *narrower* sense and, in relation to sensibility, to the understanding in the *narrowest sense*.

The *categories* are *a priori* determined modes of action of the spontaneity of the capacity for representation, i.e. determinate types of binding of the represented manifold. They can be conceived as little without a *represented* manifold as the form of representation, i.e. the unity produced without a manifold in general through binding [: 464] of a manifold. But the represented manifold that *must* underlie the categories as material if they are to be represented is only a manifold represented *in terms of the general form of intuition* when it is to be related to a manifold given through affectedness and consequently to be thought as forms of cognizability. If, on the other hand, they are represented according to their original constitution as forms of *conceivability* per se, the manifold that underlies them as material may not be the manifold represented through intuition *a priori* in time, but only that manifold represented through representation of the manifold *a priori* in general which is set out in the theory of the capacity for representation in general. For insofar as the categories are determined in spontaneity per se, they merely concern the action of spontaneity, not the material of these actions. They are attributes per se of objective unity, not of a particular material, they are forms per se of binding, not forms of the manifold that is to be bound. The particular form of the manifold determined through the nature of sensibility thus pertains in no way to the attributes of the categories per se, but only to the represented manifold in general or the representation of the general form of the material in general. The categories are thus not merely conceivable independent of sensibility, without relation to the general form of the intuitions, i.e. without time per se, but must, if they are to be thought without contaminating [: 465] their original purity with foreign elements and according to their actual essence, also be thought independent of sensibility and separate from time. Thus is established the *eternity* of logical beings.

The purely represented categories thus relate through the manifold in general represented *a priori*, whose determinate types of binding they constitute through the understanding, not to sensibility but to the capacity for representation in general. They are types of binding of the represented manifold in general without consideration of whether this manifold is represented through sensibility or not, consequently they are proper modes of action of that capacity which generates representations through the binding of the represented, or – which amounts to saying the same thing – they belong to the *understanding in the narrower sense.*

The understanding in the narrowest sense is distinguished from the understanding in the narrower sense in nothing other than that the former relates to the capacity for representation *in general*, whereas the latter relates to the *sensory* capacity for representation. It is one and the same spontaneity which connects the represented manifold in general according to those same modes of determinate action in their nature (the pure represented *categories*) as the understanding in the narrower sense, and as understanding in the narrowest sense connects the manifold represented through intuition. Just these same categories, then, which belong to the understanding in the narrower sense in their relation to the capacity for representation in general, belong to the understanding in the narrowest sense [: 466] in their relation to sensibility – an understanding which is distinguished from the former (understanding in the narrower sense) only through its determinate relation to sensibility.

If the representation *a priori* of the manifold as material underlies the *categories*, they belong to the understanding in the narrower sense. If the represented general form of intuition in general underlies them, they belong to the understanding in the narrowest sense, an understanding whose nature must consist in the relation of the mode of action of spontaneity to the form of intuition.

§ LXXV.

The categories represented in their determinate relation to the general form of the intuitions (time per se) are the *schemata*, and they are listed in the following table:

1) *Quantity in time, or series in time. Number.*
2) *Quality in time, or series in time. Degree.*
3) *Relation in time or sequence in time. Duration, determinate effect, determinate simultaneity.* [: 467]
4) *Modality in time, or time in its full compass. Being at a particular time, being in a particular time, being at all times.*

1)   To persuade oneself that the pure representation of *number* consists of the representation of *determinate quality* related to the representation of time *per se*, one need only analyze the concept of *counting* in sufficient detail. Counting means: to add units of the same type to one another (successive, i.e. bound in time) and the product of this operation, the *number*, is a quantity that consists of the activity of combination completed in time, a quantity determined through all three subordinate categories in their representation – unity, multiplicity, and universality – insofar as they can be determined in time and are contained in it as essential attributes.

Only one *single* schema of quantity, that of *number*, is possible. As time per se can *only* be represented as a *manifold*, the category of *quantitative unity* cannot possibly be a direct attribute of time per se, and since time per se must be thought as an *infinite* succession, the category of *quantitative universality* – which would require it to be thought as a complete whole and therefore without continuance – in just the same way cannot be related to time per se without contradiction. [: 468] Insofar as multiplicity of subjects of the same predicate, of units of the same type, must be thought under quantitative multiplicity and only unity of this multiplicity of the same type thought under determinate multiplicity, to this extent multiplicity in time can only be represented as a unity of the multiple of the same type successively determined, i.e. *as number*, and determined on the basis of all three categories of quantity.

Quantity is only cognizable in its relation to time, i.e. as *number*. In the same way, quantity in space can only cognized through *measurement* by means of a part treated as a *numerical unity*.

2) To persuade oneself that pure representation *of degree* consists of the representation of quality determined in time, one need only demand precision in relation to the determinate concept of degree in general. Degree means, according to universal agreement, the *quantity of quality*, the dimensions of a constitution, intensive magnitude, multiplicity without extension – a multiplicity, therefore, which does not consist in the separateness of the manifold determined in space, but in its determination in time, and can be intuited not through the external sense, but solely through the internal sense. What is to be intuited in time must be given in time or must occur in the internal sense through affectedness; it must correspond to a *sensation*. [: 469] Now if what corresponds to a sensation is to be thought determinately, this can only occur through the fact that the manifold – which is intuited through the internal sense (as change within us) – is combined through the understanding according to the categories of determinate quality and consequently as a reality bound (limited) by negation, i.e. through the fact that the predicate of *degree* accompanies it.

Since all sensation occurs under the general form of sensory representation, namely time per se, *reality*, which should be more than a mere category, more than an empty form of thought, more than a logical affirmation, must have a material given through affectedness. It must correspond to a givenness through sensation, a change within us, a fulfilment of time. Cognizable (not merely conceivable, logical) reality must therefore be thought as *full time*, as *being in time*, just as *negation*, which should be more than a logical function of negating, must be thought as negation in time, *empty time, non-being in time*. The difference between this more than logical *something* and *nothing* then consists in the difference between full and empty time. One and the same part of time, namely, can be more or less full in sensation, the something in time can approach *nullity* in time to a greater or lesser degree, reality can be determined or limited more or less through negation, it can possess a greater or lesser degree, but it must in all cases possess a degree of it if it is to be cognized *in its difference* from negation per se [: 470] as a *determinate reality*. Quality in time, cognizable quality, can thus be thought neither as reality without negation, nor as negation without reality, but must be bound as reality with negation, i.e. as *limited*. There is thus only a *single* schema of quality, namely that of degree. Quality is only cognizable in its determinate relation to time, i.e. only as degree.

Number and *degree* are thus the *schemata* that result from the determinate relation of the *mathematical categories* to the general form of intuition, time per se, and therefore can themselves be called the *mathematical schemata*.

3) The relation of the categories of relation to the form of intuition in general is determined through the schemata of relation, and the three types of mutual relation of those subjects and predicates together making up objective unity are represented through the representations of the schemata as determinable in time.

   a) *Substance in time* is a subject to the extent that as subject in the strictest sense it is determined as existing in time, as the durable subject, *duration*. *Contingency* in time, by contrast, is a predicate, insofar as it is determined as a predicate in the strictest sense, as a predicate that cannot take the place of its subject, as only existing in the subject, and consequently is that which does not have duration in time: the *mutable*. [: 471]

   Since what is given in *time* per se *itself* and can be intuited is of necessity *change*, what is durable in time and consequently must be thought as lacking change must be able to be intuited in *space* if it is to be more than conceivable and more than just intuitable. The material corresponding to the durable in time must be given to external sense, and the durable itself is only cognizable in space and in time. Therefore, whatever is to be *cognized* as a substance, as durable in time, must be something outside us, must be something which fills space and is intuited. It must be able to acquire the predicate of *extension*. The subject of our capacity for representation not intuitable as *something outside us*, therefore, can and must be *thought* as a substance durable in time, but it cannot at all be *cognized*. The soul belongs in the domain of merely conceivable substances, not in the domain of the conceivable and intuitable, of the *cognizable* substances.

   b) The determination of succession, or the series of intuitable things in time, through the category of cause and effect is the schema of determinate succession, i.e. of that succession by which one element of a series is *necessarily* thought as succeeding and the other as preceding. In as much as something given in time as the ground of another thing given in time, the being in time of the latter depends on the being in time of the former in consequence of this ground, but not the other way round (the ground from the consequence). If [: 472] the predicates of cause and effect accompany *cognizable* objects, they must be represented through the schema of determinate succession as *determination in time*, or, which amounts to saying the same thing, a manifold intuited in time per se must correspond to a cognizable *cause* and *effect*.

The *cognizable effect* is therefore that whose origin in time is determined through something else *necessarily* preceding it (the cause), and the *cognizable cause* is that whose original ground *in time* is that of something else. That which in a thing is the original ground of another thing is called *causality*. Every cognizable *causality* must therefore itself arise because it can only be cognized as a ground in time. Insofar as causality arises in time, it is called *change*, and insofar as this change is the ground of origin of an effect (of another change) it is called *action*, while change, which is merely effect, is called *passivity*.

Since *causality* both of *cause* and effect is cognizable only as *change* and *substance* only as *durability*, immutable in time, it becomes clear that substance is able to exist not as substance but only in its *contingent occurrences* as cognizable causality and cognizable effect. To this extent every *contingency* can only be the predicate of a substance, insofar as a substance, whose contingent form is a causality, must admittedly be thought as the cause, but it can only be thought through its contingent form (not as a *substance*) [: 473] as a cognizable cause, in the same way as the *action* in which the actual causality of an effect in time consists can of necessity *only* be thought *as change* and therefore cannot possibly be thought as something durable. If one now takes *force* to mean the *immediately acting* substance, a causality immediately present in the substance itself, it is then established that there cannot be any *cognizable* force because each action can only be cognized as change, as accident, and consequently does not have a substantial, continuous, non-originating action. Therefore the only force that we can accord to substances cognizable to us, to durable things in space, namely, *motive force*, must in no way be thought of as present in one substance determining another to movement, but must be thought as only communicated to this substance by another substance. That which moves moves only through movement; it changes only insofar as it is itself changed; accident in the moving substance is the ground of accident in the moved substance. The spontaneity of our capacity for representation insofar as it is an attribute of the representing subject as its own proper predicate is a *force* in the strictest sense of the word, but it is *cognizable* only in its mode of action determined in the capacity for representation, i.e. in the forms of spontaneity, and consequently not as a force but as a *capacity*. Thought in its connection with the subject as substance, as the actual force of the substance, it is merely able to be conceived; it can be no more cognized than its *substantiality* could be cognized. [: 474]

Just as the attribute of cognizable causality is not immediately attributable to any substance, so no attribute of *cognizable effect* can accompany it. What is determined through another thing in time and consequently can be said to arise, cannot be what has duration, the subject, it can only be accident. Every cognizable effect can thus only be accident, and *there is no cognizable cause of substances* (therefore the old view of the eternity of matter is untenable).

c) Simultaneity, or the series of what is indirectly intuited in time but immediately intuited in space through the category of community, provides the schema of determinate concurrence with which the elements of the series must necessarily be thought not as following one another, but as connected to one another. The determinate concept of this schema is most easily obtained by conceiving it as originating from the binding of the schema of substantiality with the schema of causality. Cognizable community consists, namely, of cognizable substantiality, duration in space, and cognizable causality, the action brought together in time, related to more than one object. An object is found in *cognizable community* with another object when both are thought as elements that have duration in space and mutually affect each other in time, so that the action of the one is the ground of certain accidents in the other, and the action of the other is the ground of certain accidents [: 475] in the one. What is cognizable as concurrently present must be determined in space and time simultaneously. In consequence, both determinations in time – the negative of duration, the positive of determinate succession – must be attributable to it. Conceivable community can only be cognizable and be a community of cognizable objects insofar as the former are mutually determined, first, as cognizable objects through duration in space, and, secondly, as *cognizably connected* objects through causality in time.

On the basis of the three categories of relation, time is applicable in its three *modes* of *duration, succession,* and *simultaneity* to *objects* (objective unity), and through time the categories of relation are applied to intuitions and therefore to that which is given in intuition.

4) Through the schemata of *modality* the relation of the categories of modality to the general form of intuition is determined as possibility, actuality, and necessity of that which is intuitable in time.

a) The category of possibility or that form of *thinking* represented per se in consciousness – a conceivability bound to the per se represented form of intuition – provides the *schema of possibility,* of the conceivability of the intuitable, and insofar as the form of intuition, time per se, is a condition of susceptibility for a material, then the conceivability of what is given to susceptibility arises from this binding – a conceivability of that to which a sensation can correspond [: 476], something that can be thought (bound in consciousness into an objective unity), insofar as it can be given through affectedness, or, which amounts to saying the same thing, that accords with the condition of this being affected, with *time per se.*

Through the category per se of possibility nothing is determined but *logical* possibility, conceivability per se. This was confused with real, cognizable possibility mainly because the difference between thought and cognition remained a deep mystery up till *Kant.* Conceivability per se only becomes cognizability through its relation to intuition, and just as logical possibility consists in conceivability, so *real* possibility consists in cognizability. An object acquires cognizable possibility, i.e. real possibility, only insofar as it acquires cognizability. It is in the capacity for cognition and not, as assumed until now, in the unrepresentable *thing in itself,* that the ground of real possibility comprehensible to us must be sought.

b) The category of actuality, or the thinking undertaken in cons-ciousness, in its relation to real intuition or to the material present in the mind under the form of sensory representation, provides the *schema of actuality.* This is a thinking of what is given through affectedness and what is directed at the material that has become an intuition through the general form of affectedness; an objective unity generated from the manifold intuited under the form of succession, [: 477] the object thought at a moment in time determined through affectedness, the being of a particular time.

Through the category per se of actuality nothing is determined but *logical actuality.* What of its nature can be thought is what is logically *possible*; what is logically *real* is what is thought. *Some thing* does not *exist* merely on account of the fact that it is thought. And just as the conceivability of an object must relate to its intuitability if it is to acquire real possibility, so the conceivability of this object must be related to real intuition if it is to acquire real *existence*. To maintain the cognizable (more than just the conceivable) existence of an object means to accord to it the predicate of *cognizability*.

Existence is called *actuality* because, insofar as it is representable, it can only be a product of *effecting*[1]. Logical *existence* occurs through thought, the action per se of spontaneity and the real action through *thinking* and *intuiting*, effecting and being affected in our representation. The existence of our representing I is representable through an affectedness that is an *immediate* effect of spontaneity per se. The existence of objects outside us through an affectedness that is an *immediate* effect of the things outside us – notwithstanding the cognizable existence of our representing I, for which we can have no other predicate than the capacity for representation per se – depends, according to the condition of its cognizability, on an affectedness from without (in which the forms of represention are initially expressed). [: 478] The cognizable *existence* of things outside us (which can only be thought through the binding undertaken by the understanding of the manifold given through affectedness and represented in an intuition) depends, according to its cognizability, *indirectly* on the action of spontaneity.

Existence is called *reality* not because it is a quality of the object (for through existence nothing is posited in the object), but because it can be maintained as logical *existence* only of a subject that is thought as object, and consequently is determined through a positive predicate, i.e. has *logical reality*. It can be maintained as real existence only of a subject accruing cognizable reality, namely what an affectedness in the mind corresponds to.

Since until now one was not able in precise terms to distinguish conceivable from cognizable actuality, and logical from actual actuality, it is easy enough to understand why one group of philosophers explained the representation of *existence* in obviously mistaken ways, and why another group considered it simply inexplicable. Most reached agreement about the fact that *existence* was a constitutive element of the *thing in itself* independent of our mind, a thing accruing the predicate of *being* which they derived from

---

1 Wirken.

the represented and from which immediately after that they derived the capacity for representation, without having a clear conception of either. Under *being* something distinct from representation per se is thought as *determinate*, something thought as distinct from representation per se [: 479], an *objective unity* which is either a product per se of spontaneity from the represented manifold in general, i.e. *logical being* – which in judgment is expressed by the little word *is*, the sign of the binding between predicate and subject – or which is a product of spontaneity and of the receptivity affected by a thing outside us, a real, a *cognizable being*.

c) The category of *necessity* or the thinking represented and carried out in consciousness in relation to both intuitability as well as actual intuition provides the schema of necessity that consists in the binding of the schema of possibility with the schema of actuality, i.e. with that which is cognized connected to cognizability per se, with being at any time in connection with being at a particular time. An object acquires cognizable necessity insofar as its being-cognized is determined through the form per se of cognition. In this way a cognized cause acquires the predicate of necessity insofar as that which is cognized as a cause depends on the form of cognition (of determinate succession) determined in the schema of causality. The categories and the forms of intuition acquire cognizable necessity because their connection with what has been empirically cognized is determined through the form per se of thinking and intuiting. In as much as the forms of thinking, intuiting, and cognizing determined in the nature of the mind [: 480] constitute true and original *laws* of conceivability, intuitability, and cognizability, to this extent *logical necessity* is the connection of what is thought (of the logically real) with the laws of thinking (the determinately logically possible), and *real, cognizable necessity* the connection of what is cognized (the really real) with the laws of cognizability (the determinately really possible); and what is cognizably necessary is everything that connects with the real according to the laws of cognizability.

In philosophy, the extremely important concept of *necessity*, in regard to the general dissolution of problems concerning our rights and duties in this life and the basis of what we expect from a future life – problems which could not possibly be attended to without this concept – has gained little from the fact that, until now, *necessity* has been generally used for the singularly possible (whose opposite is impossible) and for determinate possibility. For all these explanations presuppose a quite indeterminate concept of *possibility* according to which either the indeterminate *"is able to* *be thought"* was circularly derived from the just as indeterminate *"is able to be"*, or the determination of what is able to be thought and what is able to be was sought in the unrepresentable *things in themselves*. Here one either had to stop at the *thing in itself* and hypostasize determinate possibility or necessity and thus make these into an essential property of *things in themselves*, i.e. into the nature of things, and so take blind inexplicable necessity as the [: 481] source of everything possible and real as well as the final basis of determination of all laws of thought and being, or else one had to distinguish between the *original* thing in itself and the *derived* thing in itself and derive the necessity of certain predicates accruing to the latter from laws prescribed for created things by virtue of the reason of what has not been created. The doctrine that does not base laws on necessity, but necessity on laws, and seeks these out through the operation of reason*, has admittedly come closer to the truth. However, since here the concept of a law itself again presupposes the concept of necessity, and the whole system is built on the untenable fundament of the unrepresentable thing *in itself*, it is no wonder that it has found support only from *one* section of the philosophical world, and been rejected by *three* others.

In the purely represented categories of modality only logical possibility, actuality, and necessity per se, and thus the forms per se of thinking, can be thought. The application of these to time grants to these forms of thought the status of forms of cognition through the relation of what a given material in representation corresponds to, [: 482] and which therefore is neither representation per se nor the form of this, but a cognizable object. On the other hand, however, what a given material corresponds to and what is immediately represented through intuition is only possible, real, and necessary in *thought* through the three categories of modality.

The schemata of *relation* and *modality* all concern the *binding* per se of the intuitable in time and arise out of the *dynamic* categories and can consequently with justification be called the *dynamic schemata*.

§ LXXVII.

The schemata are the forms of cognizability determined in the nature of the *cognitive capacity a priori*; the pure representations of these are *cognitions a priori*, and the judgments in which they are immediately resolved are the

---

*   Supporters of this system generally forget that divine reason can only be thought insofar as a determinate form of thought is present as human thought in our minds.

original laws of the understanding in the narrower sense and of *possible experience* determined in the nature of the understanding.

The cognitive capacity consists of the union of sensibility and understanding, and cognition in a thinking connected with intuition. The schemata which are nothing but the connected forms of thinking and intuition are therefore the actual forms of cognition, and in as much as the object of a representation is only cognizable in relation to the schemata, [: 483] they are the actual *forms* of *cognizability*. In them the attributes determined for cognizable objects both through the nature of the understanding and through sensibility *a priori* are unified, the categories *sensualized*, the forms of intuition *determined* through the understanding, and conceivability and intuitability are raised to the level of cognizability. *Thus, no object that the schemata contradict is cognizable, and every object is only cognizable to the extent that the schemata can be attributed to it as predicates.*

The schemata consisting of the concepts *a priori* and the *a priori* represented form of intuition in general can only be represented *a priori*, and their representations are actual *cognitions*, i.e. *cognitions a priori*. They are *cognitions* because the schemata cannot be represented other than by connecting concepts with intuition, relating the purely represented categories to purely represented time, and thinking the intuition of time determinately through concepts, that is, relating it to objective unity determined through the categories, which is actual cognition. The schemata are *cognition a priori* because the object is determined not through an *a posteriori* given material, but prior to all representation in the cognitive capacity, in its forms.

As objects of cognition *a priori* the schemata acquire *necessity* and *generality* in that they are the forms which each *a posteriori* given material must assume in the mind [: 484] if cognition is to arise from it, and in that they relate with this material to what corresponds to it, or to the objects, general attributes of cognizable objects – objects that are only cognizable insofar as these attributes can be accorded to them.

Since every cognition consists in the relatedness of the representation to the determinate object and thus in a *judgment*, the representations of the schemata must, as *a priori* cognitions, be resolved into as many *judgments* as there are schemata – judgments which, to the extent that they are determined according to both their content and their form in the nature of the cognitive capacity, are *necessary* judgments; and to the extent that all cognizable objects in general must acquire their *predicates*, *general* judgments; and, as necessary and general judgments, they are also real *laws*. I call them laws of the *understanding in the narrower sense* because they are determined by the understanding in relation to sensibility, and I call them laws of *possible experience* insofar as they are the expression of conditions determined in the nature of the mind under which empirical cognition – also called *experience*, according to general agreement – is possible.

These judgments are *principles* in the actual meaning of the word, original judgments of the understanding, and require a proof as little as they are capable of one. They are *original judgments* because they immediately consist of representations having no other object, since they are determined in the mind, than the form of [: 485] thought and intuition, and because they are thus also not derived from other higher judgments. They are *not capable of proof* because proof would have to come from higher principles than the judgments themselves and consequently from judgments from which they were derived. They do not *require* proof because they carry with them the ground of their necessity and generality in their *priority*, or, which amounts to the same thing, because through them nothing is represented other than what is determined in the cognitive capacity and consequently cannot be cognized in any other manner than the way it is cognized.

Since I have already investigated cognitions expressing judgments in a determinate manner in the schemata, such judgments require no further explication, and I will content myself with simply enumerating them.

The purely represented schema of quantity provides the following judgment: the cognizable object, the appearance (the object under the form of intuition) has magnitude determinable on the basis of number, i.e. *extensive* magnitude.

The schema of quality: what is real about the appearance (that which in the appearance corresponds to sensation) has a magnitude of quality determined in time, *intensive* magnitude, *degree*.

The schema of substantiality: something of what is real of the appearance is represented as substance in time, as durable, and as accident in time, as mutable. [: 486]

The schema of causality: an occurrence of what is real of the appearance (thus a contingency per se) has a cause in time (presupposes something distinct from itself in time which it necessarily follows).

The schema of community: what is real of the appearances is present at the same time and stands in a mutual relation.

The schema of possibility: what is conceivable of the appearance and intuitable (cognizable) is possible (*can exist*).

The schema of actuality: what is cognized of the appearance, actually is (*exists*).

The schema of necessity: what of the appearance is connected with the cognized according to the laws of cognizability, is (*exists*) necessarily.

If the *a priori* determined necessity and generality of these judgments are expressed in formulations by the words "every appearance" and "must", then the *formulae of the laws of the understanding* and of *possible experience* arise from them whose further development and whose derivation of the constituent predicates of conceivability and cognizability from their original

3

conditions make up the content of the *theory* of *a priori* determinate *objects*, or of *metaphysics*.

I have called empirical cognition *experience*, and the indeterminacy of the concept of experience till now requires me to say clearly in what sense I ascribe to empirical cognition the name experience. Writers of philosophy up to the present [: 487] have usually considered it superfluous to explain how they want the term *experience* understood. It would be a vain pursuit to attempt to uncover a determinate concept of experience from what has been said by some of the most famous thinkers. *Locke* seems to me, as in so many other ways, to be an exception. Regardless of the fact that, to the best of my knowledge, he gives no express formal definition of experience, one can nevertheless say clearly enough from the entire thrust of his investigations in which he was at pains to derive the origin of the representations from *experience* that he understood *experience* as the givenness of the material of our representations through affectedness. "Whence", he writes in Book II, Chapter I, "does the mind receive all its MATERIALS of reason and knowledge? To this I answer, in one word, from EXPERIENCE. Our observation employed either, about external sensible objects, or about the internal operations of our minds perceived and reflected on by ourselves, is that which supplies our understandings with all the MATERIALS of thinking. – First, our senses, conversant about particular sensible objects, do convey into the mind several distinct perceptions of things, according to those various ways wherein those objects do affect them. – [...] the other fountain from which experience furnisheth the understanding with ideas is, – the perception of the operations of our own mind within us, as it is [: 488] employed about the ideas it has got; – which operations, when the soul comes to reflect on and consider, do furnish the understanding with another set of ideas, which could not be had from things without. And such are perception, thinking, doubting, believing, reasoning, knowing, willing, and all the different actings of our own minds; – which we being conscious of, and observing in ourselves, do from these receive into our understandings as distinct ideas as we do from bodies affecting our senses. This source of ideas every man has wholly in himself; and though it be not sense, as having nothing to do with external objects, yet it is very like it, and might prpoperly enough be called INTERNAL SENSE"[2]. – One

---

2 Reinhold's translation might be translated back into English as follows: "From where does the mind receive all its materials of reason and cognition? Here I answer: from *experience*. – Our observation that is busy either with *outer sensible* [cognizable] objects, or with *inner* actions of the mind, is that which provides our understanding with the materials of thought. – Our senses, namely, which have to do with individually *sensed* objects, deliver to the mind various determinate perceptions [*Wahrnehmungen*] of things according to the *different ways* in which they are *affected* by them. – The other source through which *experience* provides

can see from this that Locke, admittedly in the way of all his predecessors up to *Kant*, confused the material and the form of representation with representation itself, and did not allow the material per se to be given but only the representation itself through affectedness. And one can also see that he does not allow any other objects of experience than *bodies outside us*, and *changes within us*, and consequently does not allow precisely what we cognize as the only cognizable objects, the appearances of external and internal sense. And regardless of the fact that he confuses the action of the mind (which occurs through inner affectedness in its representation) with the *mode of action* determined prior to all action in the capacity for representation per se, he at least derives *cognition* of *real changes* of our mind (the empirical cognition of internal sense) from the affectedness of internal sense which for him, together with the affectedness of external sense, is *experience*. Locke thus considers affectedness, sensation, to be an essential condition of experience, and to this end [: 489] he has *language usage* on his side which has determined the word *experience* in the meaning not of cognition in general and not as cognition of real things but only as cognition insofar as it depends on sensation*. However, precisely this use of language distinguishes *experience* from *sensation*. Experience for Locke is *cognition* occurring through the material given in sensation (cognition *a posteriori*, empirical cognition), and sensation for him is only that essential component of cognition on which the material per se of an empirical cognition depends.

There are therefore two sorts of *internal conditions* (constitutive components of *experience* of which one is the *form* and the other the *matter* of experience: first, the *schemata*, or the *forms of cognizability* determined in the nature of the cognitive capacity, and, secondly, *sensation* which delivers the material of empirical cognition corresponding to these forms). In accordance with this explanation the *highest principle* of actual empirical cognition, which is at the same time the first law of the understanding in the narrower sense and of possible experience, will need to be described in what follows. [: 490]

Every cognizable object distinct from the capacity for representation per se stands under the formal and material conditions of possible experience.

---

the mind with representations is perception of the actions of the mind itself, or the *way in which* the mind [: 488] *concerns* itself with the received representations. – By making ourselves aware of these actions and noticing them in ourselves, the mind receives just those determinate representations of them as of bodies that affect our senses. Each person has the source of representations *solely in himself*, and although it is *not an actual* sense (in that it does not have to do with external objects), it is nevertheless quite similar to sensibility and can with good justification be called the *inner sense.*"

*   "Sensation of the real provides clear knowledge [*das Erkenntnis*] of individual things and cases, and this is called *experience*." *Reimarus*: Vernunftlehre Part II. Ch. I. § 212 and § 213: "Experience is knowledge [*das Erkenntnis*] of real, sensed things."

This principle is the determinate concept per se of an actual cognizable object (that is not an *a priori* represented form of the capacity for representation) resolved into the judgment through which it is thought. The cognizable empirical object, namely, is the objective unity of the manifold represented in an intuition and given through affectedness (in *outer* experience from without) determined through the categories (the schemata) related to the general form of intuition. Now, since this concept is the *most general* concept of cognizability, the concept of the cognizable object *in general*, so the principle that is nothing but the expression of this concept through a judgment cannot have any higher principle above it. It is thus the highest principle, grounded in the nature of the cognitive capacity, of knowledge of cognizable objects in the strictest sense, or of that part of metaphysics which concerns itself with these objects and is deservedly known as *ontology* κατ' εξοχην.

In place of this first principle – quite misunderstood till now – the so-called principle of *contradiction* (the *Principium contradictionis*) was posited whose actual, and entirely mistaken, meaning must now be established. According to this view, all cognizable things must be conceivable, that is, the intuited manifold [: 491] must be bound into an objective unity if an object is thereby to be cognized. The concept of cognizability thus presupposes the concept of conceivability, and just as the latter, resolved into a judgment, provides the *principle of cognizability*, so the principle of conceivability in general is obtained from the concept of conceivability resolved into a judgment, now expressed in the following form: if an object is to be conceivable the represented manifold must be bound or, expressing the same in a negative way, an object of the represented manifold that is unable to be bound is not conceivable, from which the following statement is now obtained: no conceivable, and consequently no conceived, object, *can acquire contradictory attributes*. This statement apparently expressing, in all such formulae, nothing but the represented category, the *a priori* determinate concept, of *logical possibility*, of conceivability in general, was hitherto put forward in a formula that entirely matched the muddled concept of thinking and cognizing generally prevailing and cleverly obscured the inconsistency lying in the confusion of logical and real possibility, namely: *No one thing can at the same time exist and not exist (Impossible est idem simul esse et non esse)*. The sheer allusiveness of the indeterminate expression of *being able to exist* renders this formula useable for any speculative need. At one moment it was meant *logically* in the sense of being thought per se and being able to be thought, logical being and being able to be, and at another moment it was meant *metaphysically* in the sense of actual existence [: 492] and the capacity to exist; and the deceptive representation of the *thing in itself* to which the concept of *actuality*, *reality*, and *existence* independent of the capacity for representation and determining our representations was connected obscured the unphilosophical circle by which the being-able-to-be-thought was derived from being-able-to-exist, and vice versa.

The principle of contradiction, which, after the concept of *thinking* and *logical being* has been clarified, cannot possibly still be expressed through that formula – this principle which must lose the position in *metaphysics* it has commanded till now and, instead of that, must assume the status of the *first* principle of *logic*, is the *highest law of conceivability* and belongs to the understanding in the narrower sense, whereas the *principle of cognizability* is proper to the understanding in the narrowest sense.

At this point I could conclude the *theory of the understanding* without fearing that I had neglected to treat any original *representation a priori* grounded in the form of the understanding and representing this form. In my *deduction* of the *forms of judgments* all possible relations determined *a priori* both with respect to the material as well as the form of a judgment have been fully explored. Through them the actual region of the understanding in the narrower sense has been set out, as well, in the *table of the schemata*, as the actual region of the understanding in the narrowest sense. All remaining representations belonging to the understanding in both senses [: 493] are constituted and derived from those original representations of the *categories* and the *schemata*, and their development and enumeration lie quite outside the bounds of the theory of the cognitive capacity per se in general. If, then, I additionally include explanation of certain representations grounded in the nature of the understanding in the narrower sense, I do so because the origin of these representations in the *four moments* of the *forms of judgment* is harder to appreciate than with all other representations derived from these sources, and because more than one opponent of the *critical philosophy* has found them wanting in *Kant's table of the categories*, where they would appear to belong with just as much right as they did in the representations set out in this same table.

The manifold that must underlie the *pure represented categories* as *material* is the *manifold in general* determined in the receptivity of the capacity for representation in general and represented a priori. The manifold belonging to the *pure represented categories* as material is the manifold determined in the nature of sensibility and represented by the representation *a priori* of the form of intuition. From this manifold constituting the material of the categories and the schemata a manifold must be distinguished of a quite different nature determined through the *mode of action per se* of the understanding in the narrower sense according to the four moments of judgments and determined through the understanding per se in the representations in which it [: 494] occurs. This manifold constitutes, as *pure representation*, the material of the concepts of *identity*, of *agreement* of the *inside* and of the form, as will become evident in the following.

a) The manifold nature determined by the understanding per se consists, in its moment of *quantity*, of the *multiplicity* of *subjects* determined through the *unity of the predicate*. Subjects are called *identical* insofar as they have unity according to their *predicates*; the representation of *identity* consists in the representation of multiplicity of the subjects of a single predicate, and *identity* occurs only when one and the same object (or one and the same conceived attribute of several objects) has unity with respect to itself – unity which is only produced by the object's being represented previously (in reflexion) through the understanding per se as a multiplicity. *Multiplicity*, by contrast, which is not determined by the understanding per se but through what is *given*, is not a multiplicity of the subject per se determined through unity of the predicate grounded in the understanding, but a multiplicity of subjects determined through the multiplicity of predicates grounded in the *given*, and the representation of this provides the concept of *difference* (diversity). These *differences* are not able to be *produced* in our representations, but are only *found*, they must therefore be based in the *given* and not in what is *generated* by the understanding.

b) The manifold nature determined by the understanding per se in its moment of *quality* consists [: 495] in the multiplicity of the predicates constituted in a subject, consequently in a multiplicity determined through the unity of the subject. Predicates are considered *in agreement* insofar as they have unity in a subject. The representation of *agreement* consists in the representation of multiple predicates insofar as they are bound in a subject through combination, and agreement only takes place insofar as the multiple is constituted in one (positively posited), and therefore multiplicity in the one has its ground in combination, and is represented as a multiplicity not of the given but of the thought. – By contrast, insofar as the multiplicity of the predicates in a subject is not determined by the understanding per se but through the *given*, and certain predicates are excluded from the subject through its activity of combination in the objective unity of the subject, and consequently are posited negatively in the same, to this extent such multiplicity (not determined through the understanding per se) of predicates (only negotiated by way of negation) is called *conflict*. The representation of *conflict* is admittedly only possible by way of the understanding, through a combination that excludes, but its material must be determined solely in the *given* insofar as this does not assume the form of the manifold determined through the nature of the understanding.

c) The manifold nature determined by the understanding per se in its moment of *relation* consists in the difference of the subject and the object combined into objective unity and mutually determined. Insofar as subject and [: 496] predicate do not, as it were, pertain to an object, but constitute it, to this extent their multiplicity is solely determined in this object through the understanding per se in the unity of the object. The multiple in one object, through whose combination the object becomes a single determinate object, is called *inwardness*. The representation of *inwardness* consists in the representation of the many in the one insofar as it constitutes an object existing for itself through its connection. Inwardness only takes place in relation to the multiple, whose multiplicity alone is determined through the understanding, because inwardness, *apart from* the objective unity it modifies, cannot be represented. – If, by contrast, the difference of a predicate combined into objective unity is determined not by the understanding but through the *given*, and if subject and predicate through their combination into objective unity do not constitute a *single* object but many objects *merely pertaining* to one object, the ground of their *connectedness* lies solely in the understanding, but the ground of their *multiplicity*, being more than one object, lies in *the given*. The representation of this multiplicity of the manifold connected, and yet belonging to, more than one object, is the representation of the *outside*, of the common predicate of such attributes accruing to one object only through their binding with one of the things distinct from them. The *outside* can only be represented through the understanding, but its material cannot be a manifold determined through the understanding per se but must be a manifold grounded in the given. [: 497]

d) The manifold nature determined by the understanding per se in its moment of *modality* consists in the merely logical difference of the predicate and the subject (to the extent that they must be a represented manifold, two representations, if they are to be thought, i.e. bound) and consequently in the manifold determined through the form per se of thinking. The representation of this manifold determined not through the given, but through the mode per se of representability (the unity of representation per se), is the representation of the *form*, whereas the representation of the manifold determined through being given is the representation of the *material*, of *matter*.

These strange representations are called *concepts of reflexion* because the action through which they arise in consciousness is (not a synthetic combination, but) the logical function of analytical judgment, which is called *reflexion* or *comparison*.

When attributes conceived through these concepts are transferred from the *things under the form of representation* (the appearances), in regard to which they are actually determined, to *things in themselves*, this is called an *amphiboly of the concepts of reflexion*. The way Kant derives the origin of Leibniz's system in all its parts from this misunderstanding belongs among the finest passages of the *Critique of Reason*; references should be made directly to this work.

[: 498]

Theory of Reason

§ LXXVII.

Representation that arises through the binding of the conceived manifold (represented through concepts) is called an *idea*. – And the capacity to succeed through this binding of the conceived manifold to representations is called *reason* – in the narrower sense.

The *concept* in the *narrower* sense, or the representation that arises through the mode of action of spontaneity from a *represented* manifold, is a species encompassing: *first*, the concept in the narrowest sense, i.e. the representation arising through *intuition*, and *secondly*, the *idea* in the narrower sense, i.e. the representation arising from the manifold represented on the basis of *concepts*. The material of the *idea* is the *conceived* manifold bound by the understanding, whereas the material of the actual concept is what has been intuited – the intuited manifold bound by apprehension per se. The material of *sensory representation* is the manifold *given* through affectedness. The material of the concept in the narrowest sense is certainly also a represented manifold – a manifold thus bound through spontaneity, but it is a manifold that is determined through the manner per se of affectedness as [: 499] the material of representation, and that through spontaneity of the first degree is bound according to the form of sensibility. The material of the *idea*, by contrast, is a manifold represented by the understanding through several concepts which the understanding, the second degree of spontaneity, has bound according to its proper form, and which – through the third degree of spontaneity bound to the unity of the conceived (not of the intuited) and bound to the unity of the already bound in concepts according to the form per se of spontaneity – becomes *rationality*. Whereas intuition relates immediately to the object corresponding to its material and the concept relates to the intuition out of which it was generated through spontaneity, the idea refers to concepts per se through whose binding it has arisen. The object of an intuition is the immediate object; the immediate object of the concept is an intuition by which the object becomes an *indirect* object of the concept; concepts are the immediate object of the idea and through these concepts intuition can be an *indirect* object of the idea. What is represented through the idea, therefore, is neither an empirical object that can only be intuited nor an immediate attribute of it that can only be conceived by the understanding, but only an attribute of this attribute which reason has created through the binding of the attributes conceived by the understanding.

The action of spontaneity through which the idea is generated is the same action that has been characterized in logic by the name *inference* [: 500] and is accorded to *reason* in the narrower sense, namely, the action of indirect judgment by which an attribute is only related to the object through another attribute (the middle concept), after a predicate of the predicate (the attribute of the attribute) is generated by reason from the predicate (the attribute of the object) generated by the understanding (the intuition). The idea is thus a representation proper to reason, and the capacity to succeed to representations through the action of deduction or through the connection of *concepts* is called *reason in the narrower sense*.

I say *in the narrower sense* in order to distinguish the meaning I am determining here from two others: the *wider* meaning in which the word *reason* is used without distinguishing it from the understanding, and the narrowest which will be determined in the next paragraph.

§ LXXVIII.

The representation which arises through the binding of what is conceived *a priori* is called the *idea* – and the capacity to attain representations through binding of what is conceived *a priori* is called *reason* – *in the narrowest sense* of the word.

Every representation arising through binding of what is represented through concepts is called the *idea* in the narrower sense; it may have come from concepts *a posteriori* or from concepts *a priori*. [: 501] Since ideas emanating from these different sources are in essence different from each other with respect to their *material*, and since we lack a special expression for this difference, we will give the representations generated by reason from concepts *a posteriori* (from concepts that relate through the schemata to an empirical material) the special term of *ideas in the narrower sense* and the representations produced from *a priori* concepts per se the term *ideas in the narrowest sense*.

Thus we now have a threefold sense of the word *idea* requiring elaboration. The *wider* meaning (§ XXXVII) refers to *representation in general* insofar as it is representation per se and is viewed with respect to its subjective reality, i.e as something actual in the representing subject on the basis of active and passive effects. The *narrower* sense encompasses representations stemming from the connection of ideas that are mere products of the understanding according to their form but are related to a material (the intuitions) which is the product of affectedness and which is also spontaneity (in the first degree) acting according the forms of sensibility. The idea in the narrower sense thus only has subjective reality on account of its immediate material (the concepts) to which reason binds only what is the product per se of the understanding. The idea, however, is indirectly capable of objective reality through the relation of concepts to intuitions. The *narrowest* sense limits the word *idea* to representations [: 502] generated through the binding of concepts *a priori*, that is to say, the binding of concepts relating to a merely *a priori* represented *manifold in general*. In the concepts *a priori* the represented manifold in general is bound by the understanding, but in the *ideas* in the narrowest sense the concepts *a priori*, insofar as they are a manifold determined by the understanding, are unified, yet this is not the work of the understanding but of a higher degree of spontaneity (of *reason*) called *rational unity*.

This rational unity constitutes the form of the ideas in general, i.e. the form common to ideas in the narrow and the narrowest senses and determines these through the nature of reason *a priori*.

§ LXXIX.

The form of the idea in general determined in the original mode of action of reason consists in the unity of a manifold contradicting the forms of intuition, in the unity of a manifold determined *of* the forms per se of judgments, and in the unity of a manifold, consequently, unconditioned by the conditions of the empirical material, which for that reason is called *unconditioned* or *absolute unity*.

Concepts are the material of the ideas insofar as they are concepts per se, i.e. products of the understanding. As products per se of the understanding, concepts are distinguished from one another only through their forms, [: 503] that is, by the manifold action of the understanding determined in the manifold forms of judgments. This manifold nature determined in the form of the understanding is exactly the opposite of the manifold nature determined in the forms of sensibility. Whereas the latter consists in externality and succession, i.e. in the modifications per se of the manifold per se, the former consists in the various types of connection, that is, in the modifications per se of unity per se. The manifold nature of the forms and the judgments and consequently also of the categories is thus a manifold nature independent of the forms of sensibility or even contradictory toward them.

It is accorded the second degree of spontaneity solely by virtue of the nature of spontaneity and not in virtue of sensibility; in this degree of spontaneity it is independent, and consequently it is present without the condition of an outside capacity. To the extent that the concepts are distinguished from one another (a multiplicity) merely through the manifold nature of the forms of judgments, they are a manifold unconditioned by the conditions of sensibility, and to the extent that reason connects only concepts as concepts, it only connects an unconditioned manifold. The unity arising from this is a unity of the unconditioned manifold: unconditioned, absolute unity. This will be made clearer in what follows in the development of the mode of action of reason in relation to the connection of concepts. [: 504]

§ LXXX.

The action by which reason connects concepts is an *indirect judgment* or a *syllogism,* the general form of which consists in the unconditioned connection of the first two forms of judgment according to each of the four moments, namely of unconditioned universality, limitation, concurrence, and necessity.

The action of spontaneity through which the connection of two representations (concepts) generated by the understanding is determined is called indirect judgment or syllogism. In as much as this connection is determined in consciousness as an occurrence that has already taken place, i.e. is represented, the syllogism is called *analytical,* but to the extent that it is undertaken *prior* to consciousness through the action of spontaneity (generated from concepts), the syllogism is called *synthetic* (see p. 438). Insofar as they consist of one and the same connection carried out synthetically and represented analytically, both have precisely the same form of connection – a form of connection, however, which because it is only represented in an analytical syllogism, can only be abstracted from this.

Now, in an analytical syllogism a predicate (the predicate of the conclusion) is represented as connected through another predicate – which in logic is called the middle term – with a subject (the subject of the conclusion), and consequently an object is conceived through the attribute of its attribute. A *judgment* is made *indirectly.* [: 505] The connection of the predicate and subject with the middle term is expressed through two judgments called premises, whereas the conclusion expresses the subject and predicate represented in the prefacing statements in its connection with the middle term. We shall see how this analytically expressed connection is determined synthetically.

Every judgment is determined in the nature of the understanding according to four moments, or, which amounts to the same thing, every judgment must have quantity, quality, relation, and modality, and so too must indirect judgment or the syllogism. The syllogism consists of the connection of two concepts, that is, of two products of the understanding, through two modes of action – products which must be determined according to all four moments. The syllogism can thus connect the two concepts only through a mode of action in which the modes of action by which the two concepts are determined are connected. In reality, the major premise in each syllogism consists of a *general statement* in relation to which the minor premise behaves in the manner of a particularizing statement, while the conclusion behaves in the manner of an individual statement, and so it is clear enough that *the form of the indirect judgment consists of the two connected first forms of direct judgment.*

In my attempt to prove this conclusively and thereby to delve more deeply into the nature of the syllogism than perhaps hitherto, [: 506] I think it advisable to point out to readers who have had less practice in abstract thinking that they do not lose anything if they skip over the next four numbered (internal) paragraphs. The others I would call upon to consult carefully the following schema of the ordinary syllogisms and the deduction of the forms of judgment in the theory of the understanding without which the following paragraphs can scarcely be comprehended.

M – P

S – M

S – P

The general form of syllogism referred to here, or of indirect judgment, is determined according to all four moments of judgment.

First, the subject of the indirect judgment is not immediately determined, but is determined as multiplicity and unity together (general) only through the agency of the middle term in the major premise. With respect to its predicate in the minor premise (where it is not connected with this predicate, but with the middle term) it is determined as multiplicity. In the conclusion where it is connected immediately with its predicate, it is determined as unity. The form of the indirect judgment is thus determined by the middle term determined as the logical subject* in the prefacing statements as multiplicity and unity together, and [: 507] is therefore *general.*

Secondly, the predicate of the indirect judgment is not immediately determined as a predicate, but only by means of the middle term with which it is immediately connected in the major premise – a predicate, which behaves toward its subject in the conclusion where it is brought together with it as a unity. In the minor premise where only the subject and the middle term

---

* As *logical subject*, that is, here, a subject that itself is (in the minor premise) a predicate per se of another subject.

are connected and the predicate is consequently excluded from the middle term, it is determined as multiplicity, whilst in the major premise through its connection with the middle term determined as the logical subject it is determined as unity and multiplicity together. Therefore, the predicate is brought together with it to the extent that the middle term is the subject, and in as much as the middle term is only such a subject that must itself be conceived as a predicate in the subject of the conclusion, the predicate is excluded from the direct unity of the actual subject by being connected with the middle term. The form of indirect judgment is thus determined by a predicate that behaves toward its subject as multiplicity and unity, and by its being connected with it through the middle term is only posited in the subject indirectly, therefore it is excluded from the subject by the middle term connected with the subject and posited in it. The form of indirect judgment is determined on the basis of *limitation**.

Thirdly, the relation of the subject and object *brought together* is not immediately determined in indirect judgment toward objective unity as unity and multiplicity, but only through the middle term. In the conclusion subject and object constitute a single object whose attribute is the predicate. In the minor premise, where the middle term occurs as an attribute of the subject, they constitute *two* objects, of which the one determined by the middle term, i.e. the subject, contains the basis of the other, i.e. the subject determined by the predicate. This occurs because, in the connection of the middle term with the subject in the minor premise, a ground obtains by which the connection of the predicate in the conclusion with the subject is determined. In the major premise the middle term is determined both as subject and as ground of the predicate: as subject, insofar as the predicate is bound with it as its attribute, and as ground, insofar as the predicate is determined at the same time as the attribute of the subject by its being the attribute of the middle term. The form of indirect judgment thus consists in the fact that two representations are excluded and bound by a third, [: 509] and to this extent is determined by the form of disjunction or concurrence.

Fourthly, the relation of the combination of subject and predicate to consciousness is not immediately determined, but only through the agency of the middle term as unity and multiplicity together. As *unity* in the conclusion, where the predicate is *actually* connected with the subject. As multiplicity in the minor premise, where the middle term alone is actually connected with

---

* The form of limitation determined in pure understanding per se consists in an *exclusion by way of* [: 508] *a positing* that only becomes a *negation* in the strict sense when the manifold excluded through this positing is determined on the basis of *what is given* (see p. 494 b.), i.e. where an actual *conflict* occurs. However, if the manifold excluded through this positing is a determination in *thought* only, a manifold is posited by positing what is to be excluded, and in this case *no conflict* arises despite its being a manifold.

the subject, and through that, the connection of the predicate connected with the middle term in the major premise is conceived as *possible* with respect to the subject. In the major premise this connection is determined as possible and actual together, and consequently as necessary, and the form of indirect judgment is *necessity*.

We have already encountered in the *table of the forms of judgment* forms which consist of the connection of the two first forms of judgment arising from each of the four moments. However, the form determined through this connection merely belongs to the forms of *indirect* judgments and is determined in the capacity per se of indirect judgment or the understanding per se. The categories of universality, limitation, concurrence, and necessity arising from them are attributes per se of objective (not of unconditioned) unity and can be related through this unity, in consequence, to *intuitions*, and therefore constitute in this relation the predicates of conditioned universality, limitation, concurrence, and necessity confined to the form of intuition [: 510]. Here *universality* is the unity of the multiple determined in time (or *number*), *limitation* the reality determined in time (or *degree*), *concurrence* the connection of several objects determined in *time* and in *space* (or *determinate coincidence*), and, finally, *necessity* the possibility in time inseparable from actuality determined in time.

Just as *universality, limitation, concurrence,* and *necessity* become <u>comparative</u> and <u>conditioned</u> insofar as they are determined by the understanding in the *narrowest sense* and consequently must be represented in their relation to the form of sensibility, so they become *absolute* and *unconditioned* insofar as they are determined by the understanding and consequently must be represented as something that *contradicts* the form of sensibility. They are determined, however, by reason, that is, the connections of the forms of judgment have their basis in reason insofar as they are determined in the form of indirect judgment or of syllogism where the connection of the forms of judgment in the middle term – a logical subject, a logical concept, a manifold conceived through understanding per se – occurs by way of a higher degree of spontaneity, whereas just this connection, when it occurs in a direct judgment and consequently occurs through the understanding in the narrowest sense (to the extent that, e.g. universality is predicated on the intuition of number and conceived as a direct attribute of number), is undertaken in relation not to any manifold conceived by the understanding per se [: 511] but in relation to a manifold determined through the form of sensibility. Consequently it can only be an action of spontaneity of the first degree that processes intuitions (i.e. of the understanding), not of a degree whose material is concepts, i.e. of reason.

The categories set out in the table of categories and determined *a priori* in the nature of the understanding in the narrower sense – those of *universality, limitation, concurrence,* and *necessity* – are thus capable of quite opposite determinations according to the manner of their relation to the form of *sensibility* or the form of *reason*. To the extent that they belong to the understanding as *forms of judgment* per se in the narrower sense, they are neither conditioned nor unconditioned. To the extent that they are determined in the *schemata* through time, they belong to the understanding in the narrowest sense and are *conditioned*. To the extent that they are determined, finally, in the form of indirect judgment or of syllogism, they belong to reason and are *unconditioned*.

§ LXXXI.

The representation of unconditioned unity determined in the form of syllogism *a priori* is the *idea in the narrowest sense* – the highest and most general idea, and the attributes of the object of this idea determined in the nature of the understanding, or pure, represented unconditioned unity, are *totality, infinity,* the *all-encompassing,* and *absolute necessity.* [: 512]

The *idea* in the *strictest* sense is a representation arising from the connection of concepts *a priori* (see LXXVIII). The representation of unconditioned unity, however, arises from the connection of the pure, represented, initial two categories according to all four moments and is thus the *idea* in the *strictest sense*. In as much as the object of this representation is nothing but the pure, represented form of the most general mode of action of reason and the form which all objects must assume insofar as they represented through pure reason, to this extent there cannot be any higher and more general idea than that of unconditioned unity.

I have set out the idea of *unconditioned unity* as it is originally determined in the nature of reason and consequently according to all four moments of pure understanding that provide pure reason with its material. It is important that this complicated and thoroughly determinate representation is not shifted aside unnoticed in the minds of some readers and replaced by a simpler and less determinate representation of unconditioned reason, where one will feel oneself tempted, for example, to conceive of nothing but the unity of the manifold in general not determined through sensibility. However, in that case, one has not really thought *unconditioned unity* – a unity which by no means is the unity of the manifold in general represented without sensibility (which would be the concept *a priori* of *objective unity* determined by the understanding in the narrower sense), but, on the contrary, is the unity of manifold determined by the understanding per se according to the forms of the concepts and represented only by reason. [: 513]

The representation of unconditioned unity per se remains forever in error and indeterminate where it does not have the general form of the ideas determined in the nature of the syllogism as its object. In this aspect, however, it must be conceived in accordance with all four of its moments through the connection of the first two categories, and, more particularly, through that connection's not applying to an intuition but to concepts per se, i.e. through *unconditioned connection*. Its essential characteristics are therefore unconditioned universality or *totality*, unconditioned limitation or exclusion of the limiting condition, i.e. *infinity*, unconditioned concurrence or the* *all-encompassing*, and unconditioned *necessity*.

Unconditioned unity, as the object of any *a priori* representation, is necessary for all rational beings. In the same way as reason evolves, so it too must be conceived more and more determinately. In this way it is a general attribute of all objects represented by means of reason.

Unconditioned unity must be conceived by all who avail themselves of their reason not only necessarily, but also as something *necessary* in itself, *excluding of all boundaries, all-encompassing*, and *total (complete)*. These moments have surely been apparent to every philosopher [: 514]. Yet some believed themselves to have recognized the *deity* in them, others *Nature* or the *universe*, until the *philosopher of Königsberg* discovered them in the nature of the syllogism – the first to do so.

Since unconditioned unity contradicts the form of intuition, it cannot be any attribute of cognizable objects**. Since at the same time this unity is an essential attribute of all objects conceivable through reason, it is apparent that objects, insofar as they are conceivable through reason, are not cognizable, and that reason cognizes nothing. Totality, infinity, all-encompassing, and unconditioned necessity are attributes per se of the unity of the concepts generated by reason and determined in the nature of reason. They are thus also attributes that contradict intuition and consequently any object insofar as it is intuitable, and they therefore cannot be attributed to any cognizable thing insofar as it is cognizable. Unconditioned unity and its proper attributes are thus also neither an object of *experience*, nor direct attributes of the objects of experience – objects whose content must consist of nothing but subjects and predicates under the form of an intuition contradicting all unconditioned things. On the other hand, unconditioned unity is an *indirect* attribute of cognizable objects, of appearances, [: 515] and of experience – an attribute, namely, relating to objects through the agency of the concepts that occur in them and pertain to their form, concepts that, through reason, receive a unity that the understanding connecting with intuitions cannot give them: *rational unity*. Reason binds

---

*   Under *infinity* and the *all-encompassing* must be conceived neither space nor time, nor any intuition of them underlying these two ideas.

** Not to the extent that they are cognizable, but to the extent that they are conceivable.

to cognizable objects that feature of them which is a product per se of the understanding and thereby generates not a unity of the cognizable (insofar as it is cognizable, conceivable, and intuitable at the same time), not an objective unity, but unity of the cognizable insofar as the cognizable is *merely conceivable* and is unconditioned unity. This is a context through connected concepts that exceeds all experience, but a context against which all experience must be measured insofar as concepts occur in it that inhere in the form of reason. *Objective* unity, which is determined by the understanding, relates immediately to intuitions that receive through them the essential attribute of determinate objects. It constitutes in its connection with intuition the cognizable object, and is to this extent, along with intuition, an essential *constitutive* component of experience. *Unconditioned* unity, by contrast, which is determined by reason, relates immediately to *concepts per se* subsumed under a higher unity through it. This is a unity consisting of the connection not of what is intuitable of the appearances, but only of what can be conceived of them through the understanding and which is consequently no constitutive component of experience, but a *law per se* according to which [: 516] the conceived objects of experience have to be systematically ordered in a totality of knowledge, in a scientific relation. And this is what the author of the *Critique of Reason* wanted to characterize through the very apt words: "Reason in experience is not used *constitutively*, but merely *regulatively*."

Unconditioned unity relates in a mediated way to the form of intuition, namely by means of the categories. In other words, it relates to the schemata by means of the form of understanding determined with each of them. And by those means the cognizable objects, the appearances, are subjected to the form of reason in a mediated way (indirectly). Unconditioned unity is consequently restricted indirectly to intuitions; the four attributes of unconditioned unity, by means of the four aspects of the categories, become four *conceivable* attributes of the intuitable; and judgments, which express the relations of these attributes of the appearances which are determined indirectly by reason, or, which is nearly the same, the relation of the appearances by means of the schemata to absolute unity, are formulated as the following *rational laws of the systematic unity of experience*:

1) *All extensive magnitude of the appearances must be conceived as unconditioned.* The totality of unconditioned unity is restricted here through the concept of quantity to the form of intuition, and the form of intuition is extended toward totality through the concept of quantity conceived as unconditioned (by reason). [: 517] Extensive magnitude conceived by the *understanding* is represented as a magnitude determined, conditioned and limited in time, i.e. as *number*;

conceived by *reason* it is represented as an indeterminate magnitude in time determinable ad infinitum, as numberlessness, as a magnitude which is determined through multiplicity in time alone and has no limit of multiplicity but is a magnitude extending to infinity. Reason excludes from possible experience, to this extent, every absolute limit of extension, i.e. a limit not determined in time by the understanding. In the sensory world nothing unextended, no hole in extension itself can be thought: *In mundo non datur hiatus.*

2) *All intensive magnitude of the appearances must be conceived as unconditioned.* The limitlessness of unconditioned unity is confined here through the concept of reality to the form of intuition, and the form of intuition is extended through the concept of quality, conceived as unconditioned, toward limitlessness. Intensive magnitude conceived by the understanding is represented as a magnitude of quality determined (conditioned) in time as degree; conceived by reason it is represented as an indeterminate, yet determinable ad infinitum, magnitude of quality in time, as continuity in the degrees of the real. Reason excludes from possible experience to this extent every absolute limit of *intension*, i.e. every limit not determined by the understanding in time. In the sense-world nothing can be conceived without degree, neither absolute reality, nor absolute negation, and no jump among the various degrees [: 518] themselves can be thought: *In mundo non datur saltus.*

3) *Every connection among the appearances must be conceived as unconditioned.* The all-encompassing, all-connecting nature of unconditioned unity is limited by the concept of relation to the form of intuition; this form is extended through the concept of relation conceived as unconditioned (by reason) in the direction of the all-encompassing. Any relation conceived in time by the understanding is represented as a sequence which is determined, conditioned, and limited in time. Reason thinks a relation as sequence, time series, and simultaneity which is not determined – yet determinable ad infinitum – in time; this relation is represented as a connection in time without limit. Reason, to this extent, excludes all absolutes from possible experience, i.e. it is the limit of connection not determined by the understanding. All appearances in the sensory world are connected with appearances, and nothing that is *isolated*, and consequently, no *absolute* beginning, can be conceived in this sensory world: *In mundo non datur casus purus.*

4) *All necessity inhering in the appearances* (the being of the appearances at all times) *must be conceived as unconditioned.* The absolute necessity of unconditioned unity is limited by the concept of modality to the form of intuition; this form is extended by the concept of necessity, conceived as unconditioned (by reason), in the direction of unconditioned being in

limitless time. Modality conceived in time by the understanding [: 519] is represented in the connection of its two first forms in the category of necessity as a necessity determined, conditioned, and limited in time, and as conditioned being represented in limitless time. Conceived by reason, it is represented as an indeterminate – but determinable ad infinitum – being in unending time where its determinations extend into limitlessness. Reason excludes from possible experience to this extent every absolute limit of conditioned necessity not determined by the understanding. No absolute and necessary thing can be conceived in the sensory world, however, every appearance in possible time must necessarily be conceived as conditioned, and consequently as the being-conditioned of everything that extends into limitlessness, i.e. as *unconditioned*. In the sensory world, every possible event is therefore determined by other events going forward, sideways and backward according to the laws of experience. *In mundo non datur fatum.*

These four laws of rational unity consist of the same number of laws of rational unity represented on the basis of reason and consequently extended toward the unconditioned. They are laws conceived by the understanding and are thus related immediately to the form of intuition. They are *constitutive* laws of experience (according to their form) which are nevertheless conceived by reason and consequently related only indirectly through the agency of the concepts to the form of intuition. They are merely *regulative* laws of experience, in the first respect determining the *objective* unity of that which is conceivable and intuitable in experience, of [: 520] the *cognizable* manifold, and in the second respect determining the *unconditioned* unity of the manifold merely conceivable in experience. As laws of the understanding they express the unity determined according to the four moments of immediate capacity for judgment and conditioned by sensibility, the unity of the understanding of the appearances. As rational laws, as the unity determined according to the four moments of indirect capacity for judgment and not conditioned by reason, they express the rational unity of the appearances.

Just as the *constitutive* laws of experience are included under the highest law, "every object cognizable in experience stands, insofar as it is cognizable, under the objective unity of the manifold represented by intuition", so the *regulative* laws of experience are included under the highest law, "every object cognizable in experience, insofar as it is *conceivable* in a systematic connection, stands under the unconditioned unity of the manifold represented by concepts", or, which amounts to the same thing, "nothing can be *conceived* in the *totality* of experience in the systematic unity of the sensory world which does not accord with unconditioned unity, i.e. which can be connected through reason according to this law". This highest law which reason prescribes for experience and which is the law of the systematic unity of all empirical knowledge is immediately accompanied by three great principles through which reason guides [: 521] the understanding in the investigation of nature and through which it orders its findings in a scientific context.

1) The principle of *homogeneity*, or the law of *genera*: *multiplicity determined by the understanding per se has unconditioned unity*. Multiplicity determined by the understanding per se consists of the multiplicity of the subjects of *one* predicate, the multiplicity *of the same kind*. From this multiplicity reason generates the unity of the many of the same kind, the *genus*.

2) The principle of *specification*, or the law of *kinds*: *unity determined by the understanding has an unconditioned manifold nature*. The unity determined by the understanding per se consists in the unity of the subject insofar as it is determined through unity per se of the predicate. If this predicate is an intuition unity is *individual*; if it is a concept per se the unity is a *kind*, i.e. a unity which cannot relate to an individual indirectly, but through an attribute common to several individuals and consequently can only be represented by reason.

3) The law of the *continuity of logical forms*, consisting of the conjunction of the laws of homogeneity and specification, and a *continuous* (uninterrupted) transition from one kind to another, both in the ascension to higher species and in the descent to lower ones, and on account of both making a *thoroughly systematic context* necessary. All three *principles* are determined *a priori* in the nature of the capacity for representation insofar as it has reason – as an unconditioned unity of the manifold [: 522], as an unconditioned manifold, and as unconditioned unity and manifold together*.

§ LXXXII.

The *general* form of syllogisms encompasses three *particular forms* determined likewise in the nature of pure reason, namely, the form of the

---

* The law of continuity applies to intuitions by means of concepts and is thus another way of formulating the general law of the *rational unity* of appearances. According to this law 1) continuity of *extension*, 2) of *degree*, 3) of *causal conjunction*, 4) of conditioned necessity, or of *contingency*, cannot be *cognized* as unconditioned (unlimited), but must be *conceived* in the service of a systematic unity which, (through reason), is demanded of the essential nature of the cognizable by unconditioned (by the understanding in the narrowest sense) conditioned being.

categorical, hypothetical, and *disjunctive* syllogism, through which the general form of the ideas in general, or unconditioned unity, is determined more closely in three particular forms of particular ideas – ideas which, represented purely, constitute the objects of three ideas in the narrowest sense, namely the idea of the *absolute subject,* the *absolute ground,* and of *absolute community.*

Just as the general form of judgment, or the combination of the represented manifold in objective unity, encompasses particular forms of judgment [: 523] determined in the nature of pure understanding, so the general form of syllogism, or of indirect judgment, encompasses particular forms of syllogisms determined in the nature of pure reason. And just as through the general form of the syllogisms the representation of unconditioned unity in general is determined as the highest idea of pure reason, so the representations of the kinds of unconditioned unity determined in the nature of reason are determined through the particular forms of the syllogisms, as we will demonstrate in the following.

The basic form of the syllogism in general is determined according to the four moments of indirect judgment, and consequently also according to the moment of *relation.* (In every syllogism in general the middle term must behave toward the predicate of the conclusion as *subject* and as its *ground.*) Since there are three sorts of determinate types in the moment of relation determining how predicates and subjects can be connected with one another in an objective unity, namely according to the categorical, hypothetical, and disjunctive form, the predicate of the conclusion in the major premise of the syllogism can be bound with the middle term as the *subject of the judgment* in three types of ways. The middle term can function as the subject in the strictest sense in relation to the predicate, i.e. as the object of its *attribute,* or as the *ground* leading toward *consequence,* or as one *part* to the *other* with which it constitutes a common whole. [: 524] The syllogism in the first case is *categorical,* in the second *hypothetical,* and in the third *disjunctive.* The genus syllogism thus encompasses three kinds within itself, which, insofar as they are based on the capacity for direct judgment, on the capacity to bind concepts per se through connected forms of judgment, constitute just as many forms of particular direct judgments or deductions and just as many particular modes of action of pure reason. The general mode of action of reason consists in the combination of a subject and predicate in unconditioned unity; its particular modes of action consist in the combination in unconditioned unity, whereby the subject is determined either as object and the predicate as attribute, or the subject as ground and the predicate as consequence, or the subject as the one part of a common whole and the predicate as the other. And just as the representation of unity determined through the most general mode of action of reason is the idea of unconditioned unity in general, so the representations of the three unities determined through these three modes of action of reason are the ideas of unconditioned unity of the subject, of ground, and of community, or, which amounts to the same, of the *absolute subject*, the *absolute ground*, and *absolute community*.

The categories determined in the nature of the understanding in the narrower sense – of *substance, ground*, and of *community* – to the extent that they have their ground in the understanding in the *narrower* sense, are mere forms in which to conceive [: 525] objects in general, attributes per se of the unity of the represented. In this respect they can be applied both to *sensibility* and to *what is represented* by *reason*. Through their relation to the form of sensory intuition determined in the nature of the mind *a priori*, they move into the *region of the understanding in the narrowest sense*, into the region of the empirical capacity for cognition where they constitute the *forms of cognizability* in their inseparable union with space and time, and are forms and attributes of the unity of the intuitable. Through their relation to the form of reason likewise determined in the nature of the mind *a priori*, through unconditioned combination and unconditioned unity thereby generated, they move into the *domain of reason* where in inseparable union with unconditioned unity (the unity of those attributes that have their material in the understanding per se and their form in reason) they constitute the form of the *the totality of relations* that occur among empirical cognitions and are attributes of that unity in which not the intuitable through the understanding, but what is *conceived* – what in the intuitable is produced by the understanding – is combined: the forms and attributes of *rational unity*.

External and *internal sense* converts an empirical perception, which rational unity renders complete, into a cognition. Only through external sense are *objects* – appearances of things outside us – *cognizable* in the strict sense, [: 526] and that which is intuitable through internal sense, the appearances in us, is nothing but modifications within us, *representations* per se. The rational unity of empirical cognition is thus converted into *objective* and *subjective* rational unity. Through the one the intuitable of external sense, the *objects* outside us, and through the other, the intuitable of internal sense, the *representations* within us, are brought into a *complete relation*. The three attributes of rational unity – the *absolute subject*, *absolute ground*, and *absolute community* – thereby acquire two types of essentially dissimilar objects insofar, on the one hand, as they are related to the intuitable of the internal or of external sense, and, on the other hand, as they are attributes of the unconditioned unity of representations in us or of the objects outside us, i.e. determinations of *subjective* and *objective* *rational unity*.

§ LXXXIII.

The absolute subject, the absolute ground, and absolute community determine the *objective* rational unity of experience insofar as it is *indirectly* related to things represented *a posteriori* in empirical cognition. They determine the *subjective* rational unity of experience insofar as they are *immediately* related to the representing subject represented *a priori* in distinct consciousness.

Only in empirical consciousness of the objects of external sense are cognizable *substances*, [: 527] cognizable (effecting) grounds, and cognizable *communities* (reciprocal effects) possible. The *schema of substantiality* determined in the nature of the understanding in the narrower sense can only be applied to a material given to external sense, only to what has sequence in space, to the extent that what is given in time per se is change and not permanent. The *schema of causality* at first sight, insofar as it is represented *a priori* only *as a determinate consequence in time*, appears not to be confined to objects in space. But since the determination of consequence in time is only brought about through a ground in time, and this ground in time is itself another consequence, and consequently must be *accident* per se – the accident is only cognizable insofar as it can be perceived and its substance is cognizable –, the schema of causality is likewise only applicable to accidents, that is, to accidents affecting sequence in space. Thus all *cognizable* consequence is nothing but change in space, *motion*, just as all cognizable ground is nothing but the ground of motion, to the extent that it is itself cognizable in space, i.e. itself arises through motion. The schema of community, finally, or of determinate simultaneity, apparently presupposes the form of external sense, i.e. space, in that without the relation of time (in which nothing is determined as succession per se) to space no *simultaneity* is possible. Cognizable community consists in the reciprocal effect in space of intuitable subjects on one another [: 528]. All cognizable substance, ground, community is thus *objective*, that is, relates through an objective, *a posteriori* given material to things which must be distinguished in consciousness from the representing *subject*, its *representations* and its *forms*. The *objective* substance, ground, and community related through the objective material given in intuition to objects are only *on their own cognizable* to the extent that they are objective. The schemata of substance, ground and community are the attributes of *objective unity* determined in the nature of the faculty of cognition – objective unity of the things outside us represented through intuition, and consequently of the *individual* unity of substance and accident, ground, and consequence, and the parts of community, insofar as substance, together with accident, constitute an individual, and insofar as ground and consequence and community are attributes through which two individuals reciprocally determine their individuality. The ideas of absolute substance, ground, and community of the external sense are those attributes – determined in the nature of reason – of the unconditioned unity of things outside us determined by the understanding, i.e. of objective things insofar as they are determined by the understanding as having a manifold nature on account of the variety of combination into objective unity and then bound anew by reason. They are thus not attributes of *individual* unity, of that unity by which an individual is determined as individual, but of *universal* unity by which the connection of all individuals is determined. They therefore relate [: 529] to cognizable *individuals*, things outside us, not like schemata, immediately by intuition itself constituting a component of the schemata, but, on the contrary, only indirectly through the schemata, and only through that component of them which is determined in understanding per se through the concept, through objective unity determined as substance, or as ground, or as community – a unity which is elevated toward unconditioned unity by reason. That which is represented in intuition as unconditioned is conceived as unconditioned in the idea. All cognizable things are cognizable only insofar as they are represented as conditioned, but, insofar as they are merely conceivable, i.e. represented by reason, are represented as unconditioned. The understanding cognizes individuals, reason conceives of their connection, i.e. generality – which *apart* from individuals is nothing but a *form* of thought, an empty idea – only in an *indirect* manner through the agency of the understanding in the narrower sense, and has the objective relation of affectedness.

Empirical cognition of *internal* sense per se has no objects in a strict sense, only representations toward objects which can be represented neither as something with sequence in space, as cognizable *substances*, nor as *accidents* with sequence in space, as cognizable accidents. That which is *empirically cognizable* in our representations is nothing other than the manifold given through affectedness and represented under the form of internal sense – *change within us*, which can only become an object of internal sense in *clear consciousness*. [: 530] With clear consciousness (see §XXXIX) representation is represented as representation per se within us, consequently it is represented under the form of internal sense, i.e. intuited and related through a representation – the internal intuition – to the representing subject. Representation thereby receives *subjective unity*, i.e. connection with the representing entity and in the representing entity, but it only receives a conditioned unity, a conditioned connection. It is related to the representing entity only insofar as it is determined according to the form of sensibility and determined in time.

Unconditioned subjective unity of representations is only determined by reason in *distinct consciousness*. In *distinct consciousness* (see § XL,

XLI) representations are related to the *represented I* which can only be represented as the *absolute subject of the capacity for representation a priori* and therefore can only be conceived on the basis of reason.

The *subject* of the capacity for representation as subject can only be represented on the basis of reason because it cannot be determined as subject through any predicate representable in a possible intuition, or, which amounts to the same thing, because the attribute of the subject cannot be related to the representing *I* through any intuition, as is the case in the object with the subjects of external sense where the attribute *subject*, related to the intuitable in *space per se*, determines the representation of the permanent in space and the conceivable and intuitable of the *cognizable subject*. What is cognizable *a posteriori* through internal sense [: 531] are the representations, insofar as they are appearances within us, objects under the form per se of internal sense, mere *modifications* within us which, since they cannot be related to any empirically cognizable substance representable in space and time, i.e. cannot also be conceived as empirically cognizable contingent occurrences. – What is cognizable *a priori* through internal sense is the form per se of internal empirical intuition, purely represented *time*, which is as little able to be the attribute of the representing subject as the form per se of external empirical intuition or purely represented *space* is able to be. Neither a manifold in space per se (cognizable durability), nor a manifold in time per se (change within us, representation) can constitute the representing subject, can be a property of the subject constituting its substance – a subject that must be distinguished both from things outside us, appearances on the outside, and all representations within us, the appearances of internal sense in consciousness. Space per se and time per se, *insofar as they can be intuited*, are forms per se of sensory representations and consequently are predicates per se of subjects which must be distinguished in essence from the representing entity if they are to be representable; they are predicates of representations per se insofar as these are representable and distinct from representing representations, i.e. of empirical intuitions. *Space* and *time*, insofar as they can be intuited, cannot possibly be related to the representing subject. Through them neither the representing subject nor its attribute [: 532] is represented, but only an attribute per se of the appearances distinct from the representing subject. The *unity* occurring in purely represented space and purely represented time is a product per se of spontaneity. This unity even contains the *manifold* in space and time insofar as the manifold is represented *a priori*. Consequently unity is determined in representation not through any affectedness from without, but through a spontaneity affecting its own receptivity – a product of spontaneity according to its actuality as the material of representation which is active according to the form which is determined in receptivity per se solely according to its possibility. That which of purely represented space and purely represented time is thus not a product per se of spontaneity but belongs to receptivity per se is the *possibility* per se of the form of externality and succession (not of the representing subject, but) of a *material* of a representation *given* to receptivity – the possibility per se of the form of a sensory representation *a posteriori*, the possible, the conceivable, that which is representable of *intuitability* through spontaneity per se, not intuitability itself, not the form per se of the empirical material, not the predicate per se of the appearance which is representable not through spontaneity per se but only *a priori* through sensibility. Insofar, then, as space and time can be represented by sensibility, they are not conceived as predicates of the representing entity but only of the sensorily representable. They become predicates of the representing entity, insofar, through *the category per se of possibility*, as they are conceived not as intuitable, but as [: 533] conceivable in the *representing subject*. They are *intuitable* as forms of externality and succession of possible material in the mind according to their possibility *in what is represented*. On the basis of their intuition the possibility of externality and succession of the given manifold is represented. According to their possibility in the *representing entity* they are only *conceivable* on the basis of their ground determined in the capacity for representation. They are not present in the representing entity as its forms, but it is only their determinate possibility, their conceivable ground which constitutes one of the forms of the capacity for representation, namely sensibility. This conceivable ground of space per se and time per se, *not space and time themselves*, is therefore the predicate on the basis of which the representing subject as the subject of sensibility is determined. As the subject of sensibility this ground can only be conceived, not intuited. Even sensibility as a predicate of the representing entity is not an intuitable predicate, but a merely conceivable one, and the subject is determined through this predicate on no account as a conceivable and intuitable subject, i.e. a cognizable subject. The subject of the capacity for representation is thus not immediately representable through the understanding but only through reason, and cannot be conceived as anything determinable in space and time but only as an absolute subject.

Everything determinable in space and time is a material per se of a possible representation, something that can be given to the receptivity of the representing subject. The subject itself can never be the given because, with all givenness, it must be presupposed as the something to be given *to* [: 534] distinct from the given. The representing subject can thus never occur in an intuition, and representation, by which the subject thinks itself, can only be a product per se of the autonomy of the subject, of reason. Incidentally, it is also clear enough from *the theory of the capacity for cognition* that *everything cognizable* must either be an *appearance* of the external or the internal sense, the permanent in space, the extended, the body, or that which in time per se is not external to us: the representable, change within us, representation. Only by distinguishing the representing subject from everything intuitable in space and time are consciousness and cognition possible, and the representing entity can neither be conceived as something intuitable in space nor as something intuitable in time. Its representation as subject thus becomes the task of reason per se.

The attribute of the unconditioned is thus *immediately* related to the represented representing subject, i.e. not, as with the objects of external sense, by means of the concept – determined in the schema of substantiality – of cognizable substance determined in space and time. The representing *I* is able to be represented only through an *idea in the narrowest sense*, as absolute subject.

This absolute subject acquires the attribute of *absolute ground* only with respect to what is produced by reason per se in the representations, and consequently [: 535] is representable as an *effect* only through reason in an *idea*. The absolute subject must be conceived as *active* insofar as it is the subject of spontaneity which brings forth the form of representation in general, or the unity of the manifold. The *genus* representation itself encompasses three essentially distinct *kinds* within it: sensory representation, the concept, and the idea, or the representation of sensibility, of the understanding, and of reason. Each of these types has their own proper *form* distinct from the others: unity of apprehension, unity of the understanding, and rational unity. Spontaneity expresses itself in three different degrees of activity in the process of producing them: as the capacity for apprehension, as pure understanding, and as pure reason. The action of apprehension consists in the synthesis of the manifold given through affectedness, and spontaneity is determined toward this synthesis through affectedness. It thus acts in the actual understanding as *compelled*, indeed *utterly* compelled insofar as receptivity is affected *from without*, and *relatively* compelled, insofar as spontaneity itself affects receptivity, and thus in its own action is the source of affectedness through which it impels the production of the form of representation. With each sensory representation the action of spontaneity acts as counter-effect to effect; it is a necessary consequence of this action, and if this consequence happens through something quite distinct from the representing subject the representing subject is not even able to be conceived as the absolute ground of the *occurrence* of the representation. [: 536] The action of the *understanding* consists in the binding of the manifold represented by intuition, an action toward which spontaneity is determined not through affectedness, but solely through itself – it acts therefore in an *uncompelled* way. The *concept* arises not through an effect on sensibility and a counter-effect of spontaneity, but through the binding of what has already become a representation and what is presented through the manifold to the understanding by intuition. Consequently, the concept arises through an action that has its ground neither in something outside the mind nor in the mind itself, not in sensibility, but solely in the *understanding* which gives the representation being through its *autonomy*. Since the understanding (if this is conceived of not as the categories per se but only as the forms of thought of the understanding) only binds through a manifold represented by intuition – it is, in its action, *bound* to the form of intuition insofar as it only binds what is presented to it under the form of sensory representation. The unity which it produces is only comparative and relates only to the form of intuition and thus only extends as far as the manifold determined through this form. The understanding, it is true, is *uncompelled* in the production of the concept, but it acts by being *bound* to the form of sensibility and must therefore be conceived as the absolute ground of the *occurrence* – but not of the *form* – of a concept in its narrowest meaning. It acts as the understanding in the narrowest meaning only in unification with sensibility.

The action of *reason*, by contrast, consists in the binding [: 537] of the manifold determined in the nature per se of the understanding and through the form per se of the concepts insofar as they are products per se of spontaneity to the second degree. The *idea* arises through spontaneity's giving unity to the manifold forms of the understanding (a manifold determined through spontaneity per se). It consequently binds a material which is presented to it not through sensibility, with which it is not bound to any condition of sensibility, but acts according to the forms per se of spontaneity, and therefore as unconditioned spontaneity not determined and limited by anything distinct from itself, i.e. as *absolute autonomy*. To the extent that the representing subject acts through reason, it acts as *absolute ground*, as *uncompelled*, *unbound*, determined through nothing but its own autonomy, i.e. it is *free*. The representing subject must be conceived as a *free* ground insofar as it is the subject of *reason*. *Rational unity* is the only conceivable absolute effect of the representing subject – something which is conceivable in no other way than as the absolute effect of this unity. (In the *theoretical* capacity for representation the *systematic nature* of cognition is determined through this rational unity; in the *practical* capacity for representation the moral nature of acts of will is determined.) The action of *reason* is the only possible action which can be conceived of as *free*, and it also cannot be conceived of as *free* in any other way. But this freedom, this absolute effect of reason, is only conceivable through reason per se, [: 538] through an idea. It does not belong among the cognizable actions, and is not comprehensible according to its *real* possibility, or, which amounts to the same, it has no cognizable (conceivable and intuitable) possibility for us.

The absolute subject of the capacity for representation acquires the attribute of *absolute community* only insofar as it is conceived of as a member of a whole consisting of *rational beings* – a system whose members are joined not through *cognizability*, i.e. through a reciprocal effect determinable in space and time, i.e. *simultaneity*, but through the *common agreement* of their free actions determined by one and the same action of reason. This is the *moral world*, the free state of rational beings, whose binding among one another consists in the *harmony* per se of their thought and action. It is the work of their own reason, their free effectiveness – a world which is ruled according to no other laws than those prescribed to themselves by each citizen; laws which are determined through nothing but their own autonomy, and which they obey in an uncompelled, unbounded and consequently *free* way.

The rational unity of experience (the connection of the appearances both of external and internal sense determined by the nature of reason) is represented through *six ideas*, of which three concern the *objective unity* of external, and three the *subjective unity* of internal experience; three are related through the schemata and consequently indirectly to *objects*, three indirectly through [: 539] reason to the representing *subject*; three have *indirect* objective reality insofar as they relate through the schemata to an *objective material*, and so are merely ideas in the narrower sense; three, by contrast, insofar as they relate immediately to the subject – representable through reason – of the capacity for representation, have *subjective* reality based on the subject per se and its reality, and to this extent are *ideas in the narrowest sense*. Through the first group, cognizable objects are *conceived* in a systematic context. Through the second group, representations per se are *brought* into a systematic context; through the first, what in experience is merely objective and independent of us, and through the second, what is merely subjective and dependent on us, is represented in a consistent relation.

Since the origin of these six ideas based in the nature of reason, which we therefore call *necessary* ideas, was completely overlooked until the appearance of the *Critique of Reason*, nothing was more natural than to seek the *objects* of these ideas partly in experience among cognizable things, and then – since one failed to locate them there – either to deny them immediately or find them in a *realm of the understanding* held to be quite distinct from the *realm of sensibility*. In this realm of the understanding, which was set against the realm of sensibility, one could have believed oneself to have cognized things *as they are in themselves* on the basis of reason. In the other world, things were represented as they appeared through the deceptive medium of *organization*. [: 540]

In regard to the *enduring subjects* of *external experience*, i.e. in regard to bodies, the attribute of the *absolute*, which *reason* is obliged to add to these bodies, was soon found to be missing. The attribute of bodily substance occurring in intuition – extension – revealed itself to be the opposite of the absolute and the unchanging, namely as something relative and mutable, whereas on the other side in the enduring subject of *internal experience* no attribute of its reality could be summoned up in intuition.

The attribute of the absolute, which reason is obliged to add to the *effective causes* of *external experience*, was also found to be missing from them. Every substance whose effects occur in space acts by means of a *motion* in relation to which it must be determined, likewise through motion, by another substance. No ground can therefore be perceived as absolute. In the entire compass of external experience no *first cause* of an effect occurring in this experience can occur. By contrast, on the other side, in the cause that is able to be represented in *internal* sense – *the will* – the capacity to be self-determined, the freedom that no intuition can represent according to the *real possibility* of such freedom, cannot itself be grasped.

In *community* among the objects of *external* sense, in the *physical* world, it was soon the case that the attribute of the *absolute*, which reason is obliged to add to this community, was found to be missing. From absolute concurrence, a completely [: 541] systematic ordering of all bodily substances, no other result can be conceived than the completely regular procession of the *physical events of the world*; from absolute concurrence, a complete ordering of all rational beings, no other result can be conceived than completely regular procession in *the moral world*; and, finally, from the binding of absolute community among physical substances and absolute community among rational beings, insofar as these two commonalities are ordered together, no other result can be conceived than the blissfulness of finite beings – and therefore those rational beings endowed with *sensibility*. These demands of reason are contradicted in experience through *physical and moral evils*.

All philosophical systems until now are attempts to solve the great puzzle of an *absolute* that reason demands in the service of experience, and which is sought in vain in experience. These have been *abortive* attempts, insofar as they have all thoroughly misconstrued the true meaning and ground of this *absolute*, although they were indispensible *preliminaries* leading to its ultimate discovery.

§ LXXXIV.

Through the idea of the absolute subject, that which lies at the basis of the appearances of external sense *objectively* and of internal sense *subjectively* is not represented as the *thing* [: 542] *in itself* but is represented under the form determined in the nature of reason.

The objectivity that lies at the basis of the appearances of external sense is that to which the material per se given in intuition belongs without the form which it has assumed in the mind. The unrepresentable *thing in itself*, however, through the fact that all its predicates of the appearance determined through sensibility have been dispensed with and only those predicates that understanding per se has determined of it are gathered together, is represented as a rational being per se, i.e. under the form of *rational unity*. Without a relation to the *appearance*, the absolute subject is a mere logical thing, the empty form of an idea without application. For only in its appearance does that given material occur which, through its being present in the mind, gives the conceived absolute subject application to something which is not a representation per se, nor the form of representation per se.

The quarrel of philosophers in regard to the question "whether bodily substances must be conceived of as infinitely divisible or as an aggregate of simple substances without bodies" is merely a consequence of the mistaken representation of the *absolute subject*. The objects of external sense are *cognizable, conditioned* subjects with *extension*, intuitable in space, filling space, yet, insofar as space is infinitely divisible, they are merely *conceivable, unconditioned subjects*, representable through reason and *not* [: 543] *extended*, because the predicate of space contradicts them, and the form of the idea under which they are conceived is *absolute unity*. But through this *unity of the subject* the *thing in itself* is as little able to be represented as through the *multiplicity of the spatial*, and consequently this absolute unity can as little mean *simplicity* as *absolute multiplicity* means the *extension of the thing in itself* – a thing not representable as the thing in itself, and of whose predicates, therefore, we can speak with as little justification as the congenitally blind of the colours of the rainbow.

What *subjectively* underlies the appearances of external sense, the representations, insofar as they are represented within us as changes, is the *thing in itself* to which the capacity for representation belongs. But this is able to be represented neither as *thing in itself*, nor as the thing under the form of intuition, as appearance, but only as the thing under the form of the idea, as the subject of predicates which are not representable through intuition, namely of the forms (not of the representations, but) of the *capacity for representation*, i.e. as the subject of the possibility – representable only through reason – of being affected, as the subject of thought.

The quarrel of philosophers regarding the question "whether the representing subject is simple or compound, a spirit or a body" is thus, likewise, merely a consequence of the mistaken representation of the *absolute subject*. The absolute subject of the capacity for representation is determinable neither in space nor in time. It [: 544] can thus be represented neither under the form of space, as something filling space, i.e. as *extended*, nor under the form of time, as something temporary, but it must be represented as absolute immutable unity excluding the entire manifold. Since this unity is a product of spontaneity determined in the *mode of action* per se of reason and generated through the action of reason, so it is the case that the thing in itself underlying the capacity for representation is represented on no account as the *thing in itself*, but only under the form which reason determines in regard to the representation of it, and the representing entity acquires absolute unity only insofar as it is representable (through reason). This entity thus indicates the *simplicity* of the representing subject as a *thing in itself* – a *thing in itself*, neither simple nor compound, but at the same time completely unable to be represented.

The *absolute subject* is the attribute, determined in the nature of reason, common to that which *subjectively* lies at the basis of the appearances of internal sense and *objectively* at the basis of the appearances of external sense. In relation to the appearances of external sense it designates that to which the objective material of empirical intuition belongs, but which, through this material, is only representable under the form of intuition in the appearance, yet which in its difference from the appearance is only representable through the binding of what in the appearance is present not under the form of intuition, not under the form of the attributes of the appearance determined by the understanding per se, [: 545] not under the form of the manifold of the intellectual form of these attributes, that is, it is representable through an *idea* that represents the *thing in itself* without all its material corresponding to it in intuition, i.e. through the form per se of rational unity and thus not as the *thing in itself*. In relation to the appearances of *internal sense*, the absolute subject designates that to which representation belongs as pure representation, the thing in itself, which, through its capacity for representation, is the ground of possible representation representing itself only through its capacity for representation and thus through that capacity by which it is able to represent independent of sensibility, that is, *through reason*.

Since the representation of the absolute subject signifies the unrepresentable *thing in itself* insofar as it lies at the basis of the appearances, it can easily be understood why, through this representation, one believed oneself able to represent *the thing in itself* as *thing in itself*, and why one sought its ground in the *thing in itself* so long as this ground was not found as the result of a correct analysis of the capacity for representation in the nature of reason. And since both the representing subject and the cognizable substances determined by the understanding in space must be conceived as absolute subjects by reason, one can easily understand how it happened that representation of *cognizable substance* (conceivable through the understanding and intuitable through sensibility) – the representation of *substance in the appearance* (*substantia phaenomenon*) – was confused with the representation of substance conceivable merely (through reason) [: 546] (*substantia noumenon*), i.e. of the absolute subject. Both the absolute subject of the predicates of internal sense and those of external sense were considered to be cognizable, and the cognizable elements in them were taken to be the *thing in itself*.

Since, until now, one sought the ground of the representation both of *cognizable* and *absolute* substance not where it could be found, in the capacity for representation, but where it could not be conceived without contradiction, namely outside the capacity for representation in the unrepresented *thing in itself*, the ways in which the question, "in what does the ground of our representations of the substances reside?" was answered ended up being quite varied and contradictory.

1) The ground of our representation of *substance* can be found in mere fancy [*bloße(n) Einbildung*] per se, says the *dogmatic skeptic*, and the necessity of thinking such substances is a mere consequence of *custom*. We are able to satisfy ourselves only of the actuality of our representations, but not at all of our representations of *independent things*. In order to cognize an independent thing as independent, it would have to be distinguished from everything that is not independent about it; the substance would have to be separated from all its accidents. If this happened, however, the independent thing would remain an empty representation, a merely *pseudo subject*. "One does not raise the objection", the skeptic would continue, "that the accidents are only separable from the substance in representation per se; in [: 547] the *thing in itself* they would be inseparable." But this inseparability is precisely what would have to be *proven* if I am not to consider the representation of the enduring subject to be baseless. We cannot conflate our representations of things with the *things in themselves* and then assure ourselves that we agree about this. All agreement between the thing, insofar as this is represented, and the thing, insofar as it is not represented, is impossible. We can thus speak about substances and their accidents only insofar as these occur in our representations. All accidents which occur in our representations can be separated from their substances and indeed must be separated from them if we wish to give account to ourselves about what we conceive substance to be. Now if the *dogmatic thinker* calls the subject separated from all its predicates a *pseudo subject*, he must concede that no other subjects are *cognizable* or even *representable* to us than mere pseudo subjects.

2) The basis of our representation of substance, the *materialist* answers, lies in the *extension of things in themselves*. All actual objects distinct from our mind in consciousness, all knowable *individuals*, are bodies, things

that fill space, extended things. Extension is the attribute of substance, for when we have separated all accidents from bodies we must allow them extension if they are not to be [: 548] destroyed in our thoughts, if they are still to be conceived as something. Extension, too, contains the basis of the possibility of all remaining properties of individuals, of *impenetrability, figure*, etc. That we have no representation of extension in the representing substance, admittedly, cannot be denied, but that does not result from its immateriality, but merely from the impossibility of representing what must be presupposed in every possible representation. Since, therefore, the substances of which we have representations are extended, we cannot do otherwise than deduce that those of which no representation is possible must also be extended.

3) The basis of our representation of *substance*, the *dualist* answers, lies in the *durability of things in themselves* – which are present in two essentially distinct *kinds*, namely as extended and as unextended (simple) *things in themselves*, but through their common attribute of *durability* constitute the species of *substance in general. Extended things in themselves* subsist in a space independent of our mind insofar as they – whatever changes they undergo in their constitution – must continue to remain extended and to fill space. *Unextended things in themselves* do not subsist in space, which they cannot fill, but in *time* per se, that is, they remain unchanged despite all change in their accidents, in their representations, in the same way that every person can testify to a sense of self by which he is conscious of his own *I* that continues through time and is distinct from its [: 549] organization.

4) The ground of our representation of substance, the *Spinozist* answers, lies in the *necessity* of the *single thing in itself*, which on its own is the object of the representation of an enduring and absolute subject. The *enduring* and substantial element of *bodies* is *extension*, of representing beings is the *power of thought*. The enduring element of extension and of the power of thought is the necessity existing in the *thing in itself*, the *immutable*, in which extension and the power of thought have their basis as attributes in being. All mutability in bodies is not their substance, but a mere accident. When everything that is subject to change in bodies is removed from them in thought, the only substantial element they have left is extension. The extension of a single body is distinct from the extension of another body only in its magnitude and its position in space. These two differences only concern *predicates* of extension, not extension itself, which, when it is conceived as being distinct from its accidents, only constitutes a *numerically single* extension. This is also the case with representing beings. Their numerical multiplicity is only determinable through contingent differences on the basis of accidents,

and these must fall away when one distinguishes the substantial from the accidental, the transient from the permanent. The *essential feature* in all of them is the one and the same [: 550] power of thought that manifests itself through manifold accidents in manifold appearances. Singular *extension* and singular *power of thought* are admittedly distinct from one another, but only insofar as they are essential predicates (attributes) of the *permanent*, not insofar as they are *permanence* itself. What of them is *subjective* is that through which they subsist: the permanent, immutable, necessary, i.e. one and the same *singular thing in itself*. Or one indicates a difference between what is permanent in the power of thought and permanent in extension – a difference that would concern what must be conceived of them as belonging to the subject and does not restrict *extension* and *power of thought* as predicates, and consequently, independently of them, would be determined as something existing for itself. Since no difference is conceivable between *several* so-called substances, insofar as they are justifiably given the name of *substance*, that is, are possessed of that which is *permanent, immutable*, and *necessary*, and since all representable difference in them concerns merely *accidents*, so everything, insofar as it is substance, is a *thing in itself*, a singularity. What is multiple in things is merely accidental, what is singular in them is substance; the multiple are contingencies, the singular necessary things; the multiple is mutable, the singular durable; the multiple finite, the singular unending; the multiple within time, the singular eternal. The mutable alone occurs only in the immutable, the temporal only in eternity, the contingent only in the necessary, the finite only in the infinite, the multiple only in the one, the accidents only in the substance, which is unchanging, [: 551] necessary, eternal, infinite, and singular; ἑν και παν!

5)   The ground of our representation of *substance*, the *idealist* answers, lies in the *representing thing in itself*. Substance must be distinguished from a representation per se. The *representing entity* alone occurs in consciousness as an *independent thing* distinguished from all its representations. The substances represented through external sense in space, by contrast, are only representations per se when they are distinguished from the representations and conceived according to their difference from these. For they can be represented according to this difference only when one takes away the mere accidents under which they occur in intuition, or, which amounts to the same, when one changes the shape of the intuition of them to form an empty idea which cannot be anything that exists outside the mind. All *idealists* agree that there cannot be any other *substances* than *representing* substances, and no other *accidents* than *representations* per se. They differ from one another

in that the *solipsist* only considers a *single* representing individual, the *Berkeleyan idealist* only a single *kind*, and the *Leibnizianer several kinds* of representing things in themselves as being *demonstrable*. The *solipsist* by no means denies *real* being, only the *demonstrability* of other substances apart from his *I*. In consciousness, he maintains, only the *representing entity* and the *representation* occur, and no *thing in itself* distinct from them. The represented thing *outside me*, insofar as I am able to think it, is only another [: 552] type of representation, something in me, a thought, which I am unable to compare with what does not occur within my mind; it is something, therefore, of which I cannot know whether it corresponds to something outside me. To him the *Berkeleyan idealist* replies: "It is established that there are representations and that representations presuppose a representing entity. Now in consciousness representations occur which we are obliged to distinguish from *our own representations* and whose origin we must seek in other representing entities. And I am conscious that I *generate* representations but cannot *create* them, that the material of them and therefore other substances must be present outside me, substances which, since I do not know any other type of substance than a representing substance, I can only consider to be substances of the same type as my *I*, i.e. to be apparitions."

The *Leibnizianer* acknowledges no other substances than *representing* substances, and to this extent is a true *idealist*. The representation of substance, for him, is the representation of the *thing in itself*, a thing he considers representable and cognizable through the understanding per se. He therefore declares all predicates determinable through sensibility to be mere apparitions, and, instead, all predicates conceivable through the understanding per se to be properties of the *thing in itself*. The understanding per se is not capable of conceiving any *extension*; extension is thus nothing but a mere sensory appearance, and extension *in itself* is nothing but an aggregate of unextended *things in themselves*. However, the mere simplicity of these things in themselves cannot possibly constitute their reality, [: 553] that which is *substantial* about them. This can only consist in their *internal power* – a power through which every *thing in itself* is operative for itself alone, as substance, independent of other things, a power that can only be the *representing entity*. *Motion* is only a change of external relations, and the moving power moves only through motion and cannot be, to this extent, a substance.* Every substance is thus a *power* representing

---

* There are only *two types* of representable predicates of *subsisting things*: that which *fills* space per se, *extension*; and that which *fills* time per se, *representations*. If the one does not belong to the *thing in itself*, all that is left is the other, the representations.

the world, but not a power of one and the same kind. The *infinite monad* represents distinctly all that is possible and real. The *finite rational monad* represents only what is capable of being distinctly represented according to the position of the organic body to which it is bound. The *irrational monad bound to an organic body* has this body (since it is limited through this body to determinate objects) to thank for the *clarity* of the representations that must be lacking in the representations of that monad which is a mere element of a body and whose power to represent the world is not restricted to any determinate object in this world.

In each of these idealistic systems the ground of representations of *substance* is considered – *quite properly* – from its own vantage point. Each of these vantage points has its own incontrovertible basis [: 554] – a basis challenged in vain by supporters of the other systems and thus unable to be refuted by them. In each system, however, the basis of representations of substance is only explained from a *single* vantage point and is thus *one-sided*; the explanation given by each about this basis, with only one exception, continually provokes the attacks of all the others. Our theory of representation of substance puts us in the position of identifying both the true and false in all other philosophical systems up till now. From this the following results:

1) That the *dogmatic skeptics* are quite correct when they maintain that no demonstrable object existing *outside* our mind corresponds to the representation of substance per se, or, which amounts to the same thing, that through the representation of substance the *thing in itself* is not represented as *thing in itself*; yet they are clearly incorrect when they maintain that it cannot be proven that the unrepresentable *thing in itself must* be conceived as substance.

2) That the *materialists* are quite correct when they maintain that every cognizable substance must be *extended*, but they are clearly incorrect when they transfer the predicate of extension proper to the appearances of external sense to the absolute subject, and from this to *things in themselves*.

3) That the *dualists* are quite correct when they *distinguish* the durable in space from the not durable [: 555] in space and in time per se, yet they are clearly incorrect when they attribute this distinction, which concerns the appearances per se of external and internal sense, to absolute subjects and to the *things in themselves* confused with these subjects.

4) That the *Spinozists* are quite correct when they take absolute necessity to be an exclusive attribute of the absolute subject, when they only assign a *single object* to the representation of the absolute subject distinguished from all its accidents, and when they consider the absolute subject with

respect to its predicates both of external and of internal sense to be the *same thing* (a common attribute of extension and of the representing subject); yet they are clearly incorrect when they consider this object, which is only the *form* of a representation, to be a single *thing in itself*, and the necessity of being conceived as the necessity for the existence of *things in themselves*.

5)	That the *idealists* are quite correct when they seek the basis of a representation of substance as *not* lying *outside* the representing subject, but they are clearly incorrect when they assume it to be outside the capacity for representation and its form in the unrepresentable *thing in itself*. That they, finally, are quite correct when they declare extension, considered as a property of *things in themselves*, to be a mere illusion, but clearly incorrect when they declare the unity of the absolute subject that excludes all extension to be the simplicity of the *thing in itself*. [: 556]

Finally, that every past and every future system that derives the representation of *substance* from the unrepresentable *thing in itself* – no matter what attributes of the *substance* of *this thing* are set out – can only be an abortive experiment of the human intellect that fails to recognize the limits of its powers.

Since the substances of *bodies* are not cognizable by absolute, but only by comparative subjects, as conditioned substances, as the durable in space, a possible true and actual *science* of them cannot possibly be of the *substance of the mind* itself conceivable only by way of an absolute subject through reason, a substance by which nothing at all can be *cognized*. A complete discussion of the form determined in the nature of the mind under which the representing subject must be *conceived* takes the place of the *rational psychology* carried out till now, and constitutes a part of a *higher metaphysics* that concerns itself with supersensible objects conceivable through reason per se – a metaphysics to which I must point in order to develop in more detail the *idea of the soul*.

§ LXXXV.

Through the idea of absolute cause by which reason gives complete unity to those *cognizable causes* in the sense world, a *first cause in general* is conceived of which nothing more can be determined than that it contains the entire ground of its own effect and that it cannot be a member [: 557] of the series of cognizable causes and effects.

Just as the *category* of cause determined in the nature of the understanding is nothing but the form of a concept, so the idea of absolute cause in which the category of cause is determined as unconditioned by reason is conceived as nothing but the form of an *idea*. And just as the category of cause gains direct objective reality in the schema of causality through its relation to the form of intuition, so the idea of absolute cause gains *indirect* objective reality determinable by the understanding through its relation to the *schema*. That is, along with the series of cognizable but, for that reason, conditioned and incomplete, causes, a merely conceivable, unconditioned, and complete cause must be conceived which, insofar as it is conceived as absolute, can have nothing determining its causality above it and therefore must be the *first* cause, yet, for precisely that reason, cannot be a member of the series of conditioned, cognizable causes, it cannot be related to any determinate object, and it can signify nothing but the *rational unity of causal conjunction*.

With the idea of absolute cause differences are encountered to the extent that, on its basis, an attribute of the absolute representing subject is conceived as the proper mode of action of the third degree of spontaneity of the capacity for representation or of reason. The idea of absolute cause lacks indirect objective reality when related to an objective material without a schema. [: 558] In that case, however, it has a direct relation to the representing subject, has a determinate object in the mode of action of reason, and a subjective reality which is the same as the reality of reason itself.

§ LXXXVI.

Through the idea of absolute cause insofar as this must be related to the causality of reason, the representing subject is represented as a *free cause*. The representing subject is represented as *comparatively free*, insofar as reason is involved in thinking and determines the *capacity for desire a posteriori*, and *absolutely free*, insofar as it determines the capacity for desire a priori.

Reason can only be conceived as a spontaneity acting *without compulsion* and *unbound*, i.e. as *absolute activity*. Insofar as the representing subject acts through reason, it acts through its self-activity per se, it contains the ground of its action in itself, it is determined toward action not through any being distinct from it, nor through any of its other properties distinct from its own activity, and consequently it acts *freely* (see p. 535 ff.).

This freedom is *comparative* when a certain type of outside cause determines it without necessity, and *absolute*, when no outside cause plays a role in the determination of its action. Reason [: 559] *thinks* insofar as it *generates* an idea, that is, *produces* unity (the form per se of representation) in the manifold that is presented to it by the understanding. This manifold constituting the material of ideas is determined in the *form of the understanding a priori*, and *produced* according to its constitution to this extent neither through the understanding nor through reason but is *given* in the capacity for representation. Insofar as the *idea* consists of form and material – the latter's having to be given to reason (and cannot be its own product) –, to this extent reason acts in the process of thinking *only comparatively*, that is, *freely*, *only* with respect to the *form*, unity per se, which is its activity. Yet with respect to material, it is *bound* to its given form, and consequently acts with *necessity*. Since the manifold nature of the material of reason is determined in the *understanding per se*, and therefore not *outside* the form of spontaneity, the *representing subject* acts in relation to the production of the idea only comparatively freely (insofar as the material of its action – on which the actuality of this action depends at least as much as on its form – is not its activity), but then as an *absolute cause*, insofar as the constitution of material per se is based on its *spontaneity* per se (the form of the understanding), and representation consequently is generated without compulsion through affectedness and without binding to the form of sensibility *foreign* to spontaneity.

[: 560]

Basis of the Theory of
the Capacity for Desire

That which in *the representing subject* must be conceived as ground of the possibility of representation, *the capacity for representation*, must be precisely distinguished from that which is ground of *actual representation*, which is the representing *force*. *Spontaneity itself* cannot possibly be what is meant by this *force*. No representation would be realized through spontaneity per se without receptivity. Spontaneity produces only the form per se of the representations and being affected, which is necessary *a priori* for intuition, is only produced on the basis of the given forms of sensibility. What is meant here by representing force is not spontaneity per se any more than it is the forms of receptivity and spontaneity determined as possible *a priori*; it is rather the proper ground for the actuality of the representation insofar as this must understood to be present in the representing subject. This ground of what is actualized by means of the representing subject is determined and limited by the form of the capacity for representation, which is given *a priori*, which it cannot as a finite being give itself, and to which it is *a priori* bound, [: 561] and the representing force can only express itself in accordance with the capacity given to it. The relation of the representing force to the possibility of representation determined *a priori* in its capacity, the relation of the force to its capacity, of the ground of actuality to the ground of possibility of the representation, or to representability, I call the drive of the representing subject. This consists in the connection of the force to the capacity and must be present in every finite representing entity in which the representing force is distinguished from the capacity. Being determined through the drive for the production of a representation is called *desiring*, and the capacity to be determined by the drive the capacity for desire in the wider sense.

Just as representation in general consists of two essentially distinct and essentially connected components, material and form, so too the drive to representation in general can be analyzed into two distinct and connected basic drives: the drive to material and the drive to form of representation. The first has as its object the actuality of what is given in representation, the latter – what must be brought forth in it. The first arises from the need grounded in the representing subject of a material which it cannot bring forth itself, together with the form of receptivity, as determined in the capacity; the latter from the positive power present in the representing subject, together with the form of its spontaneity, as determined in the capacity. [: 562] The first strives for being affected in receptivity and is sensory in the broader sense; the latter for expression of spontaneity, and is intellectual in the broader sense. The first is satisfied only when there is some given, and is self-interested; the latter – only through action per se, and is to that extent unselfish.

The drive is called sensory in the narrowest sense when it is determined by the forms of sensibility. The object of this drive is the representation which arises through the manner of being affected insofar as it is related to the representing subject in consciousness, i.e. is sensation. I call the capacity to be determined by the drive toward actual sensations the capacity for desire in the narrower sense. In as much as a sensory representation is related to its object, i.e. is intuition, it belongs to the cognitive capacity and is not the object of the capacity for desire, to which it can only belong in relation to the subject. Every sensation is a modification brought about through being affected and consequently empirical. (Even the pure representations of space and time are only *a priori* representations in relation to their objects determined *a priori* in the capacity for representation; in their relation to the subject however as modifications of the mind arising when receptivity is affected on the basis of its forms which are determined *a priori* they are sensations, and consequently empirical.) The drive which has sensations as its object has the empirical as its object [: 563] and is called the empirical drive.

In as much as the sensory drive strives for external sensation, it can only be satisfied from outside. In this, the representing subject behaves in respect of being affected merely passively, and spontaneity is compelled to act in the bringing forth of form. I call the drive for outer sensation *coarsely sensory* to distinguish it from the drive which has as its object just inner sensation, which I call *finely sensory* because it is satisfied by being affected when this occurs only through spontaneity, and also because it has as its object a sensation in which the mind behaves neither merely passively nor through compulsion. For this very reason, the drive, in as much as it is satisfied by inner sensation, may indeed be self-interested because its satisfaction is brought about through given material, through being affected; but only self-interested in the narrower sense, if it is to be distinguished from the coarsely sensory drive in this respect too. This drive must be seen as self-interested in the narrowest sense because it can only be satisfied by an objective material given externally and by means of something entirely different from the subject and its capacity.

I call the drive sensory in a merely narrower sense when it is determined through sensibility in connection with the understanding. The modifications which the sensory drive [: 564] undergoes when the understanding determines it on the basis of its four moments are as follows. On the basis of *quantity*: drive towards sensation through a manifold determined by means of the categories of unity, multiplicity, and totality – towards the sensorily complete. On the basis of *quality*: drive to sensation through being affected according to the categories of reality, negation and limitation, or pleasure after heavy or light occupation. On the basis of *relation*: 1) drive to persistence of the sensibly determinable subsistence; 2) drive for self-interested activity; 3) drive for self-interested sociability.* On the basis of *modality*: 1) determinability through the drive (disposition determined in the representing subject, form of desire); 2) being determined by the drive, actual desire; 3) actual desire determined by the form of desire, necessary desire, instinct.

This sensory, self-interested, empirical drive determined by the understanding is called the *rational-sensory* since its sensory form is modified *indirectly*, that is, mediated by the form of the understanding, by the form of reason; and this extends the self-interested drive conditioned by sensibility and determined by understanding to the *unconditioned*. The limitlessness [: 565] of the demand of this drive is related only by means of the sensory drive determined by the understanding to nothing but sensations and exceeds accordingly all possible satisfaction which can always only be sensory and consequently conditioned. Reason determines the capacity for

---

* In as much as these three drives are related by the external sense to empirical modifications of this sense determined in the organism they result in the drive to preservation of the body, to the body's activity, to movement, and the sex drive.

desire here merely *empirically* by means of the idea of the *unconditioned*, an idea which relates only to the objects of the sensory drive determined by understanding, and constitutes the representation of the *full array* of these thoroughly *empirical* objects. The actual object of the *rational-sensory* drive is accordingly no single sensation modified by the understanding but a *state* which would arise from the satisfaction of *all* drives extended toward the absolute as these are determined by the understanding and by reason – *happiness*; an object which can only be represented by means of an *idea* in the narrower sense. I say *idea* in the *narrower* sense, that is, by means of a representation of the unconditioned; such a representation arises only through the combination of *empirical* concepts and in which reason can only function *a posteriori* in that the unconditioned, which is essential to happiness conceived in a determined way, arises only through combination of the forms of understanding through which only objects of the sensory drive, objects of sensation, empirical objects are represented. The unconditioned, absolute, complete, unlimited, which is essential to happiness, is by no means *immediately* object of the rational-sensory drive, and is by no means desired for its own sake, unselfishly; but merely on account of the objects of sensation and of [: 566] enjoyment which the rational-sensory drive strives to bring ever closer to the idea of the absolute. Happiness is indeed to that extent the necessary object of the drive but an absolutely impossible object of experience; the state of the representing subject at any time can only exist in a satisfaction *conditioned unto the infinite*. And actual happiness, the possible satisfaction of the rational-sensory drive, can only exist in the endlessly progressive approximation[1] of the actual state to the ideal.

Reason functions in the drive to happiness only *comparatively* and only *freely* to the extent that the form of the unconditioned which it imparts to the drive is the effect of absolute self-activity. The drive to happiness itself, however, in as much as it is the result of the power of the subject determined by sensibility, understanding, and reason in conjunction, is *neither free nor unselfish*. Its original source is the need to be affected, modified by the understanding and by reason. Its direct object is the unconditioned totality by means of the understanding of determined sensations, according to its object, and its satisfaction depends on objective material being given, on being affected from outside. It is to that extent at least as much a contingent

---

1   This phrase is strikingly similar to "Unendliche Annäherung" – "endless approximation" – which occurs in Hölderlin's letter to Schiller, 4 September 1795, and which furnished Manfred Frank with the title of his major study of philosophical beginnings of early Romanticism (Frank 1997). That work is available in English translation: *The Philosophical Foundations of Early German Romanticism*, translated by Elizabeth Millan-Zaibert, SUNY Press, 2004.

effect of things which the representing being does not have in its power as it is a consequence of the instinctive and reasonable use of the faculties of the representing force. The science of the object of this drive and the means of satisfying it, [: 567] the *doctrine of happiness*, must be drawn just as much from experience, which can never be exhausted, as from the forms of the capacity for representation which can be exhausted, and the system of the rules for the use of reason determined by the idea of happiness, or *doctrine of prudence*, must be distinguished from *morality* with which it has as little in common as the *doctrine of happiness*.

Since reason, in the drive to happiness, has nothing as its object except the expansion of the state, of the sensations determined by the understanding, sensations which in their *quality* must be *pleasant*, it actually stands in this drive in the service of the sensory inclination, of the necessary inclination to pleasure, which it determines only *a posteriori* in respect to its satisfaction and only to the extent that this inclination is presupposed by it as already operative.

The capacity of the representing subject to be determined by the self-activity of the drive, or to determine itself to an action of the drive, is called the *will*; and actual self-determination undertaken with consciousness to an action of the drive is called *willing*. *Willing* is thus distinguished from *desire* in its narrower sense or from determination by the sensory drive because it is determination by reason, an action of self-activity.

Will is called *empirical* when it is the capacity of the subject to determine itself [: 568] to an action conceived by reason to be a *means* of satisfying the drive to happiness and is subordinated to this satisfaction as its *purpose*. In *willing*, an action aiming at happiness, desire is determined by reason merely *empirically*, namely under the presupposition of the drive to pleasure, to which reason gives by means of the action of willing the direction which is determined in the idea of happiness. Reason accordingly operates only *comparatively freely* in empirical willing, i.e. only to the extent that it determines the sensory drive empirically and prescribes a rule for the manner of its action which receives its sanction only through pleasure via the medium of a drive essentially different from reason.

Since the idea of happiness is determined in the representing subject partially *a posteriori* through sensations, when these are however dependent on being affected from outside and consequently on external circumstances independent of the representing subject, the idea of happiness varies in different representing subjects and even in the same representing subject does not remain constant. Reason and the understanding which determine this idea in terms of its form and only according to the given material of sensibility must remain disappointed as long as self-activity only operates in its service, i.e. as long as reason determines the capacity for desire only *empirically*, according to the *data* of an eternally incomplete experience. [: 569] Only reason has the power to determine the capacity for desire *a priori* and in this way to forestall the disappointments of the coarsely sensory drive.

Purely rational is what I call the drive insofar as it is determined by nothing but self-activity of reason, and consequently has as its object nothing but the exercise of self-activity, the mere action of reason. This action of reason, in as much as it is object of the *purely rational drive*, consists in the *realization* of the *manner of action of reason*, the *form of reason*, which is given in the subject only according to its possibility, but in terms of actuality can only be brought forth outside the subject by action of the subject. The form of reason determined *a priori* in the subject in the capacity is given to the subject and thus is not dependent on his power; but its *realization* as the form of an actual action which has no other purpose than this very *realization*, the actuality of the form of reason as object of the drive, is something that depends on the power of the subject, indeed on the mere self-activity of this power. The action of reason *in the purely rational* drive is essentially different from the action in the rational-sensory drive. In this latter drive, reason determines the representable of sensations only *a posteriori* and receives the material of its action in what is sensed as determined by the understanding. In the former drive it operates under no demand of sensation, determines the material and the form of its object, functions quite independently of [: 570] affect, does not at all presuppose the sensory drive and the capacity for sensation for the actualisation of its action, and acts consequently completely *a priori* from the fullness of its self-activity.

Reason determines the object of the purely-rational drive, the mere realization of the manner of action of reason, according to the four moments of immediate judgment, and the purely rational drive must be conceived in accordance with these determinations. It functions: on the basis of *quantity*, as the drive toward *lawful* manner of action (the form of action determined by means of absolute *universality*), toward realization of mere lawfulness; on the basis of *quality*: as the drive toward *unselfish* manner of action (the form of action independent of the sensory quality, the givenness of material, and consequently of the drive to *pleasure*), toward the realization of unselfishness; on the basis of *relation*: as the drive toward a manner of action which is 1) unalterable 2) self-active 3) in harmony with the manner of action of all rational beings; on the basis of *modality*: as the drive toward a manner of action that is 1) permitted, 2) in accordance with duty, 3) completely binding.

The object of the purely-rational drive completely determined in this way is *morality*, which consists consequently in the realization of the manner of action of pure reason intended for its own sake. The purely-rational drive is called *moral* in respect of this object appropriate to it alone.

[: 571] Reason is called *practical* in as much as the capacity lies in its self-activity to realise the object of the purely rational drive, or in other words to determine itself *a priori* toward an action which has no other purpose than the realization of reason's manner of acting, and the capacity of the representing object to determine itself through the self-activity of the purely-rational drive is called *pure will*. The *will* consists accordingly in general in self-determination to an action. If this action is subordinated by reason as a means for satisfying the drive toward happiness the will acts *empirically* in the service of sensibility, but if this action is determined through the object of the purely rational drive and if it consists accordingly only in the intended realization of the manner of action of reason, then the will acts *purely*, *a priori*, independently of the sensory drive, on the basis of no other law than the one it gives itself, in that the will merely realises the form of reason determined in accordance with its possibility through its self-activity.

The human will is accordingly *free* 1) in as much as it cannot as a capacity of spontaneity of reason be *compelled* by being affected; as the capacity of a subject which possesses apart from reason sensibility, and is able to determine itself both *a priori* and *a posteriori* and accordingly is by no means *bound* either to the law of the unselfish drive or to the law of the self-interested drive. It *acts comparatively freely* when it subjects itself to the law of the self-interested drive, [: 572] a drive which is *alien to it*; it acts on the other hand *absolutely freely* and is absolutely free in as much as it follows the law of the unselfish drive; a law which is only constituted by theoretical reason but receives its sanction as an actual law only through the self-activity per se of practical reason which submits itself to it. Morality is impossible without absolute freedom, and absolute freedom is only actual in morality[2] which is indeed necessarily determined *in its form* in the form of the capacity for reason, but *in its material*, i.e. with respect to the *realization* of this form as object of the will is a mere product of self-activity, of the positive force of the freely operating subject.

The drive to morality is *essentially different* from the drive to happiness. The first is grounded in the positive force per se, the second in the need per se modified by understanding and reason; the first is consequently completely unselfish, the second completely self-interested. For the first, the possible form per se of its object is determined in the capacity for reason, the material on the other hand through which its object becomes actualized, the realization of the purely rational manner of action, is entirely its own

---

2 The original text says: "absolute freedom is only actual in sensibility". However, Reinhold's discussion here would suggest "morality" rather than "sensibility". A simple confusion of "Sittlichkeit" with "Sinnlichkeit" in the typesetting of the original text might be the reason for the error, if indeed an error has occurred.

work; for the second the material of its object is given through sensations and indeed the objective material is entirely given through being affected from outside. It is accordingly dependent in respect of the actuality of its object on external things, and its merely ideal form which is attainable in no possible experience [: 573], the absolute of happiness, is the only thing belonging to self-activity with this drive. In the drive toward happiness reason extends the demands of the sensory drive ad infinitum; in the drive to morality it allows no validity to any demand of the sensory drive except in as much as this demand is *lawful* and compatible with the demand of the purely rational drive. Determined by the drive to happiness the subject sees itself as centre of the universe and relates everything which it is capable of effecting by understanding and reason to the state of its capacity for sensation, to *pleasure*; determined through the drive to morality however the subject sees itself only as a member of a community which consists of absolute subjects acting through practical reason who know no other purpose than the realization of lawfulness, unselfishness, etc.

Both drives are in exact contradiction with each other when they are conceived as *coordinated*; the drive to morality is annihilated when it is subordinated to the drive for happiness, this drive however is merely limited to the lawful when it is subordinated to the drive to morality. The manner of action of pure reason in as much as this is characteristic of the moral drive is called law; in as much as it is imposed upon the drive to happiness, to which it is alien – *commandment*. The determination of the sensory drive by the self-activity of the purely rational is called *necessitation*; and the necessity of subjecting the sensory drive to the law of the purely rational is called [: 574] *duty*. This necessity is heard in consciousness as the *ought* which is in respect of practical reason *free willing* of the lawful, in respect of the capacity for desire however a *commandment* which the subject freely acting through practical reason compels itself to follow only in constraining its own self-interested drive.

Just as sensibility and reason constitute in their inseparable unity the nature of the human mind insofar as this is representable, so the drive to happiness and the drive to morality constitute in their inseparable unity the *entire drive* of the human mind, and happiness combined with morality the entire complete object of this drive, the *highest good* for the human being. Combination of happiness with morality however is only conceivable if the drive to happiness is subordinated *in the subject* to the drive to morality; *in the object* of the whole drive if the measure of happiness be determined by the measure of morality, and happiness be desired and attained only insofar as the subject has made itself morally capable of it, i.e., *worthy*. Since morality is the condition under which alone happiness can be object of the striving of a subject endowed with practical reason: it is the *highest, supreme good.* – But since the rational *finite* subject must necessarily strive for happiness, morality can only constitute [: 575] the *entire* highest good of this subject in combination with the happiness it determines; and the entire highest good can not be, as the *Epicureans* hold, *mere happiness* to which virtue relates as a means to an end, nor as the *Stoics* teach can it be mere morality (virtue) the possession of which alone constituted the highest good.

How the closer definition and further development of these premises leads to the *ground of belief* for the *existence of an intelligible world* (in which the highest good is attainable only through existence and personality of the finite rational being enduring into infinity) and for the *existence of a cause of all nature different from nature and functioning in accordance with moral disposition*, this can only be adequately demonstrated in the actual *theory of practical reason* and after a completely developed *theory of the capacity for desire**. The theory of *reason in general*, insofar as it is part of the theory of the *cognitive capacity in general*, must be satisfied with establishing the mere ideas of the *intelligible world* and of the *primal being*, in as much as these are grounded in the form of the capacity for reason.

§ LXXXVII.

Through the idea of *absolute community* related to the subjects of appearances of the outer senses, the idea of the *physical* [: 576] world is determined, related to the subjects of appearances of the inner sense (the representing) the idea of the *moral world* – related to the ideas of these two worlds the idea of the *intelligible world* or of the *universe* is determined.

Just as the idea of the absolute community in general is determined in the nature of reason so too is the relation of this idea to all conceivable subjects. Reason brings all multiplicity to unconditioned unity and can only think the totality of conceivable subjects as in thoroughgoing connection, in systematic community.

With respect to the subjects of the outer sense which must already be represented as appearances through the *schema of interaction* in recognizable community, the idea of absolute community gains *indirect objective reality* in that it relates itself by means of the schema of community whose form of understanding it extends to the unconditioned, to what is given in intuition. The idea of the *physical world* is accordingly also only an idea in the *narrower* sense, and contains in its complete determination and indirect relation to actually cognizable objects the plan of a true and actual science.

---

* I am planning to follow the present theory of the capacity for representation with this.

With respect to the subjects of the inner sense, which must by no means be represented as appearances but immediately through reason as *absolute subjects*, the idea of the absolute community is capable of *subjective reality* alone grounded in the capacity for representation per se. [: 577] Since the *category* of *community* consists of the connection of the categories of *substance* and *cause*, the absolute community can also only subsist through the connection of the absolute subject with absolute causality; and the absolute subjects of the inner sense can only be conceived in absolute community to the extent that they act as absolute causes in the strictest sense, i.e. as they act through practical reason (morally). The idea of the moral world is accordingly also an idea in the *narrowest* sense and contains in its complete determination nothing that can be known except the laws of the moral world, which are no other than the laws of practical reason.

In as much as these two worlds are considered as two distinct self-subsistent subjects, reason sees itself compelled by its nature to bring them once again to absolute unity and to consider them as a thoroughly interconnected whole in absolute community. While the community is determined in the physical world by *interaction* of behaviours of reasoning beings but in the moral world by their *uniformity*, in both, that is, determined by the action of substances, that which is common to both in the intelligible world between those two worlds which constitute their material cannot be conceived as either interaction nor as uniformity. The only ground of determination of what these two worlds have in common that can be conceived as contained in them can only consist in [: 578] the determinations in the physical world having their *final causes* in the moral; a ground of determination which is inconceivable without proceeding from the idea of the intelligible world to a subject distinct from it, that is to an *intelligence* which would be conceived as the determining and efficient cause of physical and moral laws.

§ LXXXVIII.

The idea of a supreme notion of all conceivable realities, of the *universally real being*, is determined through the idea of absolute community which is related not to subjects, but to *predicates* per se (conceivable *absolute realities*) determined through pure reason.

The *predicates*, insofar as they are determined in the pure understanding *as predicates*, are conceived by means of the moment of quality and by the categories of reality, negation and limitation (p. 451). By means of the understanding in the narrower sense quality is represented in its schema as conditioned, *limited* reality connected with *negation*; on the other hand it is represented by means of reason as unconditioned, unlimited reality excluding all negation. The multiplicity conceived by reason (absolute totality) of these realities, determined by the idea of absolute community, gives the idea of the absolute essence of all realities, insofar as these have to be conceived as unlimited; [: 579] determined by the idea of the absolute subject – the representation of the ultimately real independent being – the representation of the ultimately real being as *first* cause. This highly important idea has the particular quality above all others in pure reason that its object is completely determined and consequently an *individual* is represented by reason. The complete development of the idea must be reserved for the *higher metaphysics*.

Appendices

Glossary

German term	Translation
ableiten	*to derive; deduce*
Accidenz	*accident; contingency*
Affiziertsein	*affectedness*
Anlage	*predisposition*
anschaulich	*intuiting; intuitable*
Anschauung	*intuition*
Ausdehnung	*extension*
ausgedehnt	*extended*
Ausgedehnte(s)	*the extended; extension*
Außereinanderseyn	*externality*
Bedingung	*condition*
Begehrungsvermögen	*capacity for desire*
Begriff	*concept*
beharrlich	*durable*
Beharrliche(s)	*duration; durability*
Beschaffenheit	*disposition; constitution*
bestimmbar	*determinable*
bestimmen	*to determine*
bestimmt	*determinate*
bewußt	*conscious*
Bewußtsein	*consciousness*
Beziehung	*relation*
Bezogenwerden	*relatedness*
bloss	*per se;*
	mere (adj.), merely (adv.);
deutlich	*distinct*
eigennützig	*selfish*
Eigenschaft	*property*
eigentümlich	*proper*
Empfänglichkeit	*susceptibility*
Empfindung	*sensation*
Erfahrungsbegriff	*empirical concept*
erkennbar	*cognizable*
Erkennbarkeit	*cognizability; possibility of cognition*
Erkenntnis	*cognition*

Erkenntnisvermögen	*cognitive capacity*
erzeugen	*to generate*
Folge	*effect; succession*
Formtrieb	*drive to form*
gegeben	*given*
Gegebene(s)	*the given*
Gegenstand	*object*
Geist	*spirit*
Gemeinschaft	*community*
Gemüth	*mind*
gesunder Menschenverstand	*common sense*
Gewohnheit	*custom*
Gründe	*grounds*
Grund	*ground*
Grundsatz	*principle*
Handlungsweise	*mode of action*
hervorbringen	*to produce*
klar	*clear*
Kraft	*force; power*
leidend (cf. wirkend)	*passive*
Mannigfaltige(s)	*manifold (n.)*
Mannigfaltigkeit	*manifold nature*
Merkmal	*attribute*
Nacheinandersein	*succession*
Organisation	*bodily organization*
Raum	*space*
Reizbarkeit	*sensitivity*
Rezeptivität	*receptivity*
schließen	*draw conclusions, infer*
Schluß	*inference*
Selbstgefühl	*sense of self; self-awareness*
Selbsttätigkeit	*self-activity*
setzen	*to posit*
sinnlich	*sensory*
Sinnlichkeit	*sensibility*
Sittlichkeit	*morality*
Stoff	*material*
Substanz	*substance*
Trieb	*drive*
überhaupt	*in general*
Ursache	*cause*

Urteil	*judgment*
urteilen	*to judge*
Veränderung	*modification; change*
verbinden	*to bind*
Verbindung	*binding*
Verknüpfung	*connection*
Vermögen	*capacity*
Vernunft	*reason*
Vernunftschluß	*syllogism; rational deduction*
Verstand	*understanding*
Vielheit	*multiplicity*
Vorgestellte (das)	*represented*
vorstellbar	*representable*
Vorstellende (das)	*representing entity; representing subject*
Vorstellung	*representation*
Vorstellungsvermögen	*capacity for representation*
Wesen	*entity*
Willkür	*arbitrary will*
wirken	*to effect*
wirkend	*active*
wirklich	*real, actual*
Wirklichkeit	*reality, actuality; effectiveness*
Wissen	*knowledge*
Wissenschaft	*science*
Zeit	*time*
zufällig	*contingent*
Zufälligkeit	*contingency*
Zugleichsein	*simultaneity*
zusammenfassen	*to combine*
Zusammenfassung	*combination*
Zustand	*(physical) state*

German Thinkers
Mentioned by Reinhold

Baumgarten

Alexander Gottlieb Baumgarten (1714–1762) taught at Frankfurt an der Oder. His *Metaphysica* (4th ed.) was published in Halle in 1757 and was used by Kant as the textbook in his lectures on metaphysics. He was a follower of Wolff. A useful summary of the contents of his book on metaphysics is offered in Ameriks and Naragon (eds.) 1997, xvii–xviii. Baumgarten wrote a systematic study of aesthetics: *Aesthetica*, 1750 and 1758.

Bilfinger

Georg Bernhard Bilfinger (1693–1750) was a philosopher, architect, mathematician and theologian. He adhered to the philosophy of the Leibniz-Wolff school. In 1721 he became Professor of Philosophy (without salary) at Tübingen, and in 1724 in addition Professor of Moral Philosophy and Mathematical Sciences in the Collegium Illustre. Christian Wolff assisted him in gaining a research professorship in the new Petersburg Academy. He was recalled to Tübingen as Professor of Theology in 1731.

Born

Ignaz von Born (1742–1791) is thought to have provided a model for Sarastro in Mozart's *Magic Flute*. Reinhold came into contact with him in the house of Johann Michael Kosmas Denis (1729–1800), ex-Jesuit, and highly regarded poet in Vienna (Fuchs, 147), whose work he admired and tried to imitate. His interest in poetry and aesthetics brought Reinhold into contact with the Viennese Enlightenment. Reinhold began working anonymously for the *Realzeitung*, edited after 1780 by men like van Swieten, von Born and von Scharf. The masonic lodge "Zur wahren Eintracht" (True Accord) was headed by von Born; Reinhold himself had contact with this lodge, and became a member on 30 April 1783.

Eberhard

Johann August Eberhard (1738–1809) was Professor of Philosophy in Halle from 1758. He founded and edited the *Philosophisches Magazin*, which offered a rationalist critique of Kant's work. Kant's answer to Eberhard's criticism is contained in the essay "Über eine Entdeckung nach der alle neue Critik der reinen Vernunft durch eine ältere entbehrlich gemacht werden soll", which was published in 1790.

Feder

Johann Georg Heinrich Feder (1740–1821) was Professor of Philosophy in Göttingen from 1768. He was a leading representative of "popular philosophy", and was strongly influenced by the Scottish "common sense" tradition. He was strongly critical of Kant's philosophy. With Christoph Meiners (q.v.) he edited the Philosophische Bibliothek, four volumes of which appeared in Göttingen between 1788 and 1791.

Flatt

Johann Friedrich Flatt (1759–1821) was one of the first Professors at Tübingen to lecture on Kant's philosophy, albeit critically, especially against Kant's philosophy of religion. He also wrote on natural law, and argued against the possibility of establishing a foundation for it.

Herder

Johann Gottfried Herder (1744–1803) intervened in the Pantheism Dispute with his text Gott. Einige Gespräche, published in 1787.

Hufeland

Gottlieb Hufeland (1760–1817) was Professor of Law in Jena. With Christian Gottfried Schütz he edited the Allgemeine Literatur-Zeitung. His first work was on natural law, surveying its history and its foundation, and concludes that this foundation has not yet been satisfactorily established.

Jacobi

Friedrich Heinrich Jacobi (1743–1818) published in 1785 a series of letter to Moses Mendelssohn in which he declared that Lessing had been a Spinozist. This launched the Pantheism Dispute, on which see Beiser 1987. In these letters Jacobi defended belief in revelation. See further comments in the Introduction.

Maass

Johann Gebhard Ehrenreich Maass (1766–1823) was Professor of Philosophy in Halle. He worked with Eberhard on the *Philosophisches Magazin* and wrote several essays against Kant's critical philosophy.

Meiners

Christoph Meiners (1747–1810) was Professor of Philosophy in Göttingen. He was influenced by Locke, Shaftesbury and Hume, and is a representative of the empiricist tradition favoured in Göttingen. He wrote an attack on Kant's work.

Mendelssohn

Moses Mendelssohn (1729–1786) added to the ontological and cosmological proofs of God's existence a third argument, the teleological. Cf. *Morgenstunden oder Vorlesungen über das Daseyn Gottes*, Berlin, 1785. In June 1776 Mendelssohn wrote a few pages of notes under the heading "Über das Erkenntnis-, das Empfindungs- und das Begehrungsvermögen". The essay is translated into English by Daniel O. Dahlstrom and published in *Moses Mendelssohn: Philosophical Writings*. ed. Daniel O. Dahlstrom (Cambridge: Cambridge University Press, 1997), 309–10.

Platner

Ernst Platner (1744–1818) taught medicine in Leipzig. In 1801 he became Professor of Philosophy there. Reinhold studied with him in the first months of 1784 after fleeing from Vienna and the friendship between the two lasted into the 1790s. While Platner did not reject Kant's Critical philosophy, he was in the end skeptical about its success.

Rehberg

August Wilhelm Rehberg (1757–1836) studied in Göttingen. He argued that Leibniz's system inevitably led to Spinozism, and argued against Reinhold that all dogmatic metaphysics would also lead to Spinozism. Cf. Manfred Frank, *Unendliche Annäherung*, 336ff.

Reimarus

Reimarus (1729–1814) was a highly respected doctor in Hamburg. In 1787 he published a critique of Kant's (first) *Critique*.

Schlosser

Johann Georg Schlosser (1739–1799), Goethe's brother-in-law, wrote against all absolute claims in epistemology. He was regarded by Reinhold as a supernaturalist. His work is discussed in Johann van der Zande *Bürger und Beamter Johann Georg Schlosser 1739–1799* (Stuttgart 1986).

Selle

Christian Gottlieb Selle (1748–1800) was a physician who worked in the Charité Hospital in Berlin. He became a member of the Berlin Academy of Sciences in 1786. He published works on medicine and also on philosophy where he argued in the empiricist tradition. In several short essays published in the *Berlinische Monatsschrift* he took issue with Kant's Critical philosophy.

Stattler

Benedikt Stattler (1728–1797) began teaching philosophy and theology in Straubing and Innsbruck in 1760. In 1788 he moved to Munich, where he published his three-volume *Anti-Kant*. In his continuing argument against Kant's Critical philosophy he sought to demonstrate that Christian revelation was rational and to incorporate Wolff's philosophy into Catholic theology.

Tiedemann

Dietrich Tiedemann (1748–1803) shared in the empiricist tradition favoured at Göttingen. In 1786 he became Professor of Philosophy at Marburg, becoming noted for his work on the history of philosophy. He produced a critique of Kant's work, purportedly responding to Kant's proposal in the *Prolegomena* (A 216). Controversy about the Kantian philosophy led in 1786 to a temporary ban on teaching it. Tiedemann, though opposed to Kant's work, was more strongly opposed to the ban, supporting the idea of freedom of thought.

Tittel

Gottlob August Tittel (1739–1816) was a student of Feder's. He taught philosophy in Karlsruhe, and is regarded as an adherent of "popular philosophy". He wrote two books against Kant: *Über Herrn Kant's Moralreform* (1786), and *Kantische Denkformen* (1787).

Weishaupt

Adam Weishaupt (1748–1830) was jurist, historian and philosopher. In 1788 he published arguments against Kant's ideas about time and space, and offered a critical discussion of Kant's *Critique of Pure Reason* in a work on the grounds and certainty of human knowledge.

Wolff

Christian Wolff (1679–1754) is considered to have been the most significant philosopher in the German *Aufklärung* (or Enlightenment) between Leibniz and Kant. His philosophical system relied heavily on the work of Leibniz, but has major contributions especially in the development of his systematic deductive method. He taught in Leipzig from 1703 and on Leibniz's recommendation was appointed as Professor of Mathematics at Halle. Cf. Richard J. Blackwell, "Christian Wolff's Doctrine of the Soul", in *Journal of the History of Ideas* 22/3 (July–September, 1961), 339–354.

References

Main works of Reinhold in chronological Order

"Briefe über die Kantische Philosophie." *Der Teutsche Merkur* 1786 (3), 99–141; 1787 (1), 3–39, 117–142; (2)167–185; (3), 67–88.

"Über das bisherige Schicksal der Kantischen Philosophie." *Der Teutsche Merkur* 1789 (2), 3–37.

"Über die bisherigen Schicksale der Kantischen Philosophie." *Der Teutsche Merkur* 1789 (2), 113–135.

"Fragmente über das bisher allgemein verkannte Vorstellungs-Vermögen." *Der Teutsche Merkur* 1789 (4), 3–22.

"Von welchem Skeptizismus läßt sich eine Reformation der Philosophie hoffen?" *Berlinische Monatsschrift* 1789 (2), 49–72.

Versuch einer neuen Theorie des menschlichen Vorstellungsvermögens. Prague, Jena: Widtmann and Mauke 1789[1], 1795[2]. New edition ed. Ernst-Otto Onnasch, Hamburg: Felix Meiner 2010 (Teilband 1).

Beiträge zur Berichtigung bisheriger Missverständnisse der Philosophen. Erster Band, das Fundament der Elementarphilosophie betreffend. Ed. Faustino Fabbianelli. Hamburg: Felix Meiner, 2003 (1790)

Über das Fundament des philosophischen Wissens. Über die Möglichkeit der Philosophie als strenge Wissenschaft. Ed. Wolfgang Schrader. Hamburg, Felix Meiner, 1978 (1791). Photomechanical reprint edition: Ed. Wolfgang H. Schrader, Hamburg: Felix Meiner, 1978. Partial translation: *The Foundation of Philosophical Knowledge*, trans. George di Giovanni. In: *Between Kant and Hegel: Texts in the Development of Post-Kantian Idealism.* Ed. George di Giovanni and H. S. Harris, Albany: SUNY Press, 1985, 52–106.

Beiträge zur Berichtigung bisheriger Mißverständnisse der Philosophen. Zweiter Band, die Fundamente des philosophischen Wissens, der Metaphysik, Moral, moralischen Religion und Geschmackslehre betreffend. Ed. Faustino Fabbianelli. Hamburg: Felix Meiner, 2004 (1794)

Verhandlung über die Grundbegriffe und Grundsätze der Moralität aus dem Gesichtspunke des gemeinen und gesunden Verstandes (1798). Partial translation in Sabine Roehr: *A Primer on German Enlightenment: With a Translation of Karl Leonhard Reinhold's "The Fundamental Concepts and Principles of Ethics."* Columbia: University of Missouri Press, 1995, 157–251.

Über die Paradoxien der neuesten Philosophie. Hamburg: Perthes, 1799.

Sendschreiben an J. C. Lavater und J. G. Fichte über den Glauben an Gott. Hamburg, 1799.

Beyträge zur leichtern Uebersicht des Zustandes der Philosophie beym Anfange des 19. Jahrhunderts Vol. 1–3 (1801), Vol. 4 (1802), Vol. 5–6 (1803).

C. L. Reinhold's Anleitung zur Kenntniß und Beurtheilung der Philosophie in ihren sämmtlichen Lehrgebäuden. Wien: Degen, 1805 (2nd ed. 1824).

Versuch einer Critik der Logik aus dem Gesichtspunkte der Sprache. (1806)

Grundlegung einer Synonymik für den allgemeinen Sprachgebrach in den philosophischen Wissenschaften. Kiel: Schmidt, 1812.
Ueber den Begriff und die Erkenntnis der Wahrheit. Kiel 1817.

Translations of the *Versuch*

Friedrich Gottlob Born (transl.): *Caroli Leonhardi Reinholdi Pericvlvm Novae Theoriae Facvltatis Representativae Hvmanae.* Lipsiae 1797 (Latin).
François-Xavier Chenet (transl.): *Essai d'une nouvelle théorie de la faculté humaine de représentation (Extraits).* In: K. L. Reinhold: Philosophie élémentaire. Paris 1989 (French).
Faustino Fabbianelli: *Saggio di una nuova teoria della facoltà umana della rappresentazione.* I Biancospini 7. Firenze 2006 (Italian).

Dictionaries and reference works

Adelung Wörterbuch (available on–line)
http://mdz.bib–bvb.de/digbib/lexika/adelung/text/@Generic__CollectionView;pt= 35982;lang=de
Grimm, Jacob und Wilhelm. *Deutsches Wörterbuch.* 33 Vols. Munich: DTV, 1984.
Ritter, Joachim et al. (eds.). *Historisches Wörterbuch der Philosophie.* 8 Vols. Basel: Schwabe, 1971–1992.
Sandkühler, Hans Jörg (ed.). *Handbuch: Deutscher Idealismus.* Stuttgart, Weimar: Metzler, 2005.
Von Schönborn, Alexander (ed.). *Karl Leonhard Reinhold. Eine annotierte Bibliographie.* Stuttgart-Bad Cannstatt, Frommann-Holzboog, 1991.

Translations of Kant and of other relevant works

Ameriks, Karl and Steve Naragon (trans. and eds.). *Immanuel Kant: Lectures on Metaphysics.* Cambridge: Cambridge University Press, 1997.
Dahlstrom, Daniel O. *Moses Mendelssohn: Philosophical Writings.* Cambridge: Cambridge University Press, 1997.
Gregor, Mary (trans. and ed.). *Kant: The Groundwork of the Metaphysics of Morals.* Cambridge, Cambridge University Press, 1998.
Guyer, Paul (trans.). *Critique of Pure Reason.* Cambridge, New York: Cambridge University Press, 1998.
Harris, H.S. and Walter Cerf (trans.). *Hegel, G. W. F. The Difference Between Fichte's and Schelling's System of Philosophy.* Albany: State University of NY Press, 1977.
Smith, Norman Kemp (trans.). *Immanuel Kant's Critique of Pure Reason.* London: Macmillan, 1934.
Sassen, Brigitte (trans. and ed.). *Kant's Early Critics: The Empiricist Critique of the Theoretical Philosophy.* Cambridge: CUP, 2000.
Weigelt, Marcus (trans.). *Immanuel Kant: Critique of Pure Reason.* Based on the translation by Max Müller. London: Penguin Books, 2007.

Selected discussions of Reinhold and his contemporaries

Ameriks, Karl. *Kant and the Fate of Autonomy: Problems in the Appropriation of the Critical Philosophy*. New York: Cambridge University Press, 2000.

Ameriks, Karl. "Reinhold's Challenge: Systematic Philosophy for the Public." In: Bondeli and Schrader (eds.), 77–193.

Ameriks, Karl. (ed.). *The Cambridge Companion to German Idealism*. Cambridge: Cambridge UP, 2000.

Ameriks, Karl. "The critique of metaphysics. The structure and fate of Kant's dialectic." In: Guyer (ed.), 269–302.

Beiser, Frederick. *The Fate of Reason: German Philosophy from Kant to Fichte*. Cambridge Mass.: Harvard UP, 1987.

Berkeley, Richard. *Coleridge and the Crisis of Reason*. New York: Palgrave Macmillan, 2007.

Blackwell, Richard J., "Christian Wolff's Doctrine of the Soul." *Journal of the History of Ideas* 22 (3) (July–September, 1961), 339–354.

Bondeli, Martin. *Das Anfangsproblem bei Karl Leonhard Reinhold. Eine systematische entwicklungsgeschichtliche Untersuchung zur Philosophie Reinholds in der Zeit von 1789 bis 1803*. Frankfurt am Main: Vittorio Klostermann, 1995.

Bondeli, Martin and Wolfgang H. Schrader (eds.). *Die Philosophie Karl Leonhard Reinholds*. Amsterdam, New York: Rodopi, 2003.

Böttiger, Karl August. *Literarische Zustände und Zeitgenossen: Begegnungen und Gespräche im klassischen Weimar*. ed. Klaus Gerlach and René Sternke. Berlin: Aufbau, 1998.

Breazeale, Daniel. "Between Kant and Fichte: Karl Leonhard Reinhold's 'Elementary Philosophy,'" *Review of Metaphysics* 35 (1982), 785–821.

Breazeale, Daniel. "Putting Doubt in its Place: Karl Leonhard Reinhold on the Relationship between Philosophical Skepticism and Transcendental Idealism." In: J. van der Zande and R.H. Popkin (eds.), 119–132.

Cloeren, Hermann-Josef. "Philosophie als Sprachkritik bei K.L.Reinhold. Interpretative Bemerkungen zu seiner Spätphilosophie" *Kant-Studien* 63 (1972), 225–236.

di Giovanni, George and H.S. Harris (eds.). *Between Kant and Hegel: Texts in the Development of Post–Kantian Idealism*. Albany: SUNY Press, 1985.

di Giovanni, George and H.S. Harris (eds.). "1799: The Year of Reinhold's Conversion to Jacobi." In: Bondeli and Schrader (eds.), 259–282.

di Giovanni, George and H.S. Harris (eds.). "The Foundation of Philosophical Knowledge." In: di Giovanni and H. S. Harris (eds.), 52–106.

di Giovanni, George and H.S. Harris (eds.). *Freedom and Religion in Kant and His Immediate Successors*. Cambridge: Cambridge University Press, 2005.

di Giovanni, George (ed.). *Karl Leonhard Reinhold and the Enlightenment*. London, New York: Springer, 2010.

Frank, Manfred. *Einführung in die frühromantische Ästhetik*. Frankfurt am Main: Suhrkamp, 1989.

Frank, Manfred. *Unendliche Annäherung*. Frankfurt am Main: Suhrkamp, 1997.

Frank, Manfred. *Auswege aus dem deutschen Idealismus*. Frankfurt am Main: Suhrkamp, 2007.

Fuchs, Gerhard W. *Karl Leonhard Reinhold – Illuminat und Philosoph.* Frankfurt am Main: Peter Lang, 1994.

Gerten, Michael. "Begehren, Vernunft und freier Wille: Systematische Stellung und Ansatz der praktischen Philosophie bei K.L. Reinhold." In: Bondeli and Schrader (eds.), 153–189.

Gesang, Bernward (ed.). *Kants vergessener Rezensent. Die Kritik der theoretischen und praktischen Philosophie Kants in fünf frühen Rezensionen von Hermann Andreas Pistorius.* (Kant Forschungen Bd. 18). Hamburg: Meinert, 2007.

Guyer, Paul (ed.). *The Cambridge Companion to Kant and Modern Philosophy.* Cambridge: Cambridge University Press, 2006.

Goethe, Johann Wolfgang. *Werke.* 14 Vols. Hamburger Ausgabe. Ed. Erich Trunz. Munich: C.H. Beck, 1981.

Heartz, Daniel. *Mozart's Operas.* Ed. Thomas Baumann. Berkeley: University of California Press, 1990.

Henrich, Dieter. *Konstellationen. Probleme und Debatten am Ursprung der idealistischen Philosophie.* Stuttgart: Cotta, 1991.

Henrich, Dieter. *Between Kant and Hegel: Lectures on German Idealism.* Ed. David S. Pacini. Cambridge, Mass: Harvard University Press, 2003.

Henrich, Dieter. *Grundlegung aus dem Ich.* 2 vols. Frankfurt am Main: Suhrkamp, 2004.

Herrera, Larry. "Kant on the Moral Triebfeder." *Kant–Studien* 91 (2000), 395–401.

Hinske, Norbert (ed.). *"Das Kantische Evangelium": Der Frühkantianismus an der Universität Jena von 1785–1800 und seine Vorgeschichte.* Stuttgart-Bad Cannstadt: Frommann–Holzboog, 1993.

Hinske, Norbert (ed.). "Einleitung": *C. C. E. Schmid. Wörterbuch zum leichteren Gebrauch der Kantischen Schriften.* Darmstadt: Wissenschaftliche Buchgesellschaft, 1998 (Sonderausgabe).

Jacob, Margaret. *The Radical Enlightenment.* London: Allen and Unwin, 1981.

Korsgaard, Christine M. "Introduction." In: Gregor (ed.), vii–xxx.

Kuehn, Manfred. *Kant: a Biography.* Cambridge: Cambridge University Press, 2001.

Kuehn, Manfred. "Kant's critical philosophy and its reception in the first five years (1781–1786). In: Guyer (ed.), 630–663.

Kuehn, Manfred. *Scottish Common Sense in Germany, 1768–1800.* Montreal & Kingston, London, Ithaca: McGill–Queen's University Press, 1987. Rpt. 2004.

Lamm, Julia A. "The Early Philosophical Roots of Schleiermacher's Notion of *Gefühl*, 1788–1794." *The Harvard Theological Review* 87 (1) (Jan 1994), 67–105.

Landon, H.C. Robbins. *The Mozart Compendium.* London: Thames and Hudson, 1990.

Lange, Eberhard. "Schiller und Kant." In Hinske (ed.) 1993: 121–130.

Lauth, R. (ed.). *Philosophie aus einem Prinzip: Karl Leonhard Reinhold.* Bonn: Bouvier, 1974.

Malter, Rudolf (ed.). *Kant in Rede und Gespräch.* Hamburg: Felix Meiner, 1990.

Mehigan, Tim. "'Die künftige Schule Europens': Reflections on K. L. Reinhold's *Theorie des menschlichen Vorstellungsvermögens* (1789)." In: *Moderne begreifen. Zur Paradoxie eines sozio-ästhetischen Deutungsmusters.* Ed. C. Weller et al. Amsterdam: Rodopi, 2007: 311–324

Pinkard, Terry. *German Philosophy 1760–1869: The Legacy of Idealism.* Cambridge: Cambridge University Press, 2002.

Pinkard, Terry. *Hegel: a Biography*. Cambridge: Cambridge University Press, 2000.

Reinhold, Ernst: *Karl Leonhard Reinholds Leben und litterarisches Wirken*. Jena: F. Frommann, 1825.

Roehr, Sabine. *A Primer on German Enlightenment: With a Translation of Karl Leonhard Reinhold's "The Fundamental Concepts and Principles of Ethics."* Columbia: University of Missouri Press, 1995, 157–251.

Roehr, Sabine. "Freedom and Autonomy in Schiller." *Journal of the History of Ideas* 64 (1) (January 2003), 119–134.

Roehr, Sabine. "Zum Einfluß K. L. Reinholds auf Schillers Kant-Rezeption." In: Bondeli and Schrader (eds.), 105–121.

Safranksi, Rüdiger. *Schopenhauer und die wilden Jahre der Philosophie*. Reinbek bei Hamburg: Rowohlt, 1994.

Schmid, Carl Christian Erhard. *Wörterbuch zum leichtern Gebrauch der Kantischen Schriften*. 4th edition. Ed. Norbert Hinske. Reprint: Darmstadt: Wissenschaftliche Buchgesellschaft, 1998.

Schröpfer, Horst. "Carl Christian Eberhard Schmid." In Hinske (ed.) 1993, 37–56.

Schröpfer, Horst. "Christian Gottfried Schütz–Initiator einer wirkungsvollen Verbreitung der Philosophie Kants." In Hinske (ed.), 15–23.

Schröpfer, Horst. "Karl Leonhard Reinhold – sein Wirken für das allgemeine Verständnis der 'Hauptresultate' und 'der Organisation des Kantischen Systems." In Hinske (ed.) 1993: 101–111.

Seidel, George. *J. Fichte's Wissenschaftslehre of 1794*. West Lafayette: Purdue University Press, 1983.

Steiger, Robert (ed.). *Goethes Leben von Tag zu Tag*. 8 Vols. Zurich, Munich: Artemis, 1988.

Walker, Ralph C. S. "Kant and Transcendental Arguments." In: Guyer (ed.), 238–268.

Waxman, Wayne. *Kant and the Empiricists. Understanding Understanding*. Oxford: Oxford University Press, 2005.

Wellek, René. "Between Kant and Fichte: Karl Leonhard Reinhold." *Journal of the History of Ideas* 45 (2) (1984), 323–327.

Windelband, Wilhelm. *A History of Philosophy*. Vol. II: *Renaissance, Enlightenment, Modern*. Transl. James H. Tufts. New York: Harper, 1958. Reprint. (Orig.: New York, Macmillan, 1901).

Wood, Allen W. "Kant's Practical Philosophy." In: Ameriks (ed.), 2000, 57–75.

Wood, Allen W. "The Supreme Principle of Morality." In: Guyer (ed.), 2006, 342–380.

Wunderlich, Falk. *Kant und die Bewußtseinstheorien des 18. Jahrhunderts*. Berlin, New York: De Gruyter, 2005.

Zande van der, Johan and Richard H. Popkin (eds.). *The Skeptical Tradition around 1800*. Dordrecht, Boston, London: Kluwer, 1998.

Ziolkowski, Theodore. *Das Wunderjahr in Jena: Geist und Gesellschaft 1794–95*. Stuttgart, Frankfurt am Main: Klett-Cotta, 1998.

Zweig, Arnulf. "Reinhold's Relation to Kant." In: Bondeli and Schrader (eds.), 39–54.

Name Index

Aenesidemus (see Schulze, Gottlob Ernst)
Ameriks, Karl, xvii, xxi, xxii, xxiii, xxv
Aristotle, 74, 179

Baggesen, Jens, xv
Bardili, Christoph Gottfried, xiv
Basedow, Johann Bernhard, 36
Baumgarten, Alexander Gottlieb, 2, 3, 84, 177, 178
Beiser, Frederick, xxv, 4, 81
Bilfinger, Georg Bernhard, 84, 178
Beulwitz, Caroline von, xiii
Böttiger, Karl August, x, xi,
Bondeli, Martin, ix, xxv
Born, Ignaz von, x,

Christ, Jesus, 42
Cicero, 92
Clement XIV, ix,
Corrodi, Heinrich, 8

Descartes, René, xiv, 3, 13, 14
Denis, Johann Michael Kosmas, x
di Giovanni, George, xiv, 147
Diez, Carl Immanuel, xx

Eberhard, Johann Augustus, 50, 69, 177
Epicurus, 46, 83
Erhard, Johann Benjamin, xv

Fabbianelli, Fabio, xxv
Feder, Georg Heinrich, 6, 69
Fichte, Johann Gottlieb, ix, xiv, xv, xvi, xx, xxiii
Flatt, Johann Friedrich, 51, 70
Forberg, Friedrich Karl, x, xiii, xv
Francke, August Hermann, 1
Frank, Manfred, ix, xv, xvi, xviii, xx, xxiii, xxv, 278
Franks, Paul, xxv
Fuchs, Gerhard W., ix, x, xxv

Goethe, Johann Wolfgang, x, xiii, xiv, 36

Haydn, Joseph, x
Hardenberg, Friedrich von (see Novalis)
Heartz, Daniel, x
Hegel, G. W. F., ix, xxiii
Heidegger, Martin, xviii
Henrich, Dieter, xxv, 1
Herbert, Baron Paul von, xv
Herder Johann Gottfried, xi, 4
Hinske, Norbert, 5
Hölderlin, Friedrich, xv, xvi, xxiii, 278
Hufeland, Gottlieb, xv, 51
Hume, David, 5

Jacob, Margaret, x,
Jacobi, Friedrich Heinrich, xii, xiv, xx, xxv, 4, 36
Jesuits, ix
Juvenal, 59

Kant, Immanuel, ix, xi, xii, xiv, xv, xvi, 5, 6, 7, 9, 19, 22, 23, 24, 25, 34, 42, 47, 50, 66, 73, 119, 159, 186, 188, 192, 216, 224, 231, 236, 240, 243, 251, 252, 264
Kuehn, Manfred, 1, 5, 6, 36

Lamm, Julia A., xvi,
Lange, Eberhard, xiii,
Leibniz, Gottfried, xiv, xxi, xxii, 1, 3, 4, 13, 14, 16, 17, 18, 74f., 79, 84, 96, 122, 132, 147, 148, 150, 155, 156, 178, 179, 207
Lenz, J.M.R., xi,
Locke, John, xiv, xxi, 4, 16, 17, 18, 19, 29, 74f., 83f., 89, 97, 122, 144, 147, 148, 151, 155, 237f.

Maass, Johann Gebhard Ehrenreich, 70
Maimon, Salomon, xx, xxv
Malebranche, Nicolas, xiv
Malter, Rudolf, xvi
Mandeville, Bernhard, 44
Marx, Karianne, x
Meiners, Christoph, 69, 70
Mendelssohn, Moses, 4, 6, 33, 48

Mereau, Sophie, xiii
Montaigne, Michel de, 44
Mozart, Wolfgang Amadeus, x

Newton, Isaac, 8, 9, 29, 160
Niethammer,Friedrich Immanuel, xv
Novalis, ix, xv, xx

Onnasch, Ernst-Otto, xiii, xxiii, xxv

Pascal, Blaise, 5
Platner (also Plattner), Ernst, xi, 69, 85, 127, 147, 152, 156
Plato, 74, 83
Pinkard, Terry, xv, xxv

Rehberg, August Wilhelm 4
Reimarus, 69, 85, 238
Reinhold, Ernst, xv

Schelling, Friedrich, ix, xv, xx
Schiller, Friedrich, xiii, xv, xvi, 278
Schlegel, Friedrich, ix, xx
Schleiermacher, Friedrich, xvi
Schlosser, Johann Friedrich Heinrich, 36

Schmid, Carl Christian Erhard, xiv, 6
Schönborn, Alexander von, xi
Schröpfer, Horst, ix, xiv, 1, 6
Schulz, Johann, 6
Schulze, Gottlob Ernst, xx
Schütz, Christian Gottfried, xiv, 1, 6
Selle, Christian Gottlieb, 69
Spinoza, Baruch, xiv, 5, 34, 119, 207
Stattler, Benedikt, 70
Steiger, Robert, x

Tetens, Johann Nicolaus, xiv
Tiedemann, Dietrich, 69
Tittel, Gottlieb August, 70

Vanzo, Alberto, xxiv
Voigt, C.G., x

Weishaupt, Adam, 70
Wieland, Christoph Martin, x, 1
Wolff, Christian, xi, xiv, xxiv, 1, 2, 3, 13, 14, 47, 84, 93

Ziolkowski, Theodore, xiii

Subject Index

absolute, 257, 264, 265
  absolute autonomy, 263 absolute
    cause, 273
  absolute community, 258, 264, 283f.
  absolute ground, 258, 262, 263
  absolute subject, 258, 261, 262, 264,
    265, 266
aesthetics, 2
amphiboly, 243
appearances, 12, 119, 201f., 252, 257,
  266
atheism, 30, 33, 34, 35, 56, 58, 60, 64,
  65, 66, 73
  dogmatic, 34
autonomy, 264

Baumgarten, Alexander Gottlieb,
  Metaphysics, 84, 177, 178
belief, 67
Bible, 51
binding (see synthesis)
body (see corporality)

cabbalism, 67
Cartesian system, 13
categories, 213f., 223f.
  dynamic categories, 219f.
  mathematical categories, 218f.
  modality, 216, 220, 221, 223f.
  quality, 216, 218, 223f., 277, 280
  quantity, 216, 218, 223f., 277, 280
  relation, 216, 219, 223f., 277, 280
  table of categories, 217
certainty, 53, 85
change, 196f.
Christianity, 49, 60
common-sense philosophy, 10, 31, 60,
  61, 67
concept, 97, 106, 134, 149–50
consciousness, 24, 92, 103, 111–12,
  113, 120, 121, 127, 133, 134
constitutive, 252, 254
contradiction,
  law of, 128, 239
Copernican turn, xxii

corporality (corporeality), 79–81, 90,
  94, 135, 167, 168, 169ff., 172,
  173, 174ff., 177, 178, 179, 262,
  266, 270, 273, 277
cosmology, 3
Critical philosophy, xvii

decision, 53
deism, 35
demonstration, 61
despotism, 52
  spiritual, 52
determinism, 11, 41, 42
dogmatism, 12, 40, 65, 66, 67, 118,
  119
doubt, 53, 62
  critical, 57
  dogmatic, 57, 96
  unphilosophical, 57
drive, 276
  drive to form, 276
  drive to material, 276
  drive to morality, 281
  empirical drive, 276
  purely rational drive, 280
  rational-sensory drive, 277f.
  sex drive, 277fn.
dualism, xviii, xxi, 90, 93, 96, 269f.,
  272
duty, 282

eclecticism, 1, 34, 61
ego, 92
Einbildungskraft, xviii
empiricism, 1, 2, 54, 95, 151
empirical cpgnition, 201f., 235, 237,
  259
empirical concept, 2
Epicureans, 46, 47, 48, 283
equilibrists, 30, 41
Erkenntnis, xix
Erscheinungen (see also appearances),
  xxi
Europe, 69
existence, 232

experience, 3, 59, 96, 145, 147, 175f.,
　　186, 188, 192f., 197, 224, 235f.,
　　237f., 251f., 254, 258, 264f., 280,
　　282
　　inner, 144, 147
　　outer, 147

factual knowledge, 59
faculty of representation, xxiv
fatalism, 11, 30 40
Feder, Georg Heinrich
　　Logic and Metaphysics, 69
first cause, 273, 285
Flatt
　　Ideas for the Revision of Natural
　　　Law, 51
free cause, 274
freedom, 38–42, 61, 76, 264, 265,
　　274
　　natural, 41, 42
　　supernatural, 41
　　of reason, 263f.
free ground, 263
Freemasonry, x
French philosophy, 60

Gemüt(h), xxiv
geometry, 193f.
Germany, 68
God, 55, 56, 76
　　cosmological proof of, 37
　　human dependence on, 49
　　existence of, 16, 32, 33, 34, 36, 56,
　　　61, 83
　　ontological proof of, 37
　　physico-theological proof of, 37
good and evil, 51

happiness, 46, 48, 278f.
homogeneity, principle of, 255
Hufeland, Gottlieb
　　Essay on the Basic Principle of
　　　Natural Law, 51
hyperphysics, 65, 66

idea, 243f., 250f., 263f., 264, 274
idealism, ix, 13, 17, 80, 90, 92, 95,
　　119, 141–2, 143
　　Berkeleyan idealism, 271
　　refutation of reality, 13
idea(s), 83–4, 89, 97, 122, 134, 147,
　　150
identity, 241

image(s), 112–14, 147
impression(s), 112
inference, 71, 73
innate representations, 223
innate truths (concepts),
　　doctrine of, 17, 75, 76
intuition, 80, 97, 149, 163, 164f.,
　　171f., 183f., 198f., 207f., 243,
　　265, 266

judgment, xxi, 71, 78, 85, 121
　　affirmatory, 215
　　analytical, 210f.
　　apodictic, 216
　　assertory, 216
　　categorical, 215
　　disjunctive, 215
　　hypothetical, 215
　　infinite, 215
　　negative, 210f.
　　negatory, 215
　　problematic, 216
　　synthetic, 210f.

Kant, Immanuel,
　　Grundlegung der Metaphysik der
　　　Moral, 50
　　Kritik der praktischen Vernunft
　　　(Critique of Practical Reason) ix,
　　　47, 48
　　Kritik der reinen Vernunft (Critique
　　　of Pure Reason), ix, xii, xiii, xiv,
　　　xvii, xx, 6, 7, 8, 9, 13, 16, 17, 18,
　　　20, 21, 22, 23, 24, 25, 34, 56, 62,
　　　66, 69, 96, 112, 127
　　Kritik der Urteilskraft (Critique of
　　　Judgment), ix,
　　Opus Postumum, xxiv
　　Prologomena zu einer jeden künftigen
　　　Metaphysik (Prolegomena to Any
　　　Future Metaphysics), xviii
Kantians, 69, 70
Kantian system, 5, 21, 23
knowledge,
　　reality of, 77

language use, 55, 150
law, 52
Leibniz, Gottfried,
　　doctrine of pre-established harmony,
　　　114, 179
　　Nouveaux Essais sur l'entendement
　　　humain, 147

Leibniz(-Wolff) system, 1, 2, 13, 19, 58, 75, 76, 155, 243, 271
Locke, John,
  Essay Concerning Human Understanding, xxi, 29, 84. 85, 89, 97, 122, 144, 147
logic, 71, 82
logical subject, 91

manifold, 133–4, 135, 136, 145
  unity of, 48, 133
material (see representation, material)
materialism, 9, 11, 17, 30, 40, 46, 78, 80, 83, 90, 93, 118–19, 125, 131, 135, 161, 168, 169, 174, 179, 206f., 210, 268f., 272
mathematics, 30, 50
Merkmal(e), xxiv
metaphysics, 1, 2, 3, 4, 5, 10, 11, 12, 14, 24, 30, 58, 59, 61, 65, 67, 73, 74, 77, 78, 81, 104
mind, 72, 82, 89, 92, 96, 98, 103, 121, 125–6, 131, 134, 142, 143
miracles, 72
monad, 272
morality, 29, 31, 32, 37, 38, 39, 42ff., 49, 53, 54, 55, 64, 66
moral world, 264, 265, 283
multiplicity, 146
mysticism, 67

natural law, 29, 51, 52, 54, 55, 64
natural science(s), 30
naturalism, 49, 67
nature,
  state of, 44
noumena, xxi, 268

observation, 59
ontology, 3, 11

pantheism, 16, 35, 40
  dispute, 4
perfection(ism), 47–9, 50, 51
phenomena, xxi, 268
Pietism, 1
Platner (also Plattner), Ernst,
  Aphorisms, 127, 147
Platonic system, 76
pleasure, 45ff., 50
  drive for, 43, 44, 50
political,
  prejudices, 52

popular philosophy, 8, 9, 10, 58–60, 61, 168
practical reason, 43, 281
predicate, 205f., 210
proof,
  need for, 54
property, -ies, 105
  of the body, 78
Protestantism,
  conversion to, xi
prudence, 279
psychology, 2
  empirical, 4, 98

rational theology (see theology, rational)
rationalism, 148, 149
realism, xxiii
reality of knowledge, (see knowledge, reality)
reason, 47–9, 56, 57, 67, 68, 69ff., 73ff., 79, 83, 85, 100, 101
  divine, 49
  proofs of, 67
receptivity, 123ff., 126, 127, 128, 129, 130, 131, 134, 135, 137, 138ff., 142, 143, 145, 147
regulative, 254
Reinhold, Karl Leonhard
  Beiträge zur Berichtigung bisheriger Missverständnisse der Philosophen (Contributions to the Correction of Certain Misunderstandings in Philosophy), xx,
  elementary philosophy, xx, xxiii
  Letters on the Kantian Philosophy (*Briefe über die Kantische Philosophie*, K.L. Reinhold), xi, xii, xv, xviii, 21
religious,
  prejudices, 52
representation,
  concept of, 106, 117, 139, 148
  definition of, 96, 103
  form of, 109ff., 113, 115, 117–18, 119, 120–1, 122, 129, 130, 133, 134, 142
  in general, 102, 109ff., 130, 148
  material of, 106ff., 110, 113, 114, 115, 117–18, 119, 120–1, 122, 123, 129, 130, 132, 133, 136, 138, 139, 141, 142, 144, 145
  per se, 102ff., 108, 129ff., 138, 148
  properties belonging to, 119
  reality of, 109

representing force, 89, 93ff., 124,
    126–7, 131, 148, 155, 161, 167,
    275f., 279
resemblance, 112, 113, 142
revelation, 33, 72
Romanticism, ix, xx, xxiii

Satz des Bewußtseins (see Reinhold,
    elementary philosophy)
schemata, 226f., 234f., 244
    actuality, 231, 236
    causality, 228, 234, 236, 258, 274
    community, 230, 236, 258, 283
    degree, 227
    dynamic, 234
    mathematical, 228
    modality, 231
    necessity, 236
    number, 226
    possibility, 231, 236
    quality, 236
    quantity, 236
    substantiality, 228f., 236, 258, 262
    table of schemata, 226
scholasticism, 161
sectarianism, 1
seeing, 112, 162
self, 92
self-activity of reason, 280
self-consciousness, 153f., 157f.
self-determination, 265
self-interest, 276f.
Sensus communis (see common-sense
    philosophy)
serfdom, 52
sexual desire, 176
simultaneity, 195f, 198, 230, 264
skepticism, 5, 12, 34, 35, 39, 56–8, 59,
    66, 90. 92, 141–2, 143, 161
    critical, 5, 33, 57–8, 62, 63, 65, 68
    dogmatic, 5, 9, 11, 14, 16, 30, 33,
        36, 40, 45, 56, 57–8, 60, 61, 62,
        63, 64, 65, 73, 83, 95, 96, 118,
        119, 125, 268f., 272
    unphilosophical, 58, 62, 63
solipsism, 92, 271
soul, 76, 79, 82, 89, 90, 94, 95, 98,
    124, 127, 131, 135, 137, 147, 148
space, 12, 119, 187f., 191f., 228f., 258
space and time, 195f., 202f.
specification, principle of, 255
speculation, 2, 59, 64
speculative philosophy 9, 18, 19, 20,

    21, 22, 32, 55, 65, 66, 67, 131
Spinozism, xii, 4, 10, 14, 35, 269f., 272
spiritualism, 9, 11, 17, 30, 67, 79, 80,
    83, 90, 93, 94, 119, 124, 125, 131,
    135, 137, 168, 169, 174, 177, 179,
    207f., 210
spontaneity, 125ff., 128, 129, 131,
    136ff., 138ff., 143, 145, 147
Stattler,
    Antikant, 70
Stoicism, 47, 283
subject, 92, 93,, 94
substance, 82, 91, 94, 95, 129, 135, 137
supernaturalism, 5, 9, 14, 16, 30, 33,
    35, 36, 41, 49, 50, 56, 60, 61, 64,
    65, 66, 72, 73, 125
susceptibility, (see receptivity)
syllogism, 9, 71, 72, 73, 78, 85, 205,
    246f.
    categorical, 256
    disjunctive, 256
    hypothetical, 256
synthesis, 136, 140, 153, 156, 161,
    166, 167, 170, 176, 182f., 183,
    184, 199, 203, 204, 207, 208, 209,
    210f., 211, 212, 243, 244, 245,
    262, 264, 265, 267
    of subject and predicate, 205
    of time and space, 195

Teutscher Merkur, x, 1, 22, 66
theism, 11, 16, 30, 34, 56, 61, 64, 73
    dogmatic, 33, 34, 35, 37, 41, 56, 58,
        74
theology,
    natural, 32
    rational, 3
thing(s), thing-in-itself, 12, 96, 104,
    109, 114ff., 118ff., 130, 138, 141,
    172, 177, 179, 180, 200, 202f.,
    206, 208f., 210, 221, 222f., 231,
    232, 234, 239, 264, 265, 266ff.
time, 12, 194f., 226f., 258
totality, 250
transcendental imagination, xix

unity,
    of apprehension, 262
    objective, 119
    rational, 251, 257, 262
    systematic unity of experience, 252f.
    unconditioned, 250f.
    of the understanding, 262

Vis repraesentativa, 93

Weimar classicism, xiii
Wolffian school, see Leibniz-Wolff
    system

will, 41, 50, 265, 279
    freedom of, 70, 281
    pure will, 281

CPSIA information can be obtained at www.ICGtesting.com
Printed in the USA
BVOW06s1805090716

454306BV00013B/9/P